Digitisation of Culture: Namibian and International Perspectives

Dharm Singh Jat · Jürgen Sieck
Hippolyte N'Sung-Nza Muyingi
Heike Winschiers-Theophilus
Anicia Peters · Shawulu Nggada
Editors

Digitisation of Culture: Namibian and International Perspectives

 Springer

Editors
Dharm Singh Jat
Computer Science
Namibia University of Science
 and Technology
Windhoek
Namibia

Jürgen Sieck
Computer Science
HTW Berlin
Berlin
Germany

and

Computer Science
Namibia University of Science
 and Technology
Windhoek
Namibia

Hippolyte N'Sung-Nza Muyingi
Computer Science
Namibia University of Science
 and Technology
Windhoek
Namibia

Heike Winschiers-Theophilus
Computer Science
Namibia University of Science
 and Technology
Windhoek
Namibia

Anicia Peters
Computing and Informatics
Namibia University of Science
 and Technology
Windhoek
Namibia

Shawulu Nggada
Computer Science
Namibia University of Science
 and Technology
Windhoek
Namibia

ISBN 978-981-13-3980-6   ISBN 978-981-10-7697-8   (eBook)
https://doi.org/10.1007/978-981-10-7697-8

Printed on acid-free paper

This Springer imprint is published by the registered company Springer Nature Singapore Pte Ltd. part of Springer Nature
The registered company address is: 152 Beach Road, #21-01/04 Gateway East, Singapore 189721, Singapore

Foreword

UNESCO presented its first worldwide Internet study at the UNESCO General Conference in 2015, in Paris, under the title "Keystones to foster inclusive Knowledge Societies". In the twenty-first century, the concept of a knowledge society comprises inter-connecting technology and culture. According to Klaus Schwab, Founder and Executive Chairman of the World Economic Forum in Davos, the fourth industrial revolution will "change not only what we do but also who we are. It will affect our identity and all the issues associated with it: our sense of privacy, our notion of ownership, our consumption patterns, the time we devote to work and leisure, and how we develop our careers, cultivate our skills, meet people, and nurture relationships. It is already changing our health and leading to a 'quantified' self, and sooner than we think it may lead to human augmentation. The list is endless because it is bound only by our imagination". This societal transformation changes not only all parts of the economic value chain—design, production, distribution, division, and consumption—but also communication and inter-human relationships. Thus, UNESCO advocates a humanistic vision of universal Knowledge Societies. In other words, we acknowledge cultural variations in knowledge societies embedded in universal and shared values of human rights. To indeed foster inclusive Knowledge Societies, the UNESCO Secretariat framed the concept of Internet universality, which is built on four pillars, namely human rights based, open, accessible, and multi-stakeholder driven. With Resolution 53, the concept has been adopted at the 38th General Conference. With this, each country and member state has the opportunity to use the concept as a template for a holistic and complex process of transforming and developing their societies for the twenty-first century. It also means considering the gamut of interdependencies and inter-relationships between different human rights and the Internet—such as freedom of expression, privacy, cultural participation, gender equality, association freedom, security, education.

In line with UNESCO's initiatives of fostering inclusive Knowledge Societies, this book contributes to Namibian and international perspectives, mostly based on presentations I attended at the International Conference on Culture and Computer Science in October 2016 in Windhoek, Namibia. I appreciate the efforts of the researchers and, particularly, indigenous communities who have put forward digitisation of cultures. With this said, UNESCO will continue to play a vital role in promoting an inclusive and holistic approach to a digital societal transformation following a humanistic vision.

Verena Metze-Mangold
President of the German Commission
for UNESCO

Preface

The present book comprises invited chapters as well as extended and revised versions of selected papers, which were presented at the International Conference on Culture and Computer Science, ICCCS 16, that took place at Safari Court Hotel, Windhoek, Namibia, from 25 to 28 October 2016. The conference was hosted by Namibia University of Science and Technology and HTW Berlin. Each manuscript was reviewed by at least two reviewers and was substantially revised according to reviewers' critiques before acceptance into the supplement. Our thanks go to the reviewers for their assistance in reviewing the numerous submissions.

This book provides various views and perspectives on the digitisation of culture. The contributions collected in this book represent multifaceted approaches towards modern information and communication strategies in a cultural context. They analyse, demonstrate, and, in particular, discuss current research and developments around "Digitalisation of Culture ". The authors of this volume are from different countries and hence give an extensive international overview of fundamental theories as well as best practice applications of information management, communication, interaction, visualisation, mixed, augmented and virtual reality, audio technology, multimedia, data processing, and design within a specific cultural context. Based on the best practice examples, recent developments and requirements are presented in different areas of cultural aspects, the use of data sources for augmentation as well as their visualisation and interaction.

We acknowledge the authors' efforts, and without their creativity, ideas, and hard work, it would not have been possible to compile such a diverse and inspiring publication. We promise the readers of this book new insights, the inspirations for new research and projects, fruitful discussions on the presented questions and achieved results, and much pleasure in "rummaging" through the different chapters.

The editors ensured that the book presents a variety of original developments, technologies, and conceptualisations in the digitisation of culture. The materials in this edited book provide important information and tools for cultural policy-makers, cultural and creative industries, communication scientists, artists as well as computer scientists and engineers conducting research on cultural topics.

Windhoek, Namibia	Dharm Singh Jat
Berlin, Germany/Windhoek, Namibia	Jürgen Sieck
Windhoek, Namibia	Hippolyte N'Sung-Nza Muyingi
Windhoek, Namibia	Heike Winschiers-Theophilus
Windhoek, Namibia	Anicia Peters
Windhoek, Namibia	Shawulu Nggada

Contents

About the Editors

Dharm Singh Jat received his Master of Engineering and a Ph.D. in Computer Science and Engineering from a prestigious University of India. He is a Professor in the Department of Computer Science at Namibia University of Science and Technology (NUST). His research interest spans the areas of multimedia communications, wireless and mobile technologies, SDN, network security, and roof computing. He has been the recipient of more than 16 prestigious awards. He has authored/co-authored over 160 publications.

Jürgen Sieck received his degree in Mathematics and a Ph.D. in Computer Science from the Humboldt University, Germany. Now he is the Head of the Research Group "Informations- und Kommunikationsanwendungen" and Professor of Computer Science in Berlin. His research interests are in AR, multimedia, and mobile application. In 2013, he was awarded an honorary doctorate from ONPU, Ukraine. Since 2013, he has been a Principal Investigator of the cluster of excellence "Bild Wissen Gestaltung" at Humboldt University. Since 2015, he is also a Professor at NUST, Windhoek.

Hippolyte N'Sung-Nza Muyingi is the Associate Dean: Research, Faculty of Computing and Informatics, Namibia University of Science and Technology (NUST). He acted as Dean (2014–2015) and held the Mobile Telecommunication Company (MTC) Endowed Chair in ICT (2009–2011). He led the Department of Computer Science, University of Fort Hare (UFH), and the NRF- and multi-industry-sponsored Telkom Centre of Excellence (2001–2008) and was awarded the Telkom Research Chair in ICT where an overall 100 postgraduates had competed. He is the co-founder of the South African Siyakhula Living Lab.

Heike Winschiers-Theophilus is a Professor in Computer Science and has lectured in Namibia since 1994. Her research and community development activities centre on co-designing technologies with indigenous and marginalised communities in Namibia and Malaysia. She promotes dialogical and community-based co-design following principles of action research with a transcultural approach. She has co-chaired numerous international conferences, co-authored more than 80 peer-reviewed publications, supervised local and international students, and received multiple grants.

Anicia Peters is Executive Dean of the Faculty of Computing and Informatics at the Namibia University of Science and Technology. She completed her Ph.D. in Human Computer Interaction from Iowa State University. Her research focuses on HCI, social networks, and e-participation. She has a mixture of academic and industry experience having worked in Silicon Valley and Namibia. Her research work is published, for example, in the IEEE Transactions for Visualisation and Computer Graphics, Computers in Human Behaviour, Interacting with Computers and the ACM CHI Conference. In 2016, she chaired the International Culture and Computer Science Conference as well as the Africa Human Computer Interaction Conference (AfriCHI) both organised incooperation with ACM SIGCHI.

Shawulu Nggada is an Associate Professor of Computer Information Science at Higher Colleges of Technology, UAE. He worked as Deputy Director/Associate Professor of Software Engineering at Namibia University of Science and Technology. His research interests include dependability analysis, software failure analysis, evolutionary algorithms, and optimisation. He completed his Ph.D. in Computer Science (Hull, UK), MSc in Software Engineering (Bradford, UK), and B. Tech. (Hons) in Computer Science (Nigeria).

Introduction

Dharm Singh Jat, Jürgen Sieck, Hippolyte N'Sung-Nza Muyingi, Heike Winschiers-Theophilus, Anicia Peters and Shawulu Nggada

Since the end of the twentieth century, computer technologies have become pervasive and ubiquitous in our every day life. With the introduction of wireless networks, new sensor systems, mobile computer systems and tools for the development of applications, the traditional distinction between culture and technology is superseded. In this book, we present different approaches to digitalise tangible and intangible culture as well as best practices examples, challenges and future trends in different cultural contexts. We will elaborate on several technical aspects of mobile devices, tangible user interfaces and context-sensitive services in information systems for cultural institutions and local communities. An international perspective is presented by authors from 13 different countries working with affiliated institutions in Australia, Africa, America, Asia and Europe.

D. S. Jat (✉) · J. Sieck · H. N.-N. Muyingi · H. Winschiers-Theophilus · A. Peters
S. Nggada
Namibia University of Science and Technology (NUST),
13 Storch Street, Windhoek, Namibia
e-mail: dsingh@nust.na

J. Sieck
e-mail: juergensieck@acm.org

H. N.-N. Muyingi
e-mail: hmuyingi@nust.na

H. Winschiers-Theophilus
e-mail: hwinschiers@nust.na

A. Peters
e-mail: apeters@nust.na

S. Nggada
e-mail: shnggada@gmail.com

J. Sieck
Hochschule für Technik und Wirtschaft (HTW Berlin),
Wilhelminenhofstr. 75A, Berlin, Germany

© Springer Nature Singapore Pte Ltd. 2018
D. S. Jat et al. (eds.), *Digitisation of Culture: Namibian and International Perspectives*, https://doi.org/10.1007/978-981-10-7697-8_1

Many of the existing solutions and tools for preservation and representation of Indigenous cultures and artefacts have evolved and been developed within a predominant Western design paradigm. In result, a number of text-based Indigenous knowledge management systems were developed and populated following a conventional database model [1]. Previous studies highlighted that the search for written textual and aural information in Indigenous communities is a task when researchers aim to document Indigenous history [2, 3]. In Indigenous communities, the cultural narratives are embodied in a web of tangible and intangible props, such as dances, oral stories, artefacts and conventions [4]. Nevertheless, the importance of holistic and integrated representation of the Indigenous knowledge system has been undermined in traditional approaches of technology design for preservation of culture. In this book, we have compiled local perspectives from researchers and indigenous communities on the participation in digital heritage processes. Contributions range from Australia, to Asia and Africa, more specifically Namibia showing alternative technology developments. Voices of minority ethnicities still practicing traditional rituals, such as the OvaHimba, San, and OvaHerero are expressed and amplified within the digital space.

Emerging technologies such as Mixed, Augmented and Virtual Reality, mobile devices and digital media increase the opportunities and the possibilities of the development of new applications and services within a cultural context. According to the publication of Milgram [5], Mixed, Augmented and Virtual Reality refers to the interactive medium in which representation of real objects merges with virtual components. Contents, mainly with real objects and a small proportion of virtual objects, are called augmented reality while contents, mainly with virtual and a lesser proportion of real objects, are called virtual reality or augmented virtual reality. The continued advances in computer vision technologies, tangible user interfaces, cloud computing and mobile devices have brought a renewed interest in modern computer technology for cultural institutions and communities. The integrated relationship between tangible and intangible aspects is the central part of modern information technology, and researchers acknowledged the traditional distinction between culture and technology as an obsolete phenomenon [6]. Mixed, Augmented and Virtual Reality provides the advantages of basic technologies in addition to information management, visualisation and interaction in real time between physical and virtual artefacts as well as combining a real scene with a virtual scene generated by computers. This is not only possible with real artefacts it is also possible with immaterial processes like dances, music, storytelling, ceremonies or celebrations. Nevertheless, a key challenge is to create flexible constellations between real and virtual artefacts, the real and virtual world as well as between scientific research results and Indigenous knowledge. In addition, artefacts are not only static memory spaces for material objects and real performances with some additional static knowledge. Artefacts are what we know about them, how we understand them, and how we design, present and use them. In addition, we have to analyse and understand how to interact with the artefacts in a specific surrounding space. We can create artefacts to a similar extent as the artefacts create us. The same could be said about live performances.

The chapters are grouped under four themes, namely the conceptualisation of digital heritage, digital architectures of culture, augmented reality and multimedia applications as well as interactivity in culture experiences.

The chapters featuring under the theme of 'conceptualisation of digital heritage' address issues of diversity and local perspectives presenting the need to reframe mainstream practices and concepts of digital heritage representation, preservation and integration into everyday life. One concern has been the involvement and responsibilities of indigenous communities into the process of digitalisation of their own cultural heritage, across the world. On the other hand, a meaningful dissemination of cultural knowledge requires a systematic methodology based on theoretical groundings, as such an ontological and a game-based approach are discussed.

Digital architectures of culture consider technical possibilities and constraints in collecting, storing and processing of data and information. Integrated into a national indigenous knowledge management system, challenges of representation and translation across different epistemologies are discussed. Furthermore, citizen participation of crowdsourcing applications to preserve indigenous languages and wildlife data is presented from a technical perspective.

Augmented reality and multimedia have greatly enhanced experiences of cultural heritage. While the focus in the past has been on visual representations, mostly the chapters remind us of a multitude of sensory experiences which can be enriched through acoustic or performative elements, be it virtual or real within cultural spaces. Thus, be it the experience of antique and archaeological spaces, indigenous narratives or sacred places and monuments, augmented, mixed and virtual realities have certainly attracted new audiences.

Recognising the significance of embodied experiences, an increasing trend in interactivity in the cultural sector can be observed. For example, technologies embedded in a traditional African hut installation take the visitors through an interactive role-play probing for contemporary societal ills, thereby revealing cultural tensions within familiar spaces. From a technical perspective, alternative interfaces, such as gestures, eye-tracking and control, or even visitors' clothes colours as a mechanism of interaction and selection have made strides providing new opportunities for applications in the cultural sector.

In summary, the book presents multiple facets of digitalising cultural heritage considering different concepts and epistemologies, data structures and representations, augmented, mixed and virtual realities as well as interactive systems all striving for an enhanced cultural experience. Research and developments and best practices contribute to a better understanding of cultural artefacts and practices in the digital and real world.

References

1. Yeo, A.W., Zaman, T., Kulathuramaiyer, N.: Indigenous knowledge management in the Kelabit community in Eastern Malaysia: insights and reflections for contemporary KM design. Int. J. Sociotechnol. Know. Dev. (IJSKD) 5(1), 23–36 (2013)
2. Harms, R.: Oral tradition and ethnicity. J. Interdisc., 61–85 (1979)
3. Mushiba, M., Gallert, P., Winschiers-Theophilus, H.: On persuading an OvaHerero community to join the wikipedia community. In: International Conference on Culture, Technology, and Communication, pp. 1–18. Springer International Publishing (2016)
4. Bidwell, N., Hardy, D.: Dilemmas in situating participation in rural ways of saying. In: Proceedings of the 21st Annual Conference of the Australian CHI, New York, NY, USA, pp. 145–152 (2009)
5. Milgram, P., Drascic, D., Julius, J., Grodski, Restogi, A., Zhai, S., Zhou, C.:. Merging real and virtual worlds. In: Proceedings of IMAGINA '95, Monte Carlo, pp. 218–230 (1995)
6. Schäfer, M.T.: Bastard Culture! How User Participation Transforms Cultural Production, p. 256. Amsterdam University Press (2011)

Part I
Conceptualisation of Digital Heritage

From Preserving to Performing Culture in the Digital Era

Jennyfer Lawrence Taylor, Alessandro Soro, Paul Roe, Anita Lee Hong and Margot Brereton

1 Introduction

As the computing industry goes global and access to information technology becomes ubiquitous, we are faced with enormous opportunities, and equally great challenges, to enable communities all around the world to engage with a worldwide marketplace of knowledge, services, and goods without at the same time flattening the diversity of values, practices, and aesthetics that collectively make up the culture of those communities. In this chapter, we seek to contribute to this discussion by offering a perspective on *digitising culture* that draws from a participatory design approach and advocates for a postcolonial computing agenda. The reflections we offer are largely based on our 5-year collaboration with a very remote Australian Aboriginal community on a number of projects targeted at designing information technologies for land conservation, education, and literacy.

One of the community's key values that has guided and informed the research collaboration is the ambition of the community members to 'stand in both worlds' [1], to carry forward tradition and heritage with an outlook towards the future, navigating the opportunities and tensions that may sometimes arise from the

J. L. Taylor (✉) · A. Soro · P. Roe · A. L. Hong · M. Brereton
Queensland University of Technology, 2 George Street, Brisbane, QLD 4000, Australia
e-mail: jen.taylor@qut.edu.au

A. Soro
e-mail: alessandro.soro@qut.edu.au

P. Roe
e-mail: p.roe@qut.edu.au

A. L. Hong
e-mail: anita.leehong@qut.edu.au

M. Brereton
e-mail: m.brereton@qut.edu.au

© Springer Nature Singapore Pte Ltd. 2018
D. S. Jat et al. (eds.), *Digitisation of Culture: Namibian and International Perspectives*, https://doi.org/10.1007/978-981-10-7697-8_2

peculiarities of interactions between local and global cultures. Culture, we came to learn, is not only a key aspect of the community's identity that the Elders (respected community members who are custodians of cultural knowledge) are particularly keen to pass on to the younger generations, but is also seen, in more practical terms, as one pillar of the community's future economic sustainability, enabling the creation of cultural enterprises. Thus, in many ways, above all other considerations of fitness for purpose, functionality, scalability, or economic tradeoffs, designing with culture in mind appeared from the very beginning as one crucial element for a successful design research project with the community.

This is, as we will argue in greater depth in the following sections, all but a straightforward endeavour for a number of different reasons. Firstly, despite a large body of existing work that has explored how culture (or cultural diversity) could inform design, the situated nature of technology design and use as cast by the specificities of participants, resources, and settings means that there is little agreement on these matters. Secondly and symmetrically, there are many takes on what it means for information technology to support culture and what can we expect from these designs, which in turn results from the many meanings attributed to the concept of *culture* despite being described in terms of a 'foundation stone of the social sciences' [2].

Scholars have engaged with this concept coming from very different disciplines and perspectives, starting with anthropology, business management, psychology, and including design and human–computer studies, resulting in a multitude of definitions and conceptualisations, often in conflict with one another. Kroeber and Kluckhohn in their classic review [2] traced the origin of the term back to eighteenth-century German, and in academic discourse to the work of Tylor (1871). They group the many definitions of culture based on whether they put emphasis on enumerating or describing its constituents, on the historical perspectives, on norms and rules, on habits, learning and adapting to the natural surroundings, or on artefacts, including immaterial ones such as ideas, and symbols [2].

While somewhat dated in the language, these definitions could still form the backbone of an analytical framework in that they pinpoint many key aspects of, and perspectives on culture. Attempts to operationalise culture for design have rather taken inspiration from works on cultural differences in order to make sense of how designs may need to be altered to adapt to different cultures. For example, Khaslavsky [3] elaborated on Hofstede's, Hall & Hall's, and Trompenaars & Hampden-Turner's work on cultural differences [4–6] to devise some guidelines to improve the usability of user interfaces for different cultural contexts. Such an approach seems to resonate better with the scope and goals of design research, but comes at the cost of crystallising culture to a reductive set of somewhat stereotyped measurable features, and of making intrepid statements on the preferences or needs of hypothetical users, based on the designers' own potentially shallow understandings of the users' cultures.[1]

---

[1]We assume the reader will be familiar with these issues, but those who are not may be interested in reading for example Rachel Baskerville's '*Hofstede never studied culture*' [7] and Geert Hofstede's '*What is culture? A reply to Baskerville*' [8].

One way forward was offered by Irani and colleagues in their work on *post-colonial computing* [9] that articulates culture as 'a lens through which people collectively encounter the world—a system of interpretive signification through which the world [becomes] inter-subjectively meaningful'. By seeing culture as hybrid, i.e. not bounded by national borders or ethnicities, and generative, i.e. with focus on the processes that create and transform cultural identities, Irani and colleagues shift the attention from designing to adapt to culture, to designing in conversation with culture. In doing so, they reconfigure the design process from gathering requirements and needs to orchestrating the design conversation in ways that are relevant for the culture(s) in which the design process itself is situated [9].

It should be clear by now that committing to one vision of culture equates to committing to a certain epistemological position, whether we decide to look at culture from the outside-in, in the form of taxonomies of social and psychological dimensions that can be isolated, measured and anticipated, or rather if we look at culture from the inside-out, recognising that design decisions embody particular worldviews, ethical beliefs, and values, that will eventually shape the design no matter how implicitly these values and beliefs are held. What is sometimes less evident in design research is the extent to which politics and culture intertwine to re-inscribe one another from generation to generation, and how this affects the design process, including what ideas are promoted, or even just who gets to be heard during the design encounters.

These difficulties in turn resonate with broader questions about participation in technology design, as noted for example by Irani and colleagues [9], Winschiers-Theophilus and colleagues [10], and others. Participatory design methods draw their effectiveness from a culture of democratic participation that may be common in Scandinavia, where those methods originated, but do not necessarily apply in different communities, where different sets of values may exist that determine who gets to participate, who wants to participate, and in which ways. As a result, often the individuals we engage with in cross-cultural design research, even when approaching the project from a participatory design perspective, do not necessarily represent a cross section of the people whose life will be affected by the design, and the insights that emerge from design encounters are not necessarily a reflection of the 'needs' of the community, as they also depend on what funding agencies will sponsor, what the research community will reward as innovative, and overall what the participants perceive will be eventually delivered by the project (see e.g. [11, 12]).

In this broader context, our goal in this chapter is to offer a reflection on how design can contribute to digitising culture by involving the 'users' in the concep-tualisation and realisation of projects that seek to create, search, aggregate, critique, and put to use digital information and digital tools in new ways that can be appropriated into specific cultural performances. With all the limitations hinted at above, a participatory approach that involves the community members in the design process has the potential to ensure that resulting designs embody the values and worldview of the community, rather than those of the designers alone and the institutions they work for. In doing so, these design collaborations foster the critical and technical skills that are necessary for communities to put these technologies to work by leveraging the community's existing technical capacity, and fostering technical skills development during co-design activities.

This means moving the focus to some degree from digital tools to digital literacies and from designing artefacts to designing futures. In the remainder of the chapter, we will review several different perspectives on digitising culture by discussing projects that consider culture as knowledge, as artefacts, as language and literacy, and as values (Sect. 2); we will then introduce our vision for digitising culture as digital literacy, based on a generative view of culture, and a perspective on technology and design as culturally situated (Sect. 3); and finally, we spell out a research agenda with a series of open questions related to designing for cultural processes in the digital era, including methodological and ethical considerations (Sect. 4).

2   Perspectives on Digitising Culture

2.1   *Culture as Artefacts*

From the cultural heritage perspective, one form of cultural expression is through tangible artefacts including 'buildings and historic places, monuments, artefacts, etc., which are considered worthy of preservation for the future' [13]. There are a diverse range of institutions involved in digitising tangible heritage including museums and research institutions, undertaking activities aimed at documenting, preserving, interpreting, and communicating cultural artefacts [14]. Tangible artefacts are represented through a number of technological platforms including 3D representations, virtual and augmented reality, audiovisual displays, and games and applications on mobile devices. The motivations for digitising cultural artefacts in this way are therefore primarily to document and preserve cultural artefacts in order to support research, and facilitate public awareness and cultural heritage education through museum exhibitions and displays [15].

While there are many different programmes of work relating to digitising cultural heritage, a particularly salient agenda in the discipline of computer science is that of '3D cultural heritage', involving the digitisation of existing, damaged, and absent cultural artefacts through the development of 3D models [15]. Much of the 3D cultural heritage work is currently being undertaken in Europe, with recent examples such as the *Digital Mont'e Prama* project in Italy [16]. This project comprises a physical museum exhibition of partially reconstructed prehistoric statues of people and buildings, accompanied by 3D models of the statues displayed on small and large screens that enable museum visitors to view the statues from different angles and read associated information [16].

The emphasis of digitising these cultural artefacts is on documenting *historical* objects: 'cultural heritage is a legacy from the past, which we should pass on to current and future generations' [17], though UNESCO emphasises that other aspects of cultural heritage such as intangible heritage are 'traditional, contemporary and living at the same time' [18]. Some current projects are seeking ways to make connections between historical artefacts and contemporary life. For example, the ʔeləw' k̓ ʷ– Belongings exhibit in British Columbia combines an interactive tabletop surface with tangible artefacts, and allows visitors to explore the connections between historical and contemporary artefacts when they are placed together (e.g. juxtaposing a stone adze and a modern axe), providing information about the significance of the item to Musqueam culture [19].

In the Australian context, cultural heritage researchers such as Greenop and colleagues offer new perspectives on 3D cultural heritage management including a 'cradle-to-grave' approach on the digitisation of places that enables 'a digital version of some places to be sustainably maintained, while the physical version is allowed to decay naturally' [20]. Examples of their work include 3D laser scanning of historical architecture on Palm Island in ways that faithfully represent places while maintaining the physical artefact's 'quality of abandonment' [20]. Australian cultural institutions such as the National Museum of Australia also provide a comprehensive online catalogue of artworks and objects that is accessible to the general public through its website, with each entry comprising a photograph of the object, physical description, and information about its significance [21].

2.2 Culture as Knowledge

A second aspect of cultural heritage is *intangible cultural heritage,* reflected in 'traditions or living expressions inherited from our ancestors and passed on to our descendants, such as oral traditions, performing arts, social practices, rituals, festive events, knowledge and practices' [18]. Tangible artefacts and intangible knowledge are tightly interrelated [22, 23], though some argue that intangible cultural heritage has been 'comparatively less studied' [24]. Rodil and Rehm's recent literature survey of the *International Journal of Intangible Heritage* suggests while there has been relatively even coverage of UNESCO's five domains of intangible cultural heritage, ICT research should feature more strongly on the intangible cultural heritage agenda [25].

Digitising intangible culture encompasses representing both knowledge itself and the ways in which knowledge is performed. A recent example of a project that seeks to digitise intangible heritage is Wang and colleagues' conversational agent of the Chinese philosopher Confucius based on a corpus of Confucius' texts presented through a virtual web interface [24]. The rationale for the project is that interacting with the agent will strengthen users' understanding of Chinese culture and values by gaining information about its intellectual traditions, through a conversational style that invokes characteristics of Chinese philosophical expression [24]. The ʔeləw' k̓ ʷ– Belongings project mentioned in the previous section also addresses intangible aspects of cultural heritage by casting artefacts as 'belongings' and emphasising the Musqueam knowledge in which these artefacts are embedded [19].

Outside the museum, Greenop and colleagues illustrate the potential for social media to engage the community in 'citizen heritage' initiatives such as the Lost in Brisbane Facebook site to share historical and recent photos of an urban Australian landmark [26].

Looking beyond the area of cultural heritage studies, there is a growing body of work within computer science and the HCI community that considers the digitisation of Indigenous knowledges. For example, in the African context, work has been undertaken to support Indigenous storytelling and knowledge sharing in ways that reflect oral cultural traditions [27] such as the *Homestead Creator* [28] in Namibia. In South Africa, Bidwell and colleagues developed a mobile storytelling platform that emphasises collaborative storytelling, audio/visual interface elements over text and non-textual starting points for stories [29]. From a theoretical perspective, Awori et al. contribute a conceptual model for Indigenous knowledge as expressed through people, place, and practice (PPP) [30]. This framework is leveraged for studying the role of video-mediated communication in the performance of Indigenous knowledge and intergenerational cultural transmission between Elders in Kenya and the youth diaspora in Australia [31].

In Australia, there have been a range of interesting projects aimed at digitising Indigenous knowledge and supporting intergenerational knowledge transmission, including reflecting Aboriginal epistemologies and ontologies in technology design. One such area of work is the development of custom knowledge management systems such as *Ieramugadu Cultural Information System* [32] and the *Indigenous Knowledge and Resource Management in northern Australia* (IKRMNA) [33]. In another area of work, Bidwell et al. also illustrate the ways in which existing technologies such as video cameras have been appropriated to produce grounding documentaries for the performance of situated knowledge about bushfire management on country [34]. A third area of work considers technologies that can support Indigenous storytelling and knowledge sharing, such as the use of a game engine to create 3D landscapes to communicate stories and information associated with country, and our own digital community noticeboard project with an Aboriginal community to share local knowledge in ways that reflect Aboriginal cultural perspectives, such as their literacy and event coordination practices [1].

2.3 Culture as Language

Language is a vital aspect of culture practised in 'communication between people' that embodies shared verbal and visual meaning systems [35]. According to WIPO, traditional cultural expressions '[...] form part of the identity and heritage of a traditional or indigenous community' [36], and can take various forms including verbal, musical, visual and tangible artefacts [37]. Language has been a specific focus of digitising culture, either in its own right or in association with broader cultural heritage projects.

Designing technology for language preservation, revitalisation, and instruction is another aspect of digitising culture, with a particular focus on maintaining minority and endangered languages. Holton outlines two categories of technology that can support minority languages: one is *technology products* for language learning including multimedia stories, online courses, and electronic dictionaries; the other is *online technologies* such as email lists, podcasts, and forums that foster local and geographically dispersed communities of language speakers [38]. There are a host of applications for preservation and revitalisation of Aboriginal and Torres Strait Islander languages in Australia. For example, the *Living Archive of Aboriginal Languages* is a dynamic online repository of digital bilingual education materials in English and Australian Aboriginal and Torres Strait islander languages, including illustrated children's storybooks, historical accounts, and information on topics such as bush medicine [39]. Bird and colleagues have been active in developing technologies such as the *Aikuma* mobile app that allow any Indigenous language speakers with the application to contribute their own voice recordings to digital corpora [40].

While written communication is one means of expressing languages using written literacy skills, efforts to support digital communication in different cultural contexts have also considered designing to support other types of literacy and languages with non-Roman alphabets. Extensions to existing platforms such as computer and mobile phone keyboards and screen readers in languages other than English are enhancing the ability to share content in languages that may have a non-Latin script. Numerous ICT for Development (ICT4D) projects have also considered ways to design interfaces for people from oral cultural backgrounds with low written literacy for provision of information in areas such as education and health care, including through oral, graphical, and live operator interfaces [41]. In terms of oral cultural traditions, *orality-grounded design* outlines different ways of teaching, learning, remembering, and organising information in oral languages and cultures, with resulting principles for information and technology design [42]. Zaman et al. provide an overview of other types of Indigenous language systems that can be supported through design such as smoke signals, sand drawings, sign languages, and whistle languages [43].

Designers have taken up this call to address different types of language systems and cultural expression through a range of multimodal systems, in particular by leveraging digital tools that are already in use such as SMS technology. In Australia, SMS messaging has supported creativity and language play in Aboriginal languages such as experimenting with new words, expressions and creoles [44]. Zaman et al. also illustrate how a visual SMS system is supporting Indigenous language revitalisation in Malaysia by helping youth to learn and communicate in the Oroo sign language [43, 45]. Our own digital community noticeboard project has supported cultural expression in both English and an Australian Aboriginal language by allowing users to create stories and notices in any combination of text, audio and video, with karaoke-style text highlighting supporting playback [46]. These projects emphasise the role that digital tools can play in supporting language learning and *use*, in addition to the repositories of language documentation produced by the research community such as linguists.

2.4 Culture as Values

Culture is also expressed through a community's *values*, conveyed in Hiller's definition of culture as 'the beliefs, systems of thought, practical arts, manner of living, customs, traditions, and all socially regularized ways of acting' (in [2]). Digitising culture in this sense also refers to designing digital tools in ways that reflect particular cultural values.

As mentioned in the introduction, models of cultural values such as Hofstede's 'cultural dimensions' [47] have been enlisted in design endeavours such as cross-cultural design through software localisation and internationalisation [48]. Internationalisation attempts to 'eliminate culture' from interfaces by removing 'cultural symbols [and] religious references' [49], while localisation 'caters to the needs of the local target group' (ibid.). These efforts to adapt existing interfaces to new cultural contexts have centred upon adapting various design aspects including 'language, social context, time, currency, units of measure, cultural values, body positions, symbols and aesthetics' [49]. However, this approach is being increasingly recognised as problematic by the interaction design community since the applicability of Western usability principles in cross-cultural contexts has been called into question [49], and 'transferring meaning' between cultural contexts is more complex than the technical aspects of 'translating a dialogue box or localizing an icon' [50]. More critical discussion of taxonomic cultural models from a post-colonial computing perspective [9] is included in the next section.

From another angle, digitising cultural values may also relate to how we consider cultural values in both design methods and products, particularly in participatory design. For example, Friedman and colleagues pioneered the concept of *Value-Sensitive Design* that 'accounts for human values in a principled and comprehensive manner', based on the definition of values as 'what a person or group of people consider important in life' [51]. This approach is predicated on the three pillars of 'conceptual investigations' as to what stakeholders value and how competing values should be balanced, 'empirical investigations' of values in context including through technology use, and 'technical investigations' of how computer systems can 'support or hinder human values' [51]. Recent discussions by Borning et al. have posited that value-sensitive design downplays the fact that values are not culturally universal and researchers bring their own values to design encounters [52], echoing Winschiers-Theophilus et al. arguments about the culturally situated nature of participation [10].

There are a number of Australian projects that illustrate the enactment of Aboriginal and Torres Strait Islander cultural values in the design process. This can be seen in the alignment of participatory design activities with a community's social protocols and cultural values, as in the case of storytelling workshops in our digital community noticeboard project. We noticed a preference for working in groups due to the collective nature of the local Aboriginal culture, with different people from the community contributing to notice making activities in different ways (e.g. recording the audio, translating, typing text, etc.) [53] and an emphasis on harmony and reaching consensus through group work more than usability or fitness for purpose of the interface [46]. These values can also be emphasised and celebrated in technology use, such as Christie and Verran's proof of concept for an iPad app called the 'Touch Pad Body' for health workers in Aboriginal communities that displays visual representations of the body [54]. Prospective use of the application is intended to stimulate dialogue between healthcare workers and Aboriginal people based on the values of communication as 'building shared understandings' [54]. However, we acknowledge that values may differ even between people who share a culture; recent work by Akama et al. has explored ways to navigate and represent 'heterogeneity' in a design project to stimulate conversation around the topic of Indigenous nation building [55].

3 Towards an Alternative Vision of Digitising Culture as Cultural Hybridity, Culturally Situated Technology, and Digital Literacy

3.1 From Digital Representations of Culture to Supporting Cultural Processes

In the previous section, we outline four main currents of conversation on the topic of digitising culture, with a common thread being the motivation to *save* or *preserve* aspects of culture so that they are not lost in future. For cultural artefacts, 3D models capture knowledge about the tangible properties of the object and associated knowledge in forms that may persist in spite of physical degradation of the object itself. For intangible aspects of cultural knowledge and traditions, creating digital language repositories such as databases and multimedia products supports language documentation and preservation, as well as language learning and revitalization efforts. There is a general desire in Australia and elsewhere to safeguard Indigenous knowledges for the future so that they live on after older generations have passed away [33]. From a culture as values perspective, design seeks to maintain users' beliefs and interests both through the use of design methods, e.g. participatory design, or seeking to represent them in interfaces as per the mandate of software localisation and internationalisation [48].

However, an alternative current of thought emphasises the fact that culture and knowledge is living and performed. Some cultural heritage scholars assert that 'documentary records of intangible cultural heritage *are not the heritage itself*' ([22] emphasis added), and while digital representations have the potential to support the situated enactment of knowledge, this may not be realised [22]. In the case of Indigenous knowledge, Christie and colleagues assert that digital resources such as databases contain *information* rather than *knowledge*, and that the educational value of these resources lies in the way that they support teaching and learning processes [56]. While some Australian Aboriginal and Torres Strait

Islander people may consider encoding knowledge in technology to be at odds with holistic systems of traditional knowledges that are performed 'on country', digital technologies are being developed and adopted into the knowledge practices of Aboriginal communities in diverse ways [33, 34].

If knowledge is performed, can culture be 'saved' in digital forms? The postcolonial computing agenda advocates for a shift away from viewing culture as static to understanding it as 'generative' and performed [9]. We advance the postcolonial computing notion that technology is always culturally constructed and situated, rather than neutral vessels into which culture can be loaded. Instead, we suggest a different role for digital technologies in supporting cultural processes as they are actively lived and experienced in people's everyday lives. We therefore advocate for a vision of digitising culture in which technology supports people to *enact culture in the digital age*, and people are equipped with both cultural knowledge and the skills to perform it. In this section, we unpack arguments underpinning this position: culture as generative, technology as culturally situated, and digitising culture as digital literacy, and complex interplays between digital and material forms.

3.2   Culture as Hybrid, Generative, and Performed

Firstly, the concept of culture as 'generative' has received much attention in postcolonial computing literature [9]. Irani and colleagues have highlighted the pitfalls of taxonomic cultural models such as Hofstede's cultural dimensions that present culture as quantifiable values, treat cultural traits as inherent, and use them as a way to group and differentiate between people based on 'cultural difference' [57]. In particular, they highlight that static perspectives of culture and the borders between them are increasingly questionable in light of technologically facilitated globalisation [9]. Yet, some scholars have remarked on the difficulties in developing practical understandings of the ways in which cultural generativity is experienced, and how this perspective can be operationalised in design practice [58]. A generative view of culture has been described in several different ways in the postcolonial computing literature, in terms of both individual cultural identity and collective cultural expression. These include culture as

- a '*lens* through which people collectively encounter the world' ([57], emphasis added)
- '*positions* in relation to multiple flows of people, capital, discourses...' ([57], emphasis added) and the process of 'investing in a particular (subject) position' [58];
- the 'cultural *experience*' of an individual ([9], emphasis added)
- a '*spectrum* along which a single person's cultural identity may traverse over time' in which 'the temporal movement and passage [...] prevents identities at either end of it from settling into primordial polarities' (Bhabha in [58], emphasis added);

- a *'third space* where the subjectivities of both researcher and researched are mutually constructed, and meanings and interactions are also mediated, as is knowledge itself' ([59], emphasis added).

While these definitions differ, the general implication is that culture is *lived* and evolves as it is produced and reproduced through our everyday activities. While digital representations can provide snapshots of some aspects of culture at a particular point in time, they are necessarily reductive. Viewing culture as generative, hybrid, and performed aligns with the agenda of practice-based design [60] to explore how technology is socially and culturally situated within people's everyday activities. This has been taken up by Zaman and colleagues in the development of a holistic Indigenous Knowledge Governance Framework for ICT design that approaches Indigenous knowledge as 'way of life that includes dynamic practices' [61].

3.3 Technology as Culturally Situated and Socially Constructed

Secondly, technology is both culturally situated and socially constructed in the ways that it is appropriated into particular settings and the meanings that are attributed to it, with Lindtner et al. framing technology adoption as a type of *cultural appropriation* through people 'mak[ing] the technology their own' [62]. An example of this is the uptake of mobile phones in remote Australian Aboriginal communities, where the primary use attributed to mobile phones is not placing telephone calls but instead offline sharing of multimedia content such as photographs, videos, and games with others through Bluetooth [63]. While infrastructure limitations and costs may hamper mobile phone use for making calls and sending text messages, Shaw et al. contend that mobile phones have in fact been 'creatively reconstructed and reproduced as socialized artefacts' that enact and extend the social practices within these communities [63].

Technology can be designed in ways that either explicitly or implicitly encode particular values or biases, such as particular cultural perspectives of time. Bidwell and colleagues suggest that technology can embody 'modernist' temporal values such as planning, scheduling and efficiency that resonate with Western business culture, and may not reflect alternative time practices in African communities [64]. For example, Wyche et al. illustrate that different cultural expectations around email use and response times between Kenyan workers and users in the West disrupts local temporal rhythms and preferences for 'co-present communication' [65]. In our own work, we have considered ways in which a digital community noticeboard could bring together Western time practices and those of Australian Aboriginal cultures, showing that the use of a noticeboard for advertising funeral timings in advance is at odds with a more situated approach to time management where funerals start when the 'right' set of circumstances is in place [66].

There are many other threads of HCI scholarship that explore the relationship between culture and technology, including how culture shapes our experience, e.g. with materials [67], cultures of technology making and hacking organisations, e.g. feminist hackerspaces [68] and cultures of online communities, e.g. ethnographic accounts of online gaming worlds [69]. While we are not able to address these areas here in detail, our purpose is to illustrate the entangled nature of culture and technology and suggest that processes and outputs of digitising culture are sites of cross-cultural encounters.

3.4 Digitising Culture as Digital Literacy

Thirdly, performing culture is not only about having cultural knowledge but also the *skills to carry out this knowledge* including the *digital literacy* skills to enlist technology in cultural practices. Within a myriad of definitions of digital literacy, four different components of digital literacy proposed by Bawden are (1) technology, (2) information about the world, (3) skills and competencies (e.g. locating, understanding and evaluating information) and (4) individual attitudes and perspectives [70]. While traditional definitions of literacy are concerned with reading and writing, digital technologies are giving rise to new forms of literacy by increasing the diversity of global and local cultures and paving the way for new types of text [71]. A core part of the multiliteracies perspective is the emphasis on multimodal literacy in the way that different 'modes of meaning' are combined together to construct texts, including linguistic, audio, spatial, gestural, and visual modes [71].

A multiliteracies perspective can inform technology design in ways that better account for diverse forms of cultural expression such as oral cultural traditions [42] embodied in song or storytelling, and non-Western epistemologies for teaching and learning. For example, in Australia the *8 Aboriginal Ways of Learning* is an 'Aboriginal pedagogy framework' based on principles such as 'hands-on', 'visualized' and 'narrative-driven learning' that attends to Aboriginal ways of knowing, being and doing [72]. Recent work by Mills et al. has further demonstrated features of Indigenous multimodal literacy practices as 'transgenerational, multimodal, placed, and collective', with resulting implications for both educators and technology designers [73]. Our vision for digitising culture therefore requires designing to engage with and support these situated and emergent literacy practices, including designing for literacy and orality as part of the digital community noticeboard project to support the community's aspirations for Aboriginal youth to 'stand in both worlds' [1]. In addition, designing for multimodal literacy implies also enabling the noticeboard to be maintained locally by Aboriginal people, and engaging Aboriginal people in developing technical skills so that they can create and appropriate designs from themselves.

4   Designing to Support Cultural Processes in a Digital Era

In the previous section, we have outlined a vision for digitising culture that is about designing in ways that support people to *perform their culture in the digital era* and engage with a variety of digital literacies, with all the possibilities and complexities that this entails. We reflect on some of the challenges of realising this vision by outlining some open questions that will inform our research agenda in this area in the coming years.

4.1   Design Questions

The postcolonial computing agenda advocates for designing in ways that privilege hybrid and generative perspectives of culture [9], but what does this mean in practice? One apparent tension is the focus on documenting, quantifying, accounting for and reconciling *cultural differences* in cross-cultural design. In projects that engage with Indigenous peoples, critical whiteness scholars such as Aileen Moreton-Robinson critique the apparent 'epistemic fixation with our cultural differences', arguing for a shift away from focusing on differences to reflecting the 'density' of people's experiences and multiple subject positions [74]. What are the broader implications for our efforts to 'digitise culture'? We have illustrated many different perspectives on what is meant by digitising culture, where culture can be understood as a variety of things including artefacts, knowledge, language, and values. Yet, by looking to digitise particular aspects of culture one at a time, do we risk losing a more holistic understanding of culture, as argued by Winschiers-Theophilus and colleagues [75]?

What is drawn into focus and left out of the lens of cross-cultural design is the subject of ongoing discussion in the design research community. For example, Winschiers-Theophilus and colleagues propose a *transcultural* approach for design with Indigenous communities to 'look beyond culture' by emphasising community collaborations and co-creation of meaning that are cultural 'blends' beyond individual contributions [75]. Another line of inquiry is reflected in our own efforts to design community technologies that support lived experiences of cultural hybridity. A guiding principle of our digital community noticeboards project has been to advance the community's aspirations to 'stand in both worlds' by celebrating and maintaining traditional language and culture while also engaging with the mainstream economy [1], resonating with Nakata's notion of the 'cultural interface' [76]. We are currently undertaking further empirical work to understand the 'both worlds' experience of Aboriginal and Torres Strait Islander people in urban, regional, and remote areas, and identify the role of technology in these cultural journeys.

Literacy practices in the digital era are also shifting, and the design research community is still beginning to engage with emerging theoretical perspectives on literacy, such as the multiliteracies agenda [77] previously discussed. Performing culture using digital technologies therefore goes beyond the functional skills of reading and writing, to an understanding of how to use an app, or the ability to access and use information [70]. It requires critical thinking and analytical skills to produce, access, evaluate, use, and critique digital representations of culture conveyed through new forms of text, referred to by some as 'critical multimodal literacy' [78]. However, viewing cultural processes in terms of digital literacy competencies begs the question of by whose standards these competencies will be measured, and how do we avoid deficit logics that pervade policies such the Australian Government's program to *Close The Gap* to address disadvantage among Aboriginal and Torres Strait Islander people [79]?

4.2 Methodological Questions

Designing for cultural practices in the digital age also gives rise to a number of methodological questions and challenges. A central concern of design research is ensuring long-term engagement and sustainability in technology design projects, including those aimed at 'digitising culture'. For example, there are a growing number of new digital resources and mobile applications to support literacy skills development and cultural expression in English and Aboriginal and Torres Strait Islander languages, including bilingual dictionary applications and storytelling platforms like the noticeboard. How do we ensure that such systems are both useful to and used by speakers of Aboriginal and Torres Strait Islander languages? Moreover, how do we design in ways that narrow rather than widen the gap between 'technology makers' and 'culture makers'? Key to designing for adoption and use is identifying ways in which technology can enter into the 'networks of relations' of people and resources that frame our social practices [80] as per the situated 'third paradigm' of human–computer interaction [81]. As design researchers, what design research methods can enable us to understand how digital technologies produce and are produced by cultural processes?

Many cross-cultural design projects, particularly those that engage with Indigenous people, take participatory design approaches [82] in recognising people's rights to be involved in designing the technology that they use in ways that reflect their values and perspectives. At a broader level, we relate to the idea that technology design goes beyond designing technical artefacts, to advancing Indigenous agendas in recognising Indigenous people's rights to sovereignty [11]. However, as Winschiers-Theophilus and colleagues note, 'participation' has different meanings across different cultural contexts and design methods need to contextualised to suit the local setting [10]. In the case of the digital community noticeboard project, *reciprocity* has been a guiding value which resonates with the notion of 'mutual and cooperative exchange' in Australian Aboriginal cultures [83].

We have used a number of dialogical methods such as 'yarning' [84] and 'cross-cultural dialogical probes' [85], which better align with the community's social protocols than standard interview and workshop methods, and support the co-creation of knowledge about how technology is situated within the community's social practices. Winschiers-Theophilus et al. warn against so-called 'white elephant' projects, where a lack of engagement with the community can result in the design of technologies that become a liability to users rather than an asset [86].

Yet, we continue to grapple with a number of methodological complexities. One ongoing issue is determining ways to meaningfully involve people in all aspects of the design research process who may not be design researchers themselves. This includes involvement in both designing interfaces (e.g. the noticeboard interface) and content (e.g. stories on the noticeboard) and establishing and continuing use, to documenting the design process, and disseminating knowledge generated to the design research community, as well as to the local community. This can be particularly challenging when skills and interests in the project differ to the extent that the community's objectives for the project can be 'orthogonal' to those of the researchers [87]. However, there is limited published discussion of ways to support people's participation in other aspects of the design process including establishing the project, securing the funding, documenting the design process, documenting appropriation and use, and authoring research publications. Siew and Yeo contribute the PRISMA model for participatory action research in software development, illustrating a Malaysian community's involvement in all stages of developing a mobile healthcare application including establishing the project goals, setting the project direction and developing the software [88]. A recent proposition by Molapo et al. is to allow time in the design process for people to explore design concepts and prototypes and 'develop confidence and experience' to 'productively' take part in design conversations [89].

Another area of complexity relates to evaluating the success of design interventions to support cultural practices and measuring outcomes. While evaluating usability and user experience aspects has an important place in ensuring that design products are useful and used, this may not provide a complete picture of what place technology has in these networks of relations and overlook engagement and sustainability issues [90]. Designing to support the performance of culture is inherently a project of designing cultural *futures*, and visions for futures containing technology may shift over time. For example, in the case of the noticeboard project, actual use of the noticeboard shifted from being analogous to a paper noticeboard to functioning as an educational tool in schools and a community multimedia repository [90]. Therefore, we argue that a shift in perspective is needed from evaluating design prototypes in use to evaluating whether visions for cultural futures are still desirable in light of technology, and mapping our progress towards them (ibid.). This includes identifying the role of technology in supporting a community's broader goals such as fostering sustainable rural tourism, while managing associated risks and challenges including environmental degradation [91]. Future work is needed to understand how design methods can be enlisted to put this perspective into practice.

4.3   Ethical Questions

A third area for consideration is the ethical issues implicated in designing to support cultural performances, such as the complexities of navigating intellectual property rights and ownership issues over digital representations of intangible cultural heritage [36]. Since videos and images of cultural expressions such as a ceremonial dance can so easily be created by anyone and distributed online, how do we ensure that intellectual property rights to both the dance itself and digital representations of the dance are recognised? Respecting rights and ownership over traditional knowledge is a principle in the *AIATSIS Guidelines for Ethical Research in Australian Indigenous Studies* [92]. This includes negotiating differing perspectives of intellectual property between Western and Aboriginal and Torres Strait Islander ways of knowing, including the nature of knowledge itself and individual versus communal ownership of knowledge [93]. While ownership over design artefacts such as an interface and its contents may be easy to establish, rights to co-created knowledge about technology use in context generated through the design process may be less clear-cut.

There are also sensitivities around the process of gaining informed consent, where utilitarian ethics approaches may not align well with the values and social protocols of alternative cultural perspectives such as those of Aboriginal and Torres Strait Islander people. One challenge is the fact that the work of a 'technology designer' may not be so commonly understood compared to other roles such as that of an 'anthropologist' or a 'linguist' who may be permanently employed within an Aboriginal or Torres Strait Islander community. Therefore, part of a design researcher's work is building awareness and understanding of the type of work undertaken by a design researcher, including design problems and opportunities, methods, technical artefacts and broader aspects of the research process. While we explain the project to participants and request that they sign an informed consent form, often the act of signing the form itself can present the most confronting aspect of participating in design research, particularly given many Indigenous communities are 'overresearched' communities with a historical legacy of exploitation [83].

Additionally, encounters with and responses to ethical dilemmas in design research are often not reported on within research outputs, though there is increasing dialogue surrounding ethics issues in the human–computer interaction community, including a series of workshops organised in Australia and overseas [94]. Munteanu and colleagues posit that the standard ethics protocols often do not account for ethical complexities of conducting an exploratory design approach, where a 'situational ethics' is needed to fill the void [95], extended by Frauenberger and others as an 'in-action' ethics framework [96]. Design researchers may look to alternative perspectives on ethics such as 'deontological ethics' that emphasises delivering a mutual flow of benefit to those involved in the project beyond issues such as confidentiality and informed consent that are salient in medical research [97]. In a similar vein to our discussion of methodological questions, there are open issues regarding ethics in all aspects of the design research process including documentation and publication that warrant further consideration.

5 Conclusions

In conclusion, we present a view of digitising culture as designing technology to support cultural processes in the digital era, informed by our own work on a digital community noticeboard project with a very remote Australian Aboriginal community. We have outlined many of the existing perspectives on digitising culture as artefacts, knowledge, language, and values, illustrated with local examples from the Australian context and international projects. While creating cultural repositories and digital representations is a common thread through much of this discussion, we take the postcolonial computing vision of culture as hybrid and technology as culturally situated [98] as a starting point to advocate for the position of digitising culture as designing for cultural performances and the digital literacy skills that this entails. Finally, we have posed a series of open questions and challenges relating to design approaches, methods, and ethics with which we will continue to grapple over the coming years. By contributing to the discussion on digitising culture and technology design, we hope to carry forward the vision of fostering digital skills and creativity so that every community can create digital tools to embed in their cultural performance on and in their own terms. While this may include digital repositories and representations of cultural artefacts and knowledge, digitising culture reaches beyond this to permeate the cultural performances of everyday life in all their beauty and complexity.

Acknowledgements We thank and acknowledge the Anindilyakwa community and their Land Council for the opportunity to develop this noticeboard with them, as well as the Australian Research Council for Linkage Grant LP120200329. We also acknowledge the support and generosity of those who have reviewed and given feedback on this chapter, in particular Heike Winschiers-Theophilus for her guidance.

References

1. Soro, A., Lee Hong, A., Shaw, G., Roe, P., Brereton, M.: A noticeboard in "both worlds" unsurprising interfaces supporting easy bi-cultural content publication. In: Proceedings of the 33rd Annual ACM Conference Extended Abstracts on Human Factors in Computing Systems (CHI EA '15), pp. 2181–2186. Association for Computing Machinery, New York City, New York (2015)
2. Kroeber, A.L., Kluckhohn, C.: Culture: a critical review of concepts and definitions (1952)
3. Khaslavsky, J.: Integrating culture into interface design. In: CHI 98 Conference Summary on Human Factors in Computing Systems, pp. 365–366. ACM, New York, NY, USA (1998)
4. Hofstede, G.: Culture's consequences: comparing values, behaviors, institutions and organizations across nations. Sage (2003)
5. Hall, E.T., Hall, M.R.: Understanding Cultural Differences. Intercultural Press, Yarmouth, ME (1990)
6. Trompenaars, F., Hampden-Turner, C.: Riding the Waves of Culture: Understanding Diversity in Global Business. Nicholas Brealey Publishing, London (2011)
7. Baskerville, R.F.: Hofstede never studied culture. Accounting, Organ. Soc. **28**, 1–14 (2003)

8. Hofstede, G.: What is culture? A reply to Baskerville. Accounting, Organ. Soc. **28**, 811–813 (2003)
9. Irani, L., Vertesi, J., Dourish, P., Philip, K., Grinter, R.E.: Postcolonial computing: a lens on design and development. In: Proceedings of 28th International Conference on Human Factors Computer System—CHI '10, pp. 1312–1320 (2010)
10. Winschiers-Theophilus, H., Chivuno-Kuria, S., Kapuire, G.K., Bidwell, N.J., Blake, E.: Being participated—a community approach. In: Proceedings of the 11th Biennial Participatory Design Conference (PDC '10), pp. 1–10. Association for Computing Machinery, New York City, New York (2010)
11. Tuhiwai Smith, L.: Decolonizing Methodologies: Research and Indigenous Peoples. Zed Books, London (2012)
12. Mosse, D.: People's knowledge, participation and patronage: operations and representations in rural development. In: Cook, B., Kothari, U. (eds.) Participation: The New Tyranny? Zed Press, London (2001)
13. UNESCO: Tangible Cultural Heritage. http://www.unesco.org/new/en/cairo/culture/tangible-cultural-heritage/
14. Arnold, D., Geser, G.: EPOCH Research Agenda for the Applications of ICT to Cultural Heritage (2008)
15. Koller, D., Frischer, B., Humphreys, G.: Research challenges for digital archives of 3D cultural heritage models. J. Comput. Cult. Herit. **2**, 1–17 (2009)
16. Rodríguez, M.B., Agus, M., Bettio, F., Marton, F., Gobbetti, E.: Digital Mont'e Prama: exploring large collections of detailed 3D models of sculptures. J. Comput. Cult. Herit. **9**, 1–23 (2016)
17. Hachet, M., Dellepiane, M.: Introduction to special issue on interacting with the past. ACM J. Comput. Cult. Herit. **7**, 6e (2014)
18. UNESCO: What is Intangible Cultural Heritage. http://ich.unesco.org/en/what-is-intangible-heritage-00003
19. Muntean, R., Hennessy, K., Antle, A., Rowley, S., Wilson, J., Matkin, B., Eckersley, R., Tan, P., Wakkary, R.: ʔeləwkʷ—belongings: a tangible interface for intangible cultural heritage. In: Proceedings of the Conference on Electronic Visualisation and the Arts, pp. 360–366. British Computing Society (2015)
20. Greenop, K., Landorf, C.: Grave-to-cradle: a paradigm shift for heritage conservation and interpretation in the era of 3D laser scanning. Hist. Environ. **29**, 44–55 (2017)
21. National Museum of Australia: National Museum of Australia. http://www.nma.gov.au/
22. Bonn, M., Kendall, L., McDonough, J.: Preserving intangible heritage: defining a research agenda. In: Proceedings of the Association for Information Science and Technology, pp. 1–5 (2016)
23. Lombardo, V., Pizzo, A., Damiano, R.: Safeguarding and accessing drama as intangible cultural heritage. J. Comput. Cult. Herit. **9**, 1–26 (2016)
24. Wang, X., Khoo, E.T., Nakatsu, R., Cheok, A.: Interacting with traditional Chinese culture through natural language. J. Comput. Cult. Herit. **7**, 18:1–18:19 (2014)
25. Rodil, K., Rehm, M.: A decade later: looking at the past while sketching the future of ICH through the tripartite digitisation model. Int. J. Intang. Herit. **10**, 47–60 (2015)
26. Greenop, K., Juckes, E., Landorf, C.: King George Square's citizens: social media and the intangible cultural heritage of a Brisbane icon. Hist. Environ. **28**, 26–43 (2016)
27. Rodil, K., Winschiers-Theophilus, H.: Indigenous storytelling in Namibia: sketching concepts for digitization. In: Proceeding of the International Conference on Culture and Computing, Culture and Computing, pp. 80–86. IEEE, New York City, New York (2015)
28. Rodil, K., Winschiers-Theophilus, H., Jensen, K.L., Rehm, M.: Homestead creator. In: Proceedings of the 7th Nordic Conference on Human-Computer Interaction Making Sense Through Design—NordiCHI '12, pp. 627–630. Association for Computing Machinery, New York City, New York (2012)

29. Bidwell, N.J., Reitmaier, T., Marsden, G., Hansen, S.: Designing with mobile digital storytelling in rural Africa. In: Proceedings of CHI 2010, pp. 1593–1602. Association for Computing Machinery, New York City, New York (2010)
30. Awori, K., Vetere, F., Smith, W.: Transnationalism, indigenous knowledge and technology: insights from the Kenyan Diaspora. In: Proceedings of the ACM CHI'15 Conference on Human Factors in Computing Systems, pp. 3759–3768 (2015)
31. Awori, K., Vetere, F., Smith, W.: Sessions with grandma: fostering indigenous knowledge through video mediated communication. In: Proceedings of AfriCHI 2016, pp. 1–11. Association for Computing Machinery, New York City, New York (2016)
32. Turk, A., Trees, K.: Appropriate computer-mediated communication: an Australian indigenous information system case study. AI Soc. **13**, 377–388 (1999)
33. Verran, H., Christie, M., Anbins-King, B., Van Weeren, T., Yunupingu, W.: Designing digital knowledge management tools with Aboriginal Australians. Digit. Creat. **18**, 129–142 (2007)
34. Bidwell, N.J., Standley, P.-M., George, T., Steffensen, V.: The landscape's apprentice: lessons for place-centred design from grounding documentary. In: Proceedings of DIS 2008, pp. 88–98. Association for Computing Machinery, New York City, NY, USA (2008)
35. Merritt, S., Bardzell, S.: Postcolonial language and culture theory for HCI4D. In: CHI '11 Extended Abstracts on Human Factors in Computing Systems (CHI EA '11), pp. 1675–1680. Association for Computing Machinery, New York City, New York (2011)
36. World Intellectual Property Organization: Traditional Knowledge. http://www.wipo.int/tk/en/tk/
37. Wong, T., Fernandini, C.: Traditional cultural expressions: preservation and innovation. In: Wong, T., Dutfield, G. (eds.) Intellectual Property and Human Development: Current Trends and Future Scenarios. Cambridge University Press, Cambridge (2011)
38. Holton, G.: The role of information technology in supporting minority and endangered languages. In: Austin, P., Sallabank, J. (eds.) The Cambridge Handbook of Endangered Languages, pp. 371–399. Cambridge University Press, Cambridge (2011)
39. Mamtora, J., Bow, C.: Towards a unique archive of aboriginal languages: a collaborative project. J. Aust. Libr. Inf. Assoc. **66**, 28–41 (2017)
40. Bird, S., Hanke, F.R., Adams, O., Lee, H.: Aikuma: a mobile app for collaborative language documentation. In: Proceedings of the 2014 Workshop on the Use of Computational Methods in the Study of Endangered Languages, pp. 1–5 (2014)
41. Medhi, I., Patnaik, S., Brunskill, E., Gautama, S.N.N., Thies, W., Toyama, K.: Designing mobile interfaces for novice and low-literacy users. ACM Trans. Comput. Interact. **18**, 2:1–2:28 (2011)
42. Rosenfeld, R., Sherwani, J., Ali, N., Rosé, C.P.: Orality-grounded HCID: understanding the oral user. Inf. Technol. Int. Dev. **5**, 37 (2009)
43. Zaman, T., Winschiers-Theophilus, H.: Penan's Oroo' short message signs (PO-SMS): co-design of a digital jungle sign language application. In: Proceedings of INTERACT 2015, pp. 489–504. IFIP International Federation for Information Processing (2015)
44. Kral, I.: Plugged in: remote Australian indigenous youth and digital culture. CAEPR working paper (2010)
45. Zaman, T., Winschiers-theophilus, H., Yeo, A.W., Ting, L.C., Jengan, G.: Reviving an indigenous rainforest sign language: digital Oroo' adventure game. In: ICTD '15: Proceedings of the Seventh International Conference on Information and Communication Technologies and Development, pp. 15–18. Association for Computing Machinery, New York City, New York (2015)
46. Soro, A., Brereton, M., Taylor, J.L., Hong, A.L., Roe, P.: A cross-cultural noticeboard for a remote community: design, deployment, and evaluation. In: Proceedings of INTERACT 2017. Association for Computing Machinery, New York City, New York (2017)
47. Hofstede, G.: Cultures and Organizations: Software of the Mind. McGraw-Hill USA, New York City, New York (1997)
48. Heimgärtner, R.: Intercultural User Interface Design. In: Web Design and Development: Concepts, Methodologies, Tools, and Applications, pp. 113–146. Information Resources Management Association (USA), Hershey (2015)

49. George, R., Nesbitt, K., Gillard, P., Donovan, M.: Identifying cultural design requirements for an Australian indigenous website. In: Proceedings of the Eleventh Australasian Conference on User Interface (AUIC '10), pp. 89–97. Conferences in Research and Practice in Information Technology, Brisbane (2010)

50. Sun, H.: Cross-Cultural Technology Design: Creating Culture-Sensitive Technology for Local Users. Oxford University Press, Oxford (2012)

51. Friedman, B., Kahn Jr., P.H., Borning, A.: Value sensitive design and information systems. In: The Handbook of Information and Computer Ethics, pp. 69–101. Wiley, New Jersey (2008)

52. Borning, A., Muller, M.: Next steps for value sensitive design. In: Proceedings of the 2012 ACM Annual Conference on Human Factors in Computing Systems—CHI '12, p. 1125 (2012)

53. Soro, A., Brereton, M., Lee Hong, A., Roe, P.: Bi-cultural content publication on a digital noticeboard: a design and cultural differences case study. In: Proceedings of the Annual Meeting of the Australian Special Interest Group for Computer Human Interaction (OzCHI '15), pp. 217–221. Association for Computing Machinery, New York City, New York (2015)

54. Christie, M., Verran, H.: Digital lives in postcolonial Aboriginal Australia. J. Mater. Cult. **18**, 299–317 (2013)

55. Akama, Y., Keen, S., West, P.: Speculative design and heterogeneity in indigenous nation building. In: Proceedings of the 2016 ACM Conference on Designing Interactive Systems, pp. 895–899 (2016)

56. Christie, M.: Computer databases and Aboriginal knowledge. Learn. Communities Int. J. Learn. Soc Context. **1**, 4–12 (2004)

57. Irani, L., Dourish, P.: Postcolonial interculturality. In: Proceedings of the 2009 International Workshop on Intercultural Collaboration (IWIC '09), pp. 249–252. Association for Computing Machinery, New York City, New York (2009)

58. Merritt, S., Stolterman, E.: Cultural hybridity in participatory design. In: Proceedings of the 2012 Participatory Design Conference 2012 (PDC '12), pp. 73–76. Association for Computing Machinery, New York City, New York (2012)

59. Mainsah, H., Morrison, A.: Participatory design through a cultural lens: insights from postcolonial theory. In: Proceedings of the 13th Participatory Design Conference. Association for Computing Machinery, New York City, New York (2014)

60. Kuutti, K., Bannon, L.: The turn to practice in HCI: towards a research agenda. In: Proceedings of the SIGCHI Conference on Human Factors in Computing Systems (CHI '14), pp. 3543–3552. Association for Computing Machinery, New York City, New York (2014)

61. Zaman, T., Yeo Wee, A., Kulathuramaiyer, N.: Introducing indigenous knowledge governance into ICT-based indigenous knowledge management system. In: IPID 8th International Annual Symposium (2013)

62. Lindtner, S., Anderson, K., Dourish, P.: Cultural appropriation: Information technologies as sites of transnational imagination. In: Proceedings of the ACM 2012 Conference on Computer Supported Cooperative Work, pp. 77–86. Association for Computing Machinery, New York City, New York (2012)

63. Shaw, G., Brereton, M., Roe, P.: Mobile phone use in Australian indigenous communities: future pathways for HCI4D. In: Proceedings of OzCHI 2014, pp. 480–483. Association for Computing Machinery, New York City, New York (2014)

64. Bidwell, N.J., Reitmaier, T., Rey-Moreno, C., Roro, Z., Siya, M.J., Dlutu, B.: Timely relations in rural Africa. In: Proceedings of the 12th International Conference on Social Implications of Computers in Developing Countries (IFIP Conferences), pp. 92–106 (2013)

65. Wyche, S.P., Smyth, T.N., Chetty, M., Aoki, P.M., Grinter, R.E.: Deliberate interactions: characterizing technology use in Nairobi, Kenya. In: Proceedings of the SIGCHI Conference on Human Factors in Computing Systems (CHI '10), pp. 2593–2602 (2010)

66. Taylor, J.L., Soro, A., Lee Hong, A., Roe, P., Brereton, M.: "Situational when": designing for cross-cultural time practices with an Australian Aboriginal community. In: Proceedings of

CHI 2017, pp. 6461–6474. Association for Computing Machinery, New York City, New York (2017)

67. Giaccardi, E., Karana, E.: Foundations of materials experience. In: Proceedings of the 33rd Annual ACM Conference on Human Factors in Computing Systems—CHI '15, pp. 2447–2456. Association for Computing Machinery, New York City, New York (2015)

68. Fox, S., Ulgado, R.R., Rosner, D.: Hacking culture, not devices. In: CSCW '15. Proceedings of the 18th ACM Conference on Computer Supported Cooperative Work & Social Computing, pp. 56–68. Association for Computing Machinery, New York City, New York (2015)

69. Boelstorff, T.: Coming of Age in Second Life: an Anthropologist Explores the Virtual Human. Princeton University Press, Princeton, NJ (2008)

70. Bawden, D.: Origins and concepts of digital literacy. Digit. Literacies Concepts, Policies Pract. **30**, 17–32 (2008)

71. The New London Group: A Pedagogy of multiliteracies: designing social futures. Harv. Educ. Rev. **66**, 60–93 (1996)

72. Department of Education and Communities: 8 ways: Aboriginal pedagogy from Western NSW, Dubbo (2012)

73. Mills, K.A., Davis-Warra, J., Sewell, M., Anderson, M.: Indigenous ways with literacies: transgenerational, multimodal, placed, and collective. Lang. Educ. **30**, 1–21 (2016)

74. Moreton-Robinson, A.: The white possessive: property, power and indigenous sovereignty. University of Minnesota Press, Minneapolis (2015)

75. Winschiers-Theophilus, H., Zaman, T., Stanley, C.: A classification of cultural engagements in community technology design: introducing a transcultural approach. AI Soc. 1–17 (2017)

76. Nakata, M.: The cultural interface. Aust. J. Indig. Educ. **36**, 7–14 (2007)

77. Cope, B., Kalantzis, M. (eds.): Multiliteracies: Literacy Learning and the Design of Social Futures. Routledge, London (2000)

78. Ajayi, L.: Critical multimodal literacy: how Nigerian female students critique texts and reconstruct unequal social structures. J. Lit. Res. **47**, 216–244 (2015)

79. Fforde, C., Bamblett, L., Lovett, R., Gorringe, S., Fogarty, B.: Discourse, deficit and identity: aboriginality, the race paradigm and the language of representation in contemporary Australia. Media Int. Aust. 162–173 (2013)

80. Suchman, L.: Organizing alignment: a case of bridge-building. Organization **7**, 311–327 (2000)

81. Harrison, S., Tatar, D., Sengers, P.: The three paradigms of HCI. In: Proceedings of CHI 2007. Association for Computing Machinery, New York City, New York (2007)

82. Simonsen, J., Robertson, T.: Routledge International Handbook of Participatory Design. Routledge, Abingdon, United Kingdom (2012)

83. Brereton, M., Roe, P., Schroeter, R., Hong, A.L., Lee Hong, A.: Beyond ethnography: engagement and reciprocity as foundations for design research out here. In: Proceedings of the SIGCHI Conference on Human Factors in Computing Systems (CHI '14), pp. 1183–1186. ACM, New York City, New York (2014)

84. Bessarab, D., Ng'andu, B.: Yarning about yarning as a legitimate method in indigenous research. Int. J. Crit. Indig. Stud. **3**, 37–50 (2010)

85. Soro, A., Brereton, M., Taylor, J.L., Lee Hong, A., Roe, P.: Cross-cultural dialogical probes. In: Proceedings of the First African Conference on Human Computer Interaction (AfriCHI'16). Association for Computing Machinery, New York City, New York (2016)

86. Winschiers-Theophilus, H., Zaman, T., Yeo, A.: Reducing "white elephant" ICT4D projects. In: Proceedings of the 7th International Conference on Communities and Technologies—C&T '15, pp. 99–107. Association for Computing Machinery, New York City, New York (2015)

87. Le Dantec, C.A., Fox, S.: Strangers at the gate. In: Proceedings of the 18th ACM Conference on Computer Supported Cooperative Work & Social Computing—CSCW '15, pp. 1348–1358. Association for Computing Machinery, New York City, New York (2015)

88. Siew, S.T., Yeo, A.W.: Adapting PRISMA for software development in rural areas: a mobile-based healthcare application case study. In: Proceedings of the 2012 Southeast Asian Network of Ergonomics Societies Conference (SEANES 2012). IEEE, New York City, New York (2012)

89. Molapo, M., Densmore, M., Morie, L.: Designing with community health workers : enabling productive participation through exploration. In: Proceedings of AfriCHI 2016, pp. 58–68. Association for Computing Machinery, New York City, New York (2016)

90. Taylor, J.L., Soro, A., Brereton, M., Lee Hong, A., Roe, P.: Designing evaluation beyond evaluating design : measuring success in cross-cultural projects. In: Proceedings of the 28th Australian Conference on Computer-Human Interaction (OzCHI '16). Association for Computing Machinery, New York City, New York (2016)

91. Falak, S., Chiun, L.M., Yeo, A.W.: Sustainable rural tourism: an indigenous community perspective on positioning rural tourism. Tourism **64**, 311–327 (2016)

92. AIATSIS: Guidelines for Ethical Research in Australian Indigenous Studies. AIATSIS, Canberra (2012)

93. Davis, M.: Indigenous Peoples and Intellectual Property Rights. http://www.aph.gov.au/About_Parliament/Parliamentary_Departments/Parliamentary_Library/pubs/rp/RP9697/97rp20

94. Waycott, J., Wadley, G., Schutt, S., Stabolidis, A., Lederman, R.: The challenge of technology research in sensitive settings. In: Proceedings of the Annual Meeting of the Australian Special Interest Group for Computer Human Interaction on—OzCHI '15, pp. 240–249. Association for Computing Machinery, New York City, New York (2015)

95. Munteanu, C., Molyneaux, H., Moncur, W., Romero, M., O'Donnell, S., Vines, J.: Situational ethics: re-thinking approaches to formal ethics requirements for human-computer interaction. In: Proceedings of the 33rd Annual ACM Conference on Human Factors in Computing Systems, pp. 105–114. Association for Computing Machinery, New York City, New York (2015)

96. Frauenberger, C., Rauhala, M., Fitzpatrick, G.: In-action ethics. Interact. Comput. **29**, 220–236 (2017)

97. Flinders, D.J.: In search of ethical guidance: constructing a basis for dialogue. Int. J. Qual. Stud. Educ. **5**, 101–115 (2016)

98. Philip, K., Irani, L., Dourish, P.: Postcolonial computing: a tactical survey. Sci. Technol. Human Values **37**, 3–29 (2012)

A Digital Indigenous Knowledge Preservation Framework: The 7C Model—Repositioning IK Holders in the Digitization of IK

Donovan Maasz, Heike Winschiers-Theophilus, Colin Stanley, Kasper Rodil and Uriaike Mbinge

1 Introduction

Digitally preserving and maintaining Indigenous Knowledge (IK) has received much attention from various stakeholders over the last decade. Mainstream digitization efforts have invested in database and archiving constructs, gathering information from the IK holders, recording the information, and providing access to researchers, policymakers and to the public at large, but seldom to the IK holders themselves [1]. A major paradigm shift in responsibilities having moved from external expert curators to IK holders and carriers of cultural heritage demands the development of new technologies [2]. Worldwide-limited initiatives have explored alternative procedures including indigenous communities into a long-term cultural heritage digitization process. According to [3] whom surveyed the Intl. journal of intangible cultural heritage, few actors embrace the possibilities offered by ICT in

D. Maasz (✉) · H. Winschiers-Theophilus · C. Stanley
Computer Science Department, Faculty of Computing and Informatics, Namibia University of Science and Technology, Windhoek, Namibia
e-mail: maaszdonovan@gmail.com

H. Winschiers-Theophilus
e-mail: hwinschiers@nust.na

C. Stanley
e-mail: cstanley@nust.na

C. Stanley
Computer Science Department, University of Cape Town, Cape Town, South Africa

K. Rodil
Department of Architecture and Media Technology, Technical Faculty of IT and Design, Aalborg University, Aalborg, Denmark
e-mail: kr@create.aau.dk

U. Mbinge
Otjisa Community, Otjisa, Namibia

© Springer Nature Singapore Pte Ltd. 2018
D. S. Jat et al. (eds.), *Digitisation of Culture: Namibian and International Perspectives*, https://doi.org/10.1007/978-981-10-7697-8_3

preservation and very few engage with local indigenous communities in preservation processes. This leaves a question mark on how this collected material is "understood" and how its meaning is constructed and reconstructed by outsiders and how the indigenous communities are included and represented in the phases following data collection. Rodil and Rehm [3] argue for a partnership with inside actors in continuously evaluating captured, represented, and disseminated community-collected knowledge. Yet, researchers committed to the preservation of indigenous knowledge are not always seeing the need for holistic thinking.

The Namibia University of Science and Technology (NUST) has engaged indigenous communities throughout the design and implementation process, for some years the researchers have been actively codesigning technologies with Namibian indigenous communities (e.g., the OvaHimba and OvaHerero tribes). Specific technologies were developed to support IK holders in collecting, curating, and disseminating their own cultural heritage [4]. The toolset comprises a 3D graphics homestead creator application [5], a Media Collection Tool (MCT) [6], and the Community Crowdsourcing Platform (CCSP) with a Task Management Application (TMA) as a module [7]. While as part of a national IK digitalization project, a database is being designed among other technologies to support an organized IK management initiative at national level (see chapter Chamunorwa et al. in this book).

However, the collection, curation, and dissemination tools were developed in isolation on an ad hoc opportunistic project basis rather than following an integrated approach. Considering a national deployment, adaptation, and adoption of IK preservation tools, the conceptualization of a framework becomes necessary. A guiding framework for the implementation and usage of the applications will ensure continuous and sustainable development with a focus on long-term objectives and impact. The intention of the framework therefore is to directly identify the actionable areas we are working with and relay them into a structured mechanism for future development and improvement of tools. With a holistic view on actionable capacities, new areas in need of development are identified. With a national directive, spearheaded by the National Commission on Research Science and Technology, for the implementation of a countrywide IK management system sustained by research institutes, a framework paves the way for a wider governmental structure that will regulate the national repository. Most importantly, digitalization efforts within the scope of the framework will focus on the central position of the IK holder in the overall preservation process. The framework will be generic and validated in similar contexts.

In this article, we present mainstream concepts of indigenous knowledge and knowledge management processes. Furthermore, we describe our research context and methodology leading to the development of an adequate framework for the digitization of IK to govern the implementation and design of IK preservation technologies. We describe the IK holder's toolkit briefly to exemplify the integrative approach.

2   A Theoretical Perspective

In this section, we look at the theoretical analysis of IK management, i.e., how does knowledge flow in the current implementation and the individual components thereof.

2.1   Indigenous Knowledge Management

Digital cultural heritage preservation has received much attention globally. More and more traditional practices are fading due to major rural–urban migration of indigenous youth, thereby interrupting traditional knowledge transfer and preservation mechanisms. The knowledge left with the community elders is slowly being lost as the elders are passing on.

When aiming to create a cohesive Indigenous Knowledge Management System (IKMS) with indigenous communities, there are numerous aspects that need to be considered in the overall system design and implementation. An IKMS has various mechanisms that contribute to the physiognomy of the system consisting of five phases, namely, knowledge generation, knowledge capture, knowledge curation, knowledge dissemination, and knowledge assessment (see Fig. 1).

First, we need to understand the concept of knowledge within this context. According to [8] knowledge refers to the Greek word episteme, roughly translated into knowledgeable, understanding, or to be familiar with. Terra and Angeloni [8]

Fig. 1 Indigenous knowledge management cycle

further emphasize that considering the interrelation between rationalism and empiricism leads to the more current understanding of knowledge. Accordingly, knowledge can be understood as information residing in one's mind and is derived from experience and reflection embedded in a set of individual and collective beliefs [8]. According to [9], IK in Africa is an embodiment of different modes of thought and epistemology. He defines IK as the traditional and local knowledge existing within and around specific conditions of women and men [9].

These definitions explicitly state the intrinsic nature of IK and differentiation that can be experienced from one IK holder to another as described by Bidwell and Winschiers-Theophilus [10]. Awori et al. [11] emphasize that IK is contextualized in the space between Practice, People, and Place. Considering IKs high-situated ness, tools designed with indigenous communities rarely are comparable to mainstream development.

The second component of the IKMS in the traditional sense will be the management aspect. Management systems consist of various subcomponents that form an integrated platform for collecting, curating, and disseminating the actual knowledge as described above. According to [12], a knowledge management system is an information management system with all the tools required to turn information into knowledge. Often based on organizational knowledge management theories, numerous attempts to create IK management systems exist around the globe. In most cases, those systems do not consider IK holders and communities as part of the knowledge 'organization' beyond the phase of knowledge capture. Thus, technologies developed do not provide for the indigenous community's inclusion in the digitization processes in an integrated manner. Besides, [13] who has developed a governance framework with the Penan communities to synthesize technology developments with community practices, we are unaware of similar models.

Considering the vast literature in organizational knowledge management, we briefly describe their principles as to understand which concepts could be transferable to an ongoing digital IK preservation process.

2.2 *Knowledge Conceptualization Framework*

Akbar and Tzokas [14] propose a knowledge conceptualization framework within a technological context. Based on various exploratory studies into the field, they discovered that projects studied showed similar patterns of interactions. We consider the framework relevant to our context. The derived framework is described in Fig. 2.

Stage 1: Knowledge Generation
It involves activities to experiment and create new knowledge, and results in the start of new thoughts. In our context following initial explorations of the local context as well as possibilities offered by technologies, all team members having

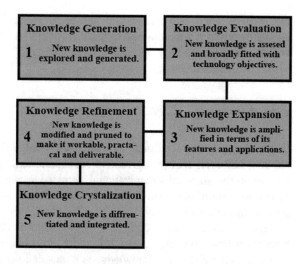

Fig. 2 Knowledge conceptualization adapted from [14]

gained new knowledge are now able to create new concepts and practices. At times following an indigenous approach to learning verbal communication and physical re-enactment (they physically demonstrate an activity) precedes, while at others conceptual understanding is required to produce new knowledge to technology design [14].

Stage 2: Knowledge Evaluation

It involves activities to evaluate new knowledge, that is, to evaluate whether it should be contemplated any further or not. The main objective of this process evolves around clarifying the goal of the knowledge being contextualized. This often results in a general discussion revolving around the daily usage of the technologies and the prospects as well as disadvantages thereof [14].

Stage 3: Knowledge Expansion

It involves activities that intensifies, or increases, new knowledge. This stage results in extending the scope of new knowledge, such as potential applications and addition of new features. This enables the IK holders to experiment and then revert back in the case where a gap was discovered [14].

Stage 4: Knowledge Refinement

This involves activities that modify, delete, or trim applications/features to make new knowledge implementable/deliverable. It results in improvement and refinement of new knowledge and its alignment with the preservation goals [14].

Stage 5: Knowledge Crystallization

This stage consists of activities that provide new knowledge in a standard format. Further, it involves two substages—differentiation and integration. In differentiation, new knowledge is partitioned in more detailed parts for specific work. In contrast, integration brings the detailed parts into a comprehensible whole. Together the differentiation and integration substages result in new knowledge getting crystallized into a concrete concept, which could be different objectives fed from various perspectives [14].

2.3 Knowledge Creation Models

In the general organizational structure, knowledge is categorized as tacit and explicit; however, IK has a profound conceptual and structural difference in comparison to the standard organizational knowledge. According to [15], knowledge travels in a spiral between different modes, namely, socialization, externalization, connecting, and embodying.

Figure 3 models the procedure of knowledge creation as a spiraling process. Noted that the knowledge creation is not a cycle but a spiral, thus the interaction between tacit and explicit knowledge is intensified through the process. The spiral becomes bigger in scale as it moves up the ontological stages. The process is defined as a dynamic process starting at the individual level and intensifying as it moves through groups of interactions.

Nonaka et al. [15] further denote that knowledge needs a context to be created. This contradicts the Cartesian view of knowledge that emphasizes the absolute and context-free nature of knowledge.

The knowledge creating process is conceptually context-specific in terms of who contributes and how they contribute. Knowledge needs a specific context to be created. According to [15], Ba as per Fig. 4 is roughly translated into "place" and this place provides the context for the creation of knowledge. This corresponds with our thinking of the creation of knowledge within the context of designing for the digitalization of IK [15].

Fig. 3 Socialization, externalization, combination, internalization (SECI) process adapted from [15]

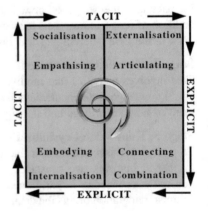

Fig. 4 Ba as shared context
in motion adapted from [15]

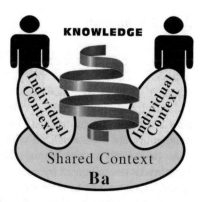

3 Research Context

Since 2008, the IK research cluster of the Namibia University of Science and Technology has been codesigning technologies with indigenous communities across Namibia. Thus, this research is based on a decade of research and development activities.

3.1 Collaborating Community

Our most current research collaborations have been with the OvaHimba communities. They reside in the Kunene region in the northern part of Namibia. The Ovahimba up to today still lives a traditional life of semi-nomadic cattle herders. Their main method of survival is by exercising their acquired experience of the land, which they have gained through an active engagement with nature and its properties through time. Elders are custodians of their largely semi-nomadic kin, while they are also crucial holders and exercisers of IK. Our engagement and codesigning are with Uariaike, our co-author, and the main elder of the Otjisa community. Otjisa is a homestead approximately 40 km outside the northern town of Opuwo. Uariaike embraces the traditional lifestyle and does the occasional city visit to purchase additional food, make use of health and other services. The homestead is quite small in structural size and is in close proximity to other similar homesteads. Uariaike is supported by his family who are also executive stakeholders in the collaboration [12, 13].

3.2 *Methodology*

Our research and development activities follow a community-based codesign approach which is based on philosophies of participatory design and action research. Endless joint activities with all research participants are pursued [16]. Following a design research approach, it addresses the intrinsic human needs that may not be easily generalized [17]. All interactions between researchers and the community are contextualized with numerous unfamiliar and uncontrollable variables promoting mutual learning. However, as part of the methodology, these circumstances are mitigated by continuous observation through both quantitative and qualitative measures to observe how the components play out [18]. Such circumstances are what conduces the mutual learning experience in the field of community-based codesign.

Our community-based codesign approach adopts fundamental principles of Afrocentricity and Ubuntu such as humanness, connectedness, and consciousness. We prevent creating a binary with mainstream research paradigms, but rather introduce a fresh perspective which enhances current research practices and foci [19].

3.3 *Research Process*

The framework presented below was developed over several steps. First, a systematic literature review was done, followed by a conceptualization based on our own empirical work. Then, the framework was refined with our research partners in Otjisa. The refinement process was initiated through a focused discussion with the community members from Otjisa. We then classified uses of the technologies they have within the scope of the phases in the framework. The explanation was started by verbally sketching the perfect technology usage scenario to the IK holder and his family and posing questions throughout the whole process. This ensured that they understand the process being presented and that they contributed meaningfully. Their inputs were integrated in the framework presented below.

4   The Digital IK Preservation Framework: 7C Model

Based on the systematic review of IK collection systems and frameworks discussed in Sects. 2 and 3 of this chapter, we have devised a framework called the 7C's. The building blocks of the 7C model are depicted below as codesign, conceptualization, collection, correction, curations, circulation, and creation.

Figure 5 shows a high-level abstraction of the functional stages involved in the digitization and preservation of IK. The following subsections elaborate the digital IK preservation framework layers in detail. The main goal of all our efforts is

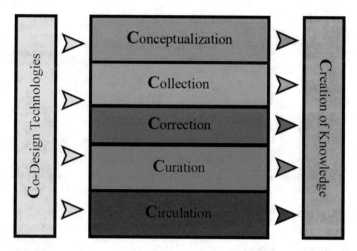

Fig. 5 Digital IK preservation framework (the 7C model)

positioning the IK holders as the main proprietors of the technologies, and digitization processes of their own IK, leading to new knowledge creation. As depicted in Fig. 5, codesign activities and creation of new knowledge are part of a continuous process of digitalizing IK.

4.1 Codesign Technologies

As mentioned, community-based codesign is the overarching methodology (with an underlying constructivist philosophy) that we follow in all our research and development endeavors. As part of the long-term engagement with communities throughout Namibia, the research cluster has refined the codesign process that has been tested and verified across various cultural tribes. The process amplifies the mutual learning environment between the researchers and the IK holders. The process also works at establishing the relationship between the researchers and the IK holders to prevent exploitation and other unfair practices as has been reported many at times in the literature, where benefit sharing was not discussed. The process outlined below works at empowering the IK holders to learn the necessary skills to design technologies that will ensure the digitalization of their cultural heritage in their own terms. Figure 6 depicts sequential activities involved in the codesign process.

Step 1: Introduction
This stage is simply intended for both parties to introduce each other and establish whether working together is an option. This stage is executed in isolation from any official recording material and a pure bonding session to ensure mutual respect.

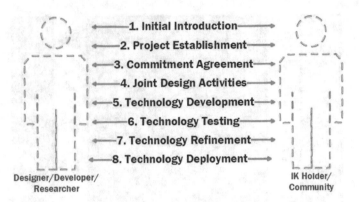

Fig. 6 Codesign process

Step 2: Project Establishment
At this stage, researchers engage with the community in discussions around the project, reveal their research and personal agendas to ensure that both the researchers and the community are on the same level. Thus, both parties elaborate on their expectations regarding the project management and outcome.

Step 3: Commitment Agreement
Based on outdated ethics rules established at institutions not familiar with equal collaborations between researchers and communities, mechanisms such as consent are required. We use the request for recording and image taking as a discussion point about rules governing the two worlds and agreements among the collaborators. This step is only required in situations where it is the first encounter with a community or individual. Commitment agreements are continuously revised as the project progresses. We often find that models for commitment differ among partners. For example, that oral contracts are not respected in academia and that paper contracts are not respected in local communities.

Step 4: Joint Design Activities
Many different techniques are used to jointly produce design concepts, such as focus group discussions, card sorting, scenario creations, walks, and real-life tech evaluations. The sessions are led or initiated by members of the team being researchers or community members. The researchers record the activities and discussions for post-situ analysis and mostly translations.

Step 5: Technology Development
The technology development stage is done in isolation from the community as this stage evolves around purely technical process such as coding, testing, refining, etc. The developments of the technologies required by the communities are based on the codesigned ideas with the communities and with the researchers. This is done to ensure that when the application is deployed in the communities that the users will

be familiar with the system to interact with the application interface as well as the functionalities that lie behind the interface. Often de facto co-creation is challenged by contextual factors such as the absence of grid power, etc.

Step 6: Technology Testing

This step is intended as an intense testing phase for the developed technology. The technology is deployed with the intended community and remains in their care for the duration of the probe. This step is vital for all types of usability testing as it provides the community with the opportunity to completely analyze the technology in their own environment isolated from the researcher's inputs.

Step 7: Technology Refinement

This step is a feedback stage that enables the community to iterate the difficulties they experienced during the probing stage. The designers can then along with the community redesign around these difficulties to improve the usability. Once this stage is completed, the technology should jump back into the probing stage to ensure that both the designers and the community agree upon the final version of the application.

Step 8: Technology Deployment

Once the probing and refinement stages have concluded, the technology is deployed with the community for their continuous use and exploitation of the technology. This allows the users to enhance their understanding not only of the developed technology but also other positive and negative social aspects of using the technology.

4.2 Conceptualization

Conceptualization in the context of digitizing IK means to understand the two epistemologies, namely one of the IK and one of the technologies to derive an appropriate mapping.

The conceptualization phase consists of a transcultural engagement approach where the focus shifts from cross-, inter-, and multicultural interactions. Thus, formulating an environment where the focus is no longer on the individual contributors, their interaction or roles, but on the smooth and elegant collaboration between stakeholders to co-develop technologies that will benefit all parties [20].

An example of this process would be the technology interface design process. This process is incorporated into a workshop, where the functionalities of the intended technology are broken down into meaningful sub-functionalities. These functionalities are then explained to the IK communities in a traditional sense. They are then tasked with selecting the appropriate depiction of the functionality that can be incorporated into the interface.

4.3   Collection

Having agreed on a workable conceptualization of digitizing IK, the correct tools must be codesigned to enable the IK holder to collect IK. This phase in the framework refers to the codesign of actual technology to be integrated and used in everyday life of the IK holders to "Record" their knowledge through the functionalities provided in the technologies. Considering the semi-nomadic lifestyle of some indigenous communities, their day-to-day activities entail much movement and physical work. Therefore, technologies must be fit in the busy schedule and be lightweight. To date, we deployed two applications that enable the IK holders to collect their knowledge via the Media Collection Tool (MCT) and collate the collected media items on the crowdsourcing Task Management Application (TMA) (see details below).

4.4   Correction

This stage in the digital IK preservation framework attains to the ability of the IK holder to use the collection tool to review and correct possibly incorrect records before the curation process is initiated. Due to the physical nature of the activities pertained to IK communities, the assumption being made is that the IK holder will collect information throughout the day and at a later stage revisit the collected information. During the revisit process, he or she will be less active and have more cognitive freedom to process what was captured and identify what needs to be corrected.

The correction process is a seemingly majestic task as all collected data needs to be validated by a local knowledgeable person to ensure that all information being released portrays the culture of the specific communities with the best of intentions as to prevent a negative perspective from being formulated by external viewers.

The feasibility of this stage revolves around the implementation of the functionality in the IK holder toolkit that would enable the IK holder to "Edit" a recording (Video or Media) by "inserting" a new recording after or in the middle of a previous recording correcting the mistake or adding on to the discussion that was being recorded. This stage is not a very complex stage but is vital in the process of ensuring that the data collected is validated before any further processes especially dissemination to the outside world.

4.5   Curation

This stage revolves around taking the collected data and putting them together into a representation which could be meaningful to a specific audience. This stage is therefore subdivided into three possible scenarios namely database curation, Homestead Creator (HSC) curation, and technology curation. Database curation is deciding which elements of the data collected are necessary, which ones belong together, etc. In other words, it is grouping unstructured information in such a way that it forms a type of collective record on a certain topic such as medicine, building, gatherings, etc.

If we want to curate HSC material, it involves formulating a specific scenario out of the collected information and then putting a 3D plot and adding a narrative or scenarios. This enables a more intuitive view and explanation of the described scenario.

The same applies for the scenario where we need to develop a whole game, you look at the data at hand, then find an all-encompassing storyline to weave the collected information into, and then just build the game navigation accordingly.

Therefore, the curation phase is the stage where the collected knowledge is put into a contextual environment for the users to interact with and learn about the cultures.

4.6 Circulation

The main reason for the initial amplification of research into the preservation of IK relates to the rise in rural–urban migration. More and more community members are diverting from their traditional lifestyles to attend schools and universities. This therefore increases the danger of their culture fading away because the knowledge holders are passing on and they have no one around to continue the legacy that was built over centuries. Thus, the importance lies in reaching out to the youth and other audiences through different means and forms. This could be access to scientific databases, games, encyclopedias, etc. This will in turn ensure that that the knowledge transition is preserved for many generations to come.

This stage therefore entails the actual contextualization of curated information into the circulation tools for dissemination to the intended focus groups. Currently, the main tools for circulation of knowledge include some small-scale 3D games, Wikipedia, etc, with further enhancement plans for Augmented Reality (AR) and Virtual Reality (VR).

4.7 Knowledge Creation

Knowledge creation is in the general sense a continuous process. Be that while developing technologies, interacting with the communities, exploring new means, etc. Knowledge is a result of human experience and reflection based on individual and collective beliefs [8]; therefore, knowledge creation is not a single-sided process. In the spectrum of this research, knowledge is not only created inside the communities but when we as the researchers engage with the communities we formulate stories in the natural sense that we share with the world and this formulates knowledge. According to [13] knowledge in indigenous communities occurs via two main processes, namely, "interaction" and "action". Whereby interaction refers to the physical exchange of existing knowledge via communication channels such as verbal communication (sharing stories) and embodied action (showing or performing a deed). Action refers to the production of new knowledge during the embodied execution of existing and acquired knowledge in a certain context [13]. Thus, within a design context of IK tools, through interaction among researchers and community members and the action of design, new knowledge is cocreated.

5   The IK Holders Tool Kit

In this section, we present the set of tools that were codesigned with the IK holder covering the different phases of the framework.

5.1   Media Collection Tool

The media collection tool was developed as the main means of IK collection through capturing various media [6]. The media is then stored on the deployed device and collected by the researchers on agreed intervals to prevent data loss from occurring. The various media forms collected in the application are images, videos, drawings, text input, and audio. The IK holders use this application to mainly document daily traditional activities that they feel worthy to preserve (Fig. 7).

Function 1: Media Collection
This function combines all the media capturing features together such as videos, images, audio, and text. This caters for all possibilities of input, to maximize the efficiency of the application in the collection phase.

Function 2: Media Review and Edit
This is a very important functionality of the application that enables the IK holder to review and edit captured media. In the event of incomplete or incorrect media, the IK holder can then add or edit the existing file to complete what is missing or correct what was incorrect. Needless to say, still images can only be drawn upon, or completely replaced where needed. This functionality contributes to the correction phase in the framework.

Function 3: Media Grouping
This is also a very important functionality of the application as this allows the IK holder to group (categorize) media relating to certain activities or topics. This allows the IK holders to categorize their captured media into meaningful

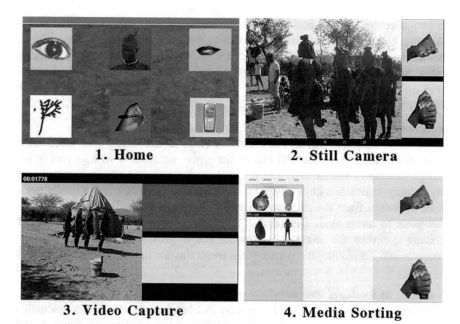

1. Home   **2. Still Camera**

3. Video Capture   **4. Media Sorting**

Fig. 7 MCT interface

classifications according to their own context. This feature contributes to the curation phase in the framework.

In summary, this technology at this junction supports the collection stage of the framework in the sense that it allows the IK communities to collect various media on their traditional activities such as building a hut. The collected data is then stored locally on the devices deployed with the IK holder, with a future addition of pushing viable information directly into an institutional database where it can be verified and pushed into the national repository.

5.2 Task Management Application

The task management application is an in-development prototype that was co-designed with the IK holders to allow them to indirectly communicate with the global crowd [7]. It will enable the knowledge holders to implicitly direct the request of 3D model designs to a global audience. These designs alternatively will then be integrated into our dissemination tools such as the Homestead creator discussed in a later section of this chapter. The following functions are supported:

Function 1: Formulate Task Request
Of all the media collected through the before-mentioned media collection tool, the IK holder must combine the related media items. The process starts with the IK

holder selecting the preferred photos of the traditional object to be modeled to 3D. After the selecting the preferred photos among the set of all captured images, the IK holder selects the audios that we recorded about those photos and the process continues in a similar manner until all related media items are assigned to the selected photos. The intention is that all media placed into a specific collection will be related to a single request. This exercise is part of a curation process.

Function 2: Process Request
This functionality revolves around the ability of the IK holder to submit a collection of media to the crowd that will enable the global community to take part in the design process of the request. The collated media items are sent as a task to the community crowdsourcing website for the translators to translate the media items such as audios from the rural communities' language to English for the graphic designers to understand. The process does not involve much except for the IK holders to review the task request content and to provide consent to upload the requests into the cloud. This is part of the dissemination process though formulates as a request.

Function 3: Evaluate Requests
The review process is also a simple process that involves the IK holders evaluating the 3D design submission. If the delivered 3D models need to be refined the IK holders, then provide details on where to improve on the 3D model or they reformulate the task request. Upon approval, the crowdsourcing platform administration is alerted as to take the necessary arrangements for the designs to be incorporated into the dissemination tools. This is part of the correction phase.

In summary, the TMA is also a type of support mechanism for the MCT as mentioned in the framework section of this chapter. The TMA mainly allows the IK holder the opportunity to group-related media files together to represent a specific object/person. This representation is then sent to the crowdsourcing platform to design a graphical representation of the object/person that will then be incorporated into one of the currents or soon to be curation tools [21].

5.3 Homestead Creator

The HSC (Fig. 8), a 3D graphics application, enables indigenous community members to depict their lifestyles and traditions by interaction and manipulation of a virtual 3D world [5]. The purpose of the HSC is to support the elders to digitally curate and disseminate IK to youths about their traditions and culture in and around their homesteads. Yet, over the years, it has become an interface, which makes space for dialog between researchers, technology developers, and indigenous elders about their conceptualizations of their own experienced lifeworlds when transferred into bits and bytes. Which in turn allows the researchers and technology developers to be more critical toward the systems they develop, when they expose their own conceptualizations of the data they "think they understand".

Fig. 8 Homestead Creator interface

The HSC is still in exploration phase due to some implications that the implementation process presents us, in the sense of importing newly created 3D objects and then redeploying. But in the current state as explained above the HSC tends to lean toward supporting the collection and curation stages more than it does the circulation stage.

5.4 Wikipedia

Wikipedia, the renowned online encyclopedia, allows in principle everybody to upload content, which would include IK holders. However, the current structure is based on written information with a very specific codification. Yet, indigenous communities have often not developed written accounts of their past and current practices as they relied on oral transmission thus making their form of information incompatible with current Wikipedia structures [22]. Several initiatives in Namibia attempting to create a Wikipedia editor community, be it of the English or the indigenous languages, have failed so far. While [23] established a persuasive approach to uploading indigenous content, it did not manifest in a continuous activity. The use of Wikipedia could be part of the curation, correction, and circulation phase.

6   Conclusion

Numerous efforts around the globe attempting to digitalize IK have shown to be a complex endeavor. And although often at time organizational knowledge management concepts have informed the development of specifically national IK management systems, the IK holder was not considered equivalent with an expert but rather an informant. Thus, technologies developed support collection from IK holders, yet processes of curation and dissemination remained inaccessible to the IK holder. In this light, we have developed a framework which suggests a continuous codesign collaboration of the tools catering for all the phases of heritage preservation thereby repositioning the IK holder. Not only will the IK holder work with the tools but has created them within his or her own context. The 7C framework has integrated codesign activities, with cultural heritage preservation phases as well as knowledge management processes based on our empirical data as well as existing theories and best practices. We have exemplified the 7C model with current technologies under development with the Ovahimba communities ensuring an integrative approach.

Acknowledgements We would like to thank the Namibian Commission for Research Science and Technology (NCRST) for their financial support over the years. More closely, we would like to thank the participants from the Otjisa village for their unwavering commitment to the project and all the contributions they have made.

References

1. Maasz, D., Winschiers-Theophilus, H.: Designing 3D representations of Namibian Flora for recognition by indigenous communities. In: International Conference on Culture & Computer Science (2016)
2. Giaccardi, E.: Things we value. Interactions **18**, 17. https://doi.org/10.1145/1897239.1897245 (2011)
3. Rodil, K., Rehm, M.: A decade later: looking at the past while sketching the future of ICH through the tripartite digitisation model. Int. J. Intang. Herit. **10**, 47–60 (2015)
4. Jensen, K.L., Winschiers-Theophilus, H., Rodil, K., Winschiers-goagoses, N., Kapuire, G.K., Kamukuen-jandje, R.: Putting it in perspective: designing a 3D visualization to contextualize indigenous knowledge in rural Namibia. In: Proceedings of the Designing Interactive Systems Conference, pp. 196–199. https://doi.org/10.1145/2317956.2317986 (2012)
5. Rodil, K., Winschiers-Theophilus, H., Jensen, K.L., Rehm, M.: Homestead creator: a tool for indigenous designers. In: Proceedings of 7th Nordic Conference Human-Computer Interaction Making Sense Through Design, pp. 627–630. https://doi.org/10.1145/2399016.2399111 (2012)
6. Kapuire, G., Winschiers-Theophilus, H., Stanley, C., Maasz, D., Chamunorwa, M., Heide Møller, R., Rodil, K., Gonzalez-Cabrero, D.: Technologies to promote the inclusion of Indigenous knowledge holders in digital cultural heritage preservation. In: International Conference on Culture & Computer Science (2016)
7. Stanley, C., Winschiers-Theophilus, H., Cabrero, D., Blake, E.: Challenges in designing cultural heritage crowdsourcing: tools with indigenous communities. In Ciolfi, L., Damala,

A., Hornecker, E., Lechner, M., Maye, L. (eds) Cultural Heritage Communities Technologies and Challenges. Routledge (2017)

8. Terra, J.C., Angeloni, T.: Understanding the difference between information management and knowledge management. KM Adv. 1–9 (2003)

9. Ossai, N.B.: African indigenous knowledge systems (AIKS). Simbiosis 7(2) (2010)

10. Bidwell, N., Winschiers-Theophilus, H.: At the intersection of indigenous and traditional knowledge and technology design. Informing Sci. (2015)

11. Awori, K., Vetere F., & Smith, W.: Transnationalism, indigenous knowledge and technology: insights from the Kenyan Diaspora. In: Proceedings of the 33rd Annual ACM Conference on Human Factors in Computing Systems, pp. 3759–3768. ACM (2015)

12. Mckenna, F.: A knowledge management system—a discourse (2008)

13. Zaman, T.: Indigenous knowledge governance framework: a holistic model for indigenous knowledge management. Doctoral dissertation, University Malaysia Sarawak, UNIMAS (2013)

14. Akbar, H., Tzokas, N.: An exploration of new product development's front-end knowledge conceptualization process in discontinuous innovations. Br. J. Manag. 24, 245–263. https://doi.org/10.1111/j.1467-8551.2011.00801.x (2013)

15. Nonaka, I., Toyama, R., Konno, N.: SECI, Ba and leadership: a unified model of dynamic knowledge creation. Long Range Plann. 33, 5–34. https://doi.org/10.1016/s0024-6301(99)00115-6 (2000)

16. Winschiers-Goagoses, N., Winschiers-Theophilus, H., Rodil, K., Kapuire, G.K., Jensen, K.: Design democratization with communities. Int. J. Sociotechnol. Knowl. Dev. 4, 32–43. https://doi.org/10.4018/jskd.2012100103 (2012)

17. Faste, T., Faste, H.: Demystifying "design research": design is not research, research is design. In: Proceedings of IDSA Educational Symposium. https://doi.org/10.1016/0167-9236(94)00041-2 (2012)

18. Collins, A., Joseph, D., Bielaczyc, K.: Design research: theoretical and methodological issues. J. Learn. Sci. 13, 15–42. https://doi.org/10.1207/s15327809jls1301 (2009)

19. Kapuire, G., Winschiers-Theophilus, H.: An insider perspective on community gains: a subjective account of a Namibian rural communities' perception of a long-term participatory design project (2015)

20. Winschiers-Theophilus, H., Zaman, T., Stanley, C.: A classification of cultural engagements in community technology design: introducing a transcultural approach. AI & SOCIETY, 1–17 (2017)

21. Stanley, C., Winschiers-Theophilus, H., Blake, E., Rodil, K., Kapuire, G.: Ovahimba community in Namibia ventures into crowdsourcing design. Proc. IFIP WG 9, 277–287 (2015)

22. Gallert, P., Velden, M.: Reliable sources for indigenous knowledge: Dissecting Wikipedia's Catch-22 (2013)

23. Mushiba, M., Gallert, P., Winschiers-Theophilus, H.: On persuading an ovaherero community to join the wikipedia community. In: IFIP Advances in Information and Communication Technology, pp. 1–18 (2016)

Cultural Heritage Semiotics

Sonia Yaco and Arkalgud Ramaprasad

1 Introduction

'Semiotics describes the process by which stimuli are transformed into information and information is transformed into stimuli; in other words, it is the process by which information is generated and dissipated' [27, p. 187]. What are the semiotics of cultural heritage? How do we disseminate information using cultural heritage? Could technology help us learn and teach cultural heritage more efficiently? This paper presents an ontological framework to conceptualize the semiotics of cultural heritage. This framework concisely describes how we currently utilize cultural heritage and can serve as a guide for using technology to learn and teach about cultural heritage. Cultural heritage may be tangible and intangible. Data about cultural heritage may be visual, aural/oral, tactile, olfactory and gustatory—corresponding to the five human senses. Advances in computers have unleashed an enormous capacity to (a) acquire this data and generate information and knowledge about cultural heritage and (b) apply the knowledge and information to promote the understanding, use and experience of cultural heritage. Computers can help augment, virtualize, visualize and comprehensively sense cultural heritage without the barriers of time and distance. Examples range from web crawlers that index digital surrogates of historical texts to remote aerial sensor technologies that detect and classify archaeological objects. While the potential opportunities of computer applications are unlimited, there is no existent strategy for humans to exploit

S. Yaco (✉)
University Library, University of Illinois at Chicago, Chicago, IL, USA
e-mail: syaco@uic.edu

A. Ramaprasad
Department of Information and Decision Sciences,
University of Illinois at Chicago, Chicago, IL, USA
e-mail: prasad@uic.edu

© Springer Nature Singapore Pte Ltd. 2018
D. S. Jat et al. (eds.), *Digitisation of Culture: Namibian and International Perspectives*, https://doi.org/10.1007/978-981-10-7697-8_4

49

cultural heritage systemically and systematically. The proposed ontological framework deconstructs the semiotics of cultural heritage. As a complement to the field of cultural heritage informatics, this ontological framework can be used to generate knowledge about and apply knowledge to the advancement of cultural heritage, using the power of modern computers. Separately, the ontological framework can be used to map the state of the research on, and practice of, semiotics of cultural heritage and to determine the gaps within and between them. Such a gap analysis will help develop a blueprint for research, practice and the translation of research to practice and vice versa.

The semiotics of cultural heritage are part of many arenas of human activities, ranging from religion to advertising to video production. A filmmaker producing a documentary on the life of Nelson Mandela, for instance, gathers stimuli and generates information that is disseminated in the film. She might use stimuli such as data from Mandela's prison visitor logs, information about Mandela's family from oral histories, and her personal knowledge of South African apartheid. She then transforms that research into a film that conveys knowledge about Mandela's life. Providing a visual map of how the filmmaker gathers and uses cultural heritage may provide ideas of how technology could enhance the semiotics of creating that film and make the process more efficient and effective.

The main arena for semiotics of cultural heritage is arguably institutions of higher education. By definition, universities are focused on disseminating knowledge. Research, teaching and service, the three core activities of universities, all require data to generate information and knowledge. For many fields, these data are about cultural heritage. As universities have cultural heritage repositories such as art galleries, libraries, archives and museums, with extensive physical and digital holdings, gathering data should be straightforward. Alas, it is not. Finding relevant data to use in research or to include in curriculum can be challenging. Faculty members (and other researchers and educators) must first locate, and then navigate, the multiple electronic search tools that describe cultural heritage resources on campus such as audio/visual resources, manuscript collections, university archives, audiovisual holdings, electronic databases, digital collections, museum holdings and so on. Anecdotal evidence suggests that faculty members (and students) are often unaware of their local holdings, let alone in those in other universities. As a result, university cultural heritage material is underutilized by its faculty. The semiotic cycle of gathering data and generating knowledge from cultural heritage, which adds value to those resources and to the university, is inhibited.

Cultural heritage professionals trying to find patrons to utilize their holdings face discovery challenges similar to researchers. An archivist who has just acquired South African protest poems often has a difficult time finding faculty, courses or projects that the collection would be relevant to. Lists of current research areas of all professors are rare. While the discoverability of course descriptions varies, at many universities even simple keyword searches of course metadata are not possible. These barriers to discovering collections and courses also hinder administrators advocating on behalf of cultural heritage institutions to legislators and donors.

Personal interactions and word of mouth remain the best ways to match cultural heritage material to researchers. Archivists almost exclusively use face-to-face methods to increase knowledge of their holdings with faculty and students, with orientation sessions for undergraduates being the most common method [1]. Other techniques include reaching out to individual faculty to suggest relevant collections and possible class assignments [16, 30, 31], collaborating with instructional faculty to develop courses [13] and acquiring collections by working with faculty [13] and students [41].

In addition to personal interactions, cultural heritage professionals, educators and digital humanities scholars explore organized approaches to link collections to research, teaching and service. Librarians investigate ways to meet cultural heritage curricular needs by conducting systematic, although not automated, analysis of course catalogues [14, 15, 20, 23]. Librarians and archivists plan services, resource acquisition to meet research needs by using faculty publications [22, 43], syllabi and other learning objects [3, 4, 9, 19, 29, 33], particularly in information literacy [6, 12, 21, 34, 39, 42] . Charles [8] advocates educators, librarians and administrators using 'curriculum mapping' to match information literacy instruction competencies to course learning outcomes.

Despite this work, literature on information-seeking behaviour of academic researchers shows a recurrent concern about the design of library discovery tools. Tibbo [36] and Anderson [2] examined historians in parallel studies in the United States and United Kingdom, respectively. Both studies find current search engines for archives to be inadequate. Anderson suggests creating a retrieval system that is in line with historians' information-seeking behaviour. Borgman et al. [5] support digital library search capability that mirrors teaching methods.

Technology applied to cultural heritage and education have created a plethora of new informatics fields such as cultural heritage informatics; library, archives and museum informatics; and educational informatics (a blend of education and library science) [10] that provide the opportunity to help researchers access and use cultural heritage repositories. Pattuelli [24], working with high school history teachers, concludes that the design of digital libraries needs to reflect how teachers think about learning objects. Data and text mining tools can also help to analyse data. Nicholson suggests that bibliomining, library text mining, [22] be used to understand patron use of digital libraries. Educators such as Romero [32] use sophisticated Educational Data Mining (EDM) to analyse various aspects of education, particularly e-learning. Ralph [26], using education informatics, concludes that having an embedded librarian in courses improves library services to doctoral students.

To take full advantage of these advances in technology, we need to understand the semiotics of cultural heritage. In this article, we suggest a comprehensive ontological framework, and subsequently a corresponding system, to facilitate the use of cultural heritage to extract greater value and more knowledge from cultural heritage collections.

2 Ontological Framework for Cultural Heritage Semiotics

This ontological framework represents our conceptualization of the problem domain—for managing semiotics of cultural heritage to enhance the human experience of the stakeholders' semiotics [11]. The framework organizes the terminologies and taxonomies of the problem domain. 'Our acceptance of [the] ontology is… similar in principle to our acceptance of a scientific theory, say a system of physics; we adopt, at least insofar as we are reasonable, the simplest conceptual scheme into which the disordered fragments of raw experience can be fitted and arranged'. [25] The ontological framework for the semiotics of cultural heritage is shown in Fig. 1 (See Appendix for glossary of terms). In simple yet holistic terms, the framework describes the building blocks of a system for generating knowledge about cultural heritage and applying it to advance education, research and service to the community.

The challenge is to construct an ontological framework that is a coherent, succinct and complete description of the problem—the systematic utilization of cultural heritage. The framework must be logical in the deconstruction of the problem, and parsimonious yet complete. It must be simple yet descriptive of the combinatorial complexity of the problem. It must be a closed description of the problem in its entirety, yet adaptable to changes in its definition.

The ontological framework is constructed by logically, hierarchically deconstructing the problem into its dimensions and elements. The ontological meta-analysis and synthesis are a new method of analysing and synthesizing domain knowledge [35]. Instead of focusing on narrow segments of a problem, it focuses attention on the whole. Meta-analysis and synthesis are especially suitable for studying complex, ill-structured problems [28]. The methods can be used to develop an ontological framework that will elucidate the problem and serve as a blueprint for its resolution.

Functions	Semiotics	Cultural Heritage	Outcomes
Acquire/Collect	[±] Data	[about] Tangible	[CH to] Investigate
Create/Edit/Delete	Information	Archaeological	Document
Organize/Arrange	Knowledge	Prehistorical	Preserve
Index/Describe/Represent		Historical	Manage
Store/Preserve/Sustain		Literary	Visualize
Secure/Authenticate		Artistic	Educate
Retrieve/Access		Scientific	Communicate
Process		Intangible	Access
Distribute		Oral	Assess
		Performance	Plan
		Social practices	Publicize
		Knowledge/practice nature	Contextualize
		Traditional craftsmanship	Enjoy

[cultural heritage

Fig. 1 Ontology of semiotics of cultural heritage

(Note: We will capitalize the words that refer to the dimensions and elements in the ontology, except in narrative descriptions of full or partial components.) We break down the problem of digitally managing semiotics of cultural heritage into four main dimensions, namely, (a) Functions, (b) Semiotics, (c) Cultural heritage and (d) Outcomes. These constitute the first level of the hierarchy. The underlying argument is that the combination of functions and semiotics about cultural heritage will help achieve the desired outcomes. At the next level, each dimension is articulated by a one- or two-level taxonomy of elements. These constitute the second and third level of the hierarchy. The dimensions are arranged left to right such that concatenation of an element from each with the adjacent words and phrases forms a natural English sentence. Each such sentence represents a component of cultural heritage. Thus, the components derived from the ontology are expressed in natural English sentences. For instance, 'Retrieve data about tangible-historical cultural heritage to manage cultural heritage'.

Thus, the argument of the framework can be expressed as

$$\text{Semiotics of cultural heritage} = f \, (\text{Functions} + \text{Semiotics} + \text{Cultural Heritage} + \text{Outcomes})$$

The Functions include traditional information systems functions for managing semiotics as well as activities of cultural heritage curators. The functions can be expressed as

$$\text{Functions} \subset (\text{Acquire/Collect}, \text{Create/Edit/Delete}, \text{Organize/Arrange},$$
$$\text{Index/Describe/Represent}, \text{Store/Preserve/Sustain},$$
$$\text{Secure/Authenticate}, \text{Retrieve}, \text{Process}, \text{Distribute})$$

The taxonomy of Functions is ordinal: the different functions usually occur in the sequence presented. However, the sequence may be interrupted by iterations of a set of Functions, for example, iterations of Store/Preserve/Sustain, Secure/Authenticate, Retrieve, Process, to assure the security and the integrity of data about a cultural heritage artefact. Similarly, the sequence may be interrupted by feedback from subsequent functions to the preceding ones, for example, from Distribute to Organize/Arrange. The functions can be performed manually, using computers, or both. The computerization of these functions, in conjunction with efforts of people, is changing the semiotics of cultural heritage in fundamental ways. It has increased the capacity, speed and the versatility of the performance of these functions.

The Semiotics of the ontology include Data, Information and Knowledge about cultural heritage. The Data include measurements and observations, both qualitative and quantitative, about cultural heritage. The Information includes relationships among collections of cultural heritage artefacts. The Knowledge includes interpretation of the above relationships in a cultural context. The three elements are ordinal: Information is derived from Data, and Knowledge is derived from Information. Thus, semiotics can be expressed as

$$\text{Semiotics} \subset (\text{Data}, \text{Information}, \text{Knowledge})$$

From the simple capability to organize data in databases, new visualizations to map the relationships between the data, to 'deep learning', computers are redefining the landscape of semiotics. Many of the techniques have been developed and applied in other disciplines. These can be imported for use in generating and applying knowledge about cultural heritage and can redefine the domain.

UNESCO categorizes cultural heritage as Tangible artefacts and Intangible [37, 38, 40]. Tangible artefacts include physical Archaeological, Prehistorical, Historical, Literary, Artistic and Scientific objects. The Intangible cultural heritage includes '(a) oral traditions; (b) performing arts; (c) social practices, rituals, and festive events; (d) knowledge and practices concerning nature and universe; and traditional craftsmanship'. [37] Thus, the taxonomy of Cultural Heritage can be stated as

$$\text{Cultural Heritage} \subset (\text{Tangible Artefacts}(\text{Archaeological}, \text{Prehistorical},$$
$$\text{Historical}, \text{Literary}, \text{Artistic}, \text{Scientific}), \text{Intangible}$$
$$(\text{Oral}, \text{Performance}, \text{Social Practices}, \text{Knowledge/Practice}$$
$$\text{Nature}, \text{Traditional Craftsmanship})).$$

Using the example of the filmmaker, one aspect of how she disseminated information and knowledge about Nelson Mandela was to 'acquire/collect information about oral cultural heritage to document cultural heritage' (Fig. 2):

$$\text{Semiotics of film} = \text{Acquire/Collect} + \text{Information} + \text{about} + \text{Oral} + \text{CH to}$$
$$+ \text{Document} + \text{Cultural heritage}.$$

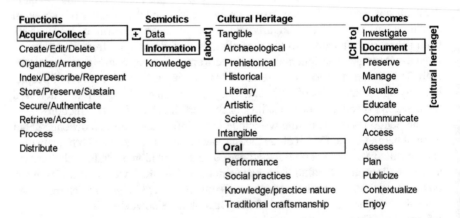

Fig. 2 One component of film semiotics 'acquire/collect information about oral cultural heritage to document cultural heritage'

The sentience of tangible and intangible culture is different. Traditionally, computers have been the strongest in managing visual data (and the associated semiotics). Their strength in managing aural/oral data (for example, voice recognition) has increased dramatically. The field of haptics has significantly advanced their capacity to manage tactile data. They are relatively weak in managing olfactory data (there are olfactory printers), and weaker still in gustatory data. The capability of computers to handle the different types of sentience critical to cultural heritage will define the role of computers vis-a-vis humans in the semiotic cycle.

Lastly, the potential Outcomes are many. Listed in no particular order, these may range from investigating (Investigate) to enjoying (Enjoy) cultural heritage as summarized below:

$$\text{Outcome} \subset (\text{Investigate, Document, Preserve, Manage, Visualize, Educate, Communicate}$$
$$\text{Access, Assess, Plan, Publicize, Contextualize, Enjoy})$$

The scale and scope of the strategies to realize the above outcomes have expanded exponentially with the advances in computer technology. It broadens the potential stakeholders in the outcomes; it can also broaden those who can participate in the semiotics of cultural heritage by allowing them to perform the various functions independently in distributed locations, thus advancing the domain.

3 Discussion

The proposed ontology is a lens to study the anatomy of the semiotics of cultural heritage. For a complex problem like this, there may be other lenses to study the problem and each can be encapsulated by a different ontology. They will provide different perspectives. We will discuss the present one in detail. Further, computers in particular and the associated information systems in general have fundamentally altered the semiotics of cultural heritage. They have the potential to create changes that are even more profound. The ontological framework can help develop a roadmap to navigate these changes.

We have discussed the individual dimensions (columns) and elements (rows) of the ontology while describing the construction of the ontology. Multiple elements of a dimension may coexist independently but may also interact with each other. Thus, Functions, Semiotics, Cultural Heritage and Outcomes may coexist and interact with each other. Knowing the independent and interacting elements is critical to generating and applying knowledge about cultural heritage through teaching, research and service.

In the hypothetical documentary on Mandela, for instance, the filmmaker would perform all the functions in the ontology except perhaps, Organize/Arrange. She would use Data, Information and Knowledge of Historical, Literary, Artistic, Oral and Social Practices Cultural Heritage. The Outcomes of the film would be to

Investigate, Document, Preserve, Visualize, Educate, Communicate, Publicize, Contextualize and Enjoy cultural heritage.

The ontology can help systematically study and manage the elements' independence and interactions. In the following, we discuss how the ontology can be used to study the interaction of (a) elements within a dimension, (b) elements across two dimensions and (c) elements across multiple dimensions, to understand the anatomy of the problem domain at different levels of granularity and complexity.

4   Combinations Within a Dimension

All possible first-order interactions among the elements of a dimension can be mapped into a table of the dimension with itself. Such a mapping can reveal strong interactions (both constructive and obstructive), weak ones, absent ones and unexpected ones among the elements. It can also highlight the direction of the interaction—one way (a to b OR b to a) and two way (a to b AND b to a). In the following, we will discuss some possible insights from such a mapping of each dimension.

The functions are sequentially dependent and iterative. Their dependencies must be coordinated for the entire sequence to be effective. Feedback from the subsequent functions to the preceding ones and feedforward from the preceding functions to the subsequent ones are important mechanisms of coordination. Thus, for example, the data that are acquired/collected about a tangible cultural heritage artefact can feedforward to securing/authenticating the artefact. Obversely, learning from processing information about an artefact can provide feedback on additional data to acquire/collect about such artefacts in the future.

The elements of semiotics are part of an ongoing cycle of generation and application of knowledge. The progression from data to knowledge is the generation phase of the cycle, and from knowledge to data the application phase. Thus, the interaction between the three semiotics elements with reference to cultural heritage will affect its effectiveness.

The elements of cultural heritage may be independent entities or entities whose interactions can provide insights into each other. For example, the oral recording of a speech may portray a document of the speech, such as a transcription or newspaper account, in a very different light. The interaction of elements may also be contained within a single cultural heritage artefact. A totem is both a carved piece of wood and a representation of religious beliefs. A dance may be a performance, religious practice and a festive event.

The outcomes are likely to be a composite of many elements interacting with one another. The interaction among the outcome elements must be mapped to manage the composite effectively. Thus, an undergraduate freshman may be interested only in accessing a cultural heritage artefact for a class assignment, whereas the cultural heritage professionals and information systems professionals are likely to be interested in all of the outcomes.

5 Combinations Between Dimensions

In addition to interactions among the elements of a dimension, all possible first-order interactions among the elements of a pair of dimensions can be mapped into a table. Such a mapping can reveal strong interactions (both constructive and obstructive), weak ones, absent ones and unexpected interactions between the elements of the two dimensions. It can also reveal the direction of the interaction—one way (a to b OR b to a) and two way (a to b AND b to a). With the four dimensions of the ontology, there are six possible pairs. In the examples in the previous section, we have some possible interactions between many of the dimensions. Here, we will summarize the six possible pairs and the potential insights from them:

Functions × Semiotics—The performance of different functions for the generation and application of data, information and knowledge about cultural heritage. Computer technology has fundamentally transformed this combination and is likely to do so even more in the future. Among the anchors of transformation are the developments of the ability to handle the full spectrum of sentient data, to manage 'big data', to automate the extraction of information and to imitate human learning.

Functions × Cultural Heritage—The performance of different functions to generate and apply data, information and knowledge about different cultural heritages. The semiotic transformations mentioned above will also transform the performance of the different functions of the various types of cultural heritage. For example, 3-D printers may aid store/preserve knowledge about traditional craftsmanship better than written documents.

Functions × Outcomes—The performance of different functions to generate and apply data, information and knowledge about different outcomes to fulfil them. Among other possibilities, advances in computers can help engage a lot more people to perform the various functions to achieve the outcomes. They can make the management of cultural heritage inclusive of amateurs and citizens, rather than keep it in the exclusive domain of curators and archivists.

Semiotics × Cultural Heritage—Generation and application of data, information and knowledge about different cultural heritage. We have highlighted some of the possibilities in the first point above.

Semiotics × Outcomes—Generation and application of data, information and knowledge about different outcomes. We have highlighted some of the possibilities in the third point above.

Cultural Heritage × Outcomes—The mapping of cultural heritage to the outcomes. Overall, advances in computers can help articulate and make visible the intangible value of tangible cultural heritage, and at the same time make tangible the value of the intangible.

6 Components of the Ontology

We have stated earlier that the dimensions of the ontology are arranged left to right with adjacent words/connectors such that the concatenation of an element from each dimension with the adjacent words/connectors creates a natural English sentence illustrating a potential component of the problem domain. Three illustrative components are as follows:

- Acquire/collect data about tangible-literary cultural heritage to investigate cultural heritage.
- Index/describe/represent information about intangible-performance cultural heritage to educate [about] cultural heritage.
- Distribute knowledge about tangible-artistic cultural heritage to enjoy cultural heritage.

The ontology encapsulates $9 * 3 * 11 * 13 = 3,861$ potential components. It would be laborious and voluminous to enumerate all of them. The ontology provides a convenient and concise visual map, showing the combinatorial complexity of the problem. A component may be instantiated in many different ways. Consider the first illustrative component above. It can be a recommender system to collect data about tangible-literary collections with reference to a course and recommend them to students to aid their investigation in the class. Obversely, an instantiation may cover many components or their fragments. Thus, there is a many-to-many relationship between the components encapsulated in the ontological framework and their instantiations.

A researcher may view each of the 3,861 components in four different ways, to advance the research agenda. Each component can be considered a proposition for description, explanation, prediction or control of a cultural heritage management system. At the base, each component may be seen as a descriptor of a system for management of cultural informatics; it describes how the outcomes of cultural heritage are achieved. At the second level, each component may be seen as an explanator of the outcomes—why the cultural heritage management outcomes are fulfilled or not fulfilled by the system. The components can be used to highlight the critical success factors of the systems and its critical failure factors. At the third level, the components can be seen as predictors of the outcomes of the system. The performance of different combinations of Functions, Semiotics and Cultural Heritage can predict particular Outcomes. Last, at the fourth level, each component may be seen as a controller of the outcomes of the system. The different combinations of Functions, Semiotics and Cultural Heritage can be used to control particular Outcomes. Whether a component is seen as a descriptor, explanator, predictor or controller of the system will depend upon the state of the research in the domain. The more advanced the state, the greater the progression from description to control.

The operation of each of the components in the ontology can be fundamentally transformed by advances in computer systems. However, each component may be affected differently, depending upon the need and the availability of technology. In summary, the ontology can be used to study the anatomy of the semiotics of cultural heritage systemically and systematically. It can be used to study both the need for and the technological potentials of doing so. Mapping the growing technological advances and needs will highlight its areas of emphasis, lack of emphasis and oversights. Mapping the use will highlight the priority of different elements and components in practice. The insights from such mappings can be used to develop a roadmap for future research and practice. We will conclude with a brief description of a program of research to follow.

7 Applications and Adaptations

The ontology can help the cultural heritage and education professionals in collaboration with other stakeholders to systematically learn from cultural heritage for teaching, research and service. Instead of focusing narrowly on matching course syllabi to data on cultural heritage, the ontology will help match the requirements comprehensively and systematically.

'Today's [cultural heritage] professionals are working toward a world in which people engage with [cultural heritage], their content and their collections in a virtuous circle where [stakeholders] are encouraged to form lifelong relationships with [cultural heritage], visiting in person when they can and visiting online when they cannot' [17, p. 29]. In such a world, cultural heritage and information systems professionals have to 'transcend the traditional boundaries ...to meet information needs in the digital age' [18, p. 613]. In this context, the ontological framework can be used to develop a cultural information literacy curriculum map for the stakeholders in higher education [8], and to integrate the primary sources of cultural heritage into the curriculum [7].

The landscape of a domain can change over time with emerging best practices and theories. The ontology-based roadmap can be amended to reflect the changing landscape. New categories and dimensions can be added, obsolete ones discarded and existing ones modified. Changes can also be introduced by the shifting focus in the domain. The finer levels of dimensions and elements can be added to the ontology to reflect the greater focus on certain dimensions or categories. For example, new outcomes can be included to reflect changing professional or institutional goals. On the other hand, sub-categories and sub-dimensions can be collapsed to echo their diminishing importance in the problem. The shifting focus and direction of research and development can be chronicled by analysing the snapshots of ontological maps over time.

The ontological framework can be used to map the state of the research and the state of the practice of cultural heritage. The maps can be at a point in time and over time. These maps will reveal gaps in research and practice, and between the two. They will also reveal the evolution of the gaps over time. These gaps must be assessed and bridged to develop a roadmap for research and practice, and for translation of research into practice and vice versa.

The gap analysis will reveal the relative emphasis on each component. Some components may be heavily emphasized, some less and some not at all. The heavy emphasis may be warranted because of the importance of the component, but also accidental, a consequence of simply doing 'more of the same'. The light emphasis on a component may be unwarranted, because of the importance of the component. Again, the lightness of the emphasis may be deliberate due to the difficulty of managing the component in research/practice or accidental—an oversight. The non-emphasized components may simply be the blind spots in research and practice, potentially unexplored and unexploited. They may also be the blank spots, logically or practically infeasible. Knowing the bright, light, blind/blank spots in research and practice, and their antecedents and consequences will help develop a roadmap for research and practice.

8 Conclusion

The ontology of the semiotics of cultural heritage illustrates the 'big picture'. The ontology can be used as a common framework to map the anatomy of a system and the research on such systems. It can also be used to compare and contrast systems. The mapping can be used to generate ontological maps that will clearly illuminate the elements or components that are frequently present, less frequently present and absent in research and practice.

Augmented reality, virtual reality and visualization technologies are fundamentally altering the sentience of cultural heritage. Experiences with cultural heritage that used to be primarily visual, static and non-interactive are being transformed into a combination of visual, aural/oral and tactile experiences, which are often dynamic and interactive. In the future, our filmmaker may be able to gather all of the cultural heritage information that went into the documentary systematically and remotely and be able to recreate the temperature of a South African jail in winter and the smell of Mandela's homecoming dinner for the 'film' viewer. At the same time, the technologies are reducing the location dependence of the experience, making them virtually location independent. For example, cultural heritage can be experienced from the computer desktop in lieu of visiting a museum —sometimes in greater detail and with more versatility. Such developments require new infrastructure to advance the protection, preservation and propagation of cultural heritage through teaching, research and service. They increase and transform the inter-dependence between the management of cultural heritage, computers and information systems. New technologies can pose novel and complex ethical questions, while creating new versions of the age-old cultural heritage issues— authenticity, ownership and conservation/preservation. The ontology of the semiotics of cultural heritage provides a systemic and systematic basis to articulate and address these issues ex-ante, in-praesenti and ex-post.

9 Appendix: Glossary

Function	The functions of the system.
Acquire/Collect	To acquire/collect data/information/knowledge about cultural heritage.
Create/Edit/Delete	To create/edit/delete data/information/knowledge about cultural heritage.
Organize/Arrange	To organize/arrange data/information/knowledge about cultural heritage.
Index/Describe	To index/describe data/information/knowledge about cultural heritage.
Store/Preserve/Sustain	To store/preserve/sustain data/information/knowledge about cultural heritage.
Secure/Authenticate	To secure/authenticate data/information/knowledge about cultural heritage.
Retrieve	To retrieve data/information/knowledge about cultural heritage.
Process	To process data/information/knowledge about cultural heritage.
Distribute	To distribute data/information/knowledge about cultural heritage.
Semiotics	Symbolic representations of cultural heritage at different levels of abstraction.
Data	Measurements and observations, qualitative and quantitative about cultural heritage.
Information	Relationships among the data about cultural heritage.
Knowledge	Interpretations of the relationships among the cultural heritage data in a context.
Cultural Heritage	The heritage of a culture.
Tangible	Tangible cultural heritage artefacts.
Archaeological	'Products of archaeological excavations (including regular and clandestine) or of archaeological discoveries' [37].
Prehistorical	Property predating history such as prehistorical tools, structures, paintings, etc.
Historical	'Property relating to history, including the history of science and technology and military and social history, to the life of national leaders, thinkers, scientists and artist and to events of national importance' [37].
Literary	'Rare manuscripts and incunabula, old books, documents and publications of special interest (historical, artistic, scientific, literary, etc.) singly or in collections' [37].

Artistic	'Pictures, paintings and drawings produced entirely by hand on any support and in any material (excluding industrial designs and manufactured articles decorated by hand); original works of statuary art and sculpture in any material; original engravings, prints and lithographs; original artistic assemblages and montages in any material' [37]
Scientific	Scientific and technological objects, instruments, devices, etc. significant to the advancement of science and technology.
Intangible	Intangible cultural heritage.
Oral	'Oral traditions and expressions, including language as a vehicle of the intangible cultural heritage' [37].
Performance	Performing arts.
Social Practices	'Social practices, rituals and festive events' [37].
Knowledge/Practice nature	'Knowledge and practices concerning nature and the universe' [37].
Traditional Craftsmanship	Traditional craftsmanship.
Outcome	The outcomes of cultural heritage semiotics.
Investigate	To investigate cultural heritage.
Document	To document cultural heritage.
Preserve	To preserve cultural heritage.
Manage	To manage cultural heritage.
Visualize	To visualize cultural heritage.
Educate	To educate cultural heritage.
Communicate	To communicate cultural heritage.
Access	To access cultural heritage.
Assess	To assess cultural heritage.
Plan	To plan cultural heritage.
Publicize	To publicize cultural heritage.
Contextualize	To contextualize cultural heritage.
Enjoy	To enjoy cultural heritage

References

1. Allison, A.: Connecting undergraduates with primary sources: a study of undergraduate instruction in archives, manuscripts, and special collections. Master's paper for the M.S. in L. S. degree. School of Information and Library Science, University of North Carolina at Chapel Hill (2005). http://ils.unc.edu/MSpapers/3026.pdf
3. Anderson, I.G.: Are you being served? Historians and the search for primary sources. Archivaria 81 (2004)
2. Anderson, R.N.: Using the syllabus in collection development. Technicalities **8**, 14–15 (1988)

4. Bean, R., Klekowski, L.: Course syllabi: extracting their hidden potential at DePaul university's suburban campus libraries. In: Sixth Off-Campus Library Services Conference Proceedings. Central Michigan University, Mount Pleasant, Michigan, pp. 1–9 (1993)
5. Borgman, C., Leazer, G.H., Gilliland-Swetland, A., Millwood, K., Champeny, L., Finley J., Smart, L.J.: How Geography Professors Select Materials for Classroom Lectures: Implications for the Design of Digital Libraries. IEEE, pp. 179–185 (2004)
6. Boss, K., Drabinski, E.: Evidence-based instruction integration: a syllabus analysis project. Ref. Serv. Rev. **42**, 263–276 (2014)
7. Carini, P.: Archivists as educators: integrating primary sources into the curriculum. J. Arch. Organ. **7**, 41–50 (2009)
8. Charles, L.: Using an information literacy curriculum map as a means of communication and accountability for stakeholders in higher education. J. Inf. Literacy **9**, 47–61 (2015)
9. Dewald, N.: Anticipating library use by business students: the uses of a syllabus study. Res. Strat. **19**, 33–45 (2003)
10. Ford, N.: Web-Based Learning Through Educational Informatics: Information Science Meets Educational Computing. IGI Publishing (2008)
11. Gruber, T.: Ontology. In: Liu, L., Ozsu, M.T. (eds.) Encyclopedia of Database Systems, Springer (2008)
12. Hubbard, M., Lotts, M.: Special collections, primary resources, and information literacy pedagogy. Commun. Inf. Literacy **7**, 24–38 (2013)
13. Kennedy, L.: Partners or gatekeepers? Archival interactions with higher education at University College Dublin. In: Holland, A.C., Mullins, E. (eds.) Archives and Archivists, pp. 219–231. Four Courts Press, Dublin Ireland (2006)
14. Leighton, H.: Course analysis: techniques and guidelines. J. Acad. Librariansh. **21**, 175 (1995)
15. Lochstet, G.: Course and research analysis using a coded classification system. J. Acad. Librariansh. **23**, 380–389 (1997)
16. Maher, W.: The Management of College and University Archives. Scarecrow, Lanham, MD, London (2001)
17. Marty, P.: Unintended consequences: unlimited access, invisible work and the future of the information professsion in cultural heritage organizations. Bull. Am. Soc. Inf. Sci. Technol. (Online) **38**, 29 (2012)
18. Marty, P.: Digital convergence and the information profession in cultural heritage organizations: reconciling internal and external demands. Libr. Trends **62**, 613 (2014)
19. McDonald, J., Micikas, L.: Collection evaluation and development by syllabus analysis: the must-ought-could (MOC) method at Holy Family College: Acquisitions In: '90: Conference on Acquisitions, Budgets, and Collections. St. Louis, Missouri, United States, May 16 and 17, 1990
20. McGrath, W., Durand, N.: Classifying courses in the university catalog. Coll. Res. Libr. **30**, 533–539 (1969)
21. Morris, S., Mykytiuk, L., Weiner, S.: Archival literacy for history students: identifying faculty expectations of archival research skills. Am. Archivist **77**, 394–424 (2014)
22. Nicholson, S.: The basis for bibliomining: frameworks for bringing together usage-based data mining and bibliometrics through data warehousing in digital library services. Inf. Process. Manage. **42**, 785–804 (2006)
23. Pancheshnikov, Y.: Course-centered approach to evaluating university library collections for instructional program reviews. Collect. Build. **22**, 177–185 (2003)
24. Pattuelli, M.: Teachers' perspectives and contextual dimensions to guide the design of N.C. history learning objects and ontology. Inf. Process. Manage. **44**, 635–646 (2008)
25. Quine, W.V.: From a Logical Point of View, p. 16. Harvard University Press, Boston, MA, USA (1961)
26. Ralph, L.L.: Using education informatics to improve library services to doctoral students: an embedded approach. Int. J. Doctoral Stud. **7**, 235–244 (2012)

27. Ramaprasad, A., Rai, A.: Envisioning management of information. Omega: Int. J. Manag. Sci. **24**(2), 179–193 (Omega 24, 2, April 1996, 179–193) (1996)

28. Ramaprasad, A., Syn, T.: Ontological meta-analysis and synthesis. Commun. Assoc. Inf. Syst. **37**, 138–153 (2015)

29. Rambler, L.: Syllabus study: key to a responsive academic library. J. Acad. Librariansh. **8**, 155 (1982)

30. Robyns, M.: The archivist as educator: integrating critical thinking skills into historical research methods instruction. Am. Archivist **64**, 363–384 (2001)

31. Rockenbach, B.: Archives, undergraduates, and inquiry-based learning: case studies from Yale university library. Am. Archivist **74**, 297–311 (2011)

32. Romero, C., Ventura, S.: Educational data mining: a survey from 1995 to 2005. Expert Syst. Appl. **33**, 135–146 (2007)

33. Shirkey, C.: Taking the guesswork out of collection development: using syllabi for a user-centered collection development method. Collect. Manag. **36**, 154–164 (2011)

34. Smith, C., Doversberger, L., Jones, S., Ladwig, P., Parker, J., Pietraszewski, B.: Using course syllabi to uncover opportunities for curriculum-integrated instruction. Ref. User Serv. Q. **51**, 263–271 (2012)

35. Tate, M., Furtmueller, E., Evermann, J., Bandara, W.: Introduction to the special issue: the literature review in information systems. Commun. Assoc. Inf. Syst. **37**, 103–111 (2015)

36. Tibbo, H.: The impact of information technology on academic archives in the Twenty-first century. In: Prom, C.J., Swain, E.D. (eds.) College and University Archives: Readings in Theory and Practice, pp. 27–53. Society of American Archivists, Chicago (2008)

37. UNESCO: Convention on the means of prohibiting and preventing the illicit import, export, and transfer of ownership of cultural property 1970. (1970). http://www.unesco.org/new/en/culture/themes/illicit-trafficking-of-cultural-property/1970-convention/text-of-the-convention/

38. UNESCO: Intangible Cultural Heritage. (2003). http://www.unesco.org/culture/ich/en/convention#art2

39. Van Scoy, A., Oakleaf, M.: Evidence vs. anecdote: using syllabi to plan curriculum-integrated information literacy instruction. Coll. Res. Libr. **69**, 566–575 (2008)

40. Vecco, M.: A definition of cultural heritage: From the tangible to the intangible. J. Cultural Heritage **11**, 321–324 (2010)

41. Wagner, J., Smith, D.A.: Students as donors to university archives: a study of student perceptions with recommendations. Am. Archivist **75**, 538–566 (2012)

42. Williams, L., Cody, S., Parnell, J.: Prospecting for new collaborations: mining syllabi for library service opportunities. J. Acad. Librariansh. **30**, 270–275 (2004)

43. Wormell, I.: Matching subject portals with the research environment. Inf. Technol. Libr. **22**, 158–164 (2003)

Insights and Challenges in Digitalization of a Secret Sign Language of the Penan on Borneo Island

Tariq Zaman and Hasnain Falak

1 Introduction

Nowadays, Information and Communication Technology (ICT) tools have been developed to document and maintain indigenous languages all over the world [1]. The target of these initiatives is creating databases and sharing indigenous language material online so the wider research and development communities can access it [2]. In this whole process, very often the local communities have been motivated to participate as "data bank" or "content providers". The major audience for these initiatives was felt to be the people from literate backgrounds. Hence, in results, the targeted language content has been decontextualized and by the following complex language frameworks it is recorded in the form of dictionaries. The scope of these dictionaries is limited as well as the structure of the content is generally complex, so it is of very limited use for local communities. In addition, main target of the digitalization initiatives is spoken languages.

With this background and challenges, we, the researchers from Universiti Malaysia Sarawak and Namibia University of Sciences and Technology with partnership of Penan local community of Long Lamai, embarked on a project for digitalizing and preserving Oroo'. Oroo' language is a combination of signs which the nomadic Penans use to communicate with each other during their forest journey. Due to unique structure of the language, it of extreme value to society. However, the young Penan generation does not consider it useful and the old generation is slowly dying out, so the Oroo' digitalization project is started with the main goal of

T. Zaman (✉)
Hochschule Für Technik Und Wirtschaft (HTW) Berlin, Berlin, Germany
e-mail: Tariq.Zaman@htw-berlin.de; zamantariq@gmail.com

T. Zaman · H. Falak
Universiti Malaysia Sarawak (UNIMAS), Jalan Datuk Mohammad Musa,
94300 Kota Samarahan, Sarawak, Malaysia
e-mail: hasnainflk@gmail.com

© Springer Nature Singapore Pte Ltd. 2018
D. S. Jat et al. (eds.), *Digitisation of Culture: Namibian and International Perspectives*, https://doi.org/10.1007/978-981-10-7697-8_5

"preserving" and "reviving" the old sign language and to make it more relevant in changing lifestyle of community.

2 Background

Penan is one of the indigenous communities living in Sarawak (Malaysia), Brunei and Kalimantan (Indonesia). Sarawak is located on the island of Borneo and is one of the two states of East Malaysia that is separated from West Malaysia (Peninsula Malaysia) by the South China Sea. With an area of 124,449.51 km^2, Sarawak is the largest state in Malaysia, making up some 37.5% of the country's total area. On top of that, Sarawak is a home to 28 ethnic groups and 63 languages (DBP), communities each with their different language, culture, and lifestyle [3]. Penans is part of the Orang Ulu ethnic group, a conglomeration of more than a dozen sub-ethnic groups, which comprises 5.5% of Sarawak population. Long Lamai is one of the oldest settled Penan communities in the area of upper Baram river. It is a true picture of remote and rural area, accessible by an hours' longboat journey upriver from the nearest small airport. The community's population is approximately 598 individuals and 116 households and there is limited electricity supply and telecommunication service [4]. The community of Long Lamai settled in this area for over 50 years ago and today mainly dependent on farming but still travel to forest for collecting daily livelihoods. In 2009, Universiti Malaysia Sarawak established Telecentre project for addressing the information and communication needs of the community. However, very soon a debate has been initiated about "next step", which is how to use digital access for the socioeconomic development of local community? Hence, since then a number of research and development projects have been initiated in the field of rural ICTs and infrastructure in order to nurture a sustainable socioeconomy.

3 Status of Oroo' Language

We conduct a survey to examine the threat and endangerment level of Oroo by exploring language use patterns. The survey also captured Penan adults' opinions and attitudes about the Oroo' in contemporary society as well as the extent to which Penans commit themselves to fostering the Oroo' language.

The participants in this study were 80 Penan people from 5 different villages Long Lamai, Long Tungan, Long Selatong, Long Apu, and Long Palai (see Fig. 1).

The sex distribution was 25% female and 75% male while the age distribution was 20–25 years, 49%; 25–50 years, 31%; and 50 years and over 20%. 16% of the respondents were based in villages and 39%; Penan diaspora living in towns.

The survey questionnaire had three sections. The first section was an in-depth exploration of the participants' biographical information. The second part explored

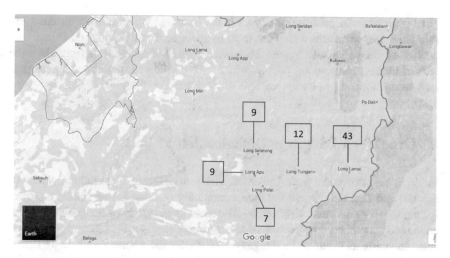

Fig. 1 Map, the location of the villages and no. of participants

participants' perception and level of Oroo' language endangerment, seeking information on preferred languages and it is used in various contexts. The third part had several items that surveyed language diversity, vitality, relationship with modern technology, and use in contemporary context. The questionnaires were distributed to all willing participants along with necessary instructions.

In terms of results, and to explore the status of Oroo' language and intergenerational knowledge transmission, most of the participants considered Oroo' language as endangered, 39%; severely endangered, 29%; definitively endangered, 6%; critically endangered and 6%; and extinct. The remaining 20% considered the language safe (Fig. 2). According to UNESCO, definitively endangered are the languages used mostly by the parental generation and up, severely endangered are the languages used mostly by the grandparental generation and up. Critically endangered are the languages used by very few speakers, mostly of

Fig. 2 Status of Oroo' language

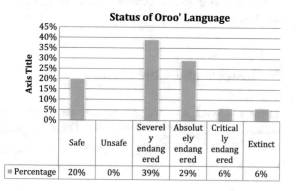

	Safe	Unsafe	Severely endangered	Absolutely endangered	Critically endangered	Extinct
Percentage	20%	0%	39%	29%	6%	6%

great-grandparental generation, extinct is the language which has no speakers and safe languages are those which are used by all ages, from children up [5].

90% of the participants agreed that main reason of language endangerment is the lack of interest from young people, while 34% considered that Oroo' language is only useful for old generation such as grandparents.

4   Oroo' Sign Language Digitalization Project

In 2013, the researchers from Univeristi Malaysia Sarawak, Namibia University of Science and Technology and the local community of Long Lamai started a project for digitalizing and preserving Oroo'. The main target group of the project is local community members irrespective of age and gender. As a first attempt, to understand the currents status of the language, we conducted a survey with Long Lamai community. The results showed that today, only a very small number of community members can communicate with Oroo' signs [6]. Hence, in addition to documenting the language, we enquired how to make the Oroo' language more relevant in changing the lifestyle of Penans so it can be sustained. Hence, in addition to developing repositories of photos, videos, drawing, and textual description of signs, we also developed three different ICT solutions for three distant age groups.

For intergenerational knowledge exchange between the parents and kids, an Oroo' Tangible platform has been developed. The platform comprises capacitating sensing tangibles, made from a mixture of real and artificial material and attached to a corresponding 2D representations of images on mobile tablets screen [7]. A PC-based Oroo' adventure game has been developed for 8–10 years old children. The game has multiple levels, on the first level different Oroo' signs as part of imaginary story, followed by an interactive component of treasure hunt to find hidden signs. These signs are hidden in the background scenery of the rainforest. In the third stage, users are instructed to shoot the right sign with a blowpipe, which is corresponding to an animal [6]. In the third attempt, we codesigned the Penan Oroo' Short Messages Signs (PO-SMS) app with a group of Penan youth in Long Lamai [6]. The app allows the Penan youth to send each other Oroo' messages, by arranging 2D graphical representations of leaves and twigs to create meaningful messages.

5   Insights and Challenges

In the following sections, we present the insights and challenges of our multiple endeavors to document and digitalize Oroo' language.

5.1 Multiple Approaches

The initial survey results showed different levels of Oroo' language proficiency based on age group in Penan villages. It also reflects quick and rapid language loss; therefore, we developed multiple solutions to address the needs of each age group (Fig. 3). For elder community members, we developed Oroo' Tangibles platform so they can use it to teach their young children of age 9 year and below. We discovered 10- and 11-year-old children in Long Lamai, interested in playing computer games so we developed Oroo' adventure game for them. For the youth, we developed PO-SMS and integrated Oroo' language communication in mobile devices so they can use Oroo' as their medium of communication in virtual world. We found that loss of Oroo' language is visible in all age groups, for that a single solution may not work so we developed different interventions based on age groups and their interests.

5.2 Reflection on Actions

The nature and scope of the project are not common. This gives us an opportunity to go beyond rigid rules of inquiry, and to generate new rules in situations that are uncertain and unique. We had different cycles of designing multiple solutions and a mode of reflection (Fig. 4) is entered when the flow of action is broken by these events. The researchers turned into critical observer of their actions. The reflections helped us to redesign the next steps; for example, after Oroo' adventure and Oroo' tangibles, we discussed if it is "enough" to develop game or database for language

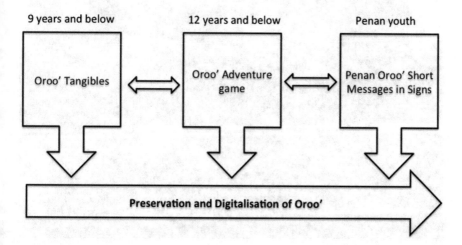

Fig. 3 Multiple solutions for different age groups

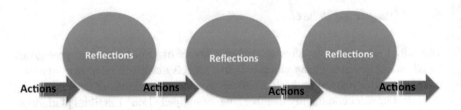

Fig. 4 Continuous reflections of actions

preservation. This leads us toward designing a new solution and integrating Oroo' in common digital medium of communication.

5.3 *In Situ Design Process*

In situ design process was another important aspect of our journey. We experienced forest walks, community dialogs (Fig. 5), and visual representations which are very effective tools for getting insights and to enhance community participation. To teach us the importance of community in sit design process, a community elder shared, "if I want to teach hunting to my children I will bring them forest and will not teach them in Telecentre".

Fig. 5 Community meetings for re-confirmation of design

5.4 Counter-Narrative

The common narrative about Penans is "anti-government", "anti-development", and "people living in the forest". They are considered always dependent on other communities and the people with no modern skills to survive in settled life. However, in our engagement with Long Lamai community, we observed the community acceptable of taking challenges, adaptable, and receptive of technologies, nevertheless emphasizing on their conditions of engagement. We also observed that community of Long Lamai utilizing this opportunity of using digital technologies for Oroo' language preservation as a means to create counter-narrative. Hence, the Oroo' digitalization is not a sole purpose of the community but also a way to reconstruct their image in outside world.

5.5 Co-learning and Co-creation

Co-learning and Co-creation of multiple solutions was an integral part of the project. We found an eagerness for knowledge and skill in the community members, which could be also the reason of need to cope with the challenges of settlement from nomadic life. The community has a principle of "working with" researchers instead of "working for" researchers. In a discussion with village headman, he mentioned that the documentation of Oroo' language will help the younger generation but also the elders to refresh their memory.

5.6 New Opportunities of Livelihood

We also created new means of livelihood for local community by integrating Oroo' as learning package in tourism activities. This could activate the interest of youth who returned from towns after completing their education and looking for income opportunities. In addition to tourists, we also offered this as an activity for service learning students who visited Long Lamai for a 2-week educational program.

6　Conclusion

The results of this study show that the majority of Penan community and especially the old generation consider Oroo' language as central to their Penan identity, history, and culture. The language establishes their relationship with the ecosystem which is endangered by the changing lifestyle. Furthermore, there is concern about the future of the language and explicit demand of using new means and technology to revitalize the language. However, if due care is not taken and the focus is just on developing technology-based solution it can lead toward new challenges the local communities becoming more vulnerable. One of the ways to avoid these challenges we practiced community-based intensive participatory approach in which community takes a lead role to shape research and development agenda. This may be a lengthy and time-consuming process; however, we found this approach more sustainable in long run.

Acknowledgements The Oroo' project was carried out with the aid of a grant from the ISIF Asia. I also thank all the community members and my co-researchers who participated in the one or other of our research activities.

Consent An informed consent was obtained from the participant for publication of accompanying images.

References

1. Dyson, L.E.: Cultural issues in the adoption of information and communication technologies by Indigenous Australians. In: Proceedings Cultural Attitudes Towards Communication and Technology, pp. 58–71. Murdoch University, Perth (2004)
2. Buszard-Welcher, L.: Can the Web help save my language. In: The Green Book of Language Revitalization in Practice, pp. 331–45 (2001)
3. Saee, S., Yeo, A.W.: Sarawak ethnic languages: revitalisation and maintenance. In: The First Regional Conference on Computational Science and Technology. Universiti Malaysia Sabah (2007)
4. Zaman, T., Yeo, A.W., Jengan, G.: Designing digital solutions for preserving Penan sign language. Adv. Hum. Comput. Interact. 4 (2016)
5. Brenzinger, M., Yamamoto, A., Aikawa, N., Koundiouba, D., Minasyan, A., Dwyer, A., Smeets, R.: Language Vitality and Endangerment. UNESCO Intangible Cultural Unit, Safeguarding Endangered Languages, Paris. http://www.unesco.org/culture/ich/doc/src/00120-en.pdf. Last accessed July, 1, 2010 (2003)
6. Zaman, T., Winschiers-Theophilus, H.: Penan's Oroo'Short Message Signs (PO-SMS): co-design of a digital jungle sign language application. In: Human-Computer Interaction, pp. 489–504. Springer International Publishing (2015)
7. Plimmer, B., He, L., Zaman, T., Karunanayaka, K., Yeo, A.W., Jengan, G., Blagojevic, R., Yi-Luen, E.D.: New interaction tools for preserving an old language. In: 33rd Annual ACM Conference on Human Factors in Computing Systems, pp. 3493–3502. ACM, New York, NY, USA (2015)

Digital Game-Based Learning as Digitization of Learning Culture

Martin Steinicke

1 Introduction

In [1], I have participated in defining digital game-based learning comparatively wide as:

"Digital game based learning is the process of being taught and/or learning via digitally enriched play-/gamelike activities or by playing/designing/creating/modifying digital games."

As argued in [2], digital game-based learning thus covers three more or less distinct scenarios: To begin with, learning by playing a digital game. Either framed with or without individual reflection or group discussion. This scenario covers learning in formal as well as informal settings—e.g., "stealth learning" [3] or "interest-driven learning" [4]. The second scenario is learning by designing or creating [5] as well as modifying (e.g., [4, 6]) digital games. The produced game or mod might be created to generate either an entertainment or learning experience for the prospective player but the focus is that creators learn through their work. The third scenario covered by our definition is learning framed by playful interaction with digital media or game components. One approach that fits into this scenario is digital aesthetic learning.

Obviously, this definition covers quite a number of approaches to teaching and learning with technology supported or enhanced forms of play and games. This brought me to the point, to question whether digital game-based learning is actually a method as oftentimes simply stated (e.g., [7–9]). In the context of teaching and learning, Meyer—in his seminal work on "Unterrichtsmethoden" (approx. methods of class/instruction/education)—defines these as the forms and procedures that students and teachers use to appropriate their natural and societal reality under institutional conditions [10]. Considering this definition, digital game-based learning

M. Steinicke (✉)
University of Applied Sciences HTW Berlin, 12459 Berlin, Germany
e-mail: martin.steinicke@HTW-Berlin.de

© Springer Nature Singapore Pte Ltd. 2018
D. S. Jat et al. (eds.), *Digitisation of Culture: Namibian and International Perspectives*, https://doi.org/10.1007/978-981-10-7697-8_6

in itself does not perfectly fit. Thus, I subsequently explore whether it might actually be more than a pure method, but rather a "Didaktik". The goal of this exploration is less of claiming a final position, but to stimulate discussion on this point of view.

2 Psychological Paradigms of Learning

The field of "Didaktik" (didactics) is—primarily in Germany—a broad field of epistemology, models, and oftentimes heated disputes. To cover the numerous concepts, approaches and frontlines would go well beyond the scope of this article that as one part aims to situate Digital Game-Based Learning (DGBL) in this academic field.

Indeed, didactics are always created or adapted in relation to historic educational and sociocultural trends as well as psychological paradigms of learning. Interestingly, especially the latter and the related beliefs of what is scientific as well as what is worth researching, in combination with a diverging approach of how to educate future teachers and their forms of employment resulted in the fact that Didaktik is a thriving and diverse field in Germany, but close to nonexistent in the Anglo-Saxon and French domain [11].

Thus, the three paradigms relevant to this inquiry are briefly presented below. On one hand to lay the groundwork for the presentation of the models of didactics in (3) and on the other due to the fact that these paradigms are also relevant when discussing methodological concepts such as project-based learning (etc.) in (4).

2.1 Behaviorism

Behaviorism is a paradigm of learning and individual development that focuses primarily on the observation and experimentation on behaviors and behavior acquisition. In contrast and at some points in time very probably in opposition to the success of psychoanalysis, it focuses on observable and measurable behaviors (black-box approach) instead of hypothesizing on hidden mental processes or structures—which was deemed unscientific at best [12, 13]. Based upon the notion that individual behaviors are consequences of (previous) interactions with the world, one main focus was the prediction and control of the behavior of an individual [14]—the latter primarily by influencing the relation between stimuli and responses. This type of learning is fostered primarily by the manipulation of the (co-)occurrence of stimuli—as in classic conditioning—or by administering rewards and punishments—as can be seen in operant conditioning.

The behavioristic model of teaching mirrors this, in that the main mode of teaching, is instruction that focuses on passive reception and reproduction of "true" content or facts [15]. Behaviorisms strong focus on quantitative empirical research, with the scientist as a neutral observer of contrived experiments that should yield standardized/reproducible results, strongly influenced the science of education especially in the US—as Ellen Lagemann was saying "[...] one realizes that Edward L. Thorndike won and John Dewey lost" [11].

2.2 Cognitivism

While behaviorism was very influential at the time and could explain some forms of learning exceptionally well, others did not fit this paradigm. As one of the dissenters, Bandura highlighted the reciprocal nature of the relation between individual and environment and later included individual and social psychological processes [16]. This led to a renewed interest in the inner workings of the ignored black box. The opening to qualitative scientific approaches and theories on the inner, mental, and cognitive processes led to a fundamental change in the psychological and educational fields that focus on thinking, learning, and action [17]. This "cognitive turn" also made learning psychology compatible with didactics again [17]. This was due to the fact that cognitivism evaded the behavioristic view of the learner as a guinea pig that has to be skillfully manipulated into adopting a predefined behavior —which was a capital sin for most pedagogues in Germany.

The cognitivist view of learning, in accordance to this, focuses on information-oriented learning, in which content needs to be actively processed instead of reinforced [15] as well as lead to (inter alia) general problem-solving skills and metacognition [17]. A further point of interest is that in contrast to the behavioristic approach of defining optimized structures for teaching any learner (see e.g., "programmed instruction" in 3.2), cognitivists focus(ed) on choosing media that fits the individual patterns of cognition, decoding/understanding, and processing of the given audience [15]. Notwithstanding this, the processing metaphor and lingo (still) resembles the working of an information-processing device [17] and evokes the idea of transportability of learning content [15] in relation to information theory.

2.3 Constructivism

Constructivists propose that humans are active, intervening and patterns of reality generating observers, participants, and protagonist who create realities that suit themselves [18], which implies that knowledge cannot be transmitted and processed as in the behaviorist and cognitivist views but rather needs to be (re-)constructed by every individual.

Additionally, radical versions of constructivism provokingly propose that the world—as we perceive it—is our own invention [19, 20]. A consequence of this and radical constructivism in general is that learning cannot be generated from outside the individual: it can only be triggered and even this may have (1) no,

(2) expected, or (3) unexpected results [17]. For didactics, this ends in a number of problems—most notably that it is impossible to decide which knowledge/content is worth to be covered, that the process of teaching and processing cannot be organized in an orderly fashion/at all, and that a distinction between/measurement of successful and less successful learning is impossible [17].

Nonetheless, tempered versions of constructivist psychologies of learning and constructivist didactics try to combine the constructivist and the instructionalist paradigm [17]. Versions of recommendations for learning environments/class in this context generally propose three central elements [17]:

1. The learner is/should be active and take action.
2. Learning is/should be situated in concrete contexts of experience and problems.
3. Learning is/should be situated/embedded in small social entities or communities.

Reading these, it certainly becomes clear why the constructivist paradigm offers such high conceptual fit with views of (especially German) pedagogues as these are basically renewed/reformulated versions of classic methodological postulates of the reform pedagogy movement [17]. Interestingly, this shift from content to methodological questions [17] is not well received by every school of thought in the field of didactics.

3 Didaktik/Didactics

Didaktik in itself focuses on all aspects of teaching and learning in a general sense [17]. It is "a model or a system of how to envisage the teaching-learning process as well as a kind of metatheory where the various models can be compared with each other" [11].

Following Terhart [17] one primary distinction in the field of Didaktik is between the "Allgemeine Didaktik" (general didactics) and a plethora of "Besondere Didaktiken" or "Spezialdidaktiken" ("special didactics") [21]. The former broaches the issues of teaching and learning on a general basis and in all its preconditions, processes and results inside as well as outside of institutions [17]—albeit, due to the fact, that the primary period of formal learning is located between the age of six and eighteen, even general didactics has traditionally a strong focus on teaching and learning in school [17].

Special didactics, in contrast, focus on specific questions of teaching and learning regarding a special target group, institution, or subject matter (etc.).

In the field of general didactics, a number of theories (or theory groups/theory families/models [17]) can be discerned. As a matter of principle, each of these comes with/defines its own view(s) on what learning as well as teaching is and how it should be—as well as how it should be planned, conducted, analyzed, discussed, and researched. Following, the most prevalent theories/models according to [17] and the special didactics related to this enquiry are highlighted.

3.1 *"Bildungstheoretische Didaktik"*

The core concepts of the Bildungstheoretische Didaktik are "Bildung" and "Inhalt".

Bildung refers to the idea of individual/self-development (as a process) in relation to normative goals that need to balance requirements and demands of the society and future generations. Such goals have always been bound to the current view on the ideals of the individual in/and society [17]. These change (and alternate), e.g., from the disciplined worker bowing to crown and church in absolutism [17] to the ideal of a self-determined individual that is able to emancipate itself [22] or (later) to show/act in solidarity [23] as well as be willing and prepared for moral action [24]. The idea of Bildung through the encounter with culture [17] via "Bildungsgüter/Inhalte" (educational content)—elements of culture and knowledge that are deemed worthy of covering—is central to the Bildungstheoretische Didaktik. This has been explicated by Klafki in his statement of the "Primat der Didaktik vor der Methodik" (primacy of didactics over methodology) [25], which promotes the idea of starting from the educational content and using a didactic analysis to analyze its "Bildungsgehalt" (educational substance), its critical reflection, and justification and only subsequently create a lesson plan—all deduced from the imperative inner logic of the content [17]. But this deduction is problematic at best as every content needs to be considered in relation to the situation of the class, needs to be transformed into a lesson topic by stetting it into context to/ with a problem or question [23], and because it can be staged/enacted differently by a/each teacher [17]. Klafki later modified his thesis to the primacy of the goal decision over all other aspects—i.e., over content, methods, and media. But he accepts the interdependence of all of these constitutive factors of instruction, as long as they are not considered equal to the significance of the critical–emancipatory goal question [23]. In this context, he also distinguishes between potentially emancipatory and instrumental topics [23]—the latter being knowledge or skills (e.g., reading) that might be used for emancipatory goals or anything else. These should be set into the context of critical–emancipatory themes to showcase their relevance to the students. A further option would be the usage of teaching methods that directly tie to these themes even when the content itself is instrumental. Thus, the instrumental character of the content is counterbalanced by the emancipatory elements of the chosen method [23]. This might be a concession to methodology-oriented critics like Meyer [26] and others that identified a "peaceful coexistence" of didactic models and practical teaching [27] as well as a discontinuity between theory building and relevance to practice [28].

3.2 *"Lehr-/Lerntheoretische Didaktik"*

One empirical-based school of didactic theory/models is the "Lehrtheoretische" [17] or "Lerntheoretische Didaktik" [10]. Founded by Heinemann with his

"Berliner Modell", these models take on the perspective of the teacher who should be supported with scientific knowledge when planning and analyzing lessons/class [17]. It was developed based on empirical research and as a counterpoint to the Bildungstheoretische Didaktik and its approach of deducing all other aspects of teaching from the educational content—or later the educational goals, respectively. Instead, it proposed the interdependence of goals, content, methods, and media [17] to such a degree that one could start planning/analyzing from any of these fields. Furthermore, it proposed that no matter at which planning stage, changing/ developing one field always leads to potential issues or changes in the other fields [29]. Critics found fault with the ignored general societal conditions and normative positions, which led to the adaption of the model. In general, the Berlin model is considered to focus on class as an instrumentally rational and measurable organization of teaching–learning processes [17]. It was developed further by Schulz [30] to the "Hamburger Modell" (Hamburg Model), which underlined the interactive/ interactionist nature of lessons/class and proposed a participatory planning by teachers and students—and thus exhibits a "quasi-therapeutic form" [17].

3.3 "Kybernetische Didaktik"

The "Kybernetische Didaktik" or "Kybernetische Pädagogik" bases itself on a marriage of the concepts of cybernetics and information theory—inter alia information-processing and feedback loops—as well as the behavioristic paradigm of learning [31]. It owed its short-lived prominence not only to the applicability of these concepts to didactics and pedagogy but to a number of further factors, namely, the prevalence of cybernetics and artificial intelligence in the science and pop cultures of the 1970s, its proposal of a new (technicistic) idea of man, as well as a perceived German educational disaster that seemed to require to double the number of "Abiturienten" (pupils gaining their certificate of general qualification for university entrance) to support the economical growth [31]. The latter consequently seemed to necessitate an optimized (efficient and effective) and cost-efficient schooling that the cybernetic pedagogues seemed to offer. This was the claim that teaching is basically objectifiable [32] and thus a technological solution could replace the informational system that supports the learner [32]—the replaced "Lehrsystem" (teaching system) clearly being the teacher. While the description of the teaching component as "teaching intelligence" was already apparent in the work on the Berliner Didaktik [17], it is now clearly the focus of the pedagogic approach.

Interestingly, Frank distinguishes between two general forms of teaching, namely, "anbietendes Lehren" (offered teaching) and "strategisches Lehren" (strategic teaching) [32]—both are again subdivided as can be seen in Table 1.

Strangely, Frank proposes that the "Lehren durch lernverhaltensabhängige Lehrstoffvermittlung" (2.2.2 Learning-behavioral content transmission) is the most

Table 1 Cybernetic forms of teaching with content—synthesized from [32b]

1. "Offered teaching"			2. "Strategic teaching"		
Choosing a correct simplification			Defining the sequence of content elements		
1.1 Responder	1.2 Simulation	2.1 Controlled learning	2.2. Regulated learning		
Learner may query system	Learner may manipulate model with reduced complexity	No user influence	2.2.1 Socratic model	2.2.2 Learning-behavioral content transmission	
System responds with facts	Learning through experience	e.g., Lecture, radio/TV	System queries	Presenting facts and truths to user, sequencing progress depending on user input (programmed instruction)	

important of all forms of teaching [32]. This clearly underlines the view on teaching and learning as well as on the user of such learning automata—being clearly a reductive and mechanistic one [31]. Probably also due to this and a number of additional factors, the cybernetic pedagogy did not persist long. Contributing factors have certainly been, e.g., the depreciative as well as arrogant view on other schools of didactics [31], the hyper-/pseudo-scientific lingo, and probably most of all the low practical success/dissemination of programmed instruction approaches and systems in the German-speaking countries—inter alia due to high production costs and workload as well as needed technical/programming expertise [33, 34].

While today, introductory works on didactics like [17] not even mention the cybernetic didactics and others—like Meyer [10]—criticize the cybernetic school's reduction of methodological questions, it nonetheless left its mark. This is visible in approaches to concepts such as "Computer Based Training" [!sic] [35]. Although in these, especially games and simulations are given as the more promising alternatives to simple tutoring systems [36, 37]—the latter equal mostly 2.2, while the former were introduced as 1.2 of Table 1. But it also left scorched earth that made/makes discussions on digital game-based learning nontrivial, especially in/with a field of didactics and pedagogy that should have a natural fit: the "Spieldidaktik".

3.4   *"Spieldidaktik/Spielpädagogik"*

Before plunging into the discussion of the "Spieldidaktik", one hurdle needs to be taken. While in English a distinction between play and games is found, this is not the case in German. Here, "Spiel" can denote all forms/categories/continua of both activities and objects as well as free and rule-based processes. While in English the distinction of play and game is also not clear-cut—for a discussion see e.g., [1, 38, 39] and for a comparison to Scandinavian languages e.g., [40]—diving into this would go beyond the scope of this paper. Thus, below play and/or game will "simply" be used as a translation of "Spiel" without any discussion here.

The concept of using play and games in education is certainly not a new one [41–44]. Personal experience of school time will probably include memories of teachers trying to motivate their students by using games and by competition, especially in physical education. But the appliance of play and games in educational contexts is inarguably older than our current educational system. Chess, for example, originated in India some "thousand years ago" [45]. The play pieces of chess depicted the four divisions of the Indian Army, and the game was basically a simulation of battle [46]. Notably, the original version of chess was "part of princely or courtly education in acquiring [...] culture" [46], since at least the enlightenment, play, and games as a potential tool for learning came into the wide societal focus. While some forms of games—especially gambling—were ostracized, others like billiard became legitimated, and well-known games—like the Game of the Goose—stuffed with educational content [47].

A serious problem for digital game-based learning in didactics and pedagogy is strangely one primary point that speaks for the usage of play and games in the first place: its relevance to the development of the child/human, which goes hand in hand with a certain utopian glorification that is visible, e.g., in Schiller's bon mot of "[...] das der Mensch nur da ganz Mensch ist, wo er spielt." ([...] only there man is truly man, where he plays.) [48]. This lays the groundwork for the ambivalent views on play/games in education. On the one hand, its natural relation to learning and its emancipatory potential, which makes learning "kindgemäß" (fitting the child's nature) and human [49], are highlighted. On the other hand, the question is oftentimes posed, whether the potential or overly encroachment of didactics on play can be justified from a pedagogic point of view [50]. The latter goes hand in hand with a notion of an ideal notion of "pure" play [50] that must not be endangered by an instrumentalization of play/games.

The discussion on explicit "Lernspiele" (learning games) is thus equally heavy with conflict. While most reform pedagogues of the twentieth century viewed it as a valuable part of the "Pädagogik vom Kinde aus" (child/student-oriented pedagogy), others critiqued the closed structure of games [50] in contrast to play and its focus on clearly describable and measurable cognitive learning goals. The latter in combination with two following points shed light on what is discussed under the term of learning games. First, as Popp [50] argues, that (school) pedagogues mainly base their hopes on the motivational affordances of games that foster intensive and enduring repetition of action [50]. Second, learning games are considered a special case/subset of "Spiel" (play/games) based on rule-based parlor/board games. In line with this is the notion/warning that educational content "dressed" in the form of games does not guarantee the experience of play [51], as well as that educational content (and learning games) is only programmed instruction or digital versions of print media [52].

All these points indicate a rather narrow interpretation of learning games as conceptually embedded games (see below) and oftentimes not even digital ones

[50]. The critique on these games as well as on its digital versions—see e.g., [53]—certainly cannot and should not be denied.

Nonetheless, it may have contributed to the fact that "Spieldidaktik" and "Spielpädagogik" (didactics and pedagogy of play/games) in general rather focus on distinctions of historic and valuable forms of play (not games) and how to promote these. Thus, "Spieldidaktik" is actually a didactic of teaching play rather than a didactic for teaching with play/games—see e.g., [54]—and is certainly in need of updating [55].

4 Examples Under Investigation

Subsequently, a number of examples of digital game-based learning treatments and approaches developed by the Creative Media group will be presented and set into relation to the presented paradigms of learning and didactic models as well as further related methods and theories.

4.1 DGBL Scenario One and Conceptually Embedded Versus Integrated Games

In the discussion of learning games in 3.4, it was argued that these games could be considered Conceptually Embedded Games (CEG), which denotes to simply embed the learning "content" into a given game [56, 57]. On the one hand, using a given game mechanic or genre and trying to squeeze a non-related learning content into it has the commercial advantage of being able to reuse the developed game system. Simply paste another content into the game mechanics and the next learning game is done. This drastically reduces the workload of preparing such a game and is thus in the interest of "Do it yourself"-oriented teachers, too.

But on the other hand, this leads to a number of serious issues:

1. The game feels like chocolate-covered broccoli [58 citing 59] as the game is like a "sugar coating" [59] to hide the educational objective.
2. The user plays the game, but as the core game mechanic does not match the thing to learn, a huge chunk of time can be spent without encountering the intended content. This is a salient feature of adventure style games like "Winterfest" [60] or "Physicus" (see [3] for a discussion).
3. The player feels the separation between game and learning and thus tries to evade the learning content to play the game part [53, 61], thus increasing the problem of point two. Additionally, the student learns that gameplay equals fun and learning equals boring.
4. When considering a learning game as medium for teaching, then the postulate of Meyer should be heeded. In contrast to separate concepts of Media in the

Bildungstheoretische, cybernetic, and Lehr-/Lerntheoretische Didaktik, Meyer proposes that these are "deep-frozen" (i.e., fixed) constellations of decisions on learning goal, content, and methods [10]. Thus, simply changing the content would break the composition and thus would be a violation of all presented didactics.

Instead, we are interested in researching the design of core mechanics that actually are the thing the player should learn in the first place—thus making it a Conceptually Integrated Game (CIG) [56, 57]. The research on developing and applying CIG—or games with the intrinsic integration [62, 63] of concepts, behaviors, or systems (etc.) that should be learned—might be traced back to Papert [63]. Nonetheless, there seems to be a dearth of such digital games, especially when subtracting the (Newtonian) physics-centered games such as Supercharged! [3], SURGE I and II [62, 63], or FormulaT Racing [64].

But the actual distinction between CEG and CIG is not always straightforward, indeed. The two following examples underline this.

Exhibit Number One is the Game "Crazy Robots". The single-player game Crazy Robots was developed as a prototype in a design-based research process in parallel to and with a software framework for mobile games [65]. Due to the fact that the game should be used by and tested with a private tutoring company, some factors of the didactic conception were set in advance—e.g., media: "mobile game" and goal: "correctly associating countries to continents", while the latter does not correspond to an emancipatory goal.

This could have been done with a quiz-show-like game, but we decided to create a game that has a faster flow and does additionally train the visual recognition of the continents and their spatial relation on the globe. In Crazy Robots, small robots fly over the screen and collide with the currently displayed continent (see Fig. 1). Correctly associated matches gain the player points that are awarded in relation to the predefined difficulty of the country. In contrast, incorrect matches cost lives depicted as light bulbs. Players thus use their fingers to nudge robots either onto the current continent or away.

Crazy Robots is obviously a purely behavioristic skill and drill/practice approach [61] that fits to a certain degree the concepts of the cybernetic didactics. The game was developed in conformity with the interdependence of goals, content, methods, and media in mind. Evangelist of the "Spielpädagogik" would probably have a fit.

The game mechanics were developed for this game and its content and thus could be considered a conceptually integrated game (CIG). Nonetheless, the mechanics feel a bit too generic to be a really good example of CIG. On the other hand, simply switching the country names with foreign language words that need to be associated to "part of speech" labels—e.g., "running" to "verb" instead of "Germany" to "Europe"—would definitely break the game from an aesthetic point of view as well as from a logic one (location of labels on a 3D sphere).

Fig. 1 Crazy Robots: Swiping country names onto continents (correct earns point, incorrect deducts lives)

Exhibit Number Two is the Stoichiometry Game "Chemmetry". Stoichiometry consists in fact of simple cross-multiplications, but interviewed teachers told us that many students fail to see this as they get confused over chemical reactions and correlated units. Thus, the game "Chemmetry" was designed to help students see through the abstraction in order to find the simple math. By playing the game, the student is encouraged to match ratios over seven abstraction layers, which eventually lead toward solving complete chemical equations.

Throughout the game, the player is first encouraged to find a certain ratio by experimenting. For instance, there are no hints as to how many crates a ship can hold, the player has to find this out by placing crates on top of a ship until it sinks. Following, the game lets the student use the recently acquired knowledge in order to solve a related task. Starting with this basic example, the students progress to levels that start to look like chemical equations, but have either a relation to the common sense world of students or represent a chemical experiment that results in a clearly visible outcome. Figure 1 showcases a montage of such a level, in which the player needs to find the amount of honey and cocoa that need to be added to a fixed amount of milk to create a well-tasting cocoa drink.

To support the usage of model-based in contrast to constraint-based thinking, a solution similar to the one employed by SURGE II [62, 63] was chosen. The player needs to choose the amount of cacao in a planning sequence (part d.), before the player can afterward test his solution as shown in part e. of Fig. 2.

Fig. 2 Collage of game screens in different stages of the "mix cocoa" level [66]

Last but not least, students reach a level, where they actually are using the mass of a chemical element in order to solve a given equation by employing the trained approach of identifying the relevant elements and the corresponding ratios. Notable is the fact that the last level is actually congruent to a task that students need to solve in a written exam. After playing the game, such tasks have been solved by students that had not yet covered stoichiometry in school [66].

The game mechanics and aesthetics as well as the sequencing of the levels, to build up the required understanding of the mathematical procedures, were tailored for Chemmetry. Using these to teach any other content would be hard and would require serious reworking. Hence, the game can be considered a CIG.

While the game uses some behaviorist feedback (like any game), it strives to build on frames of the target group (cognitivist). Nonetheless, it could be considered an instruction-focused Skinner algorithm (cybernetics) [32], in which players need to finish a level before advancing to the next task. In contrast, its conception was based on a didactic analysis based on teaching and learning goals that would fit the Bildungstheoretische Didaktik with the limitation that the game was created in a student project on DGBL, so the general medium/method was a kind of predestined. The setting and workflow were chosen with the prevalent method "experiment" of the subject-specific didactic in mind. The game complies with the elements one and two of learning environments that tempered versions of constructivist psychologies of learning and constructivist didactics recommend, but would not be a love match for the "Spielpädagogik".

4.2 DGBL Scenario One and Experiential Learning Theory with a Kinect Game

The following method and example showcase that scenario one of the DGBL definition is neither bound to single-player games nor to games that have been created with an educational application in mind. The method combines the approach of "system-focused game-based learning" with the "digital embodied game-based learning" strategy [2]. In this combination, participants of workshops or interventions explore the rules and mechanics of a given (game) system via embodied interaction.

In general, this approach actually requires comparatively short bursts of gameplay—approximately less than three minutes. This is on the one hand due to the required physical interaction that may exhaust players too much otherwise, which is especially true in case of training settings in business contexts. On the other hand, it is due to the fact that this method is generally used with groups of learners—oftentimes with only a fraction of them being players at any given moment. Longer play sessions would thus be too taxing to the non-playing participants (NPPs), too, as they have an active observation task and should give concise feedback after each round.

The first cycle of digital embodied system-focused game-based learning starts with a short introduction of the game and optionally influences the perception of players by giving well calculated "hints" on how to play or what may be of interest while playing—both of which may be used as priming (on contextual priming see e.g., [67]). The players thus play a game round or level, while the non-playing participants (NPPs) observe. After completing the game sequence—oftentimes by failing or modest success—the discussion sections of this method start with querying the players on their experience—in latter rounds especially on the success of beforehand agreed-upon strategies (etc.). This is then, in general, naturally enriched by the feedback and opinions of the NPPs that share their observations with the players. This again fuels discussions in the whole group. In workshops, these discussions always led to the desired effect that the group argued on the two planes of the concrete play experience and their (work) life—highlighting the similarities and differences.

Building upon the development of this discussion and/or on probing of the workshop facilitator, players and NPPs then debate new strategies as well as rule or goal changes—in some cases by changing the game's settings or modus; in others by layering these changes on top of the social interaction without any technical implementation. The consequences of the thus changed game system are experienced in the next round/level and again discussed and reflected upon afterward.

A digital embodied system-focused game-based learning thus starts in the "Active Experimentation" stage of the learning cycle of Kolb's [68] experiential learning theory. Based on the "Concrete Experience" of gameplay, participants reflect themselves, upon the game system as well as the results of the applied strategies or the emergent patterns of action ("Reflective Observation").

Aided by the support of or even led by the workshop facilitator, new findings and insights are distilled ("Abstract Conceptualization"). Based on these, implications for future actions [69] can be inferred. As soon as (some of) those concepts or hypotheses are actively tested in the action system (i.e., game or game-/playful-enriched intervention), the learning circle is closed—or following Kolb [69], the spiral restarts on a new level (Fig. 3).

Rafting Game Example: To exemplify the above-described method, consider the rafting mini-game in the commercial-of-the-shelf (entertainment) digital game collection "Kinect Adventures" as described and applied in [64] highlighted in a slightly adapted version in the following two paragraphs.

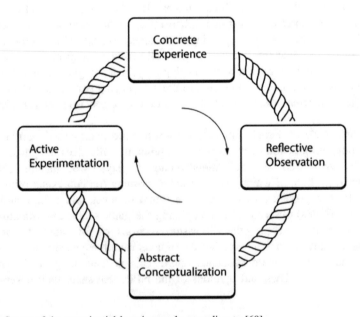

Fig. 3 Stages of the experiential learning cycle according to [68]

The game can be played either as a single player or with two players steering a raft down a white water. The players have to physically jump up and down to overcome obstacles. They steer by moving their entire body left or right in front of the Kinect sensor. If one player moves right and the other left, the boat continues straightforward. Thus, both need to coordinate their behavior to steer the boat in such a way as to collect as many silver coins as possible. While sometimes there is a single course to follow, generally multiple options are available. Thus, players need to explicitly agree either on actions (left, right, jump) or on a targeted path before gameplay or under extreme time pressure during play.

Both the setting and the core mechanics lend themselves very well to experience leadership. Additionally, it can be used to discuss related issues in change and innovation processes. While the core mechanics reward good coordination, the setting invokes the powerful metaphor of sitting in the same boat. Furthermore, it generally gives rise to questions like: How does an "ideal" type of leadership look like in the game? Is this congruent with (my) working-life experience?

When applying the game in workshops again and again, a specific peculiarity in relation to Kolb's "Experiential Learning Theory" became obvious: Indeed, the specific learning processes triggered by the application of the digital embodied system-focused game-based learning method/approach are characterized by an "integrated duality". First, players learn about the game system in accordance with Kolb's cyclic, respectively, spiral model—as can be illustrated by typical utterances such as follows:

- "When I tried to steer left at the junction, my teammate leaned to the right so that the raft crashed against the central outcrop." (Concrete Experience)
- "So where did we go wrong? What could we have done to prevent this?" ("Reflective Observation")
- "We need better coordination—every boat needs a skipper!" ("Abstract Conceptualization")
- "It might work out, if you take the lead. I'll do as you say!" ("Active Experimentation")
- "That didn't work out too well … my teammate always reacted too late." ("Concrete Experience").

Especially in the reflective observation from concrete experience to abstract conceptualization as well as when choosing one hypothesis to test in the next iteration ("Active Experimentation"), previous real-world knowledge is incorporated—as can be illustrated by typical utterances such as follows:

- "On ships a strong hierarchy exists and the skipper needs to utter the commands. That should work out in the game as well!"
- "As a manager I do not give commands, but rather specify goals and rules. We should give this a try. It might perform better than the skipper approach…"

Coming back to the proposed "integrated duality" of this approach, the point is that knowledge about both the game system and real (work) life is developed. But while reflection and debate generally shifts from generating knowledge about the game system first to discussing the situation in real (work) life second, the point is that the duality of the experience of this intertwines in the active performance of the play act ("Active Experimentation" and "Concrete Experience"). This enables the workshop participants to actually develop and test modes and strategies of actions even though the game system or playful interaction does not replicate the real (work)-life situation faithfully (Fig. 4).

For this reason, digital embodied system-focused game-based learning stands in contrast to other simulation- and/or game-based learning approaches which focus on creating a simulation model/game system that is as congruent with the targeted real-life system as possible—i.e., featuring a "High Simulation Fidelity" [70]. The latter generally is aspired to due to the fact that it is assumed to foster or even guarantee that developed or acquired knowledge can be transferred into the real (work)-life context—see e.g., [70]—and/or cater to the (perceived) preference of trainees especially in business or medical contexts—see e.g., [71].

In contrast, the introduced method uses a strategy of de-familiarization comparable to aesthetic-performative approaches—such as [72] use—to trigger insights. Nevertheless, the game system fosters the emergence of experiences that are either congruent to emerging experiences in the designated real-world system or are their

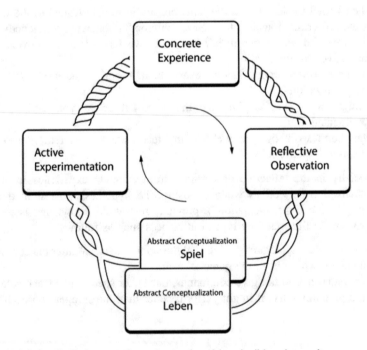

Fig. 4 "Digital embodied system-focused game-based learning"-learning cycle

explicit antipode. The former facilitates transfer of successful strategies to the goal system while the latter—similarly to approaches like the "headstand" creativity method [73]—lead to a divergent or new perspective on the goal system thus elucidating alternative strategies and patterns of action. This can be related to Klafki's point [23] that some contents have a certain "Vorwegbestimmtheit" (predisposition). The point here is that some or even most topics have a connotation of/trigger specific sociocultural themes/values/attitudes. This need not be ignored, but can be made fertile for the educational process.

Using the rafting game can be considered DGBL, but would not fit definitions of "learning game", "serious game", or "edutainment" [1]. The game uses (like any game) behavioristic feedback, but the application of the game can be associated with the constructivist paradigm of learning as it enables and requires the reflection on and re-enactment of specific constructions of social reality—see "integrated duality" above. Furthermore, the game complies with all three elements or learning environments that tempered versions of constructivist psychologies of learning and constructivist didactics recommend. It would additionally be a perfect fit for the "kommunikative Didaktik" (communication-oriented didactics) [17]. The freedom of social layering of rules and role-play could make the treatment acceptable to the "Spielpädagogik".

4.3   DGBL Scenario Two and Project-Based Learning and Learning by Teaching

Scenario two is the usage of (learning) games to teach something—but actually not to the players but to the creators of the game. To discuss this scenario in relation to didactics, consider its slightly adapted description from [2] in the following paragraph.

In the DGBL course I taught for some time [74], students were expected to gain insights concerning game studies, learning theories, and digital game-based learning on the one hand. On the other hand, they had to realize a practical project: Either creating a digital game that could be used to cover working-life relevant themes like leadership, teamwork, and conflict management or modifying a commercial off-the-shelf digital game (COTS-DG). In the latter case, the goal was to create an experience that could be used to reflect and discuss the stages of the Hero's Journey. A story pattern that highlights processes of individual and social change processes. No matter which option students choose, they became acquainted with key issues of digital game-based learning by practical experience in a project-based learning [75] setting. Especially, the "relatively long-term, problem-focused" [75] and authentic project task seemed to motivate the students. Additionally, their inherent interest in games as well as the task to create something of value to others but in a self-directed way (as proposed by [75]) made them pour their heart and soul into the creative process. In addition to these motivational issues, the key point is that to make a good game or mod, students have to develop a solid understanding of the content they are covering. The consequence is that students have to learn what their games shall teach—thus touching the concept of "learning by teaching". The latter has been shown to be very promising both in educational [76] and business [77] contexts and comes as an added advantage when focusing on learning games as the product of the projects.

DGBL scenario two ties the "Methodische Großform" (main/basic type/form of teaching/class) of projects [10] to learning by teaching. Thus, it requires and promotes a comparatively high student activity and a conjunction of cognitive and affective learning. It thus fits perfectly into the constructivist learning paradigm. Due to the fact that the project form was chosen to (additionally) foster relevant professional, social, and self-management competencies, it can be considered to have a natural fit to the Bildungstheoretische Didaktik.

4.4 DGBL Scenario Three and Constructionist Learning

Creative/aesthetic methods—e.g., in workshops on change and innovation processes—typically use techniques from fine and performing arts to create artifacts or experiences that are personally meaningful to the participants and, in the majority of cases, are presented to and discussed by workshop participants [2, 72]. To discuss this scenario in relation to didactics, consider its slightly adapted description from [2] in the following paragraphs.

In creative/aesthetic methods, both creation and discussion explicate implicit ideas, opinions, fears, knowledge, etc., thus enabling the individual and the group to share, learn from, and work with them.

One specific exercise that may exemplify this concept is the visualization of the hero at the respective stages of the Hero's Journey. How does the hero look like, e.g., when in "The Ordeal"? How are their feelings mirrored in their posture and appearance? This again can be executed either with or without digital means—e.g., using the posture of a workshop participant [72].

A corresponding digital version of this exercise is using the "Spore Creature Creator"—the latter being an integral part of the COTS-DG "Spore". While part of the game system, the editor itself would typically not be considered a game. Nonetheless, through its appearance and in combination with the task of creating a hero or workshop participant in monstrous form, it induces an observably playful attitude of mind. Using an easy to learn interface, the editor enables participants to build creatures. These can be customized in body statue, skin texture, and color as well as number and appearance of extremities and accessories. Created creatures can even be animated with a special selection of moves and emotional mannerisms. We applied the digital version of the exercise in both our work with SMBs and in one-time workshops, where it proved its potential for enabling participants to express their implicit ideas and feelings as well as discuss key points of innovation and change processes.

Another example of the potential in augmenting a creative exercise with digital means is the use of the game Minecraft. The latter places the player in an open world with its own rules and physics, but without any specific goals. The only implicit goal is to survive by collecting or growing food and building a shelter to hide inside during nights. In its "creative mode", it provides an ideal setting to focus on the core of Minecraft: creativity. Players can choose from building blocks to assemble structures or reshape entire landscapes in a Lego-like manner.

Again the modus operandi was to give workshop participants a short tutorial, then between 10 and 20 min to build and subsequently discuss their results in the group. While the same exercise would have been much more physical using real materials like paper, plastic, or clay, the digital version has the advantage that it overcomes the spatial and material limits of the non-digital settings.

This is, e.g., due to the fact that while the building blocks in Minecraft come in a broad variety of natural materials ranging from wood and cobblestone to ice and gold, these can be arranged in physically eccentric ways—e.g., impossible arcs or blocks of ever flowing magma, thus allowing the players to be free in creating the artifact that matches their idea of the respective issue best. Furthermore, the resulting artifacts are explorable and walkable for the player characters, thus making them easier to present and explain. Participants generally enjoyed working with Minecraft, sometimes so much so, that they got lost in just playfully exploring their digital environment and had to be reminded of their actual task. We also found that similarly to manual crafting exercises, participants became very creative in improvising with the given material.

The described scenario bears a similarity to the Lego Serious Play method [78] and ties into the constructivist paradigm of learning. Due to the fact that participants recreate knowledge of/views on the questions by actually creating models of these as artifacts, this scenario can be understood as constructionist [79], too. It could be used in conjunction with the Bildungstheoretische Didaktik, but very probably not with cybernetic approaches—due to their focus on quantifiable measurement and low focus on social learning. This scenario, I daresay, is the only one that a "Spieldidaktik" would be really comfortable with. Although it still uses a computer (or another digital device), it can plainly be seen as "Konstruktionsspiel" [54] (constructional play).

5 Discussion

The goal of this paper was to explore whether digital game-based learning (DGBL) might actually be more than a pure method, but maybe a "Didaktik". I hope to have shown that each approach that falls under the considered definition of DGBL is compatible with at least one Didaktik. This in itself is nothing special—it would actually be quite strange to find a method that could not be used in a single context of didactics for planning and executing a lesson plan. What is noteworthy, however, is that the individual approaches that are united under the umbrella of DGBL do so clearly fit very different didactics as well as paradigms and theories of teaching and learning.

This may simply highlight the fact that our definition is not a very good one, but I feel that the scenarios and approaches actually create something bigger through their conjunction. Nonetheless, DGBL could simply be a family of methods and that's the end of it.

But again a "but": Consider the presented idea of Klafki [23] that some contents have a certain "Vorwegbestimmtheit" (predisposition) to certain topics that can be used to reach specific learning goals. Add that the idea of creating conceptually integrated games is identifying the core of a content/topic and sculpting the game mechanics that make this content and thus the integrated learning goals experienceable/experiential. Combine this with the argument that a game as a medium is a "deep-frozen" constellation of learning goals, content, and method [10].

And the tasty result would be that the conception of a conceptually integrated game would be a didactic analysis, indeed.

But a didactic analysis cannot be done without a frame of reference—i.e., a Didaktik. Admittedly, this Didaktik need not be a new DGBL-Didaktik but could be an existing one that "only" needs to be adapted to encompass all aspects of DGBL.

Considering the theories/models of general didactics, this seems to be a utopian (or dystopian) proposition. A very special Didaktik in contrast should actually be waiting in the wings but balks at this idea: "Spieldidaktik". It should fit the most but fitted the least.

The question is thus: Is DGBL going to advance the digitization of learning culture(s) hand in hand with a renewed Spieldidaktik or without?

References

1. Bodrow, W., Busch, C., Steinicke, M.: Digital game based learning. In: Proceedings of the International Conference on E-Learning and the Knowledge Society, pp. 171–176 (2011)
2. Busch, C., Conrad, F., Steinicke, M.: Digital games and the hero's journey in management workshops and tertiary education. Electron. J. e-Learn. **11**(1), 3–15 (2013)
3. De Freitas, S., Maharg, P.: Digital Games and Learning. Continuum International Publishing, New York City, NY, p. 113 (2011)
4. Squire, K.: Video Games and Learning: Teaching and Participatory Culture in the Digital Age. Teachers College Press, New York City, NY, (a) 19–22, (b) 174f, (c) p. 90f (2011)
5. Marlow, C.: Making games and environmental design: revealing landscape architecture. In: Proceedings of the 6th European Conference on Games Based Learning. Academic Publishing International Limited, pp. 309–316 (2012)
6. Monterrat, B., Lavoué, E., George, S.: Learning Game 2.0: Support for Game Modding as a Learning Activity. In: Proceedings of the 6th European Conference on Games Based Learning. Academic Publishing International Limited, pp. 340–347 (2012)
7. Pivec, M., Dziabenko, O., Schinnerl, I.: Aspects of game-based learning. In: 3rd International Conference on Knowledge Management, Graz, Austria, pp. 216–225, July 2003

8. Rondon, S., Sassi, F.C., de Andrade, C.R.F.: Computer game-based and traditional learning method: a comparison regarding students' knowledge retention. BMC Med. Educ. **13**(1), 30 (2013)
9. Idris, W.I.S., Hamzah, H., Ahmad, A.M., Zaki, S.: Teaching complex theoretical subjects using digital game-based learning in the faculty of creative industries, UTAR. In: 7th International Conference on University Learning and Teaching (InCULT 2014) Proceedings, pp. 141–148. Springer, Singapore (2016)
10. Meyer, H.: UnterrichtsMethoden I –Theorieband. Frankfurt am Main, Cornelsen Scriptor Verlag, 8th ed., (a) p. 44, (b) p. 24, (c) p. 150, (d) pp. 143–145 (1995)
11. Kansanen, P.: The Deutsche Didaktik and the American Research on Teaching. In: Kansanen, P., Meri, M. (ed.) The Didactic Relation in the Teaching-Studying-Learning Process. Didaktik/Fachdidaktik as Science (-s) of the Teaching Profession, vol. 2, no. 1, pp. 107–116 (1999)
12. Boeree, C.G.: Behaviorism. http://webspace.ship.edu/cgboer/beh.html
13. Plassmann, A.A., Schmitt, G.: Lern-Psychologie. Essen: Universität Duisburg-Essen, Campus Essen (2007). http://www.lern-psychologie.de
14. Watson, J.B.: Behavior: An Introduction to Comparative Psychology. Henry Holt and Co., New York, NY, US, p. 3 (1914)
15. Mair, D.: E-Learning—das Drehbuch. Handbuch für Medienautoren und Projektleiter. Springer, Berlin, cited in [13] (2005)
16. Bandura, A.: Social Learning Theory. General Learning Press, New York City (1971)
17. Terhart, E.: Didaktik: Eine Einführung. Stuttgart, Reclam, (a) p. 33 (b) p. 34, (c) pp. 36–37, (d) p. 38, (e) 99–101, (f) 130 & 133f, (g) 108–111, (h) 26, (j) 140 (2009)
18. Reich, K.: Konstruktivistische Ansätze in den Sozial- und Kulturwissenschaften. In: Hug, T. (ed.) Die Wissenschaft und ihr Wissen, Bd. 4. Baltmannsweiler, pp. 356–376 (2001)
19. Foerster, H.: Das Konstruieren einer Wirklichkeit in Watzlawick, P. (Hrsg.) Die erfundene Wirklichkeit: Wie wissen wir, was wir zu wissen glauben. Beiträge zum Konstruktivismus, 13, pp. 39–60 (1986)
20. Kelly, G.A.: Psychologie der persönlichen Konstrukte, cited in [13] (1986)
21. Seel, H.: "Allgemeine Didaktik" ("General Didactics") and "Fachdidaktik" ("Subject Didactics"). In: Kansanen, P., Meri, M. (1999) The Didactic Relation in the Teaching-Studying-Learning Process. Didaktik/Fachdidaktik as Science (-s) of the Teaching profession, vol. 2, no. 1, pp. 13–20 (1999)
22. Benner, D., Brüggen, F.: Theorien der Erziehungswissenschaft im 20. Jahrhundert. Entwicklungsprobleme-Paradigmen-Aussichten, pp. 240–263. In: Benner, D., Tenorth, H.-E. (eds.) Bildungsprozesse und Erziehungsverhältnisse im 20. Jahrhundert. Weinheim, Beltz 2000, (Zeitschrift für Pädagogik, Beiheft; 42), p. 250 (2000)
23. Klafki, W.: Zur Unterrichtsplanung im Sinne kritisch-konstruktiver Didaktik, pp. 11–48 In: Adl-Amini, B., Künzli, R. (eds.) Didaktische Modelle und Unterrichtsplanung. Weinheim, München: Juventa (a) p. 14, (b) p. 17, (c) pp. 21–22, (d) p. 23, (e) pp. 18–19 (1991)
24. Klafki, W.: Neue Studien zur Bildungstheorie und Didaktik – Zeitgemäße Allgemeinbildung und kritisch-konstruktive Didaktik. Beltz Verlag, Weinheim, 6th ed., p. 30 (2007)
25. Klafki, W.: Studien zur Bildurgstheorie und Didaktik. Beltz: Weinheim (1963) cited in Terhart, E.: Didaktik: Eine Einführung. Stuttgart, Reclam, p. 109 (2009)
26. Meyer, H.: Rezeptionsprobleme der Didaktik oder wie Lehrer lernen. In: Adl-Amini, B., Künzli, R. (eds.) Didaktische Modelle und Unterrichtsplanung. Weinheim, München: Juventa, 3rd ed., pp. 88–118 (1991)
27. Adl-Amini, B., Künzli, R.: Vorwort. In: Adl-Amini, B., Künzli, R. (eds.) Didaktische Modelle und Unterrichtsplanung. Weinheim, München: Juventa, 3rd ed., p. 7 (1991)
28. Adl-Amini, B.: Grauzonen der Didaktik – Plädoyer für die Erforschung didaktischer Vermittlungsprozesse, pp. 210–237 In: Adl-Amini, B., Künzli, R. (eds.) Didaktische Modelle und Unterrichtsplanung. Weinheim, München: Juventa, 3rd ed., p. 210 (1991)

29. Klein, I.: Gruppen leiten ohne Angst – Themenzentrierte Interaktion (TZI) zum Leiten von Gruppen und Teams. Auer Verlag – AAP Lehrerfachverlag, Donauworth, 12th ed., p. 111 (2011)
30. Schulz, W.: Ein Hamburger Modell der Unterrichtsplanung – Seine Funktion in der Altagspraxis, p. 49–87 In: Adl-Amini, B., Künzli, R. (eds.) Didaktische Modelle und Unterrichtsplanung. Weinheim, München: Juventa, 3rd ed. (1991)
31. Karcher, M.: Schüler als Trivialmaschine, pp. 99–122. In: Caruso, M., Kassung, C. (eds.) Jahrbuch für Historische Bildungsforschung 2014. Schwerpunkt Maschinen. Sektion Bildungsforschung der Deutschen Gesellschaft für Bildungsforschung. Verlag Julius Klinkhardt, Bad Heilbrunn, (a) p. 103, (b) p. 114, (c) p. 99 (2015)
32. Frank, H.G., Meder, B.S.: Einführung in die kybernetische Pädagogik. Deutscher Taschenbuchverlag, München, (a) pp. 22–23, (b) pp. 24–25, (c) pp. 30–50 (1971)
33. Zabel, N.: Die Lehrmaschine und der Programmierte Unterricht – Chancen und Grenzen im Bildungswesen der DDR in den 1960er und 1970er Jahren, pp. 123–152. In: Caruso, M., Kassung, C. (eds.) Jahrbuch für Historische Bildungsforschung 2014. Schwerpunkt Maschinen. Sektion Bildungsforschung der Deutschen Gesellschaft für Bildungsforschung. Verlag Julius Klinkhardt, Bad Heilbrunn (2015)
34. Hoffmann-Ocon, A., Horlacher, R.: Technologie als Bedrohung oder Gewinn? Das Beispiel des Programmierten Unterrichts, pp. 153–172 In: Caruso, M., Kassung, C. (eds.) Jahrbuch für Historische Bildungsforschung 2014. Schwerpunkt Maschinen. Sektion Bildungsforschung der Deutschen Gesellschaft für Bildungsforschung. Verlag Julius Klinkhardt, Bad Heilbrunn (2015)
35. Seidel, C. (ed.): Computer Based Training. Erfahrungen mit interaktivem Computerlernen. Göttingen, Stuttgart: Verlag für Angewandte Psychologie (1993)
36. Seidel, C.: Trends beim Computer Based Training, pp. 9–29 In: Seidel, C. (ed.) Computer Based Training. Erfahrungen mit interaktivem Computerlernen. Göttingen, Stuttgart: Verlag für Angewandte Psychologie, p. 20 (1993)
37. Sageder, J.: Didaktische Aspekte des Einsatzes von Computern für Lehren und Lernen, pp. 59–86 In: Seidel, C. (ed.) Computer based training. Erfahrungen mit interaktivem Computerlernen. Göttingen, Stuttgart: Verlag für Angewandte Psychologie, p. 74 (1993)
38. Salen, K., Zimmerman, E.: Rules of Play: Game Design Fundamentals. MIT Press, pp. 79–80 (2004)
39. Frasca, G.: Play the message. Ph.D. Dissertation, IT University of Copenhagen, Denmark (2007). http://www.powerfulrobot.com/Frasca_Play_the_Message_PhD.pdf
40. Juul, J.: Half-Real—Video Games between Real Rules and Fictional Worlds. MIT Press, p. 29 (2005)
41. Abt, C.C.: Serious Games. University Press of America, p. 10 (1970)
42. Perler, P.P.: The Art of Wargaming: A Guide for Professionals and Hobbyists. Naval Institute Press (1990)
43. Andlinger, G.R.: Business games-play one! Harvard Bus. Rev. **28**, 115–125 (1958)
44. Schleiermacher, F.D.E.: Pädagogische Schriften. 2 Bde. Schulze, T., Weniger, E. (eds.) Küpper (former Bondi Düsseldorf) p. 50 (1957) cited in Meyer, H.: UnterrichtsMethoden II – Praxisband. Frankfurt am Main, Cornelsen Scriptor Verlag, 15th ed., p. 345 (2010)
45. Forbes, D.: The History of Chess: From the Time of the Early Invention of the Game in India Till the Period of its Establishment in Western and Central Europe. W. H. Allen & co., p. 37 (1860)
46. Darayee, T.: Chess. In: Meri, J.W., Bacharach J.L. (eds.) Medieval Islamic civilization: An encyclopedia. Routledge, p. 148f (2006)
47. Schädler, U., Strouhal, E.: Das schöne lehrreiche Ungeheuer –Strategien der Eingemeindung des Spiels in der Kultur der Bürgerlichkeit – Eine Einleitung. In: Schädler, U., Strouhal, E. (eds.) Spiel und Bürgerlichkeit: Passagen des Spiels I. Springer, Wien, pp. 9–21 (2010)
48. Schiller, F.: Fünfzehnter Brief, pp. 56–57. In: Jung, A. (ed.) Schillers Briefe über die ästhetische Erziehung des Menschen. Teubner, Leipzig. p. 57 (1875)

49. Meyer, H.: UnterrichtsMethoden II–Praxisband. Frankfurt am Main, Cornelsen Scriptor Verlag, 15th ed., p. 344 (2010)
50. Popp, S.: Das Lernspiel im Unterricht. Pädagogische Welt 7/90. pp. 306–311 + 293, (a) p. 307, (b) p. 308, (c) p. 309 (d) p. 310
51. Popp, S.: Das Lernspiel in der Schule/Pädagogische und didaktische Überlegungen zu "den didaktischen Materialien mit Spielelementen"(Einsiedler), pp. 8–15. In: Drescher, R. (ed.) unterrichten/erziehen Nr.4. Wolf Verlag, Regensburg. p. 12, July 1992
52. Peschel, F.: Vom Edutainment zur kreativen Herausforderung/Der Computer als Werkzeug im Offenen Unterricht. Multimedia-Didaktik. Springer, Berlin, Heidelberg, New York, p. 14 (2003)
53. Egenfeldt-Nielsen, S.: Third generation educational use of computer games. J. Educ. Multimedia Hypermedia 16(3), 263, Research Library p. 263, (a) p. 267 (2007)
54. Renner, M.: Spieltheorie und Spielpraxis: eine Einführung für pädagogische Berufe. Lambertus, 3rd ed., (a) pp. 104–143 (2008)
55. Hauser, B.: Spielen und Lernen der 4-bis 8-jährigen Kinder. Das Spiel als Lernmodus. Positionspapier Spiel zu Gunsten des Entwicklungsprojektes "Erziehung und Bildung in Kindergarten und Unterstufe". Pädagogische Hochschule Rorschach PHR (2006)
56. Clark, D.B., Martinez-Garza, M.: Prediction and explanation as design mechanics in conceptually integrated digital games to help players articulate the tacit understandings they build through game play. In: Steinkuehler, C., Squire, K., Barab, S. (eds.) Games, Learning, and Society: Learning and Meaning in the Digital Age, pp. 279–305. Cambridge University Press, Cambridge (2012)
57. Clark, D.B., Killingsworth, S.S., Martinez-Garza, M., Eaton, G.V., Biswas, G., Kinnebrew, J. S., Sengupta, P., Krinks, K., Adams, D., Zhang, H., Hughes, J.: Digital games and science learning: design principles and processes to augment commercial game design conventions. In: AIED 2013 Workshops Proceedings Volume 2 Scaffolding in Open-Ended Learning Environments (OELEs), p. 1 (2013)
58. Habgood, M.J.: The effective integration of digital games and learning content. Doctoral Dissertation, University of Nottingham, Nottingham, p. 6 (2007)
59. Bruckman, A.: Can educational be fun? In: Game Developers Conference 1999, San Jose, CA, p. 2 (1999)
60. Malo, S., Müsebeck, P.: Winterfest—an adventure game for basic education. In: Workshop-Proceedings Informatik, vol. 2, pp. 61–65 (2010)
61. Ke, F.: A case study of computer gaming for math: engaged learning from gameplay? Comput. Educ. 51(4), 1609–1620 (2008)
62. Kafai, Y.B.: Learning design by making games. In: Constructionism in Practice: Designing, Thinking and Learning in a Digital World, pp 71–96, p. 80 (1996)
63. Habgood, M.J., Ainsworth, S.E.: Motivating children to learn effectively: exploring the value of intrinsic integration in educational games. J. Learn. Sci. 20(2), 169–206 (2011)
64. Holbert, N., Wilensky, U.: Representational congruence: connecting video game experiences to the design and use of formal representations. In: Kynigos, C., Clayson, J.E., Yiannoutsou (eds.), Constructionism: Theory, Practice and Impact, pp. 370–739 (a) p. 371 (2012)
65. Busch, C., Claßnitz, S., Selmanagic, A., Steinicke, M.: MoLeGaF: a mobile learning games framework. In: European Conference on Games Based Learning, vol. 1, pp. 41–49. Academic Conferences International Limited, Oct 2014
66. Busch, C., Dohrmann, L., Möhlihs, M., Pasadu, M., Steinicke, M.: Design-based research on conceptually integrated games to foster chemistry skills in secondary education. In: European Conference on Games Based Learning, p. 89. Academic Conferences International Limited, Oct 2016
67. Palmer, S.: The effects of contextual scenes on the identification of objects. Mem. Cognit. 3 (1975), 519–526 (1975)
68. Kolb, D.A.: Experiential Learning: Experience as the Source of Learning and Development. Prentice Hall, Englewood Cliffs, NJ, (a) p. 41 (1984)

69. Kolb, A.Y., Kolb, D.A.: Experiential Learning Theory: A Dynamic, Holistic Approach to Management Learning, Education and Development, (a) p. 5 (2008)
70. Rooney, P.: Creating serious games at third level: evaluating the implications of an in-house approach. In: Proceedings of the 6th European Conference on Games Based Learning: ECGBL, p. 432. Academic Conferences Limited, Oct 2012
71. Issenberg, S.B., Mcgaghie, W.C., Petrusa, E.R., Lee Gordon, D., Scalese, R.J.: Features and uses of high-fidelity medical simulations that lead to effective learning: a BEME systematic review. Med. Teach. **27**(1), 10–28 (2005)
72. Trobisch, N., Scherübl, I., Denisow, K.: Innovationsdramaturgie nach dem Heldenprinzip – Narratives Wissen für erfolgreiche Veränderungsprozesse nutzen. In: Busch, C., Schildhauer, T. (eds.) Digital-experimentelle Lernkulturen und Innovationen – Texte und Aufsätze. Glückstadt: Verlag Werner Hülsbusch, pp. 67–152 (2014)
73. Wittchen, B., Josten, E., Reiche, T.: Arbeitsmethoden im Unterricht. Holzfachkunde: für Tischler/Schreiner und Holzmechaniker, pp. 538–547 (2006)
74. Busch, C., Conrad, F., Steinicke, M.: Digital games and the hero's journey in change and innovation management workshops. In: Proceedings 6th European Conference on Games Based Learning, pp. 72–81, Oct 2012
75. Blumenfeld, P.C, Soloway, E., Marx, R.W., Krajcik, J.S., Guzdial, M.: Palincsar: motivating project-based learning: sustaining the doing, supporting the learning. Educ. Psychol. **26**(3&4), 369–398 (a) p. 370 (b) p. 375 (1991)
76. Berliner, D., Casanova, U.: Being the teacher helps students learn. Instructor **98**(9), 12–13. p. 12f (1989)
77. Cortese, C.G.: Learning Through Teaching, Management Learning, pp. 36, 87 (2005)
78. Kristiansen, P., Rasmussen, R.: Building a Better Business Using the Lego Serious Play Method. Wiley (2014)
79. Harel, I.E., Papert, S.E.: Constructionism. Ablex Publishing (1991)

Part II
Digital Architectures of Culture

An Intermediary Database Node in the Namibian Communities Indigenous Knowledge Management System

Michael Bosomefi Chamunorwa, Heike Winschiers-Theophilus
and Tariq Zaman

1 Introduction

Indigenous knowledge has long been known to be a means for communities to increase and improve food production, improve wealth distribution and resolve conflicts amicably [1]. In several African countries, such knowledge was seldom documented but was instead passed down from generation to generation through oral tradition [2]. This system of spreading knowledge was effective more than a decade ago, but is now facing challenges due to several factors. Rural to urban migration is one of the major factors that have contributed to reduction in the passing on of IK from one generation to another. This is because, most youth now spend more time in the cities, due to school and work commitments, whilst the knowledge holders, who are usually older family members, remain in rural areas [3]. As a result, they end up embracing the modern way of life at the expense of their own culture that possesses unique and useful indigenous knowledge [4]. This leads to the erosion of some IK which holds intrinsic value in their respective communities [5]. In other cases, communities which remain in touch with their IK face exploitation from individuals and groups who realize the potential monetary returns of some knowledge before the communities themselves do so. As a result, several governments now actively empower communities to benefit from the

M. B. Chamunorwa (✉) · H. Winschiers-Theophilus
Namibia University of Science and Technology, 13 Storch Street,
Windhoek, Namibia
e-mail: chamunorwamichael@gmail.com

H. Winschiers-Theophilus
e-mail: hwinschiers@nust.na

T. Zaman
Universiti Malaysia Sarawak (UNIMAS), Jalan Datuk Mohammad Musa,
94300 Kota Samarahan, Sarawak, Malaysia
e-mail: zamantariq@gmail.com

© Springer Nature Singapore Pte Ltd. 2018
D. S. Jat et al. (eds.), *Digitisation of Culture: Namibian and International Perspectives*, https://doi.org/10.1007/978-981-10-7697-8_7

commercialization of their IK [6, 7]. However, if this is done with inadequate laws guiding such research, communities who provide the IK to third parties may never enjoy the benefits of their knowledge once it gets commercialized.

In a hybrid world where indigenous knowledge is still practiced in its original forms and digital representations of it can be authentically produced, the role of IK holders in the preservation process becomes essential to not only collect but also curate and disseminate within the digital world [8]. Thus, we are concerned in establishing and providing technologies which enable indigenous communities to be the agents of the digitization process of their own knowledge and to integrate these with the national IK management system. Since 2008, a research cluster from the Namibia University of Science and Technology's Faculty of Computing and Informatics has co-designed, developed and deployed several digital tools which enable IK holders to document and organize their knowledge whilst in their natural physical context [4]. These tools are installed on tablet computers which run on predominantly Android operating systems. They allow a user to capture still images, videos, drawings, text as well as audio recordings which describe different IK topics. Collected IK is stored in secondary memory of the devices used to capture it [8]. Apart from the default metadata attached to the digital media files by the devices themselves, there is no extra metadata linked to any of the collected media. However, storing this data in primary devices is not ideal, as there is a risk of irrecoverable data loss if a device is damaged or misplaced. Second, for as long as the data is stored in the devices, it is inaccessible to the outside world and therefore remains in possession of the IK holder only. As a result, researchers need to provide the ability for captured IK to be saved in a more persistent storage such as that provided for by a data centre. In addition to persistent and secure storage, the data also needs to be housed in a structured manner that allows authorized and in cases where applicable, authenticated users to access and share it in a useful and accessible manner.

Thus, in this paper we first present case studies on national IKMS as a response to previous exploitation. We then highlight structural and access right issues within a national digital context. We further introduce Namibian IK digitization efforts, consisting of a national initiative supported by our IK research clusters technology developments. Therein, we will outline the structure of data, information and knowledge created with such technology developments and explore options available for further processing. Lastly, the chapter proffers a concept of an intermediary node to bridge the technical gap between the IK holder's context and the national repository.

2 Related Work

The value of IK has motivated nations to manage indigenous knowledge following different strategies as exemplified by the two cases presented below. We detail two national IK management systems that were effected in India and South Africa, respectively. These systems have ICTs as their pillar, thereby permitting electronic storage of IK as well as fine-grained access control to the data in storage. However, with an increasing involvement of communities in the digital world new mapping processes and structures need to be formulated to cater for communities as well as national interests.

2.1 The Value of IK

To exemplify the consequences of a lack of management of IK, we draw upon the famous story of the commercialization of the Hoodia plant. The plant is a well-known appetite and thirst suppressant used by the San communities [9]. The San reside in parts of Southern Africa and had generational knowledge about the applications and use of the Hoodia plant [10] yet did not document this beyond their own tribe. As a result, the only documentation about the use of the plant was done by non-African researchers during the colonial era without attribute to the San [6]. The South African Council for Scientific and Industrial Research (CSIR) later set out to research on the possibility of extracting the active compounds in the Hoodia plant on an industrial scale with the aim of manufacturing dietary supplements [9]. They patented their findings and licensed further research and production. The entire process did not include any acknowledgement of the San, who were already users of the plant, albeit in an unprocessed form and were therefore the rightful owners of this patented knowledge [9]. Whilst a benefit-sharing agreement was later implemented, this case highlights the exclusion of IK holders from the mainstream economy. In the absence of measures to integrate the communities in the management process, there is a risk of expropriation and exploitation [6].

Several similar cases around the world which involve third parties appropriating IK at the expense of the communities from where the knowledge originated have been reported. This has led some governments to set up bodies to enforce policies aimed at protecting IK and benefiting communities in possession of it. In countries like South Africa, Australia and India, progress has been made in academia and other fields to help ensure that IK is preserved for dissemination to coming generations as well as to ensure it is protected by copyrights and patents to ensure benefits are shared fairly between communities that own it with third parties that want to realize profit from the knowledge [11–13].

2.2 India's Traditional Knowledge Digital Library

India has a vast IK base mainly associated with the use of herbs and spices for medicinal purposes [11]. Some of the knowledge about the healing properties of these herbs and spices is only shared between generations using local languages like Sanskrit and Urdu [11]. Because of this, such knowledge is inaccessible to people outside of the communities. This has led to unfortunate cases where major pharmaceutical companies misappropriate such knowledge and file for patents to give them a legal mandate to manufacture medicines using extracts from the herbs [14]. Filing for such patents resulted in these corporations solely benefiting at the expense of the communities who knew and had been using such knowledge for many generations. This once led to two protracted and expensive legal battles in the 1990s, between the Indian authorities and the European Patent Office, over the granting of patents for turmeric powder and a need-based fungicide. To mitigate continuous exploitation of indigenous communities' rights, the Government of India initiated an interdisciplinary task force to develop the concept for a Traditional Knowledge Digital Library (TKDL) [14]. The TKDL aims to provide a platform from where international patent offices and examiners can find information that already exists as IK before issuing out patents for the same to third parties [11]. This was the first time that traditional knowledge became codified in a language and in systems accessible to the patent offices. TKDL also helps safeguard India's IK by providing consistent documentation about the various IK enabling them to be accessible by future generations [11]. At least 36 cases had been identified by the European Patent Office and 40 cases by the United States Patent and Trademark Office utilizing TKDL [15]. Therefore, we can conclude that the Indian TKDL is a means to defensively protect IK, albeit without clearly asserting the rights of the local communities nor clear means to benefit them from any financial windfall arising from its commercialization.

TKDL obtains most of its information from non-Latin digital transcriptions of documents on *Siddha*, *Unani*, *Yoga* and *Ayurvedic*. Using the Traditional Knowledge Resource Classification (TKRC) of TKDL, these transcriptions are later translated into English, German, French, Japanese and Spanish [11]. It is essential to note that the TKRC does not perform transliteration but instead completes smart translations and converts abstracted data into the languages using Unicode, XML and Metadata methodology [13, 16]. Data stored in the TKDL is queried and accessed via a web-based interface, and results are returned in the available languages [11]. Some results, such as those relating to Ayurveda and Unani are available as A4 sized transcript pages from the same website. Approximately, 10 million of these transcripts are available [16]. The TKDL software also converts traditional terminologies into scientific terminologies: for example, *Jwar* to fever and *Mussorika* to smallpox.

2.3   NIKMAS

South Africa is one of the few African countries that have taken major strides in developing ICT systems to catalogue and preserve IK in a way that benefits the communities as originators of the IK [17]. The National Recordal System (NRS) was introduced to develop a system that can protect the rights to IK by providing a platform that allows IK holders and practitioners to store their knowledge and be recognized or compensated if the knowledge finds commercial uses [7]. Data is collected by field workers who are deployed in rural areas with paper-based questionnaires and digital cameras [18]. The data captured is stored in the National Indigenous Knowledge Management System (NIKMAS), which is a semantic digital repository that was developed to support the NRS. NIKMAS catalogues IK by recording the IK holders then the knowledge that they hold [19]. To ensure the process can be carried out nationally, there are several IK documentation centres (DC) which help regionalize the data collection efforts. These IK DC then upload the records captured to a central database as required [7]. NIKMAS also has a cutting-edge semantic search engine as well as security layer that ensures all users who request to access data are documented and verified as well as the reason for their data requests known [20].

2.4 Marrying Community and National Interests

Whilst India and South Africa have taken a high-level decision on the management of IK, we are suggesting an increased involvement of communities in the original design of the digital IK management process, thereby rethinking issues of access and meaningful information extractions.

2.4.1 User Access Rights in IK Management

With communities now being empowered to benefit from sharing their IK using ICTs, more problems arise [21]. Most of the problems mainly arise due to the disconnect between the structure of rules governing data sharing in a certain cultural group and standards that exist in the field of computing [22]. Most organizations can easily formulate access rights to govern how information can be shared across departments by simply enforcing rules at a database level [23]. These access requirements may be guided by company policies and are usually transferable across organizations with little or no customization at all. This is not the case with IK preservation as the rules that govern how knowledge is shared are culturally situated. For example, some IK is only supposed to be shared based on family or tribal lines, whilst some IK can only be shared based on guilds and trades prevalent in a specific community, e.g. knowledge about healing practices being shared by a healer to another healer who is next in line [24]. On the other hand, entities that spearhead the collection and curation of IK data may have their own policies that regulate how information is accessed and who can access the information [7].

The design of any ICT-based IK management system should then be based on the understanding of the traditional IK sharing aspect [25]. Zaman [26] suggests studying the cultural norms related to IK sharing inherent in a cultural group before embarking on the actual systems development process. However, to derive a unified model is challenging in Namibia, a multicultural country where diverse knowledge sharing practices exist due to the presence of different tribes. Thus, a flexible data access organization needs to be implemented to account for the various community requests.

2.4.2 Epistemological and Structural Challenges

Researchers such as [26] emphasize that most IK preservation and sharing projects which depend on ICTs fail mainly because of the approach that is taken when implementing them. ICT professionals and practitioners take on the traditional role of system designer and developer and overlook the importance of understanding how IK takes tacit and implicit forms restricted to a given community's activities and governed by its social and cultural dynamics [26]. Most IK in rural Southern Africa is created and transferred by oral and performative means. An applicable example is that of a traditional healer who instructs his apprentice on how to treat an ailment. In addition to telling the apprentice on which plants and herbs to look for, the healer usually emphasizes on other intangible aspects of the healing process, e.g. the time of the day as well as the location where the healing is to be carried out [5, 27]. These processes are somewhat easy repeat and grasp when in the natural setting and context, but challenges arise when we try to model them using technology constrained structures. Preserving such traditional practices using ICTs leads to the loss of context in some cases as technologies used to preserve and share IK rely on structured technical systems whilst IK relies on different ontologies and epistemologies which are difficult to map on current data structure models. As a result, to help improve the outlook of IK preservation projects relying on ICTs, there is need for all stakeholders to understand the IK management system in a holistic manner.

3 The Namibian Initiative

3.1 Namibian National Program

In Namibia, the National Commission on Research, Science and Technology (NCRST) is spearheading a project that is aimed at collecting, documenting and disseminating IK from the various ethnic groups in the country using digital means [28]. The Namibian Indigenous Knowledge Management Systems project was formulated to stem the loss of IK by providing persistent digital and information technology-based interventions aimed at digitally preserving and disseminating IK of the various cultural groups spread across the country [28]. Different stakeholders came together to frame policies as well as gather requirements on how best to catalogue and curate IK. The IK systems research cluster from the Namibia University of Science and Technology's Faculty of Computing and Informatics

(FCI) took on the responsibility to develop and implement the technical components. The research cluster assists in the collection of IK by engaging mainly Namibian rural communities and co-designing technologies that empower IK holders in each community to collect various digital media pertaining to their IK and practices [8].

3.2 Methodological Approach

The research cluster relies on community-based co-design (CBCD) approach comprising principles of participatory design and action research [29]. Thus, services or systems developed are not only based on the technical expertise and assumptions of the developers but instead embrace communities needs and visions [22]. Accordingly, over the years the long-term collaborating communities have become co-designers rather than informants and testers of the technologies developed. As a result, all the co-designed tools developed in the past reflect the communities' conceptual and practical models.

3.3 Collaborating Communities

Research for this study is mainly conducted with two ethnic groups, namely, the OvaHerero from Erindiroukambe in Eastern Namibia and the OvaHimba from Otjisa in Opuwo, Northern Namibia. The two communities hold significance because most of the previous work was carried out with their members. In addition to this, the ethnic groups are closely linked as they descend from the same matriclan and therefore share several traditional rituals and major dialectical language similarities [30]. These similarities as well as the significant underlying differences make it ideal to determine how technologies designed with one group can be transferred to the other [30].

3.4 IK Holder Tools

The two communities have been instrumental in the designing and development of tools that can be used to collect IK in digital formats. These tools include the Homestead Creator (HSC), Homestead Scenario Depiction Tool (HSDT) and the media collection tool (MCT). This section outlines the functions of each tool before we venture into describing how they all fit into the national IKMS.

3.4.1 The Homestead Creator

In 2014, researchers together with some elders from the Herero community in Eastern Namibia co-designed a platform known as the Homestead creator [4]. The prototype is a 3D graphics tablet application developed using UNITY 3D. It uses touch interaction and enabled users to select objects and drag them into a place on an empty canvas, and through previously established camera perspectives inspects their creation [27]. This tool allowed village elders who are community knowledge holders, to reconstruct their physical contexts in a 3D virtual environment. These representations would usually be homesteads that IK holders could relate to and were familiar with. The short-term goal of the prototype was to investigate how knowledge holders would represent their homesteads in a virtual environment whilst the long-term goal was to co-design a tool that could enable villagers to recreate a context and embed recorded multimedia IK (Fig. 1).

The HSC prototype was tested with a group of village elders from Erindiroukambe in Eastern Namibia and several design challenges and knowledge gaps which existed in the tool were exposed [27]. These challenges emanated from the difficulty in representing simulated real-life objects for users not previously exposed to 3D technologies in a manner that enables them to easily recognize the representations. HSCs design was meant to allow digital media depicting different IK-related scenarios to be embedded at various locations. The location of these scenarios was marked by a generic character making hand gestures indicating the presence of a scenario that could be viewed [4]. However, there was no standard way of enabling the users to determine the type of IK embedded at a chosen location. It was bound to present challenges when larger IK aggregates were embedded in a small area within the virtual environment [31]. Users would have more pronounced difficulty in identifying the IK class embedded at the various locations, and it would be cumbersome for a user to navigate inside the entire virtual homestead to establish the location of a certain IK class [31].

Fig. 1 A screenshot from the Homestead creator interface captured from a top-down [4]

3.4.2   Homestead Scenario Depiction Tool

The design shortfalls highlighted above were addressed in a consecutive phase with the IK holders. More co-design sessions were held and during these, appropriate visual hints were modelled. These hints were to be embedded in the virtual environment in a manner that would enable any users of the prototype to determine the type of IK embedded at any location in the environment. The resulting prototype was named the Homestead Scenario Depiction Tool (HSDT), and it was tested in the same manner as the HSC. The primary goal of the HSDT was to explore how best to provide visual hints that could guide a user navigating in a virtual environment on the type of IK embedded in a specific location. The HSDT prototype was also developed using the Unity 3D game engine, it was compiled to execute on the Android operating system [31].

Using a community-based co-design approach, the researchers, interacted with various knowledge holders from the Herero Community to model scenarios that could be recreated in a virtual environment. These scenarios were chosen owing to the nature in which they manifested in the natural context of the community members. Each of the scenarios selected is characterized by a gathering of crowds of people and sometimes livestock, thereby making it difficult to distinguish from the next when observed from a long distance [31].

In addition to these factors, all three scenarios were chosen because they each represented common events and activities that occur in and around a Herero homestead. The first scenario was modelled based on the description given for a cattle branding scene (Fig. 2) whilst the second and third featured a child naming ceremony and a community meeting to discuss water shortages, respectively. The

Fig. 2 Cattle branding scenario, note the levitating branding iron with a red halo to increase the prominence

tool was evaluated to determine if users, who were not previously exposed to hints in a traditional 3D virtual environment setting, would easily and comfortably utilize them as guides to interact with an object or would they instead formulate their own visual hints they could easily relate to.

Results gathered showed the propensity for the users to identify a scenario by observing all models in the scene as opposed to identifying an event by observing a single object on a random location in the virtual environment.

3.4.3 Media Collection Tool

Another tool the researchers co-designed with knowledge holders was the media collection tool (MCT) (Fig. 3). Just like the HSC and HSDT, this tool was developed to execute on Android devices [8]. The purpose of the MCT was to enable IK holders to digitize their IK independently from external collectors [8]. This was accomplished by unifying features such as taking pictures, videos and audio recordings, as well as providing the functionality to create drawings and text. Several design iterations were carried out with each session followed by a usage evaluation. Emphasis was placed on co-designing icons that the IK holders could relate to and easily remember as being associated with the data capturing actions they wanted to carry out. Data collected using the tool was stored in directories on the device classified by media type; therefore, images, videos and text files were stored in separate folders in the same directory on the tablet, named with the current timestamp [8]. It was realized that the IK holder had minimal technical skill level for interacting with the tool and previewing the data he collected. As a result, it was decided to do away with the default Android media gallery and instead devise a custom gallery only accessible through the tool. This gallery operated from a combination of physical file storage and an SQL Lite database to allow the IK holder meaningful and easy navigation within the tool [8].

Combined results of usability tests for the HSC, HSDT and MCT all helped improve the source of IK-related data for the researchers. The 3D-based tools led the researchers to explore the possibility of deconstructing and getting relative spatial data from homesteads in the virtual environment whilst the MCT provided them with much needed digital media centred on IK collected by knowledge holders in a natural and relaxed setting.

3.5 Structural Requirements

Test results from the HSC as well as the HSDT helped the researchers to establish the significance of place, location and navigation interweaved with social activities in mapping IK [32]. Whilst interacting with these tools, the IK holders showed the 'situatedness' of the knowledge in their communities. This realization encouraged the research cluster to renounce textual dominated technologies and instead explore

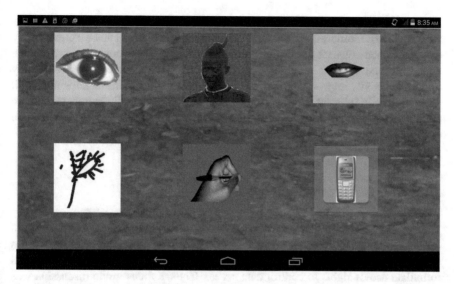

Fig. 3 Screenshot of the menu structure for the media collection tool [8]

using visual and location-based representations which provide virtual contexts for digitized IK [4, 22, 27]. As a result, the HSC also has additional background function to allow logging of all the interaction and positions of objects in the virtual environment [33]. These logs make it easy to recreate a homestead on a different device or as a map. The log files are currently in text format but they can be converted to JavaScript Object Notation (JSON) or Extensible Markup Language (XML). The log files can be rich sources of data which can be used to playback various scenarios as depicted by an IK holder, further enrichment can allow voice-overs to be added to describe these scenarios.

On the other hand, the HSDT does not store any logs, it instead concentrates on improving how scenarios can be better depicted for easy identification [31]. Through this, IK can be categorized into cultural themes based on the scenarios emanating from the provided hints. These themes can have various metadata and keywords attached to them making it easy for users to query for IK through key texts or graphical scenarios.

The media collection tool captures digital media in the form of video, image, annotations and text files. All these files are captured at varying intervals and can describe a single or multiple cultural activities or the knowledge holders' daily activities. In the case of cultural activities, the knowledge holder can combine various digital media to create an aggregate of files that belong together and share the same contexts. The IK holder can then attach access rights that determine how the aggregate created is accessed by different user groups once it is in the public domain. The various data captured using the digital tools are currently being stored either on the primary devices used to record it or on secondary backup devices. Our aim is to transfer all data into a constrained structured and reliable database system whilst allowing controlled access to it by any interested and authorized third party. Since the body of knowledge, we wish to store comes from a different epistemology, it is crucial that we preserve any of the attached contexts to ensure it remains accurate. These contexts may include intangible and difficult to digitize specifications such as time; e.g. a culturally important activity may only be carried out at a specific time of the day, together with some culturally relevant specifications, such as people or family members who are allowed to access the knowledge related to the activity. All these contexts can be classified as rules that can be used by communities to govern access to their IK.

3.6   Access Requirements

We set out to establish these access rules by consulting one of our long-term collaborators in Opuwo. Of utmost importance to us, was determining what rules existed culturally to govern knowledge sharing, we could then map these rules and formulate access rights to control data access. Thus, a focus group discussion was held with our Ovahimba co-designer and his family at Otjisa village near Opuwo. According to the knowledge holder, he does not place restrictions on who he shares knowledge with. Several scenarios were poised to him as a means of determining how he would react in each. The first scenario centred on how he decides to share knowledge with a researcher known to him. The second scenario centred on how he decides which knowledge was appropriate to share with a researcher whom he did not know prior to an encounter. The third scenario aimed at establishing how he would share knowledge with an individual who is not a researcher nor a community member, but is instead a representative of an entity which wished to monetize his knowledge. For all proposed scenarios, his stance remained the same. He highlighted that he shares knowledge freely with anyone who expresses interest regardless of any perceived or implied intentions of the person asking. This concurs with statements made by the Erindiroukambe community who equally did not identify any segregation of knowledge access but rather based their decisions on who wants to know [2]. The discussion digressed and moved on to determining how he felt his knowledge and facets about his culture should be represented to the outside world, since he could freely share this information. His response indicated that he felt neither him nor other community members had control over how an outsider presented their culture in public domain; he, however, expressed his desire to have the power to correct any misconceptions he would come across (see Maasz et al. in this book).

3.7   Consequences for Design

From the discussions with the IK holder, it was apparent that the existence of natural access rights was doubtful. Instead, the picture painted by the IK holder showed signs of most knowledge existing on an open access principle. However, we will still have more design sessions with different IK holders including those from the Nama and OvaHerero community to establish whether the open access principle is common practice among the ethnic groups. Once this has been established, the next step will involve mapping these rules into a structure akin to that used in defining user type for a relational database. This will culminate in the completion of a central system that can store IK.

4 Intermediary Node Concept

This section introduces the concept of an intermediary node between the IK context and the national IK repository system. The IK holder will have direct control over who accesses his data and be able to determine the extent to which his data is shared outside his context. All this will be accomplished whilst adhering to the access rights prescribed by the knowledge holder and the national IK policy as well as guidelines which are both still in their draft phases. The proposed database node concept will be loosely based on the national database prototype that we developed for the NCSRT in 2016. The prototype was initially developed to test the feasibility of storing the structured data originating from national surveys being carried out by the University of Namibia. The existing framework and model will be adjusted to cater for the unstructured data which is captured by the digital tools discussed earlier. The adjusted prototype will be developed in a manner that allows for separate instances of the system to be deployed at chosen institutions or regional centres across Namibia. Using the knowledge digitizing tools, the IK holders will be able to create media packages containing images, videos, voice notes or text and mimics their epistemologies, i.e. they will attach rules to govern who can access the data. Further, the media packages can be marked for access on a national level, regional level or special individual level. In addition to the media packages, other data such as the log files from the HSC and details of scenarios from the HSDT will also be handled for storage in the system. Data harvested from the hints in the HSDT may be combined with the log files from the HSC used as the foundation of keywords which can be used to query the system to retrieve 3D depictions of some culturally relevant scenarios, provided adequate information has been attached. Thereafter, the media packages and log files can be uploaded either directly to the national database or ideally to a regional centre node closest to their communities. This approach will serve as one of the ways to keep IK holders and their communities at the centre of the knowledge management process as it allows them to have fine-grained control of data.

4.1 Technical Requirements

The prototype will be a three-tier application as shown in Fig. 5. The back end will comprise a relational database responsible for storing data and profiles required for user authorization and authentication. The database will also be responsible for storing metadata of all collected digital media as well as textual input from the IK collection tools. Database resources will not be directly accessed by users, instead an intermediate tier will be constructed to handle all Create, Read, Update and Deletion operations through a Representational State Transfer Application Programming Interface (REST API) [34]. The REST approach was chosen to improve on scalability as it allows development of client applications independently from the main engine of the system. The intermediate tier will also contain a semantic search engine that is synced with the database and makes it easier for data searches to occur. Lastly, to cater for the saving, organizing and retrieval of digital media objects, a Flexible Extensible Digital Object Repository Architecture (FEDORA) will be used. This will provide an interface that abstracts all processes responsible for organizing and retrieving media files in the file system of the server. The FEDORA core will also be responsible for keeping some of the metadata for each file. Whilst Fig. 4 shows a high-level view of the proposed system architecture, the section below expands this architecture to present the concept in a semi-technical manner. Each of the three layers has at least one sub-layer (Fig. 5):

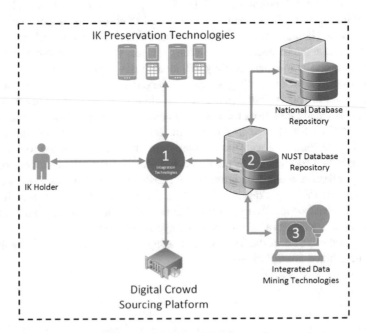

Fig. 4 Overview of the IK ecosystem showing the link between the technologies

(a) The client layer provides a user interface which allows users to interact with the underlying system. Clients can be developed in any platform including dedicated mobile (Android and iOS) as well as responsive web interfaces. Current tests are being carried out using Android-based clients. Each of the clients will consume the RESTful API when uploading, editing or retrieving data. Clients are also responsible for helping foster the first level of security, data access rights management as specified in the REST API documentation. Security will be fine-grained to also log the device IMEI number as well as user profile of the IK holder who possesses it at a given time. This will enable us to link collected data to a single IK holder and device. The client will enable the IK holders to attach access rights on their data before they post it to the database node. These rights can be applied and enforced on single files or alternatively on the entire data set. Second, the IK holders can choose to mark data as openly accessible or alternatively delegate members of the research cluster, i.e. from the institution housing their data to act on their behalf to allocate access, they can also delegate/authorize the commission to handle rights management on their behalf.

(b) The logic layer can be split further into four distinct sub-layers, namely, security layer, user management layer, file management layer and integration services layer. These sub-levels operate in tandem to provide all the logical functions of a node. The user management layer is responsible for exposing all functions that enable new users to be registered and authenticated before they

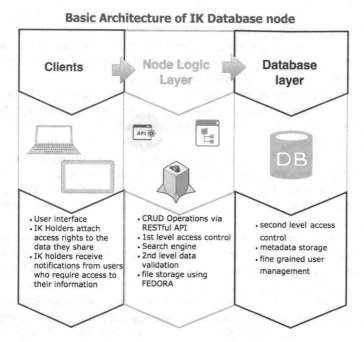

Fig. 5 Architecture of the IK database node

can access resources. By default, four user classes exist: administrators, IK holders, research cluster members and ordinary registered users. More user types will be initialized to extend from the existing classes. The security layer is closely coupled with the user management layer and is responsible for controlling access to resources on the system. Robust authorization and authentication will be executed in this layer. Users will be allocated roles and access to individual files or groups of data will be determined on this layer. Enforcement of the IK Policy is also handled by the security layer to ensure the rules specified in it are adhered to. Digital media object (file operations) handling will be executed on this level as part of the file management layer. This is based on the FEDORA architecture. This layer is responsible for providing abstracted functions that enable digital media objects to be stored on the file system of a server. A RESTful API will be used to store, describe and index any digital media as required. The layer also interfaces with the database layer to store some metadata and file indexes. The database will keep track of the relationships between the files as specified by the IK holder. This ensures that the system does not decontextualize the media and metadata thereby discarding some of the meaning associated with it. FEDORA was chosen because it helps eliminate the process of manually organizing and versioning files in the server thereby lessening burden on the system developers. The integration services layer is responsible for ensuring seamless communication between all the layers, this layer is therefore exposed as the RESTful API that is accessible to the different clients. The final component of the services layer is a semantic search engine. This search engine is synced with the database that contains the metadata to enable intelligent and linked searches for authorized users. The integration services are heavily coupled with the database and moderately coupled with the other three layers. Without the services layer, the other layers would exist as separate modules with no coherence.

The final layer is the database layer. Here, all metadata related to files as well as user profile data and user roles are stored in here. The database keeps data that is used by the security layer to control access to the system. The first level backups, syncing, data redundancy checks and disaster recovery are implemented on this level. In addition to that, all actions on the database are logged or auditing purposes on two levels, the first level is on the database itself and the second level of logging is on secure log files that are backed up to an external location. No client can have direct access to the database level, this feature is catered for by the RESTful API.

(c) As we have detailed in the previous sections, systems and collection methods that gather IK from knowledge holders through an intermediary can result in the IK holders losing control of how their knowledge is represented. Since our concept proposes to have the IK holder at the centre of the data collection, preservation and dissemination process, it aims to eliminate intermediaries thereby ensuring that data collected is correctly mapped into a database system, considering epistemological inferences. This approach will also make it possible for us to propagate and replicate the captured data into other storage facilities such as the national database, whilst maintaining the access rights prescribed by the IK holder.

5 Conclusion

Namibia can pride itself of rich sources of IK still carried by its communities. Having recognized the value of IK, like in other nations, efforts have been made to digitize, preserve and manage IK. However, a challenge remains to marry communities and national interests in acknowledging the agency of the IK holders extended into the digital world. We have presented previous technologies co-designed with indigenous communities whilst at the same time engaging in a technical development of a digital national IKMS. Thus, our current efforts centre around the bridging between those systems, for which we have presented a concept of an intermediary node. Soon, we will test and validate a prototypical implementation with selected indigenous communities to ensure community compliances.

Acknowledgements The authors would like to thank the Namibian National Commission on Science, Research and Technology for financially supporting the project. We would also like to extend our gratitude to the Otjisa and Erindiroukambe community for their commitment to this project.

References

1. Mkapa, B.: Indigenous knowledge a local pathway to global development. Indigenous knowledge local pathways to global development: marking five years of the World Bank indigenous knowledge for development program, pp. 1–3 (2004)
2. Kapuire, G.K.: An explorative action research study toward the design of a digital knowledge organisation as part of an indigenous knowledge management system with a Herero community. Ph.D. thesis, University of Cape Town (2013)
3. Jensen, K.L., Winschiers-Theophilus, H., Rodil, K., Winschiers-Goagoses, N., Kapuire, G.K., Kamukuenjandje, R.: Putting it in perspective: designing a 3D visualization to contextualize indigenous knowledge in rural Namibia. In: Proceedings of the Designing Interactive Systems Conference, ACM, pp. 196–199 (2012)
4. Rodil, K., Winschiers-Theophilus, H., Jensen, K.L., Rehm, M.: Homestead creator: a tool for indigenous designers. In: Proceedings of the 7th Nordic Conference on Human-Computer Interaction: Making Sense Through Design, ACM, pp. 627–630 (2012)
5. Winschiers-Theophilus, H., Bidwell, N.J., Chivuno-Kuria, S., Kapuire, G.K.: Determining requirements within an indigenous knowledge system of African rural communities. In: Proceedings of the 2010 Annual Research Conference of the South African Institute of Computer Scientists and Information Technologists, ACM, pp. 332–340 (2010)
6. Wynberg, R., Schroeder, D., Chennells, R.: Indigenous peoples, consent and benefit sharing: lessons from the San-Hoodia case. Springer, Berlin (2009)

7. Ngulube, P.: Embedding indigenous knowledge in library and information science education in Anglophone eastern and southern Africa. In: Handbook of Research on Social, Cultural, and Educational Considerations of Indigenous Knowledge in Developing Countries, p. 92 (2016)
8. Kapuire, G.K., Winschiers-Theophilus, H., Stanley, C., Maasz, D., Chamunorwa, M., Møller, R.H., Rodil, K., Gonzalez-Cabrero, D.: Technologies to promote the inclusion of indigenous knowledge holders in digital cultural heritage preservation. In: International Conference on Culture & Computer Science (2016)
9. van Heerden, F.R.: Hoodia gordonii: a natural appetite suppressant. J. Ethnopharmacol. **119** (3), 434–437 (2008)
10. Ohenjo, N., Willis, R., Jackson, D., Nettleton, C., Good, K., Mugarura, B.: Health of indigenous people in Africa. The Lancet **367**(9526), 1937–1946 (2006)
11. Chakravarty, R.: Preserving traditional knowledge: initiatives in India. IFLA J. **36**(4), 294–299 (2010)
12. Hunter, J.: The role of information technologies in indigenous knowledge management. Aust. Acad. Res. Libr. **36**(2), 109–124 (2005)
13. Zaman, T., Yeo, A., Kulathuramaiyer, N.: Indigenous knowledge governance framework (IKGF): a holistic model for indigenous knowledge management. In: Second International Conference on User Science and Engineering (i-USEr2011) Doctoral Consortium. Kuala Lumpur (2011)
14. Erstling, J.: Using patent to protect traditional knowledge. Tex. Wesleyan L. Rev. **15**, 295 (2008)
15. Hirwade, M.: Protecting traditional knowledge digitally: a case study of TKDL (2010)
16. Gupta, V.: Traditional knowledge digital library. In: Sub-regional Experts Meeting in Asia on Intangible Cultural Heritage: Safeguarding and Inventory Making Methodologies. Bangkok, Thailand, 13–16 December 2005
17. Hoppers, C.A.O.: Indigenous Knowledge and the Integration of Knowledge Systems: Towards a philosophy of articulation. New Africa Books, South Africa (2002)
18. Pretorius, R., Bezuidenhout, H.: National Recordal System IK Holder Catalogue Process (2011)
19. Khalala, G., Makitla, I., Botha, A., Alberts, R.: A case for understanding user experience challenges confronting indigenous knowledge recorders in rural communities in South Africa. In: IST-Africa Conference Proceedings, 2014, IEEE, pp. 1–8 (2014)
20. Van Rooyen, B.: Safeguarding the future of indigenous knowledge through ICT: ICT and society. CSIR Science Scope **5**(2), 24–26 (2011)
21. Ngulube, P.: Managing and preserving indigenous knowledge in the knowledge management era: challenges and opportunities for information professionals. Info. Develop. **18**(2), 95–102 (2002)
22. Kapuire, G.K., Winschiers-Theophilus, H., Stanley, C., Chivuno-Kuria, S., Rodil, K., Katjivirue, M., Tjitendero, E.: Community-based co-design in Okomakuara a contribution to 'design in the wild'. In: Proceedings of the 13th Participatory Design Conference: Short Papers, Industry Cases, Workshop, Descriptions, Doctoral Consortium papers, and Keynote Abstracts-Volume 2, ACM, pp. 207–208 (2014)
23. Yu, S., Wang, C., Ren, K., Lou, W.: Achieving secure, scalable, and fine-grained data access control in cloud computing. In: Infocom, 2010 Proceedings IEEE, pp. 1–9 (2010)
24. Cheikhyoussef, A., Shapi, M., Matengu, K., Ashekele, H.M.: Ethnobotanical study of indigenous knowledge on medicinal plant use by traditional healers in Oshikoto region, Namibia. J. Ethnobiol. Ethnomedicine **7**(1), 10 (2011)
25. Van Der Velden, M.: Design for the contact zone. Knowledge management software and the structures of indigenous knowledges (2010)
26. Zaman, T.: Indigenous knowledge governance framework: a holistic model for indigenous knowledge management. Ph.D. thesis, Universiti Malaysia Sarawak, (UNIMAS) (2013)

27. Winschiers-Theophilus, H., Jensen, K., Rodil, K.: Locally situated digital representation of indigenous knowledge. In: Proceedings of the Cultural Attitudes Towards Technology and Communication, Australia (2012)
28. Jauhiainen, J.S., Hooli, L.: Indigenous knowledge and developing countries innovation systems: the case of Namibia. Int. J. Innov. Stud. 1(1), 89–106 (2017)
29. Winschiers-Theophilus, H., Winschiers-Goagoses, N., Rodil, K., Blake, E., Zaman, T., Kapuire, G.K., Kamukuenjandje, R.: Moving away from Erindiroukambe: transferability of a rural community-based co-design. IFIIP WG 9 (2013)
30. Stanley, C., Winschiers-Theophilus, H., Blake, E., Rodil, K., Kapuire, G.: Ovahimba community in Namibia ventures into crowdsourcing design. Proc. IFIP WG 9, 277–287 (2015)
31. Chamunorwa, M., Kapuire, G.K.: Effective visual hints in a 3D virtual environment for an indigenous community. In: Proceedings of the International Conference on Culture and Computer Science (ICCCS-2016), ACM (2016)
32. Bidwell, N.J., Winschiers-Theophilus, H., Kapuire, G.K., Rehm, M.: Pushing personhood into place: situating media in rural knowledge in Africa. Int. J. Hum Comput. Stud. 69(10), 618–631 (2011)
33. Rodil, K.: Co-designing digital technologies for cultural heritage preservation with indigenous communities in Namibia. Ph.D. thesis, Aalborg Universitetsforlag (2016)
34. Rodriguez, A.: Restful web services: the basics. IBM developerWorks (2008)

Promoting an Open and Accessible Digital Preservation of Namibian Indigenous Languages

Heinrich Naatwilwe Aluvilu, Heike Winschiers-Theophilus
and Sarala Krishnamurthy

1 Introduction

1.1 Background

Despite a relatively small population of approximately 2.2 million, Namibia can pride itself of about 30 spoken languages Namibian languages [1]. The indigenous languages in Namibia are not yet entirely endangered due to their continuous usage in everyday life. However, it has come to our attention that little content or resources of Namibian local languages are available in digitalized formats and readily accessible to the general public. This does not only have an effect on the preservation of the languages, but also on the development of the language content and on the possible contributions which can be collected and aggregated to capture all the content of the indigenous languages in Namibia and preserve them. Even though the National Language policy of Namibia prescribes that local languages should be the medium of instruction at primary level, some schools introduce English very early on. The high status accorded to English in society poses a threat to the preservation and future of local languages. The national institutions are expected to take appropriate account of the human factor with regard to language competence and language use, people's attitude to linguistic varieties and distinct languages of the country, linguistic norms, etc. [2]. Only a few Namibians are

H. N. Aluvilu (✉) · H. Winschiers-Theophilus (✉) · S. Krishnamurthy (✉)
Namibia University of Science and Technology, 13 Storch Street,
Windhoek, Namibia
e-mail: heinrich91@gmail.com

H. Winschiers-Theophilus
e-mail: hwinschiers@nust.na

S. Krishnamurthy
e-mail: skrishnamurthy@nust.na

© Springer Nature Singapore Pte Ltd. 2018
D. S. Jat et al. (eds.), *Digitisation of Culture: Namibian and International Perspectives*, https://doi.org/10.1007/978-981-10-7697-8_8

learning their native languages at schools, particularly in urban areas, and at the universities [3].

We are therefore proposing a Collaborative and Open-Content Online Dictionary. It will function as a simple language translation platform service for several Namibian indigenous languages. It will provide an open and collaborative platform on which anyone who has an interest in learning Namibian indigenous languages can go to and moreover, can contribute to the collection, preservation, and development of these various languages. The system will be based on our current version of an online Namibian indigenous languages dictionary prototype (NIL), which we present in this paper. The digitalization of indigenous language content, designed and developed as a Namibian online collaborative open-content dictionary-like platform, allows for searching, adding, defining, translating, and storing of all the existing content of our various local languages. The main concern here is to provide a readily available, accessible, searchable, and well-defined language content structure that will serve a convenient purpose for anyone who wants to use it and look beyond language as a barrier in the Namibian context. Well aware of the efforts needed to create a dictionary we propose a crowdsourcing approach as supported by the system built. Besides ensuring an appropriate data structure, we thus focus on creating a user-friendly interface to support various indigenous language speakers to participate.

1.2   A Multilingual System

A belief in linguistic equity ensures that all languages should be protected, promoted, and preserved. The African society today is a multilingual which is a resources that we must celebrate as well as utilize. The JUBA language in education conference held in 2012 in Sudan declared that African languages should be used alongside with established languages on the continent, such as French, English, Portuguese, and others to provide multilingual education based on a mother-tongue program. The educational, social, cultural, economic, and political benefits of institutionalizing multilingual education should be discussed, evaluated, and supported by all stakeholders, including individuals and the government. All learners should be taught in basic formal and informal education through the languages that they know best. This strengthens their literacy, numeracy, and cognitive skills. Further, this helps them to develop their language skills as well. Once learners have acquired the necessary academic proficiency in reading, writing, and in numeracy, second language should be introduced in schools. This transition from mother tongues and local, indigenous languages to European languages, such as English and the others mentioned above should be gradual.

However, there are several challenges to the teaching and learning of local languages. If we take the Namibian example, English is written into the constitution and given a high status in the country despite the low numbers of people who actually speak English. Linguistic diversity creates a problem for the selection of languages for official and educational purposes. Namibia has three major language groups: Bantu languages, Khoekhoegowab, and the Germanic languages. The fear of selecting one language over and above any other was that it would trigger an inter-ethnical rivalry. Hence, English was chosen as a neutral language to foster national unity in the country. Some of the reasons advanced for choosing English as a medium of instruction across the country are the following: (1) To develop many languages as mediums of instruction would be very costly for the country; (2) Namibia lacks trained teachers in the indigenous languages to teach in those languages; (3) Sufficient materials have not yet been developed in the local languages which could be used in the language classroom; and, finally, (4) Movements of children and teachers across different regions could prove to be a major challenge in teaching indigenous languages. The example of the Zambezi region can be cited here. In Zambezi, the official medium of instruction is Silozi, but it is not the mother tongue of many children and teachers residing in this region. With the result, the children have to first learn Silozi, which is not their mother tongue, and then learn, English once they move into higher grades defeating the whole purpose of improved literacy, numeracy, and cognitive skills which come because of learning in the mother tongue. A lot of work has to still be done for the development of indigenous languages.

Furthermore, for a language to be chosen as medium of instruction, it needs to fulfill certain criteria such as [4]: its use; its level of development including orthography and standard forms and its ability to express modern, up-to-date concepts in arts, science, and technology; the availability of resources; finally, the political, social, and cultural importance of the language. Languages need to be developed in such a way that they can grow in terms of their orthography and also evolve into a standardized version cutting across the dialectical variations found in the different regions and social strata. Further, they should be developed to such an extent that they can meet all the communicative needs of the society in which they are used. Many languages are not found in the written form; therefore, the matter of preservation becomes an insurmountable problem. Also, given the lack of resources that the country is facing, diverting funds toward development of local, indigenous languages cannot be expected. Material production is another challenge that local languages face, and the private sector will not promote indigenous languages when their raison d'etre is tied to profits leading to the advancement of a culture of capitalism in the country. Further, modernization of indigenous languages is taking place at a very slow pace and is not able to keep up with the rapid advances in technology where every day new developments are taking place. This is symptomatic of poor language planning at the national level.

A significant challenge for indigenous languages is the lack of coordination of language activities across the country. At the national level, it is found that language experts and researchers are working in tandem, but totally ignorant of what is happening in another part of the country, leading to a lack of coordination and consolidation of efforts with the result that little is achieved at the corpus level. Despite advances made in acknowledging the role of local languages in education, the lack of proper implementation and monitoring has led to many lacunae in language matters. Currently, the responsibility of developing study materials is taken up by NIED who has been commissioning authors to write teaching books in local languages. But these have to be evaluated and checked for quality. Therefore, there is a need to develop mechanisms to ensure that good quality materials are made available for both learners and teachers in particular and the public at large.

Many scholars have pointed out the need for bilingual education or multilingual education system. There are several UNESCO studies and linguistic research findings that can be used to develop a bilingual education system to provide increased chances for better literacy rates and improving education in Namibia. The first step toward language development is language preservation. In order to respond to the linguistic needs of the local languages, the easiest and best option is to go for digitalization of languages. The use of technology answers all the challenges that have been raised in the foregoing section. There are several advantages in the use of technology.

2 Literature Review

2.1 Preserving Indigenous Languages

The significance of maintaining indigenous languages has been widely recognized in light of preserving world views and diverse conceptualizations. However, in the age of globalization, intangible cultural expressions, such as literatures and oral traditions, are easily overlooked and lost [5]. Zaman and Winschiers-Theophilus [6] postulated that languages can only be sustained if they are used in everyday life. Thus, they have developed a mobile app for a secret sign language only mastered by the elder Penan in the rainforest of Borneo. The app bridges generational gaps and attracted the interest of the indigenous youth to use their traditional language.

In Namibia, most indigenous languages are still spoken by old and young although current linguistic trends in urban areas and usages of technologies show that Namibian citizens often mix indigenous languages with English. Many a time the older generation has expressed their concern in preserving the original traditional linguistic expressions. We therefore support current discussions at national level which suggest initiatives for the preservation of the various indigenous languages with clear progress indicators and safeguarding the participation of community members fluent in these languages to take part in defining and executing some of the methods needed in preserving these languages [5].

The absence of a digital Namibian Indigenous language repository not only represents a threat to the preservation of native languages in Namibia but also deprives the future generation's indigenous communities off the opportunities to learn their mother tongues in schools, at home or outside of Namibia for those residing in other countries.

2.2 Current Approaches to Language Digitalization

Over the years, different methods have been defined for preserving indigenous languages, such as digital media resources like audio recording, and also electronic formats such as online open-content platforms were developed and managed by groups of indigenous communities working together in a collaborative manner. González [7] suggests that the use such technologies on the one side boosts indigenous communities pride of their cultural heritage while at the same time raises global awareness on the importance of sharing, celebrating and appreciating cultural differences.

However, with recent developments of emerging technologies as well as crowdsourcing platforms aiming for wider inclusion, we observe a general lack of indigenous communities appropriating those technologies. For example, Wikipedia, which is claiming to strive for the inclusion of all human knowledge and various contributors, has shown to be rather hostile to indigenous communities [8]. Wikipedia has developed its own mechanism of editing validation to ensure reliable information. However, current systemic biases and technical challenges have prevented indigenous communities to actively participate in Wikipedia editing, let alone develop their own indigenous Wikipedia [8]. With a rigid rule system, maintained by a selective contributor community creating a systematic bias, Gallert et al. [8] have uncovered major cultural clashes between Wikipedia and an indigenous community hampering their participation. Thus, although we promote the usefulness of creative collaborative platforms to preserve languages and especially indigenous languages, we need to ensure the participation of indigenous communities from the onset.

2.3 Creation of Online Dictionaries

Considering the large expenses for a manual construction of bilingual dictionaries requiring numerous linguistic human resources, automatic extraction has been investigated [9]. With a scarcity of parallel corpora, alternatives such as comparable corpora and Wikipedia are suggested as promising resources [9]. An example is a Wikipedia-based corpus reference tool, which is a dictionary-like reference tool designed to help users find information similar to what one would find in a dictionary when looking up a word, except that this information is extracted from large corpora [10]. Yet in the absence of large texts written in Namibian indigenous languages, we deploy a crowdsourcing approach to jointly build up a comprehensive dictionary. Thus, national initiatives need to be established for the preservation of the various indigenous languages ensuring the inclusion of indigenous language speakers to take part in defining and executing some of the methods needed in preserving these languages [5]. A good example of an indigenous crowdsourcing project is the Kamusi Project. It is a community-engaging project using the public in creating an Internet Living Swahili Dictionary (ILSD), and through the crowd, the project introduces new features as the project transitions toward a massively bilingual Global Online Living Dictionary (GOLD) [11]. "This project has always been conceived as collaborative but controlled—users are encouraged to contribute new or improved entries, but those contributions are ultimately subject to authoritative review" [11]. Lessons learned from the Kamusi project can be integrated in new developments of collaborative open-content bilingual dictionaries. Linguistic data that is submitted by independent researchers and also submissions done through crowdsourcing formed by indigenous communities will need to be validated [12]. The indigenous communities participating in crowdsourcing will have their own views of the data too [13]; therefore, careful considerations will be required at all times to be when facilitating these collaborations.

3   Development Process

The research is based in a pragmatic research paradigm following a research through design methodology [14]. It will allow us to employ design techniques during project execution which are documented to support application to similar projects. Our design methods are based on a participatory design approach.

3.1   Creation of Online Dictionaries

Designing and building an online language dictionary requires a large crowd providing entries of the different local languages, and therefore, representatives for each one of these groups should be part of this project from the very beginning.

We deploy a participatory approach with representatives from the different language groups. A participatory approach ensures that requirements of end users are considered in the early phases of design and that use appropriate technology leading to higher acceptance rates and technology adoption. Including the community in design decisions allows us to create a product with them, for them, and also ensures a higher quality of the prototype and user experience in the end.

3.2   User Survey

We conducted a semi-structured questionnaire-based survey to collect demographic information, awareness, and need for such a system as well as general technology expertise. We interviewed 54 participants through in-person, groups, and online

Table 1 Namibian Indigenous Languages (NIL) online survey

Question	Yes (%)	Maybe/sometimes (%)	No (%)
Need for NIL online dictionary?	89.4	10.6	0
Need for learning how to speak or read another local language?	80.9	14.9	4.3
Receive future updates on the NIL project progress?	93.5	0	6.5

questionnaires which they had to complete. The group of participants was very diverse in terms of gender, age cultural background.

Tables 1 show the responses that were given by the participants.

3.3   User Evaluation of Similar Systems

Rather than evaluating similar systems from a designer perspective, we invited participants to evaluate existing systems. We selected five (5) open and online content dictionaries to be evaluated by our invited participants. The following systems were selected:

- Wiktionary
- Lingro
- Merriam-Webster
- Collins Dictionary
- The Kids Open Dictionary

The aim was to introduce our participants to the concept of open-content systems and get feedback on useful features as well as usability experiences to guide our design.

According to the observations made during the evaluation sessions of the above-mentioned dictionaries, the participant's explored different features and indicated which of the features on the systems they liked using and would like to see in the dictionary prototype as well.

3.4   Dictionary Design

3.4.1   Data Structure

Based on common features found in similar systems and the requests by the participants, a data structure for the dictionary was created as represented in the Fig. 1.

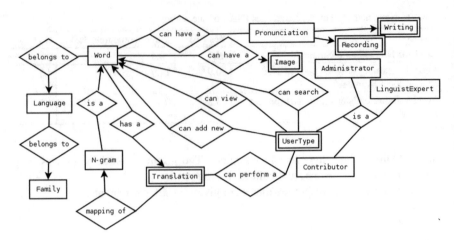

Fig. 1 Namibian Indigenous Languages (NIL) online dictionary ER diagram

3.4.2 System Features

Figure 2 shows a use case diagram depicting the different interactions of users with the system

Figure 2 shows the different use cases and their actors who will be making use of the NIL dictionary.

3.4.3 Process Flow

- A user wants to see translate a word from one local language to another.
- The user opens the web page/app.
- The user selects the language of the word they want to translate, and the language of they want it translated into.
- They enter the word and press the "enter" button on their keyboard.
- The system checks the database and sees if a translation (n-gram) is available.
- If a translation is available, it is displayed and the user's request is considered fulfilled.
- If no translation is available, the n-gram is sent to users who have registered themselves as contributors. A contributor is someone who speaks both languages indicated by the user requesting a translation.
- The contributor will see the translation request on the system and they translate the n-gram. Their translation is then sent back to the system, and made available to the user other system users.
- The n-gram is then stored in the database for future reference.

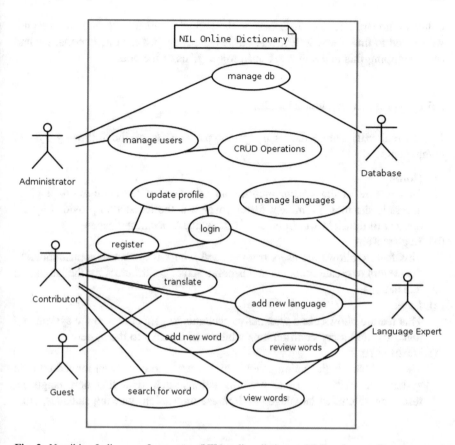

Fig. 2 Namibian Indigenous Languages (NIL) online dictionary UML use case diagram

In effect, this is a type of "real time" translation system which uses real people to translate the n-grams which, in the fields of computational linguistics and probability, is a contiguous sequence of n-items from a given sequence of text or speech. By virtue of its design, it collects only useful n-grams which people need translations for. Over time, a collection of good n-grams translations could be collected.

3.5 Implementation

This section discusses the implementation with the aims of giving the reader insight into mechanisms behind the NIL online dictionary prototype. We have broken down the application architecture into the main functional features which make up the system and explain the role they play. We have selected Ruby programming language together with the Rails MVC framework technologies to implement our online dictionary because, first, these tools worked together very well and, second, we needed to find a way to leverage our resources against the timeline that we had for developing this and still meet our project goals at the end.

3.5.1 Main NIL System Modules

Our current NIL online dictionary prototype consists of the following system components.

(a) **Home**

This feature of the system presents an overview of the application. It gives access to the most prominent feature, which is the translation provided by the options to translate word/phrases from available local languages.

(b) **Registration**

This feature allows the users from general who wish to make contributions to the system to create accounts and become active contributors for the languages translations.

(c) **Login**

This feature allows users with active accounts to gain access to the system and make the necessary contributions which will be save to the system.

(d) **Dashboard**

The dashboard is the action panel, which users who have been logged into the system can make use of to perform actions such as adding new language, resolving submitted language word/phrase translation, viewing statistics, etc.

3.5.2 The Language Translation Mechanism and System Architecture

Here, we discuss the components responsible for the translations and the steps behind the procedure. Our MVC architectural pattern for implementing has the following components:

Models

- Language—*stores the different local languages*
- N-gram—*represents a word/phrase in a local language*
- Translation_Request—*store all unresolved/untranslated language words/ phrases*
- User—*stores account user information*

Views

- Dashboard (*index*)
- Devise (*confirmations, mailer, menu, passwords, registrations, sessions, shared*)—*manage user settings*
- Home (*_language_list, index*)—*translation area on home view*

- Layouts (*application*)—*master layout of the application*
- Translation_Requests (*index*)—*view of all unresolved translations on the system.*

Controllers

- application_controller—*sets correct preference for logged in user*
- dashboard controller—*gives logged in user statistics*
- home_controller—*sets all available languages on home page for user*
- language_controller—*creates new languages in database*
- ngram_controller—*performs word/phrase translations*
- translation_requests_controller—*resolves pending translations*

With the simple components shown above, we look at the steps performed during a word/phrase translation:

Step 1—user selects from_language and to_language, these are from available languages, which may have or not have words/phrases.
Step 2—user enters word/phrase the wish to translate in the from_language input field and press enter to perform the translation.
Step 3—in the background, the entered word is search for by matching the selected from_language and matching it to a language group of the to_language.
Step 4—if the word/phrase is not found because it does not exist, it is then submitted as a request under the from_language group

3.6 Evaluation of NIL Dictionary

The online dictionary prototype was tested and evaluated by a group of participants. The screenshot below depicts the first screen the users see when opening the system (Fig. 3).

Below are a series of actions which were available to the participants when they were testing the prototype:

- **Home**—the screen of the prototype which the users (guest or registered) see first.
- **From language**—select an available language from which to translate a word from.
- **Translate word/phrase**—type the word/phrase to translate.
- **To language**—select an available language from which to translate a word to.
- **Entered word/phrase**—translate the entered word/phrase to a word/phrase in the target language.
- **Existing word/phrase**—when the word/phrase being translated exists, it is displayed to the user, and if it does not exist, this word/phrase will be logged and sent as a request to the community of contributors to respond to.

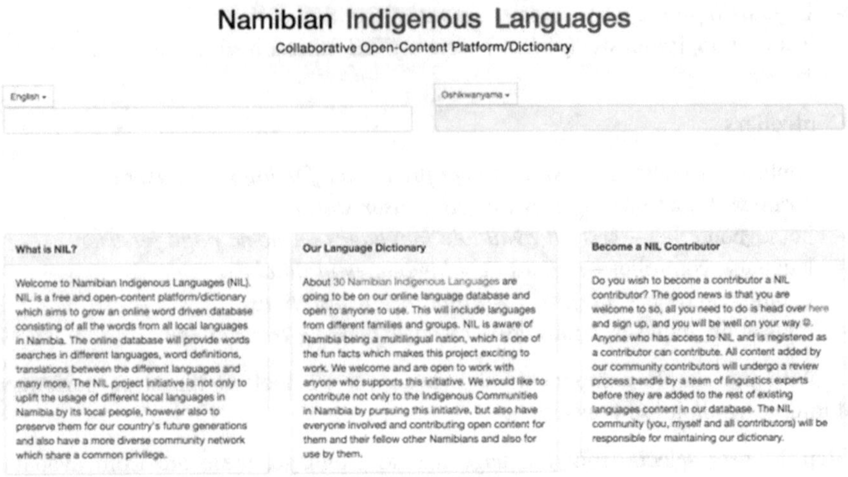

Namibian Indigenous Languages

Collaborative Open-Content Platform/Dictionary

English ▾

Oshikwanyama ▾

What is NIL?

Welcome to Namibian Indigenous Languages (NIL). NIL is a free and open-content platform/dictionary which aims to grow an online word driven database consisting of all the words from all local languages in Namibia. The online database will provide words searches in different languages, word definitions, translations between the different languages and many more. The NIL project initiative is not only to uplift the usage of different local languages in Namibia by its local people, however also to preserve them for our country's future generations and also have a more diverse community network which share a common privilege.

Our Language Dictionary

About 30 Namibian Indigenous Languages are going to be on our online language database and open to anyone to use. This will include languages from different families and groups. NIL is aware of Namibia being a multilingual nation, which is one of the fun facts which makes this project exciting to work. We welcome and are open to work with anyone who supports this initiative. We would like to contribute not only to the Indigenous Communities in Namibia by pursuing this initiative, but also have everyone involved and contributing open content for them and their fellow other Namibians and also for use by them.

Become a NIL Contributor

Do you wish to become a contributor a NIL contributor? The good news is that you are welcome to so, all you need to do is head over here and sign up, and you will be well on your way ☺. Anyone who has access to NIL, and is registered as a contributor can contribute. All content added by our community contributors will undergo a review process handle by a team of linguistics experts before they are added to the rest of existing languages content in our database. The NIL community (you, myself and all contributors) will be responsible for maintaining our dictionary.

Fig. 3 Namibian Indigenous Languages (NIL) home screen

- **Login**—registered contributors use their valid credentials to login into the prototype. Users without accounts can sign up for one new ones.
- **Dashboard**—shows the total number of registered contributors and a quick statistics overview on the system statistics, such as number of words/phrases the logged in user has translated, the number of available word entries per language, the number of word/phrase requests made, and other information.
- **Non-existing word/phrase**—happens when a user attempts to translate a word/phrase from one language to another and that word/phrase does not exist in the database yet.
- **Pending translations**—shows the users all the words/phrases that have been requested and are still awaiting translations (Fig. 4).
- **Save new entry**—newly translated words/phrases are instantly saved to the database and made available for translation for the respective languages, giving contributor feedback of new entry.
- **Correct new word incorrect spelling**—when a translation result is returned and the contributor recognizes a misspelling in the translated word/phrase, there is an option of flagging it as such, and this will cause it to be reflected back on the system that it needs to be translated again.
- **Deleted (remove) word/phrase**—allows contributors to see all word/phrase translation requests which have been removed from the pending translation list, and have an option to restore and add them back into the pending translations list.

According to our testing and feedback sessions, we have learned that the prototype still requires further development to address issues which testers came across when they tested the prototype.

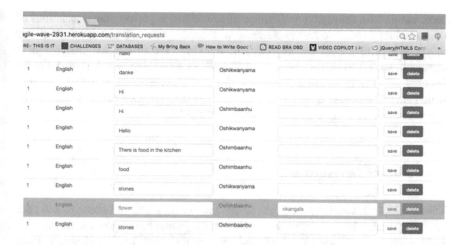

Fig. 4 Namibian Indigenous Languages (NIL) save new word

We are using software versioning to track the development of the NIL online dictionary application, which will help us log and attend to the feedback which the testers gave us.

4 Discussion

After completing our first prototype development and doing the testing, we have taken the note of all the response feedback and decided take time to analyze the feedback that we have received from the testers so that we can design the new version.

4.1 Current System's Statistics

Currently, the system contains a number of untranslated submissions. We have a 149 registered users on the system featuring 14 languages which have been added to the system. We have a total of 586 n-grams on our database added so far.

4.2 Expertise

The problem we had with the initial design thinking of the NIL online dictionary was that there was and there is still currently no guaranteed access to linguist expert contributors who are readily available and committed to perform the translations of the local languages. We had to continue with further research and development of the project with a different approach in thinking. We discovered that the new approach needed to modify what we had built to something which shared similar features of already existing platforms like stack exchange/stack overflow, etc., which are collaborative question and answer network platforms on the Internet. The experts in this case are the native speakers of the languages.

4.3 Future Development

The developments and contributions to this project are surely not going to end here or cease at all. The maintenance of ever growing code base upon which the core system implementations were built and performing optimal refactoring is the top priority on our list as we continue the development of this project. The implementation will expand and go in depth with the focus of representing and storing each local language as best as possible and creating a formal language data structure which can be maintained and optimized. Innovative approaches will be introduced to get more people on board contribute to the project, whether it is being a developer, linguistic expert, or native language speaker. In addition of words in respective languages, institutions who wish to contribute to this initiative as well too will be welcome. The focus of further implementations will be on the development of a mobile version, an API as well as the dictionary itself.

5 Conclusion

Namibian indigenous languages are still alive today and are being spoken. Even though there may not be any threat or danger of some languages becoming extinct, we felt that our research was not only going to focus on creating an online open-content dictionary for local languages to allow people from the different indigenous communities to collaborate and contribute, but rather also make provision for putting in place the necessary platform for preserving these very languages.

The development and evaluation of the system have shown that much redesigning, re-implementing, and restructuring of the collaborative open-content online dictionary for Namibian Indigenous Languages (NIL) are still necessary. A few challenges which have not been completely resolved or developed as anticipated, however, have led to other discoveries in ways of implementation and design of the local languages database.

In an extremely short period of time, namely 2 months, we have managed to develop and release numerous versions of the prototype and address different issues along the way to make sure that we presented a simple, intuitive, and usable prototype which conforms to most of the user's expectations.

The observation that we have made during this development are that in comparison to most development approaches in software projects which would require planning of how certain tasks will be executed, actually the opposite of eliminating planning or focusing too much on proved to have been more efficient and fruitful. Having a basic idea and design of a basic system in our case, the NIL system, doing a quick implementation and putting it in the wild allowed us to adapt to how the different observations simulated the system's usage and from that, we could then determine how to best adapt it to the users, by mapping response and user actions.

A major challenge remains to ensure a continuous usage of the online dictionary to guarantee the building of a comprehensive dataset.

Acknowledgements We thank Abrie Abrie for collaborating on the development of the prototype and for doing a review of the work as well, respectively. We are also thankful for all 54 participants who took part in the interview and testing sessions of the research project and for giving us feedback for the future development of this project.

References

1. Namibian Languages: Retrieved 18 June 2017, from http://biodiversity.org.na/NamLanguages.php (n.d.)
2. Legère, K., Trewby, R., Graan, M. van.: The implementation of the Namibian language policy in education: lower primary grades and pre-service teacher education. Retrieved from http://www.nied.edu.na/assets/documents/06Archive/01NationalCurriculumGuide/Po_Implementation LanguagePolicy_2000.pdf (2000)
3. Kamwanyah, N.J.: Mother tongues' days are numbered. Retrieved 20 Feb 2015, from http://www.namibian.com.na/index.php?id=133835&page=archive-read (2015)
4. Wiley, D., Dwyer, D.: African language instruction in the United States: directions and priorities for the 1980s. African Studies Centre, Michigan State University, Michigan (1980)
5. Sakti, S., Nakamura, S.: Towards language preservation: design and collection of graphemically balanced and parallel speech corpora of indonesian ethnic languages. In: Proceedings of the Oriental COCOSDA, Gurgaon, India (2005)
6. Zaman, T., Winschiers-Theophilus, H.: Penans' Oroo' short message signs (PO-SMS): co-design of a digital jungle sign language application. In: Proceedings of INTERACT, Germany, Sep 2015
7. González, M.I.: ViTu, a system to help the mexican people to preserve and celebrate their culture. Methodology 971–976 (2011). http://doi.org/10.1145/1979742.1979502
8. Gallert, P., Winschiers-Theophilus, H., Koch Kapuire, G., Stanley, C.: Clash of cultures, clash of values: Wikipedia and indigenous communities. In: van der Velden, M., Strano, M., Hrachvec, H., Abdelnour Nocera, J., Ess. C. (eds.) Culture, technology, communication: common worlds, different futures? In: Proceedings of the Tenth International Conference on Culture, Technology, Communication. London, UK, 15–17 June 2016, pp. 200–213 (2016)
9. Erdmann, M., Nakayama, K., Hara, T., Nishio, S.: Improving the extraction of bilingual terminology from Wikipedia. ACM Trans. Multimedia Comput. Commun. Appl. 5(4), 1–17 (2009). https://doi.org/10.1145/1596990.1596995

10. Ginsburg, J.: A Wikipedia-based Corpus Reference Tool, 1–7. In: Proceedings of the 2012 Joint International Conference on Human-Centered Computer Environments, ACM New York (2012)
11. Benjamin, M.: Lexicography without lexicographers: Crowdsourcing and the compilation of a multilingual dictionary. Retrieved from www.elexicography.eu/wp…/03/Benjamin_lexicography-without-lexicographers.pdf (2016)
12. Benjamin, M., Radetzky, P.: Small languages, big data: bilingual computational tools and techniques for the lexicography of endangered languages. In: Proceedings of the 2014 Workshop on the Use of Computational Methods in the Study of Endangered Languages, (pp. 15–23). Baltimore, Maryland, USA (2014)
13. Gorjanc, V., Gantar, P., Kosem, I., Krek, S. (eds.): Dictionary of modern {S}lovene: problems and solutions. Retrieved from http://www.ff.uni-lj.si/sites/default/files/Dokumenti/Knjige/e-books/dictionary_of_modern_slo.pdf (2017)
14. Zimmerman, J., Forlizzi, J., Evenson, S.: Research through design as a method for interaction design research in HCI. In: Proceedings of the SIGCHI Conference on Human Factors in Computing Systems, pp. 493–502 (2007)

Animal Tracking

Elisabeth Thielen, Alexander Kremer, Tobias Krüger, Bastian Hermann and Jürgen Sieck

1 Introduction

Tourism is an important economic activity for many countries in the world. For example, more than 1.3 million tourists visited Namibia in 2015 [1]. One of the country's most important attractions is the Etosha National Park. Etosha National Park is a 22.270 km^2 large wildlife sanctuary located in the north of Namibia, Southern Africa [2] and is home to 114 different mammals, which can be observed in their natural habitat [3]. Visitors can either explore the park on their own, if they bring a car with off-road capabilities, or can partake in a guided tour with a driver from the Etosha National Park staff.

Getting to see a specific animal requires a lot of luck in such a vast, open space, which is why every lodge inside the park has their own collective book of animal sightings, where visitors can inscribe their most interesting animal sightings with their location, date and time or browse through previous sightings made by other visitors.

E. Thielen (✉) · A. Kremer · T. Krüger · B. Hermann · J. Sieck
Hochschule für Technik und Wirtschaft (HTW Berlin),
Wilhelminenhofstr. 75A, Berlin, Germany
e-mail: elisabeth.thielen@student.htw-berlin.de

A. Kremer
e-mail: alexander.kremer@student.htw-berlin.de

T. Krüger
e-mail: tobias.krueger@student.htw-berlin.de

B. Hermann
e-mail: bastian.hermann@student.htw-berlin.de

J. Sieck
Namibia University of Science and Technology (NUST), 13 Storch Street,
Windhoek, Namibia
e-mail: j.sieck@htw-berlin.de

© Springer Nature Singapore Pte Ltd. 2018
D. S. Jat et al. (eds.), *Digitisation of Culture: Namibian and International Perspectives*, https://doi.org/10.1007/978-981-10-7697-8_9

Unfortunately, those books' information is often outdated since sightings are mostly inscribed long after the sighting was made. Additionally, the different books in the different lodges contain different information, since visitors only report their sightings in one of the lodges as opposed to all of them. This makes it difficult to search for specific sightings and also aggravates the creation of informative statistics.

The idea was thus to create an animal tracking application giving a user the possibility to use their smartphone in order to upload a sighting with its corresponding geolocation data to a server and to quickly access other people's sightings.

Animal tracking has been done for far longer than technology is around. Since the beginnings of mankind, animal tracking was used when hunting for food. When looking at African countries and especially Namibia, there are still tribes that to this day have remarkable skills when it comes to animal tracking.

One of those is the native Namibian tribe of the San [4] who have expert knowledge when looking for 'spoors', a term used to describe animal tracks. Experienced trackers can utilise 'ground spoor, vegetation spoor, scent, feeding signs, urine, faeces, saliva, pellets, territorial signs, paths and shelters, vocal and other auditory signs, visual signs, incidental signs, circumstantial signs and skeletal signs' [5] in order to track down animals. During a study with four San hunters, they demonstrated their incredible knowledge and were able to correctly identify the animal species from a spoor in 147 cases [6]. In most of the cases, they were also able to identify the sex, age and if the animals were individuals.

The San traditionally use bow and arrow when hunting for animals. First, they have to try to find animals spoors, track down the animal, shoot it with a poisonous arrow and then follow the animal until the poison takes effect.

However, acquiring such a complex skill takes many years of learning and immense knowledge of the animals and nature. While expert hunters may recognise spoors immediately, unknowing tourists might completely overlook them [5].

In National Parks like Etosha, tourists have the possibility to book tours with expert guides who are still able to interpret spoors in order to find animals. But many tourists also use the opportunity to discover the park on their own in their private cars and could greatly benefit from an application that uses crowdsourcing in order to record and share sightings of interesting animals.

Even the approach of leaving information for others is not a modern concept, the nomadic Penans in Malaysian Borneo use Oroo', an incredibly complex forest sign language, in order to leave messages for others [7]. The Penans use combinations of twigs and leaves in order construct messages, leave them in the forest and other Penans coming upon them know how to interpret the messages.

The goal of our project is similar: to enable people to use their smartphone to record animal sightings and give them the possibility to make this information available to other visitors coming after them.

2 State of the Art

Digital animal tracking and habitat monitoring have been explored during many studies. Many of them make use of wireless sensor networks (WSN). Two approaches have proven to be successful in the past:

- Tracking devices (often in the form of collars) attached to animals (or other mobile entities for that matter), that periodically send data to a base station;
- Radio frequency identification (RFID) tags attached to animals and RFID readers setup in strategic locations. Every time an animal with an RFID tag passes the reader, data is received and recorded.

The tracking device approach has been effectively used with zebras [8] and deer [9], while the RFID solution provided good result in tests with ducks [10] and badgers [11].

However, this wireless sensor network approach was not feasible for our project in Etosha National Park. The above-mentioned approaches do well in, for example, scientific studies, with a smaller number of animals (<100) needing to be tracked. While this could be used to track a specific species or group of animals—maybe endangered ones in order to ensure their well-being—it could not be used to track all of the animals tourists might be interested in.

Because of that, the decision was made to use a crowdsourcing approach, as was basically used before with the sighting books at the lodges. This analogue version should be improved using modern technology. Instead of using books to log sightings, the sightings should be recorded with a smartphone and then shared with other users via Internet.

Big advantages of this strategy are that no hardware needs to be deployed in the park, which might distress animals and would probably not be permitted by the park authorities anyway, and that a smartphone can be used as the recording device. This means that no additional hardware needs to be handed out to visitors, as nowadays most people always have their own device with them.

The idea for a crowdsourcing animal sightings app is not completely new. A similar application already exists for African animals named 'Africa: Live' [12]. This application shows a map (Fig. 1, left image), onto which users can tap in order to add sightings. The user is taken to a new view where details of the sighting (which species, their activity, etc.) can be entered (Fig. 1, middle image). The application also features an offline mode, which is, however, hidden behind a paywall (Fig. 1, right image). The coordinates of a sighting are determined by where the user taps on the map. Unfortunately, this is a very inaccurate way to determine the location of a sighting. A better approach would be to use GPS coordinates for the localisation.

The 'Africa: Live' application features a wide variety of species as well as the option to report suspicious activities (such as poaching). The collection of sightings of some endangered species is allowed, but they will not show on the map publicly.

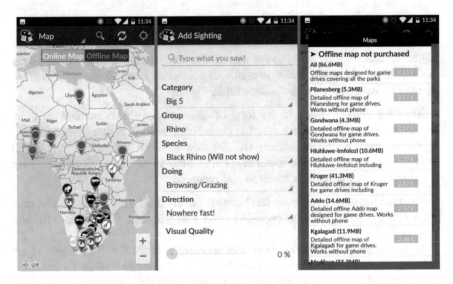

Fig. 1 Multiple screenshots of the 'Africa: Live' application

This application works well for African animals but does not allow the creation of sightings from other regions of the world. It would, therefore, be interesting to create an application that could be easily adapted to allow sightings of animal species from all over the world.

3 Requirements and Limitations

Before the start of the project, it was planned to create a client-server application with three different types of clients. The first two were meant to be native mobile applications, the third a webpage. At the very start, the general requirements and limitations had to be discussed and the project goals adjusted accordingly.

3.1 Internet Connection

One big limitation arose during the development: the poor network coverage in national parks such as the Etosha National Park. There are signal masts placed at the gates and lodges but they are not enough to cover the entire park. Internet access is available within a radius of 10–15 km of the lodges and gates but elsewhere smartphones mostly lack reception.

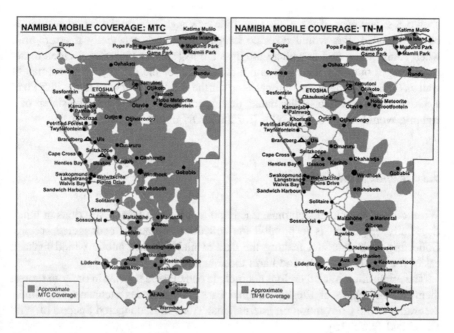

Fig. 2 Mobile network coverage of the two main mobile network providers in Namibia (Etosha National Park is outlined in blue) [13]

Figure 2 depicts the mobile network coverage in Namibia provided by MTC (Fig. 2, left side) and Telecom Namibia (Fig. 2, right side). Etosha National Park (outlined in blue) is not covered completely by the providers.

There are five lodges and four gates in Etosha National Park that each has their own signal mast providing network coverage. Since Etosha is roughly 22.275 km^2 in size and the masts only cover between 2.200 and 4.900 km^2 (using 10 and 15 km for the radius of the masts' reach), this leaves 78–90% of Etosha without network coverage.

This meant that the application needed an offline mode that stores the sighting data in a local database on the smartphone during times when the phone has no network access.

The network problem finalised the decision to only implement native mobile applications rather than a webpage. With Android and iOS running on over 90% of mobiles and tablets [14], it was decided to develop the application for those two operating systems.

At the beginning of the project, it was planned to take a photo of a sighting and store it on the server together with the sighting's location, timestamp and other information. However, because of the limited network access, this idea was dismissed. Uploading and downloading the image would take too much time. According to nurdology.com [15], uploading even a 320 × 240 pixel image would take 16 s using EDGE. Downloading the same picture from the server would only need 5.3 s; however, if there were multiple new sightings on the server waiting to be downloaded, this would take too long to download, especially if errors arise when connectivity and download progress are lost. It was therefore decided to not store images but only the name and a description of the activity of an animal, as well as GPS coordinates and a timestamp for the sighting. Opposed to the 225 kb of a 320×240 pixel image, the name, description, coordinates and timestamp of a sighting would only be 120 Bytes (for the JSON object see Sect. 4.3).

3.2 Legal Restrictions

When collecting animal sightings, it is important to keep legal restrictions in mind. Especially, important is to prohibit the collection of data of endangered species. Collecting their data and making the data available to the public would make it easier for poachers to find and harm those animals.

The application must therefore not include endangered species in order to protect them. In the region of Etosha National Park, this includes elephants and rhinos according to the Convention on International Trade in Endangered Species of Wild Fauna and Flora [16].

It would be a possibility to allow sightings of endangered species without distributing them to other users. This would mean that statistics of the data on the server could include those endangered species without having to fear poachers, since the data could never be requested from the server. However, to ensure the safety of the data on the server it would have to be encrypted.

4 Architecture

4.1 General Overview

The architecture of the application consists of multiple components. Figure 3 shows an overview of the architecture.

Sightings can be created using an Android or iOS client. The smartphone determines the current GPS location, the time and date and the user adds additional information about the sighting, e.g. which animal was seen and what the animal was doing at the time. The sighting data is then stored in the local SQLite database on the phone. Table 1 shows two sample sightings.

If the phone has access to the Internet, it can communicate with the server. The server's database and the local phone database are synchronised; new sightings made by the user are sent to the server and other users' sightings are received from the server.

Sighting data is stored in a MySQL database on the server.

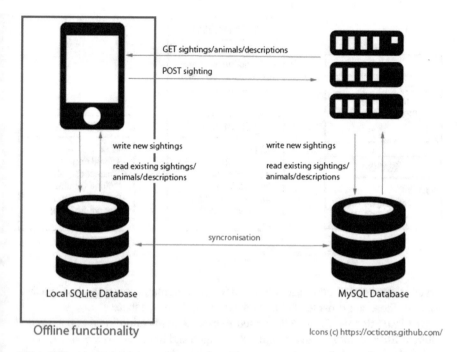

Fig. 3 The basic client-server architecture of the application

Table 1 Sample sightings

Animal	Description	Latitude	Longitude	Timestamp
Giraffe	Eating	−18.8277	16.9510	2016-04-29 06:31:17
Zebra	Running	−18.9020	16.9765	2016-04-29 06:39:59

4.2 Offline Mode

An important feature of the application is the possibility to use it offline, when no network access is given at a location. In order to achieve this, the application checks for connectivity as soon as the application is started. If the application has access to the Internet, the local SQLite and remote server databases are synchronised.

If a sighting is added in offline mode—without a connection—then it is saved in the local database. The SQLite database has, amongst others for all the animal types and descriptions, two tables containing sightings: One with all the sightings from the server and one, where only the sightings made offline and awaiting upload are stored (Fig. 4).

Whenever the main screen is accessed, the app tries to synchronise with the server. If the phone has access to the Internet, the not yet uploaded sightings are sent to the server and deleted from the upload queue. Afterwards, a request to the

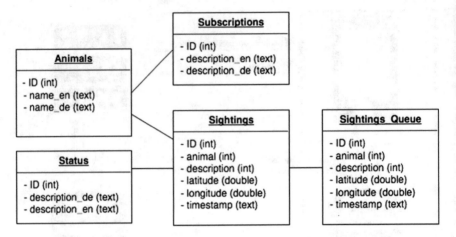

Fig. 4 The local SQLite database tables

server is sent, and if other users have added new sightings since the last synchronisation, those are downloaded and added to the local database.

One issue that needs to be addressed in case of publication in an app store is if different users should be able to upload the same sighting. Due to the vast space of the Etosha National Park, single spots are not usually crowded with many tourists, but it could occur that multiple visitors spot the same animal and try to upload a sighting of it. It would of course verify the sighting, but would also crowd the database unnecessarily. It would therefore be mandatory to detect multiple sightings at the same time from the same area and add only one of them to the database.

4.3 JSON Data Format

For the communication between the client and server, the JavaScript Object Notation (JSON) was used. The following lines show an example of a sighting in JSON format.

Example of a Sighting in JSON format

```
{"id": 0,
"name": 1,
"description": 2,
"latitude": -18.8277,
"longitude": 16.9510,
"timestamp": "2016-04-29 06:31:17"}
```

Sightings have an ID, a keyword describing the animal, a description of what the animal was doing (sleeping, hunting, running, etc.) as well as a latitude, longitude and timestamp. Name and description are foreign keys pointing to entries in the name and description tables in the server database.

Timestamps in database are often generated on the server as opposed to on the client. However, in our application, this would result in saving the moment the data has been uploaded to the server rather than the moment the sighting has actually been made. Since the desired timestamp is the one of the sighting, the timestamp has to be created on the client and sent in the JSON object.

5   Implementation and Demonstration

The final implementation consists of two native mobile applications and a remote server. The Android client is written in Java and the iOS client was developed using Swift. The server uses nginx and offers a REST API written in PHP.

5.1   Client

Figure 5 shows screenshots of the finished Android client. Their functionality is going to be described in the following paragraphs.

A.   *Starting the app*

The start screen of course shows the user all the possible functionalities of the app, in this case the four modes (Fig. 5, left image). The menu is accessible from every

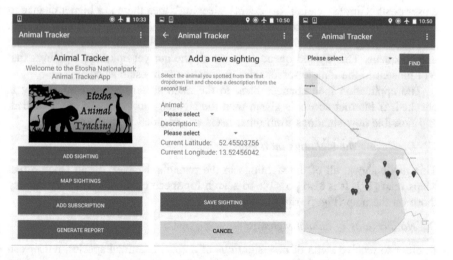

Fig. 5 Screenshots of the android application, main activity (left image), 'Add a new sighting' activity (middle image) and 'Show sightings on map' activity (right image)

screen and contains a short tutorial for every screen, information about developers and licenses, a button to change the application's language and a short notice about the exclusion of endangered species in the app.

On first access of the start screen, which marks the app start, the application checks for the required permissions (GPS and writing to external storage) and requests these from the user in case they are not given. The application also checks for network connectivity and syncs the SQLite database with the server database if it is reachable.

The local database is empty when the application is used for the first time after the installation and has to be filled with data from the server.

B. *Adding a sighting*

One of the most important functionalities of the app is the creation of a new sighting (Fig. 5, middle image). The application retrieves the user's current coordinates via a GPS manager; the user chooses an animal from a drop-down list as well as a short description of the animal's current activity from another list (e.g. 'Eating', 'Sleeping' and 'Herd 15+').

Upon clicking 'Save Sighting', an empty sighting instance and a current timestamp are created. Afterwards, the application checks if the user selected an animal as well as a description. If this is not the case, then nothing further happens and a toast is triggered, making the user aware of the missing inputs. If both have been selected, then their values and the current latitude, longitude and timestamp are added to the empty sighting instance.

It was decided to record both the species and the activity of an animal in order to give a user more information in order to decide if he could still be able to see this animal. If a user just uploaded a sighting of a 'Lion' 'running', then another user arriving after the original poster will probably not get to see the animal. However, if a user posts 'Giraffe' 'eating' or 'Zebra' 'sleeping', then there is a higher chance to still get to see this animal for users arriving after the sighting was originally created.

The sighting is then added to the general local SQLite database, as well as an upload queue. This upload queue contains all the not yet uploaded sightings that will be sent to the remote server once connection is re-established.

The application then changes back to the main screen, where connectivity is checked. If Internet access is given, then the sightings in the queue are uploaded, and possible new sightings from other users downloaded from the server.

C. *Displaying the sightings on a map*

This mode shows all of the sightings in the phone's database on an Open Street Maps map [17]. It is also possible to search for specific animals and only display those on the map (Fig. 5, right image).

D. *Notifications of animal sightings*

In order to receive alerts of new sightings of a specific animal species, a user can subscribe to an animal and get a push notification each time a new sighting of the subscribed animal is posted to the server (Fig. 6, left image). A subscription can be

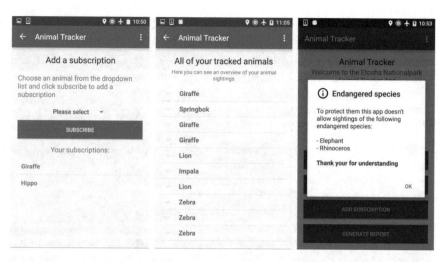

Fig. 6 Second set of screenshots of the android application, add subscription activity (left image), create report activity (middle image) and the menu item addressing endangered species (right image)

added by selecting a type of animal from the dropdown and then clicking 'subscribe'. However, this is still a theoretical feature. While it is possible to add and display the subscriptions on this page, the actual push notifications and messages from the server have yet to be implemented.

E. *Creating a report*

This shows an overview of all of the user's own sightings and enables the user to trace their own route through the sightings' GPS coordinates (Fig. 6, middle image). The overview shows all the animals seen in chronological order. On clicking on a list item, the GPS position and time the animal was seen at as well as the entered activity of the animal are being displayed.

Figure 6 (right image) shows the menu popup information for the endangered species.

Figure 7 shows the iOS client's UI. This UI differs from the Android one as both applications used the native UI components of their operating systems, giving the Android application the typical Android look and the iOS one the typical iOS look, respectively.

5.2 Server

The server handles requests from the clients. Sighting data is being collected by the client and then sent to the server via an HTTP request in JSON format. The server API can be accessed via endpoints. Each endpoint is a uniform resource locator

Fig. 7 Screenshots of the main screen (left image), show on map (middle image) and subscription feature (right image) of the iOS client

(URL), which is accessed with an HTTP verb. Valid HTTP verbs are, for example, POST, GET, PUT, PATCH and DELETE. The following endpoints are available:

GET/animals/Returns a list of available animals, e.g. lion.
GET/descriptions/Returns a list of available descriptions of animals, e.g. eating.
GET/sightings/Returns a list of sightings of the last 10 days.
POST/sightings/Accepts and saves a sighting.

The POST/sightings endpoint accepts a JSON object in the form of the JSON sighting example in Sect. 4.3.

The sightings are stored on the server in a MySQL database. This database currently has three important tables: animals—which lists all possible trackable animals, status—which lists all possible animal descriptions and sightings—which contains all the sightings ever sent to the server (see Fig. 4).

The server only returns the last 10 days worth of sightings whenever a client requests sightings. While older animal sightings from the last season or even year could possibly function as statistical data, they would only crowd the sightings map without being actually helpful for the task of finding animals.

Useful statistics might include where certain species are seen most often, if their movements follow specific patterns or if their behaviour differs from season to season, etc.

6   Field Tests of the Application

The implementation was tested during two game drives in Etosha National Park in Namibia. One of the test drives was done at the very beginning of the week before the implementation process had started and the second one at the end of the week in order to test the implementation.

The first game drive served multiple purposes. Most importantly, the students could actively experience and understand the use case of their future application. Additionally, the availability of mobile network access was documented throughout the drive. The results of this test undermined the importance to create an offline solution for the application (see Sect. 3.1).

Another task during this game drive was to collect valid sightings data that could function as test data in the database during the implementation phase of the project.

The process used to collect the test data was to take pictures of sightings and then extract GPS coordinates and the timestamp from the metadata of those images after the drive.

The second game drive was done after the implementation phase on the last day of the coding week. This drive was used to test the application that had so far been developed. After only few days of development not all of the features were fully implemented. However, the core features of creating a sighting, storing it in the local database and displaying them on the map were working.

Both times the drives started and ended at the eastern *Von Lindequist Gate* and had roughly the same route. It lead from the *Von Lindequist Gate* to *Fort Namutoni* and from there along the rim of the *Etosha pan* towards *Halali* and then back to the *Von Lindequist Gate*.

The following describes the results of the testing of the application's previously described core features during the second game drive.

Sightings could be created with correct GPS location, timestamp, animal name and description, added to the local SQLite database and shown on the map.

While most of the sightings were collected correctly, two of the sightings were missing GPS coordinates. It appears that the respective smartphones were unable to retrieve test data at that moment. To prevent such faulty sightings from entering the database, a check for valid GPS data was implemented after this game drive.

Due to the short development time of only 4 days, the applications were only running locally on the Android and iOS test devices, but were not yet connected to a server. The connection to the server had to be implemented after the game drive.

Nevertheless, the server was tested in Berlin after the end of the coding week and no issues were experienced with getting animals, status or complete sightings and new sightings were correctly posted to the server database.

7   Result

The goal of the project was to create an application that would allow users to create and share animal sightings as well as retrieve other users' sightings in the Etosha National Park. The project has been implemented for both Android and iOS devices and has been connected to a server and works both online and offline. All the components of our system have been tested and showed positive results. The application can be used with minimal setup—it is only necessary to instal the application on the smartphone—and without the distribution of additional hardware in the park, which might distress animals.

The project can therefore be seen as successful.

We had the possibility to discuss our application with the owner of a private game farm just outside Windhoek. While the reaction to the application was overall positive, he mentioned concerns about the possibility of poaching, if endangered species could be tracked with our application. He was pleased to hear that our application does not allow the tracking of those animals.

8   Future Work

The project resulted in a solid prototype of an animal tracking application that can be used both on and offline in the Etosha National Park. While this prototype provides a user with basic functionality, there exist multiple ideas in order to extend this prototype in the future.

For one, it would be possible to connect the application to an animal recognition tool. Instead of choosing the type of animal from a list, the user could take a photo of the animal and the correct type would be identified by the application itself. This could prevent faulty statistics due to wrong identification of an animal by the user.

While a tourist could of course distinguish a lion from a giraffe and add those sightings correctly, it might be more difficult to identify different species of antelopes. So while a user might not even want to add a false sighting, faulty sightings could still find their way into the database. Of course, crowdsourcing also gives users the possibility to intentionally add false sightings.

Image recognition could be a very good approach to solve this problem, while other mechanisms such as moderators cannot be used, as moderators would have to be at the site of a sighting at the same time as the user in order to be able to verify a sighting.

However, it might not be easy to implement image recognition in this context. Often, when seeing animals in the wild, it is only from afar. This means that one might not be able to get a clear picture of the animal, making animal recognition harder.

Additionally, the problem of limited network access would remerge. For the image recognition to work offline, information about all the detectable animals such as comparative images would have to be downloaded in advance and stored on the phone locally.

At the moment, the server only contains animal species specific to Namibia and the Etosha National Park. The different types of animals that can be used in the application are retrieved from the server and not hardcoded in the app. This means that the available types of animals could be easily adapted to the part of the world the user is currently in. Different packages of animals could be created for different regions of the world (e.g. animals such as lions, elephants, springboks, etc. for Namibia, bison, cougars, moose, etc. for Canada, kangaroos and koala bears, etc. for Australia and tigers, water buffalos, etc. for Asia). The server would then hand out the packages corresponding to the user's GPS location.

Along with this, the application should also be internationalised. So far, the application features only two languages, English and German.

Another future task would be the implementation of the still theoretical feature of receiving push notifications for 'subscribed' animals, as mentioned in Sect. 5.1.

Finally, the overall users' captured data could serve as an imperative input in animal studies and wildlife statistics on various topics such as animal movements in different seasons.

In case of publication of the application in an app store, it would also be necessary to enter a dialogue with the National Parks as to how they could benefit from such an app without having to fear that their rangers and guides might become obsolete. Those rangers of course can offer a lot of more in-depth knowledge to tourists than an application like Amtrack ever will. The application should therefore rather function as an addition to those rangers instead of exchanging them.

References

1. Ministry of Environment and Tourism, Namibia: Tourist statistical report (2015)
2. General Information on a Etosha National Park Website. http://etoshanationalpark.co.za
3. Information on the Wildlife on a Etosha National Park Website. http://www.etoshanational park.org/wildlife
4. Lee, R., Hitchock, R.: African hunter-gatherers: survival, history, and the politics of identity. Afr. Study Monogr. Suppl. **26**, 257–280 (2001)
5. Liebenberg, L.: A Field Guide to the Animal Tracks of Southern Africa. David Philip Publishers, Claremont (1990)
6. Stander, P.E., Ghau, I.I., Tsisaba, D., Oma, I.I.: Tracking and the interpretation of spoor: a scientifically sound method in ecology. J. Zool. Lond. **242**, 329–341(1997)
7. Zaman, T., Winschiers-Theophilus, H., Yeo, A.W., Ting, L.C., Jengan, G.: Reviving an indigenous rainforest sign language: digital Oroo' adventure game, ICTD'15 Article 69 (2015)
8. Juang, P., Oki, H., Wang, Y., Martonosi, M., Peh, L.-S., Rubenstein, D.: Energy-efficient computing for wildlife tracking: design trade-offs and early experiences with ZebraNet, ASPLOS X, pp. 96–107 (2002)
9. Jain, V., Bagree, R., Kumar, A., Ranjan, P.: WildCENSE: GPS based animal tracking system, ISSNIP (2008)

10. Mainwaring A., Culler D., Polastre J., Szewczyk R., Anderson J.: Wireless sensor networks for habitat monitoring. WSNA'02, pp. 88–97 (2002)
11. Dyo, V., Ellwood, S.A., Macdonald, D.W., Markham, A., Mascolo, C., Pásztor, B., Scellato, S., Trigoni, N., Wohlers, R., Yousef, K.: Evolution and sustainability of a wildlife monitoring sensor network. In: SenSys'10, pp. 127–140 (2010)
12. Africa Wild Live Website. http://www.wildafricalive.com/
13. Network Coverage of the Two Main Mobile Network Providers in Namibia. http://www.tourbrief.com/cms/index.php?option=com_content&task=view&id=919
14. Market Shares of Different Mobile/Tablet Operating Systems in 2016. https://www.netmarketshare.com/operating-system-market-share.aspx?qprid=8&qpcustomd=1&qpsp=2016&qpnp=1&qptimeframe=Y
15. Comparison of Upload and Download Speeds for Different Image Sizes. http://nurdology.com/2012/08/20/upload-speeds-of-3g-4g-lte-and-hspa/
16. Convention on International Trade in Endangered Species of Wild Fauna and Flora. https://www.cites.org
17. OpenStreet Maps, Open Source, Free Card Material. http://www.openstreetmap.org

Automated Animal Recognition Platform

Bastian Hermann and Jürgen Sieck

1 Introduction

Let us assume that you like to travel and are a naturalist. If possible, you love to observe animals in their natural habitat. You are neither an expert nor a professional biologist but you like this for hobby purposes. We were in this situation in May 2016 when we stayed for a project in Namibia for 1 week. At that time, we explored the Etosha National Park on our own for several times. That was our first time in Namibia and the first time that we were able to observe African animals in their natural habitat. Therefore, it was not easy for us to determine the different animal species. The manual classification of animals is usually a difficult task for inexperienced observers. While the differences of well-known animal species like elephants and lions are clearly recognisable, this task is more difficult, for example for the different antelope species. If the observer is not able to determine the photographed animal by himself, he needs some kind of external help. Currently, there exist several mostly impracticable and outdated possibilities. For example books and websites which show an image and a description for each species sorted in top-level groups like mammals and insects. In the best-case scenario, the service provides a decision tree to enclose a small group of possible animals with some concatenated questions. The disadvantage of these approaches is that all users have to invest a lot of time to get a result.

B. Hermann (✉) · J. Sieck
Hochschule für Technik und Wirtschaft (HTW Berlin),
Wilhelminenhofstr. 75A, Berlin, Germany
e-mail: bastian.hermann@gmail.de

J. Sieck
Namibia University of Science and Technology (NUST), 13 Storch Street,
Windhoek, Namibia
e-mail: j.sieck@htw-berlin.de

© Springer Nature Singapore Pte Ltd. 2018
D. S. Jat et al. (eds.), *Digitisation of Culture: Namibian and International Perspectives*, https://doi.org/10.1007/978-981-10-7697-8_10

This paper describes a new approach to determine animal species based on pattern and colour recognition. The prediction result of the pattern recognition will be cross-validated by colour recognition, so that a success of the cross-validation results in a high probability, that the returned proposal is correct. A failure on the other hand signals missing uniqueness of the animal in the picture, which leads to more recommendations for the user. Additionally, the user is able to choose the correct recommendation out of the provided pictures and send this feedback back to the service, which will improve the prediction in the future. The recognition component can be accessed by the user through a web application, which also contains a location-based pre-processing for an improved recognition performance.

2   State of the Art

At present, the computer-assisted animal recognition is little studied. The major part of the published paper of the broad field automated recognition is focused on objects, buildings, and faces. Nevertheless, there exist two papers which deal with the specific topic 'species recognition' and are related to this work. The first one 'Automated identification of animal species in camera trap images' by Yu et al. [1] is based on a combination of the scale-invariant feature transform algorithm and the cell-structured local binary pattern classified by a linear support vector machine. They tested this method with a database containing over 7000 camera trap images of 18 species and achieved an average classification accuracy of 82%. This result confirms that SIFT and local binary pattern are valid techniques for an automated animal recognition system in real and complex scenarios [1].

The second paper by Spampinato et al. deals with the automatic fish classification for underwater species [2]. They also combine two well-known algorithms for feature extraction to achieve a better accuracy compared to a single usage of one of them. At first, texture features are extracted by using statistical moments from the grey-level histogram like mean, standard deviation, correlation and more. Additionally, a Gabor filter which is generally used for edge detection is also used for the texture feature extraction. Finally, a gray-level co-occurrence matrix (GLCM) is used to characterise the texture of an image by analysing pairs of pixel with specific values and specific relationships occur in an image. The results of a GLCM are statistical indicators like energy, correlation, entropy and more [2, 3]. All the information of the above-named methods will be used for a feature vector which describes the texture of the image. The second type of features is based on the shape of the fish which are extracted by using the Curvature Scale Space transform and the histogram of Fourier descriptors of already dissolved boundaries. The resulting completed feature vector consists of 120 components which will be reduced by the principal component analysis to 24 features. They tested this system on a database with 360 images of 10 different species and achieved an average correct rate of about 92% [2].

2.1 Differences to Our Work

The main difference between the two above-mentioned paper and our work is the field of application. While these papers are focused on automated processing and labelling of a high data volume input to assist professional biologist, for example with preliminary sorting, our application is designed to assist non-professionals to determine the species of photographed animals. In general, we can say that the first case is construed to achieve the highest classification accuracy, but in the second case, we have to take care of non-professionals' user needs. Therefore, we decided to design a cross-validated method which is able to achieve a high classification accuracy most of the times, but also be able to detect non-unique input data to return more than one result to the user.

For the automatic fish classification, Spampinato et al. were able to use video input data to track the fish over consecutive frames by using the Adaptive Mean Shift Algorithm [2]. In contrast, in our work, the result depends on a single photograph the user submits. The method has to be robust toward typical problems like changing background, different illumination, complex pose of the animals, and more which could be softened by analysing many video frames instead of one picture.

Finally, our method will extract and analyse colour features of the photographed animals which is excluded in both the papers but mentioned by Spampinato et al. in their future work.

2.2 Similarities to Our Work

All papers have in common that they have to extract features from pictures or video frames. This extraction is based on specific characteristics, which are close to the human perception. Yu et al. are using the local binary pattern algorithm to extract pattern features and Spampinato et al. are using statistical methods for texture feature extraction. Due to the good results of pattern recognition related to animals, our method will use the local binary pattern algorithm too. Additionally, we combine the pattern recognition with another natural distinctive feature: The colours of the animals. This so far ignored differentiator will be responsible for an approval or rejection in our cross-validation method.

3 Technical Basis

3.1 General Requirements

As already mentioned in the previous chapter, this application has to take care the application's context. Due to the fact that this service is oriented for non-professional users, the target position is not to provide a single proposal of a species for each time. The service has to be able to detect non-unique or difficult input images and return more than one proposal if necessary.

These are the following requirements for unknown input images:

- The animal shall fill most of the picture.
- The animal shall be photographed from the side, whereby the direction is not important.
- The size of the image shall be 500 × 500 pixels. Pictures with other sizes will be scaled and cropped if necessary.

We prepared a testing database which matches these requirements. For the first phase and for the proof of concept, this database contains the following six different animal species:

- Elephant
- Giraffe
- Lion
- Zebra
- Kudu
- Springbok

The database contains 15 images for each class. We varied the number of training images, starting at two and ending at 14, for the testing results at the end of this paper.

The returned output of this service is a species proposal based on the calculated results. To assist the user to decide whether the proposal is correct or false, every proposal will be displayed with an image of the specific species.

3.2 Pattern Recognition with Local Binary Pattern

The idea of extracting texture features for pattern recognition is motivated on two facts: First of all, other papers achieved good results with this approach and especially with the local binary pattern algorithm. Second, our approach is based on extracting natural distinctive features, which contain differentiators like shapes, colours and also textures. Using the local binary pattern for our work will cover the pattern part in our concept. The idea behind taking this method is that the composition of micro-patterns of an animal can be described very well by such an operator. The high performance of this algorithm in the field of texture description, an invariance to monotonic grey changes and a computational efficiency could be proved by Ojala, Pietikâinen and Harwood in a comparative study of texture measures with classification [4].

The basic version of the local binary pattern histograms was designed for texture description and the basic idea is to summarise the local structure of a greyscale image by comparing each pixel with its eight neighbours. If the intensity of the

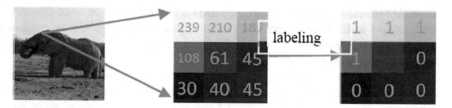

Fig. 1 Operation step of the local binary pattern algorithm

neighbour pixel is greater or equal, it will be labelled with a 1 and 0 if not. You can see an example of this process for one centre pixel in Fig. 1. The result is an 8-digit binary number like 10000111 (started at the upper right corner of the example in Fig. 1 and continued in the clockwise direction), which will be merged with all other pixels of the image in a histogram. Based on this textual description, a formal description of the local binary pattern operator can be given as

$$\text{LBP}(x_c, y_c) = \sum_{\{n=0\}}^{\{N-1\}} 2^n s(i_n - i_c). \tag{1}$$

The 8-digit binary for a pixel is calculated as the sum of each neighbour's (N: number of neighbours) result of the s-function, which returns 1 if the intensity is higher than the central pixel and 0 if not. Additionally, the result of the s-function is multiplied with 2^n, to switch the affected digit in the binary representation for each neighbour. Therefore, a maximum of 2^n different results are possible for a pixel.

Due to the fact that the operator cannot handle the same textures at different scales, the algorithm was extended to use a variable neighbourhood [5]. The local neighbourhood is defined as a set of sampling points placed on a circle around the centre pixel. The radius of the circle around the central pixel, which defines the neighbourhood, is variable to cover different scales of a pattern to be able to recognise animals with diverse sizes or photographed on various distances. If a sampling point does not fall in the centre of a pixel, bilinear interpolation can be used to determine this point, but also any other interpolation algorithm can be used [6]. Following Ahonen et al., the last step is to divide the image into a variable number of regions, where each region produces a histogram [5]. The feature vector consists of the concatenated histograms, which can be classified by a support vector machine.

3.3 Colour Recognition

The second part of our approach is the extraction of colour features to cross-validate the pattern recognition. The program flow of this part contains several individual steps. At first, the image will be converted to a suitable colour space, since OpenCV loads images as RGB by default. Afterwards, a part of the image will be cropped out and the average colour calculated. Finally, the Euclidean distance between the unknown input image and the trained classes will be determined.

The existing and suitable colour models can be categorised into two major classes. Technical and physical models which create colours from real or idealised substances. RGB and CMYK are typical and well-known representatives of this class. It is important to record the following limitations of the most popular colour space RGB according to Sarifuddin et al. [7]:

- The presence of a negative part in the spectra, which does not allow a representation of colours by overlapping the spectra.
- Difficult to determine colour features like the presence or absence of specific colours.
- Inability of the Euclidean distance to capture colour differences.

The second major class contains models which are designed to be human perceptual oriented. Colours are described by natural features like hue, saturation and brightness. For example, HSV and Lab are part of this major class. The first criterion hue refers to the pure spectrum colours corresponding to the dominant colour as perceived by humans. Compared to the RGB colour space, HSV models are able to recognise the presence or absence of colours in given set of colours [7]. Therefore, this paper focuses on the HSV, Lab and RGB colour space to achieve comparable results.

The second processing step crops out a tile of the given previously converted images and calculate the mean colour. This paper will compare different tile sizes starting from 1×1 pixels over 20×20 pixels to the whole image. Due to the fact that we do not know the shape of the animal in the given picture, we have to set a fixed cropping position for the 1×1 and 20×20 pixel extraction, which is the centre of the image. A smaller tile size increases the probability to only include pixels from the animal in the picture but, as a disadvantage, it is possible to fully hit the background. On the other hand, a bigger tile size increases the probability to include pixels belonging to the background as a side effect. The influence of different tile sizes will be tested and discussed in Chap. 4: 'Tests and Results'.

The last step is the calculation of the distance of the given unknown picture and the already trained images. There exist many possibilities to measure distances based on the existing colour models. The Euclidean distance, for example is frequently used for cubic representation spaces such as RGB and Lab but occasionally in cylindrical spaces like HSV too [7]. To achieve a comparable result, we use the Euclidean distance for all colour spaces, however future work could focus on different distance measurement methods to improve the colour recognition part.

3.4 Processing User Feedback

In a previous paper, we have shown that the results of the local binary pattern histograms can be improved by a higher number of training images [8]. We tested the local binary pattern histograms with the standard face database AT&T and varied the number of training images. The AT&T database contains 10 images for each of the 40 persons so that we were able to start with 1 training image and increment by 1 until 9 images [9]. The achieved correct rate starts at 65% at 1 training image, increases to 87% at 3 images and reaches the maximum at 9 images at 95%. These results show that the correct rate can be increased by a higher number of training images, however they also show that the rate is already on a very high level at 9 images of the AT&T database. But we have to record some major differences between images of the AT&T database and animal pictures provided by users as you can see in Table 1.

Based on the comparison of the different application contexts, we expect that the recognition of user-provided images of animals is harder to perform. Therefore, the global maximum of the recognition rate can be reached only if the number of training images is very high. That is the reason why our concept includes an additional processing step after the visualisation of the result. The user is able to return a feedback to the software whether the given proposal was correct or wrong. If the proposal was correct, the new image will be integrated into the training source. Otherwise, the user will get a new proposal and he is able to choose again.

3.5 Program Flow

The program flow of the animal recognition service, as you can see in Fig. 2, can be described as an endless loop. After the start of the service, the pattern recognition model and the colour recognition model will be trained. The services than stay in an idle mode until an incoming request wakes up the program. The incoming image will be processed as mentioned before and based on the pattern recognition an

Table 1 AT&T images compared to animal images

AT&T	Animal images
Contains 400 images of human faces. This standard database is known as one of the easier databases	In this paper, we will work on animal images provided by users which include the typical difficulties
All images were taken against a homogeneous background	The background is changing
Faces are in an upright, frontal position with some small side movements	Based on the precondition the animal is photographed from the side
The lighting slightly changes at different times	The lighting can change

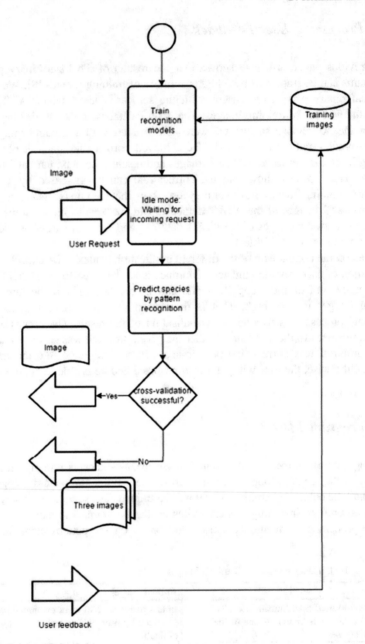

Fig. 2 Program flow

animal species will be predicted and cross-validated by the colour recognition model. If it is successful, the result will be returned to the user. Otherwise, the service will return the three best matching proposals. The user is able to confirm a correct proposal in both cases. The feedback will be processed by the service and the given input image added to the database of known animals.

4 Recognition Accuracy

4.1 Pattern Recognition

Our test database consists of 90 images with 6 different animals. As you can see in Fig. 3, we trained the recognition model with a different number of training images per class and determined the classification accuracy afterwards with the images we did not use for training. We started with 2 images per class and achieved a correct rate of 36%. The number of training images was incremented by 3 for each step except the last one. The best rate was reached when the model was trained by the maximum of the number of training images.

We finished the test with 13 training images for each class and achieved an overall classification accuracy of 83%. The second line in Fig. 3 shows the corresponding logarithmic trend line which matches well except one outlier at 5 training images per class. The trend line was fitted based on the given correct rates, to visualise an interpolation and a potential extrapolation, which has to be approved in the future. Overall, we can see that a high number of training images is necessary to achieve a good recognition result. Based on the logarithmic approximation, we expect that a higher amount of training images are useful to improve the correct rate until a limit value, whereby the interpolation and especially the extrapolation do not prove any unverified points.

Fig. 3 Classification accuracy of the local binary pattern histograms

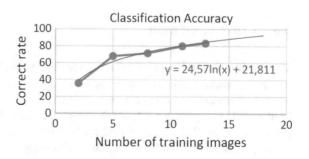

Fig. 4 Classification
accuracy of colour
recognition

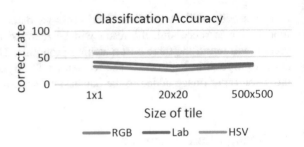

4.2 Colour Recognition

The colour recognition model was tested with the same database mentioned above. It is important to record that it was not possible to improve the overall correct rate with a number of training pictures from 10 images and more. The correct rate stagnated at this point with small outliers up and down. Therefore, our tests were performed with a fixed size of 13 training images per class and a fixed size of 12 validation images. We tested, based on a cross table, all possible variations of colour spaces and tile sizes.

As you can see in Fig. 4, the HSV colour space produces the best results for this setup and context. As expected, the RGB colour space is limited in determining colour distances. The Lab colour spaces produced not the good results we expected due to the reason that the Euclidian distance is not the best measurement method for this model. We are surprised that the variation of the tile size does not have a big impact on the result. The correct rate decreases at 20×20 pixels for the RGB and the Lab colour space but is stable for the HSV colour space. Overall, a correct rate of 58% for the HSV colour space is a good value and enables the further processing of the colour recognition results without having a negative impact on the pattern recognition result. It is important to mention that the combination of two statistic outputs cannot improve the overall result. Therefore, our approach focuses on filtering pattern recognition results which show a strong difference in the colour recognition.

4.3 Cross-Validation

The combination is implemented as a cross-validation based on the results of the pattern recognition and colour recognition. As described in the implementation chapter, there are several parameter options for the cross-validation which have been tested. The pattern recognition model and the colour recognition model are parameterised so that we can expect the best recognition rates based on the results of the previous sections. So the number of training images was set to 13 per class and the used colour space of the colour recognition was set to HSV. As we can see in Fig. 5, three different cross-validating criteria were tested as follows:

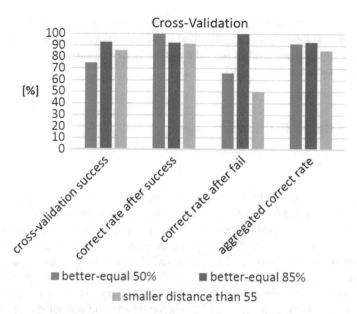

Fig. 5 Cross-validation success and correct rate in percent of different cross-validation variants

1. '**better-equal 50%**' fails when more than 50% of the other classes have a smaller colour distance than the pattern recognition result.
2. '**better-equal 85%**' is similar to the first one, but only fails when more than 85% of the other classes have a smaller colour distance than the pattern recognition result.
3. '**smaller distance than 55**' adopts another approach and fails when a fixed limit is exceeded.

The first category 'cross-validation success' shows the probability that a cross-validation for this criterion is successful. The next category 'correct rate after success' presents the correct rate if the previous cross-validation was successful. On the other hand, the category 'correct rate after fail' presents the correct rate if the previous cross-validation failed, but it is important to note that the user gets the 3 best matching results in this case. If one of them is a correct proposal, this will increase the correct rate. Due to the fact that this category contains the probability of 1 correct proposal out of 3 attempts, it is not directly comparable to the second one. Finally, the last category shows the aggregated correct rate of the correct rate after success and the correct rate after fail, both weighted by their probability of occurrence. As we can see in Fig. 5 and as expected, the probability of a cross-validation success is higher when the limit will be increased from 50 to 85%. The consequences of such an increase are a lower recognition rate after a successful cross-validation, but a higher recognition rate after a failed cross-validation. The aggregated correct rate is very similar and kept very constantly in other tests. At least, the fixed distance does not stick out with a better performance than the other criteria, but it is the only scalable criterion which does not change when the number of classes will be increased in the future. That is the reason why we have such a solution in mind for future work.

5 Web-Based Platform

5.1 Overview

The web application builds on top of the animal recognition service and provides an interface between the user and the system. The user starts the process by uploading a taken photo of an animal on the web application. If available, the Exif data will be extracted and forwarded to the geospatial data service component which will be explained in the next section. The geospatial data service component determines and returns the country, the photo was taken, and based on that information all animal species which are usually existent in this country. As the next step, the web application sends the raw image and the selection of valid animal species via web socket to the animal recognition service. This component, as explained in the chapters before, reduces the training sources, based on valid animal species for this image, respective the country where it was taken, and determines one or more predictions of animal species. The predictions will be returned to the web application which visualises them for the user. If the user provides a feedback, whether the proposal is correct or wrong, it will be fed to the system and internally forwarded to the animal recognition service component (Fig. 6).

5.2 Geospatial Data Service

Geographic databases are known as a part of spatial databases, which are optimised on saving and loading of geometrical objects. In general, these databases allow, contrary to common databases, the instantiation of geographic data types and a provision of special functions related to these data types. Such functions are defined for example by the Open Geospatial Consortium, which was founded in 1994 as Open GIS Consortium. The goal of this organisation is the development of spatial information processing based on common standards and a high interoperability [10]. The proof of concept of this paper uses CartoDB as a geographic database, which supports the data types of the Simple Feature Access Standard of the Open Geospatial Consortium [11]. CartoDB provides a preconfigured REST-API for the capsulated component access and a library of spatial datasets like administrative country borders [12].

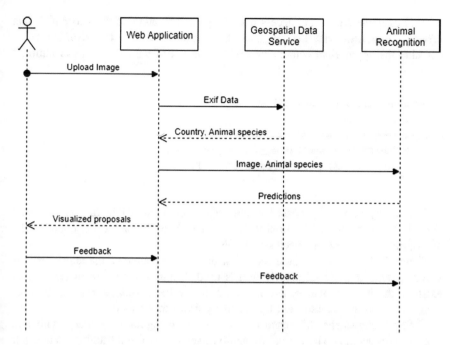

Fig. 6 System overview as a data flow diagram

For the prototype the following tables and its content were created:

- **Countries**: The spatial data of all country borders.
- **Animals**: A list of available animals, like Lion, elephant, giraffe, zebra, kudu, springbok, deer, beaver, wild boar and weasel.
- **Animal_in_Country**: This table links animals with countries in which they are existent. The first six animals were linked to the country Namibia, while the other four animals were linked to the country Germany.

Following the data flow diagram in the previous section, the first step after an image upload is the extraction of Exif data. For this purpose, the open-source JavaScript library 'exif-js' can be used. The extraction of specific tags, more specifically their values presupposes that the desired tag identifiers are known. The extracted longitude and latitude are sent via jQuery and the *getJSON* command to the geospatial data service as shown in the following listing:

```
$.getJSON(``https://host/api/sql?q=
    SELECT name
    FROM world_borders
    WHERE ST_Intersects(the_geom,ST_SetSRID(
            ST_Point(X,Y),4326))'')
```

This example shows the access and the parametrisation of the geospatial data service component with the longitude and latitude (X, Y). The returned value contains the appropriate country as JSON. The list of animal species is returned with the same principle as the following listing shows:

```
$.getJSON(``https://host/api/sql?q=
     SELECT name
     FROM country_and_animal_joined
     WHERE ST_Intersects(the_geom,ST_SetSRID(
              ST_Point(X,Y), 4326))'')
```

This query accesses prepared a table which contains a join of countries and animals based on the table *Animal_in_Country*. The returned value contains the appropriate list of animal species as JSON.

Figure 7 shows the potential reduction of training source of the animal recognition system, if a spatial preselection is used. While a maximum of ten classes exists in the implementation and dataset, it is possible to reduce this selection for Namibia down to 6 classes and for Germany down to 4 classes.

Figure 8 shows the difference of the average recognition accuracy with and without preselection. The animal recognition service used ten training images per class, while five images per class were used to validate the results. The recognition rate with ten classes (without preselection in Namibia and Germany) is at 66%, but increases to 80% in Namibia with six classes (as already shown in previous chapters) and to 85% in Germany with four classes.

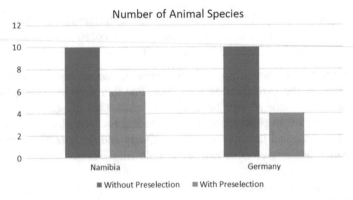

Fig. 7 Number of animals with and without preselection based on the implementation and dataset

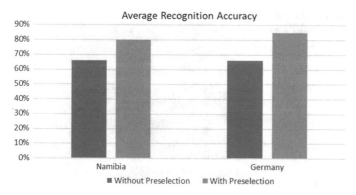

Fig. 8 Recognition accuracy of the local binary pattern histograms in percent with and without preselection based on the implementation and dataset

5.3 Result

The initial screen of the web application contains the upload functionality, visible in Fig. 9. The user is able to upload an image by drag and drop the file into the marked area, or browse and select an image from the local file system.

After the image upload, the result of the geospatial data service is visible. The example in Fig. 10 shows a picture of a zebra which was taken in Namibia and uploaded to the web application. The result of the Exif data extraction is presented below the image under the heading 'EXIF-Daten'. Next to the date, when the image was taken, the latitude and longitude are shown. The result of the geospatial data service is visible below, whereby the country and occurring animals in this country are presented. Based on the prototyping dataset the returned results of the geospatial computation are valid (Fig. 11).

Fig. 9 Upload function of the web application

Fig. 10 Functionality and
result of the geospatial data
service

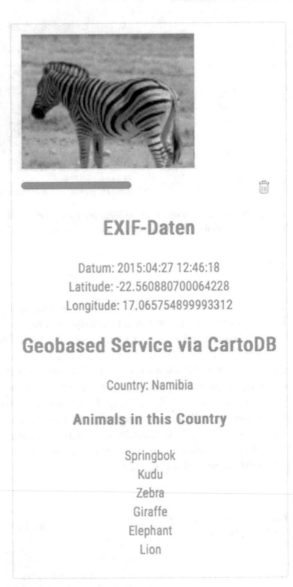

The last step is, as mentioned in the data flow diagram in a previous section, the visualisation of the returned prediction of the animal recognition service. The web application contains one image for each animal species which is shown, when the animal recognition service returns a corresponding result. The web application is able to visualise more than one proposal next to each other, if the animal recognition service returns more predictions.

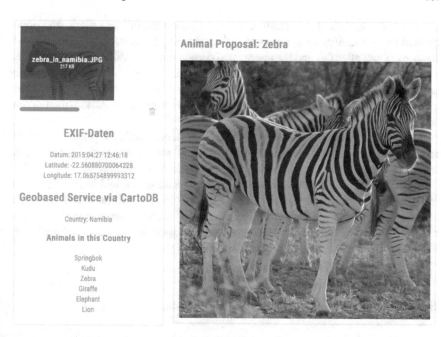

Fig. 11 Visualisation of the animal recognition service result

6 Summary and Future Work

This paper focused on a user-oriented concept to recognise wildlife animal species. We wanted to provide a service, which is able to process user-provided images of animals and returns a proposal as an image of the calculated species. This service shall also be able to analyse images, which are non-unique or hard to recognise and provide more than one proposal. Finally, the user's feedback of correct proposals should be recorded to improve the pattern recognition in the future.

We showed that the pattern recognition achieves good results, especially if trained with a high number of images. We tested the model with a maximum of 13 training images per class and achieved a correct rate of 83%, but a logarithmic extrapolation supports our thesis that the correct rate can be improved with a larger amount of training images until a limit value, which shows the utility of processing the user feedback, whereby the interpolation and especially the extrapolation are assumptions, which have to be verified in the future.

The colour recognition model has been tested with different colour spaces and several tile sizes. It seems that the size of the cropped tile does not have a big impact on the result but the used colour space already has. For this context and setup, the HSV colour space produced the best results.

The combination of both recognition models is implemented as a cross-validation, where the result of the pattern recognition will be tested against the result of the colour recognition. We tested different failure criteria and documented the probability of a cross-validation success, the correct rate after success, the correct rate after fail and the aggregated correct rate. The different criteria can be seen as a controller to move the rates up and down, but keep in mind that normally an increase of the one category will produce a decrease of the other category. There exist different suitable options and at the end, it is a matter of taste which option suits best.

In future work, we will focus on different distance methods within the colour recognition model. Distance measuring methods are available for some colour spaces like the Lab, which fit better than the Euclidean distance.

We will increase the test database for this application and add more classes and more images for each class. The cross-validation criteria will be tested again and examined how they scale with a higher number of classes. The recognition models will be tested as well especially, to verify the extrapolation based on a logarithmic formula made for the pattern recognition.

References

1. Yu, X., Wang, J., Kays, R., Jansen, P.A., Wang, T., Huang, T.: Automated identification of animal species in camera trap images. EURASIP J. Image Video Process. **2013**(1), 1 (2013)
2. Spampinato, C., Giordano, D., Di Salvo, R., Chen-Burger, Y.-H.J., Fisher, R.B., Nadarajan, G.: Automatic fish classification for underwater species behavior understanding. In Proceedings of the First ACM International Workshop on Analysis and Retrieval of Tracked Events and Motion in Imagery Streams, pp. 45, 50. ACM (2010)
3. MATLAB: Texture analysis using the gray-level co-occurrence matrix (glcm)
4. Ojala, T., Pietikâinen, M., Harwood, D.: A comparative study of texture measures with classification based on featured distributions. Pattern Recogn. **29**(1), 51–59 (1996)
5. Ahonen, T., Hadid, A., Pietikâinen, M.: Application to face recognition. IEEE Trans. Pattern Anal. Mach. Intell. **28**(12), 2037–2041 (2006)
6. Ojala, T., Pietikâinen, M., Mäenpää, T.: Multiresolution gray scale and rotation invariant texture classification with local binary patterns. IEEE Trans. Pattern Anal. Mach. Intell. **24**(7), 971–987 (2002)
7. Sarifuddin, M., Missaoui, R.: A new perceptually uniform color space with associated color similarity measure for content-based image and video retrieval. In Proceedings of ACM SIGIR 2005 Workshop on Multimedia Information Retrieval (MMIR 2005), pp. 1–8 (2005)
8. Hermann, B., Sieck, J.: Personenidentifikation mit Sensorsystemen (2016)
9. AT&T Laboratories Cambridge: The Database of Faces. http://www.cl.cam.ac.uk/research/dtg/attarchive/facedatabase.html (1994)
10. Open GIS Consortium: Standards (2016)
11. Herring, J.: Opengis implementation standard for geographic information simple feature access. Common architecture. OGC Doc. **4**(21), 122–127 (2011)
12. Carto: DOCUMENTATION. https://carto.com/docs/ (2017)

Part III
Augmented Reality and Multi Media Applications

Saxa Loquuntur: The Function of (Multi-)Media for Antique Architecture

Christian Kassung and Sebastian Schwesinger

1 Media of Archaeology

A common expectation of the sciences is that they should have no relation to media, or at most a neutral and independent one. In fact, the exact opposite is true. Let us have a look at two prominent examples. The first is the famous copperplate of the Forum Romanum produced by the Italian painter and architectural historian Giovanni Battista Piranesi in the middle of the eighteenth century (Fig. 1). What we see in Piranesi's engraving is more an overflowing architectural fantasy than a faithful rendition of the site of the Forum as he would have found it. We see the monumentally exaggerated remains of ancient constructions, some half-immersed in the flood of time, and between them people, tiny as ants. Yet we also see something else, or more precisely, there is something we do not see: whatever is behind the Arch of Titus is simply concealed by it. To put it differently, Piranesi can choose a perspective for his drawing that permits him to not represent things he does not wish to show. And we, in turn, cannot look behind the arch; it fails to give any testimony of

The research results presented below are the product of an interdisciplinary project at the Image Knowledge Gestaltung Cluster of Excellence, a cooperative undertaking of Classical Archaeology (Susanne Muth), Virtual Acoustics (Stefan Weinzierl) and Cultural History and Theory (Christian Kassung). For specific questions relating to archaeology or acoustics, please see our colleagues' publications listed in the bibliography [1–5]. We would also like to thank the members of the project team, who enriched the project from the very outset with their ideas and innovative impulses.

C. Kassung (✉) · S. Schwesinger
Institut für Kulturwissenschaft, Humboldt-Universität zu Berlin, Unter den Linden 6, 10099 Berlin, Germany
e-mail: ckassung@culture.hu-berlin.de

S. Schwesinger
e-mail: sebastian.schwesinger@culture.hu-berlin.de

Fig. 1 G. B. Piranesi 1748: Vedute di Roma: Campo Vaccino copperplate print of the Forum Romanum. http://www.zeno.org/nid/20004223756

those things that lie beyond it. Even the use of perspective and the chosen section of the city convey the desired impression of faded monumentality .

This brings into view two medial aspects of archaeology. The first is historical. As a child of his times, Piranesi naturally used the medium of the copperplate print to communicate his knowledge and, as we have also noted, to enact it. When contemporary archaeologists use other media, such as photography or three-dimensional models, different logics of knowing and not-knowing are generated. A 3D model, for instance, cannot hide anything, because it can be viewed from all sides. If there is uncertainty in respect of some feature, and in a fundamental sense there always is, other strategies of veiling and unveiling must be chosen. Hence, the frequent tendency to represent only those features one possesses adequate knowledge to reconstruct. This is why models such as that of the Agora of Athens in Fig. 2 are populated only by a few solitary figures, their vegetation sparse at best. And the buildings for which sources are lacking are merely hinted at by rectangles. To put it differently, every historical reconstruction must come to terms with knowing and not-knowing, with the fragmentary character of all historical transmission, and come up with media-specific solutions. Consider for instance the cardinal difference between 2D and 3D media, as demonstrated by our two examples.

Fig. 2 J. Travlos 1966: Museum of the Ancient Agora: model of the Agora of Athens, second-century AD. http://www.agathe.gr/

Now, one could—to return to our initial suspicion—suppose that the aim of science is to produce knowledge that is independent of the logic of its media. That is, that science must necessarily use media, but that it should then abstract from their use. Against this supposition, we would like to posit systematically that there is no media-independent knowledge, or more pointedly: that the acquisition, communication and preservation of knowledge are genuine functions of media. As a demonstration of this thesis, consider the question of what Julius Caesar 'really' looked like. To answer this question, we need sources, and these, in turn, need media in order to be considered sources: coins, statues, drawings, films and so on. So, first of all, we have nothing else but media to transport the image of Julius Caesar through time. Who or what Julius Caesar was thus depends upon the knowledge of these media.

Now, if media have their own histories, what Caesar looks or looked like at a particular moment is to some extent contingent. Someone who possesses an ancient coin with his portrait and knowledge of its transmission has a different image of Caesar than someone who only reads comics. Yet whether or not this coin or that bust was handed down over the long course of history is purely a matter of chance. Taking the average of these media representations would as little correspond to historical truth as the attempt to crystallize a 'true likeness' on the basis of their genealogies. This is to say that we must—and this is the second, systematic aspect of how archaeology's media function—conceive of media as a constitutive element of a history of knowledge. Even when we 'ourselves' traverse the Forum Romanum or some other archaeological site and behold it with our own 'eyes', we are part of a specific medial constellation: the stones and scenery of a walkable excavation site transmit and emphasize a particular knowledge, our eyes see particular things, periods and reconstructions. Above all, we see—as opposed to hearing, feeling or tasting.

2 Geometry of Seeing

In 1985, the French philosopher Michel Serres published a book on 'The Five Senses' [6]. There Serres argues, not unlike the way we have in our introduction, that an appropriate knowledge of our world cannot be severed from our sense perceptions. In so doing, he is writing against a philosophical tradition that tended to treat the five human senses as a rather perilous source of knowledge. Like other scientific pursuits, philosophy sought a reality 'independent of the subject'. That is to say, it sought the Julius Caesar that really existed, independently of our ideas, our perceptions and our media. Against this phantasm of an external world, Serres posited 'A Philosophy of Mingled Bodies', the idea that the five senses interpenetrate in every perception and that this interpenetration is the very element of human knowledge.

Before the background of Michel Serres' urgent plea, let us go back briefly in the history of the senses, or of the senses' disconnection from those regularities that were 'observed' behind them and rationally formulated as laws. It should first be noted that in the main currents of European intellectual history—aside from a few exceptions, such as Johann Gottfried Herder—sight, the optical sense, is the privileged source of knowledge. The other senses were accorded, on account of their alleged specificity, complementary functions appropriate to a more subjective, involuntary and passive mode of accessing the world.[1] This explains why, in the history of knowledge, the sight was investigated first.

The laws of optics were approached for the first time systematically in the early modern period, by Leonardo da Vinci among others. In this drawing (Fig. 3), we see a so-called camera obscura, a dark chamber between the points o, p, q and r, into which light falls through a small aperture m, n. Known since antiquity, the camera obscura now became a model of the eye and of the mechanism of seeing, just as it would later be used to explain the construction of cameras and other optical media. Or to put it differently: the eye was recognized by its underlying laws as one medium among others. Joseph Vogl refers to this medialization as the 'denaturing' of the senses [9]. What is crucial here for our concerns is how transferring the senses from the body to a model, experiment and apparatus created the very condition of the possibility of their simulation.

---

[1]Examples of such an opposition of sensory capacities can be found in Ong [7], among others. A critique of this way of thinking has been undertaken by Sterne [8], to name one example.

Fig. 3 L. da Vinci 1508–09:
course of lines of sight in a
camera obscura.
Manuscript D 8r, https://
upload.wikimedia.org/
wikipedia/commons/8/8f/Da_
vinci_camera_obscura_%
28from_notebooks_71%29_
0071-q75-644x596.jpg

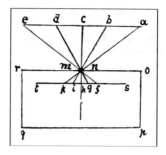

It is all the more important to understand which laws were now taken as the basis of a given act of sense. The central element, on which Leonardo's drawing is based, is the rectilinear propagation of light. We see the rays of light coming out of an external object *a*, *b*, *c*, *d* and *e* and falling straight through the aperture. Behind it, in the darkened chamber, they hit a screen on which they reproduce the object optically. The fact that light rays propagate in a straight line is anything but trivial; for how does a single ray or even particle of light know which direction is 'straight'? The mechanism of rectilinearity was not discovered until much later, and can safely be left aside here. What counts is not why light propagates in a straight line, but simply that it does. How is this ascertained? By using a camera obscura or a screen to make the light ray visible on its course.

Whereby the point and the line emerge as the decisive elements of optical laws. And, since the point becomes the spot where the line is turned or reflected, geometry comes into play and becomes the definitive knowledge of all the behavior of light. What we see in Leonardo's drawing is thus, first and foremost, not a camera obscura at all, but a geometric argument: the external object appears mirrored on the screen. Nobody understands how an image can be compressed into a single, mathematical point, how a beam can be infinitely condensed. The point here, however, is precisely not understanding, but a description—a conception of natural science that will be explicitly propagated by Isaac Newton.

And the application of this knowledge is always also at stake. The geometry of seeing thus became the medium of drawing when, in 1525, no less an artist than Albrecht Dürer placed a barely clothed, indeed lasciviously depicted woman before a camera obscura and proceeded to plot her literally point for point ('Instruction on Measurement with Compass and Ruler') [10]. Dürer did not draw in any lines of sight. We, the viewers, imagine them. It is we ourselves who aim past the ruler at the object, the semi-nude woman. The more robust the separation between the space of the nude and the space of the draftsman, the more penetrating the gaze. This is not looking; it is optical palpation. Seeing and touching coalesce, constituting what Michel Serres calls a mingling of knowledge.

Encroaching further upon modernity, we find, in the posthumous 1677 'Treatise on Man' [11] by the mathematician and philosopher René Descartes, the vexing illustration seen below (Fig. 4). It is taken from a section in which Descartes explains the vision. What is missing here, as compared to the renditions of

Fig. 4 R. Descartes 1677:
model of vision. In:
Descartes, R.: The World and
Other Writings, p. 133.
Cambridge University Press,
Cambridge/UK (2004)

Leonardo and Dürer, is the division into two separate spaces. Instead, the seer is operating—assisted by two sticks—immediately in the external world. The sticks symbolize lines of sight, but no longer as uninvolved mediators between the inside and the outside; they are now direct, feeling actors. The underlying geometry is identical: the sticks are straight lines, meaning that it is less the sense of touch than the relation of segments and angles that is decisive. And this is precisely what Descartes then says: 'Notice also that if two hands *f* and *g* each hold sticks *i* and *h* with which they touch the object *K*, then even though the soul is otherwise ignorant of the length of the sticks, nevertheless, [...] it will be able to tell, as if by a natural geometry, where the object *K* is'. [11: 133–134] But if the role of geometry is unchanged, there is still a second, crucial difference compared to the previous scenario presented by Leonardo and Dürer: the person is looking with two eyes. Reality is felt out with two sticks, and it is precisely this situation that first permits of the 'natural' calculation of the distance between beholder and beheld. Hence Descartes' rationale: 'because it can tell the distance between the points *f* and *g*, and the sizes of the angles *fgh* and *gfi*'.

If you think back to your school days, you can immediately solve the puzzle of what is behind Descartes' text and 'natural geometry': trigonometry. Though known since antiquity, trigonometry was not fully elaborated until the Renaissance, where it was developed above all in the context of applied military ballistics. In any case, we need the tangent function in order to rationally understand what our body effects automatically, according to Descartes: a calculation of the distance between subject and object by multiplying half the eyes' or arms' distance by the tangent of the angle comprised by the object. The decisive thing is that calculation takes place, that mathematics appears to underlie reality. Or that, behind the infinite diversity of processes, there is mathematical identity. For the mathematical description of 'natural' processes constitutes an essential step towards the establishment of numerically operating media systems capable not only of representing, but also of designing processes of perception. This is to say, to put it differently once again, that particularly clever people are less concerned with diversity than they are with laws. Which brings us back to Michel Serres' critique of philosophy and the sciences.

3 Geometry of Hearing

What we naturally cannot see in the illustration is the fact that the aged, groping man is blind. According to Descartes, it is possible to see even without being able to see, because the geometry behind the two senses is identical. Seeing can be explained and understood as touch, as palpating the world with two more or less physical sticks. For a sense to become a sense of direction you need—seen mathematically—two sticks, two eyes or two ears. Seeing and hearing function equally as palpation, as exploring the world by feeling one's way across its surfaces. It is above all this symmetry of seeing and hearing that Descartes' text recalls, and in doing so it calls into question the above-mentioned dominance of the eye. More often than not, it is in exceptional situations that hearing seems to assert itself, namely when nothing can be seen.

War may well be the most notorious situation of exceptionally restricted sense perception. Even when the enemy cannot be seen, he can still be heard in the incessant, deafening 'infernal concert' Ernst Jünger described so powerfully in his journals [12: 127]. In the spring of 1915, the German psychophysicists Erich M. von Hornbostel and Max Wertheimer discovered that the disparity between the travel times of acoustic signals to the right and left ears enables so-called 'directional hearing'. Depending on the angle between the source of sound and the median plane of the head, the signal has a longer or shorter path to each ear. Two things are essential for Hornbostel and Wertheimer's experiments. The first is that irregular noises are easier to localize than well-defined tones. Or, as Hornborstel very clearly expresses it: 'Directional perception works better for noise than for sounds or simple tones. [...] The sharper characteristics of noises make them appear more concrete and easier to locate' [13: 603, 612]. Modern room acoustics thus begins with a more empirically based optimization of concert and lecture halls, on the one hand, and with the scientification of our ability to localize sounds, on the other.

Second, the goal of Hornborstel and Wertheimer's experiments was not merely to understand the mechanisms of human hearing, but also—and perhaps above all—to improve our ability to hear with the help of technological media: 'The dependence of perceived directionality on the time delay with which a sound pressure wave hits both ears leads us to the idea that acoustic localisation could be improved by increasing the time delay artificially. This can be achieved if the sound receivers—the microphone or ear trumpet—are placed at a greater distance from one other (directional listener)' [14: 389].

As in the geometry of light rays, a creative leeway emerged in this history of hearing that went far beyond our biological disposition. While pre-digital means had already enabled us to look and listen to the depth and breadth of space and into the short and long of time, computer-aided numerical procedures today enable the simulation of entire worlds. If we recall Michel Serres' plea, this involves the challenge of taking the models of the senses—which, historically, were developed autonomously—and fusing them back together in a virtual sphere, so as not to let the knowledge of the world flow anew into artificially separated channels.

This short historical remark will have to suffice to bring us back to the topic at hand and the primary thesis of this article: in archaeology and its media, we have until now seen much too much, and heard too little. We have thus far merely beheld the stones, while utterly neglecting the possibility that they could have also had another function, first and foremost an acoustic one. Now, naturally, we can see the stones, but how can we hear them? To answer with Descartes, and in anticipation of the further trajectory of this article and the digital media to come: since we know the underlying laws, we do not need the stones! The reconstruction of a historical reality thus becomes a construction of a historical possibility. We test how different architectural configurations may have functioned acoustically by simulating the propagation of sound waves. Just like Leonardo, who plotted the course of rays in his camera obscura (which was not even a real apparatus), we can simulate acoustic waves in digital spaces with the help of cutting-edge computer technology. We can hear what ancient city-dwellers may have heard in public plazas, i.e. we can investigate the acoustic function architecture may have had. We have no traces to read and interpret; rather, we create traces in order to compare the plausibility of various possible events, situations and configurations.

4   Visual Reconstruction

Every acoustic construction begins, however, with a visual reconstruction. On the basis of existing sources and testimony, architectural space must be reconstructed as such. We do not want to go into any more detail here about the challenges and difficulties of such reconstructions. Our project was able to draw here on the digital models, and attendant research questions and problematics, developed under the direction of Susanne Muth in the framework of the research project 'digitales forum romanum' at the Humboldt-Universität zu Berlin. The digital model of the Pnyx, to which we will return in our conclusion, was created by our research fellow Jana Beutler in cooperation with project team members Una Schäfer and Dirk Mariaschk.

This brings us to our first case study, an investigation of political communication and its medial, i.e. architectural conditions in the late Roman Republic of around 100 BCE. At that time, the Forum was the centre of public life in Rome. It was where the magistrate convened popular assemblies in order to make political announcements or discuss drafts of legislation. While the precise function of such *contiones* is a matter of debate among researchers, there is no question that oral communication was decisive on the Forum plaza.

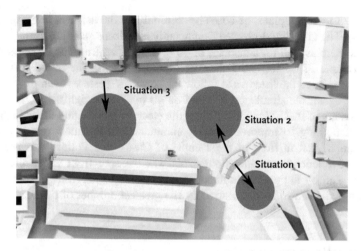

Fig. 5 E. Holter, A. Müller, S. Muth 2016: aerial perspective of the Forum Romanum in the late Roman Republic, ca. 100 BCE, digitales forum romanum, Winckelmann-Institut at Humboldt-Universität zu Berlin, project head: Susanne Muth, 3D model: Armin Müller, http://www.digitales-forum-romanum.de/

It can be demonstrated that over the course of the second century BCE, public addresses were held from three different spots on the Forum Romanum (Fig. 5). Although the sources verify the various locations, they permit no conclusions as to the functional reasons for the switches, such that representational interpretations have classically held sway among researchers. The earliest location of the *contiones* was in the Comitium, the open space directly before the Curia, the seat of the Senate. The Curia, the Comitium and the Rostra—the first orator's platform on the Forum—together constitute an architectural unit. A person speaking from this spot could address the citizens gathered in the Comitium in the knowledge that the Senate would be watching in the background.

It can be gathered from the sources that this situation began to change around the middle of the second century BC. Presumably, Rome's expanded dominion had brought about such a growth in population that the Comitium became too crowded, and the speaker on the rostrum consequently turned to face south in order to address the people on the open plaza of the Forum. One further area of the Forum was also used for public speeches at this time, and its importance grew over the course of the second century: the Temple of Castor and Pollux on the opposite side. These, then, are the three architectural spaces in which we conducted our virtual experiments to find out how well the orators could communicate, both optically and acoustically, with their audience.

The digital models made it possible to generate various views of the respective speaking positions. These images clearly show that the three positions differed starkly in terms of visibility. A speaker standing on the Rostra and facing north to the Comitium could be seen on the slightly sloping site by a great number of listeners, even those standing further away. The example shown simulates a distance of 40 metres from the speaker (Fig. 6, left). Now, if this speaker turned in the direction of the open plaza, he could be seen only by the listeners in his immediate proximity. His visibility decreased significantly as citizens standing further away, as simulated here as well for a distance of 40 m (Fig. 6, centre). The situation in front of the Temple of Castor and Pollux was quite different. The raised rostrum that stood here enabled the listeners to follow the speakers' gestures even from a greater distance—again, the simulation is based on 40 m (Fig. 6, right).

The results of these simulations are quite clear. While turning towards the open plaza did nothing to improve visual communication, the most recent historical configuration, that in front of the Temple of Castor and Pollux, was not least a product of functional considerations. This was the spot from which the speaker could be seen by the greatest number of listeners and—according to our thesis— therefore perhaps also be understood by the greatest number of listeners.

5 Acoustic Reconstruction

Even if these reconstructions have led to more questions, for example about the Romans' height and the quality of their eyesight, or about objects such as banners impeding their view, we can at least devise plausible scenarios for how well or poorly the citizens of Rome could have seen the speakers. But how can we investigate acoustic intelligibility? Experimenting with the acoustic properties of reconstructed architecture requires the creation of a virtual acoustic space. This enables an estimation not only of a speech's audibility but also of its intelligibility. Virtual acoustics was originally developed to the end of improving the acoustic properties of existing spaces as well as spaces yet to be built. We have adapted these tools in order to experiment with different spatial configurations in a way that allows us to draw conclusions about the acoustic function—or dysfunction—of historical spaces that no longer exist.

Virtual acoustics requires three central, interconnected components. First, a signal must be present. For this, we recorded a speech of Cicero's in an anechoic chamber. Second, we need ambient sounds. These were recorded on St. Peter's Square during the pontifical Angelus prayer. And the third, decisive factor in acoustic transmission is, of course, the space itself as the sound's propagating medium. Generally speaking, about 90% of all aural impressions are produced by reflected rather than direct sound. So what we are above all trying to do is calculate the effects of the signal and the noise interacting with space. This can be achieved by describing and calculating the interaction as a set of complex transfer functions.

To simulate these processes of spatial filtering in a virtual environment, as many as 20 million acoustic signals are transmitted from the prearranged speaking position to the digital model and computed according to the laws of physics.[2]

---

[2]This description specifies only one of the main methods in use to calculate a room impulse response. These methods are usually combined in acoustics software [15: 244–248].

Fig. 6 J. Bartz, E. Holter, D. Mariaschk, A. Müller, S. Muth 2016: audience simulation on the Forum Romanum, digitales forum romanum, Winckelmann-Institut at Humboldt-Universität zu Berlin, project head: Susanne Muth, 3D model: Armin Müller, graphic: Jessica Bartz and Dirk Mariaschk, http://www.digitales-forum-romanum.de/

What happens inside the computer resembles—naturally only in a very rough way —the drawing of lines in Leonardo's camera obscura. Only that it is the computer that draws these lines, while also incorporating into its calculations the acoustic properties of the sound source, of the listeners, and even of the air. The result of this calculation is a so-called impulse response, an acoustic 'fingerprint' with which every sound wave is tagged on its path through the virtual model. Finally, all the sound waves that arrive—directly or indirectly—at a virtually positioned listener are included in the calculation of the acoustic impression for that point (room impulse response). Then, the signal at these points is assessed according to specific parameters for the intelligibility of speech, on the basis of which a diagram of intelligibility is generated for each spatial configuration. Naturally, it is still at least as important to rate the intelligibility calculations of the various spatial positions with 'real' ears.

The three diagrams below visualize the results of the acoustic simulations and the listening test for the three different speaking situations in the late Roman Republic. The zone within the dotted line denotes the area in which a speaker is understood very well by his listeners. We use the dashed line to surround the zone containing those positions in which the speech is intelligible only with great concentration and in the absence of further interference.

Here, the catchword 'further interference' indicates a not unproblematic assumption. We assume that the citizens kept as quiet as they could—even though we know that the opposite was often the case, i.e. that in the late Republic, in particular, speakers were often intentionally, and severely, interrupted. In this sense, the diagrams characterize bounded scenarios that are intended less to be interpreted in themselves so much as to be used as a key for comparing the three different scenarios of public address.

To now compare the three scenarios, a speaker standing on the Rostra could easily address himself to space as far as the Curia (Fig. 7, top). By turning to the open plaza of the Forum, he could theoretically reach a larger audience than in the closed off area of the Comitium. Yet this new space, in fact, offers no improvement over the previous situation. On the contrary, owing to architectural properties, the area of good intelligibility is smaller than before. The area with satisfying acoustics is greater, but the impact of interfering noise is more disruptive (Fig. 7, centre). The greatest number of listeners can be reached in situation 3, from in front of the

Temple of Castor and Pollux. If we assume an average of about four people per square metre, then in this configuration, around 12,000 people can follow a speech without any problem, and a further 12,000 can follow it with some effort (Fig. 7, bottom).

These enormous numbers make it easy to discern the architectonic functionality of the various speaking positions. The Temple of Castor and Pollux was of decisive importance for political communication in the late Republic, for it let—to put our title, *Saxa Loquuntur*, into play—the stones speak. At this point, we would no doubt have to get into historical detail in order to adequately interpret the shifts of speaking position. Yet this we will leave up to our project colleague Susanne Muth, so that we for our part can point out once again how valuable such simulations of the multisensory properties of places and spaces are for generating new questions and theses. For the question of the acoustic functionality of spaces is a question that only becomes adequately poseable through the interdisciplinary cooperation of archaeology and virtual acoustics. And this naturally gives rise to the question of what other approaches to the experimentalization of historical spaces can be conceived.

6 Audiovisual Construction

We can finally return to Michel Serres and the mingling of the two senses, or to the question of other forms of experimentalizing historical spaces. The preceding simulations taught us to conceptualize political communication in ancient Rome as a multisensory event. It makes no small difference for language intelligibility whether the listener sees the speaker or not.[3] To which it must be added that, although the graphic visualizations suggest clearly defined zones of varying intelligibility, the borders were much more porous in our own listening test. The areas of intelligibility also varied according to listeners' familiarity with the content matter of Roman politics. The dynamic of a given speech is also decisive for its intelligibility. Certain catchwords and noises were still identifiable at much greater distances, and the emotional tenor of a speech is easily communicated even without word-for-word intelligibility. Which for its part leads to the question of to what extent, or what degree of, literal understanding is even necessary for political participation. Perhaps other, more performative forms of communication were even more important; and not least for that reason a fixed component of rhetorical training. Positing this thesis would naturally mean we have to include the performative dimension of political communication in the design of the simulation.

---

[3]Investigations of the interdependence of language intelligibility and (manipulated) visual impressions go back to the McGurk effect, which was first published in 1976 [16]. To date, this has not been developed in the direction of applying it to total bodily performance in virtual environments.

Fig. 7 C. Böhm, S.
Weinzierl 2016: auralizations
of the Forum Romanum,
diagram by the research group

Which brings us to our most recent case study: a dynamic simulation of the ecclesia, the popular assembly in ancient Athens (Fig. 8).

After the founding of Attic democracy at the end of the sixth-century BC, the polis resolved to designate the Pnyx hill as the sole site for popular assemblies. In its original layout, the natural slope of the Pnyx was exploited to create a theatre-like situation with the citizens looking down on the city to the north. Later, at the end of the fifth century, walls were erected on the northern side so that an embankment could be raised, which also mirrored the direction of the slope and thus of the assembly: the city was now positioned behind the ecclesia. In a third phase, this situation was further expanded in order to accommodate larger crowds.

We are now trying to integrate our digital reconstructions into the computer game environment Unity. This enables us to simulate not only light and sound,

Fig. 8 D. Mariaschk, U. Schäfer 2017: virtual simulation of the ecclesia in Unity, diagram by the research group

but also movement. Diagrams and static listening situations are thus replaced by interactive, walkable worlds. This also means that procedures can be implemented and investigated. For instance, we are currently working on one scenario that encompasses the entire process of a popular assembly, including climbing the Pnyx, finding a free seat, interacting with other agents and even the audiovisual impression made by the speech.

Naturally, the use of these technologies involves specific problems. Game environments were not developed to do historical research. But the variety of obstacles and questions that arise in the course of such an implementation are an integral component of the research process itself. Which brings us full circle. The sciences have tended to use media such as photography, diagrams or drawings in an unreflected way. But if one confronts a science such as archaeology with a media technology as new as the VR game engine Unity, there is no way around a constant reflection on the relationship between media and the production of knowledge. And it is only natural that we should also be driven by the hope that with these new media, we may discover things and interrelations simply overlooked, or concealed, by traditional media.

References

1. Kassung, C., Schwesinger, S.: How to hear the forum Romanum. On historical realities and aural augmentation. In: Busch, C., Sieck, S. (eds.) Kultur und Informatik. Augmented Reality, pp. 41–53. Verlag Werner Hülsbusch, Glückstadt (2016)

2. Muth, S.: Das Forum Romanum: Roms antikes Zentrum neu verstehen. Antike Welt **46**(6), 34–40 (2015)
3. Muth, S., Schulze, H.: Wissensformen des Raums: die schmutzigen Details des Forum Romanum – Archäologie & Sound Studies im Dialog. Cluster-Zeitung **55**, 7–11 (2014)
4. Weinzierl, S.: Beethovens Konzerträume. Raumakustik und symphonische Aufführungspraxis an der Schwelle zum bürgerlichen Zeitalter. Verlag Erwin Bochinsky, Frankfurt am Main (2002)
5. Weinzierl, St (ed.): Handbuch der Audiotechnik. Springer Verlag, Berlin (2008)
6. Serres, M.: The Five Senses. A Philosophy of Mingled Bodies. Continuum, London (2008)
7. Vogl, J.: Becoming-media: Galileo's telescope. Grey Room **29**, 14–25 (2007)
8. Ong, W.: Orality and Literacy. The Technologizing of the Word. Methuen & Co., London (1982)
9. Sterne, J.: The Audible Past. Cultural Origins of Sound Reproduction. Duke University Press, Durham (2003)
10. Dürer, A.: Underweysung der Messung mit dem Zirckel und Richtscheyt (1525)
11. Descartes, R.: The World and Other Writings. Cambridge Texts in the History of Philosophy. Cambridge University Press, Cambridge (2004)
12. Jünger, E.: Kriegstagebuch 1914–1918. Klett-Cotta, Stuttgart (2010)
13. von Hornborstel, E.M.: Das räumliche Hören. In: Bethe, A., et al. (eds.) Handbuch der Normalen und Pathologischen Physiologie mit Berücksichtigung der experimentellen Pharmakologie, 11th vol.: Receptionsorgane I, pp. 602–617. Springer, Berlin (1926)
14. von Hornborstel, E.M., Wertheimer, M.: Über die Wahrnehmung der Schallrichtung. Sitzungsberichte der Preußischen Akademie der Wissenschaften, pp. 388–396 (1920)
15. Ahnert, W., Tennhardt, H.-P.: Raumakustik. In: Weinzierl, S. (ed.): Handbuch der Audioakustik, pp. 181–266. Springer, Berlin (2008)
16. McGurk, H., MacDonald, J.: Hearing lips and seeing voices. Nature **264**, 746–748 (1976)

The Metamorphosis of Kishikishi: Exploring Audience Experiences Telling the Same Story Just Different Media

Helvi Itenge-Wheeler, Heike Winschiers-Theophilus, Alessandro Soro and Margot Brereton

1 Introduction

Traditional African stories remain an integral component and tool used to educate, entertain, and provide guidance on cultural norms to African youth. "Storytelling in Africa provides entertainment, satisfies the curiosities of the African people, and teaches important lessons about everyday life. It is essentially a communal participatory experience" [1]. However, in Namibia, rural–urban migrations and compulsory schooling have shifted traditional and especially rural communal living styles. In villages often the elderly and toddlers remain while school-going children are at distant boarding schools and the middle-aged generation is in town working. Thus, the nostalgic scene of intergenerational story-telling and listening around the fire has become a scarcity. Children are introduced to stories at school through books, which mostly did not originate from Africa [2]. Our preliminary survey conducted in a Namibian rural school showed that when children were asked for their favorite stories, they named European fairy tales such as "The Three Little Pigs", "Rapunzel", and "Snow White", which they had read at school rather than referring to indigenous stories.

H. Itenge-Wheeler (✉) · H. Winschiers-Theophilus
Namibia University of Science and Technology, 13 Storch Street, Windhoek, Namibia
e-mail: hwheeler@nust.na

H. Winschiers-Theophilus
e-mail: hwinschiers@nust.na

A. Soro · M. Brereton
Queensland University of Technology, Brisbane, QLD 4000, Australia
e-mail: alessandro.soro@qut.edu.au

M. Brereton
e-mail: m.brereton@qut.edu.au

© Springer Nature Singapore Pte Ltd. 2018
D. S. Jat et al. (eds.), *Digitisation of Culture: Namibian and International Perspectives*, https://doi.org/10.1007/978-981-10-7697-8_12

Not only are traditional stories at risk, but there seems to be not much interest in leisure reading among Namibian children. Reading for pleasure refers to reading that we do of our own free will anticipating the satisfaction that we will get from the act of reading. It also refers to reading that has begun at someone else's request and we continue because we are interested in it [3]. Furthermore, leisure reading can be characterized as "when we are completely engaged/absorbed in what we are reading, so absorbed that time flies without us noticing it and we lose awareness of the surroundings" [4].

A survey among Namibian learners has revealed that they hardly read for leisure, they only read textbooks to study, and they have visited the library only on few occasions or never [5]. Through numerous informal conversations and observations, we realized that young people are not encouraged to read at home. Ten parents were approached randomly at a flea market in Windhoek, and asked if they were willing to purchase books for their children to read at home. Only 3 parents responded positively, the other 6 parents indicated that they preferred to buy toys. Some parents believe that when they send their children to school, it is the teacher's responsibility to make sure that their children are well educated, and the parent's job is to buy the uniforms, and pay school fees. This situation suggests that a culture of reading is not instilled at home.

As a result of a limited reading culture in Namibia, as well as a lack of literature in indigenous languages, our overarching research project intends to design technologies which enhance the reading experience and awaken a wider interest in reading. Transforming indigenous stories into a written representation enhanced by technology can ensure the preservation of the stories as well as the language. Technologies such as augmented reality (AR), public shared screens, enhanced moving images, 3D graphics, sounds, multimedia animated stories on personal tablets, and mobiles applications, have shown promising results in enhancing user experiences in many related fields, such as cultural heritage preservation, and education. These technologies can be deployed in schools, libraries, and other spaces where reading is encouraged. We postulate that lessons learnt from audience experiences of indigenous stories in various forms can guide further efforts of appropriate technology design promoting young children's reading interest.

Thus, in this paper, after considering related literature on technologies attempting to enhance reading experiences, we briefly depict the children's reading context in Namibia. Then Kishikishi, a traditional tale, which will be the narrative studied in different media is introduced. We first look at the reported and observed listener's experience of the story and then reader's experiences of the same story in a book. In a quest to explore further technologies we present three independently designed technologies. We have preloaded Kishikishi on a notice board, developed a mobile Kishikishi reading game as well as an augmented reality version of the Kishikishi book. We extract audience experiences' themes which propose to be taken into account in further technology developments.

2 Transforming Reading Experiences

Reading experiences have changed over time and mostly due to its medium. A number of digital technologies have emerged with the aim to maintain traditional books' feels and experiences that readers have been appreciating in paper books and criticizing its absence in digital books. Thus, as technology finds better alternatives to eye-straining backlit screens, many popular devices are providing an ever-more "paper-like" reading experience [6]. A study was conducted which combine positive aspects of physical and digital books specifically to enhance people's active reading [7]. QOOK is one good example of an interactive reading system focusing on visually enhanced traditional books, enabling active reading by integrating physical and digital books [8]. Furthermore, QOOK gives users the experience of flipping the pages and allows keyword searching and bookmarking.

A number of studies have investigated the benefits of digital reading over paper reading. Reference [9] claims that the use of iPads enhances the level of engagement of children. In particular, one teacher commented that: "...when children use the application, the iPad comes to life and involves the child that cannot be passive anymore but are forced to be active..." [9]. A growing trend is to augment the e-book with interactive sounds and animations—also called enhanced e-books. A study conducted with 7–12-year-old children on leisure reading, established that enhanced e-books with interactive and multimedia features, afford a better reading experience than basic e-books [4]. Reference [10] present a new type of digital book which takes a traditional book and enhances it visually and aurally, while effectively combining the physical and digital world. It provides a successful integration of a mixed reality book which presents multisensory content by keeping the physical book. The user can see a live video feed of the scene and hear augmented and spatialized sound. Users can experience the spatial sound changing according to their position and the actual content on the page [10]. Similar techniques have been deployed in public spaces such as museums, where a so-called "Living Book", consisted out of a traditional book with RFID tags on each page.

Depending on which page is open, sound and videos are played [11]. Reference [12] remarked that sound design is used to create artificial ambience, allowing audiences an embodied experience. The quality of sound to convey information and emotion is well exemplified in movies. Similarly, Ref. [13] stated that children wanted to have an e-book that is not "boring", thus the design team suggested: (a) videos that summarize parts of the text and (b) sound effects linked with words and images. The enhanced e-book read-aloud narration was by far the most appreciated feature—mentioned by the 50% of the participants. This was followed by puzzle games, videos, and interactive images (in this order) [13]. In other work, LIT KIT—a portable, cyber-physical artifact was designed to support and enhance children's picture-book reading in both physical and digital environment [14]. Furthermore, the LIT KIT employs color, sound, and movement to evocate the picture-book while it is being read. It also employs lighting, undulating fabric streamers and sounds that a child can customize during and after reading a picture-book.

Further work has explored the integration of tactile feedback into children's electronic books (e-books) through variable friction surface haptics enabled by the TPaD Tablet technology [15]. It further illustrated that e-books simply replicate the content of traditional paperback storybooks in digital form. It was further stated that Children were generally positive about the concept of haptic e-books. For example, one child noted that the textures were "fun to feel". Another child described the tactile sensation as "itchy". Several parents thought the textures would enhance the reading experience. For example, some parents said, "It helps convey information about the story to the reader. It makes it more real, more fun, more interactive and more playful". This study also tells us that in order for the user's experience to be enhanced fun must be part of the process. This TPaD was enjoyed by the children who reported that the textures were "fun to feel" [15]. In a similar study aimed to enhance story listening, and reading for younger children a haptic vest that generates vibrotactile stimulation related to story content was utilized. There is a little study on the haptic vest, yet the results provide initial evidence that "haptic effects can potentially enhance the reading/listening experience of children beyond 4 years" [16].

While much of the reading technologies have focused on recreating and enhancing traditional reading experiences, we consider audience experiences of traditional stories equally including listener and reader's experiences to inform further designs.

3   Kishikishi's Origin

In order to establish audience experience and derive design themes, we first present the current reading context in Namibia. We then introduce Kishikishi, a traditional story, which will be the content of the narrative explored throughout the different media in the following sections.

3.1   Contemporary Namibia

In Namibia, the government provides free education from primary school up until grade 12, to promote literacy as being a human right. However, according to Ref. [17], only 22.4% of learners could be classified as readers in terms of a study conducted in 36 schools among 1402 learners in seven Namibian regions. Furthermore, [18] stated that most of the students have challenges grasping and comprehending, processing reading material, and making out important points. This emphasizes the lack and inadequate literacy training in the early years of schooling. Having visited numerous schools across the country we have discovered that most of the government schools do not have school libraries, and the few that have are not functional. Surprisingly, some school libraries have few story books but the children were never afforded the opportunity to go to the library and read or borrow books, instead some libraries where used as storage.

Considering that there are 13 indigenous languages in Namibia, and only 1.2% of the population speak English, the national language and language of instruction, at home (Ministry of Basic Education and Culture, 1998), it is necessary to develop innovative ways by which to instruct learners in a multilingual country [19]. Only recently was the medium of instruction changed to indigenous languages at the primary level to accommodate non-English speakers' learning efforts. However, there are very few written materials in indigenous languages, with outdated dictionaries, no encyclopaedias, and negligible traditional stories. One of the national efforts has been the biennial Namibia Book Fair attempting to promote a culture of reading and writing among Namibians, with an emphasis on indigenous literature. A further initiative by Helvi-Itenge-Wheeler was the foundation of Yambeka Children Media (YCM), a community Social Enterprise, to promote African languages, tales, and the culture of reading (Fig. 1).

3.2 Kishikishi, a Traditional Story

While Namibian tribes have many traditional stories, Kishikishi is known to most Oshiwambo speaking people in Namibia. The story was told to scare kids away from places where they should not go. With many variations of narratives across families, the essence of the story is Kishikishi a monster, which is out to eat children. The hero of the story is a small boy who climbed a tree and eventually

Fig. 1 Children reading storybooks published by Yambeka Children Media

defeated the monster. The story transmitted an experience of fear, suspense, and the forbidden. It also allowed for imagination on how the monster probably looked like.

"When I was a child, the elders used to tell me the story of Kishikishi. It used to scare me but I loved listening to the story over and over again" [20]. Thus, [20] created her own account of the story as follows (Table 1).

In order to establish remembered experiences, we asked nine Oshiwambo-speaking women who listened to Kishikishi, when they were young how they recollect the storytelling being asked the following open-ended questions:

1. When you were a kid, do you remember listening to the story of Kishikishi?
2. If the answer is yes, how did you feel when the story was being told to you?
3. Were you scared, happy, etc. Please explain in detail how you felt.
4. Did you ask adults to recite the story over and over? If the answer is yes, why?
5. If the story was so scary why did you listen to it over and over?

A1 said "I was never afraid because I knew it does not exist, maybe because of the way my mother started the story by saying long, long time ago, also at the end of the story I knew that the heroes will always win." In contrast, the other eight

Table 1 The Story of Kishikishi	Once upon a time, there was a terrible monster called Kishikishi.
	Kishikishi liked to eat people. One day, Kishikishi came to a new land and ate everyone who lived there. Except for… one little boy called Penda. Penda climbed a very tall tree, so that Kishikishi could not get him. When Kishikishi thought that he ate everybody, he wandered around and sang: "I'm the only one in this land." (2 times) Penda started singing, too: "It's me and you in this land." (2 times) Kishikishi was very angry. He wanted to be the only one in the land. Now he had found that there was someone else! Kishikishi said to the boy, "Why don't you come down here? Then we can have fun together—just the two of us." Penda began to throw his belongings at Kishikishi. He threw a saw and a knife. Kishikishi swallowed them all, thinking Penda was among them. Kishikishi started singing again, "I'm the only one in this land." (2 times) Penda started singing, too: "It's me and you in this land." (2 times) Kishikishi was still very angry. He began to shake the tree. Penda said, "Watch out Kishikishi! I'm coming down!" As soon as Penda jumped down, Kishikishi ate him. When Penda was inside Kishikishi's stomach, he found his saw and his knife. He cut a hole in Kishikishi's stomach and let all the people out. Kishikishi went away and never ate anyone ever again. The end!
	Reprinted from Kishikishi the Bad Monster book. By Helvi-Itenge-Wheeler. Windhoek, Namibia 2012 by Yambeka Children Media

adults admitted to be scared every time they heard the story of Kishikishi. A2 stated that, "it was always scary to hear the story of Kishikishi, but at the same time I was excited to listen. Story time was also entertainment for us." Another question we posed was: If the story was so scary, why did they listen to it over and over? A3 responded by saying, "I loved the way my mother recited the story, she sang during the storytelling, and she sometimes changed her voice sound like Kishikishi. That made me excited and it was entertaining at the same time; I was always looking forward to it." A4 mentioned how this storytelling time made her feel closer to her mother "I felt loved and happy when I got a chance to sit next to my mother, and felt her closeness." A5 stated that the parents kept on changing the stories, and that made it even more interesting. "I was curious to know how it will change all the time. I was scared yet excited at the same time. I also enjoyed the story because it made me use my imagination. Since there were no pictures of Kishikishi, I always imagine how it looks like, how it runs and how big it was." The questioned adults also stated that the mystery of the story which sometimes the storytellers brought into the story by changing it every time they retell, the story made them enjoy and always look forward to hearing it over and over.

From these statements, we extract a number of listening experiences such as: enjoying the tension, curious about variations of the story, free to imagine, narration style with songs and intonations, and the context allowing closeness to the mother.

4 Kishikishi in a New World

In the following section, we are following Kishikishi through a number of media, such as the book, the digital notice board, the mobile app, and the augmented reality book, as depicted in Fig. 2. We then describe the setting used to explore each medium.

4.1 Kishikishi in the Book

Many Namibian traditional stories like Kishikishi were not written down in a format of a storybook for children. Thus, Itenge Wheeler [20] was keen on bringing the story of Kishikishi into a colorful and receptive format for children (Fig. 3).

4.1.1 The Book

The story of Kishikishi was first published in 2012 and it contains 24 pages in a soft copy. The book has been distributed to schools and public libraries throughout Namibia. The Kishikishi book is also published as an ebook, however, the ebook version of Kishikishi did not receive much attention from the end user. This is

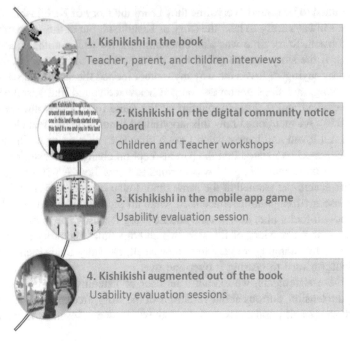

Fig. 2 Kishikishi in a new world

Fig. 3 The first two pages of Kishikishi in a book. Reprinted from Kishikishi the bad monster book. By Helvi-Itenge-Wheeler. Windhoek, Namibia 2012 by Yambeka Children Media

probably a result of it being a basic ebook digital facsimile of the print version of the printed book, which has the same text and the same illustrations.

Three major changes were made from the original recalled story to the written one. In the original story, the boy did not use a saw and a knife, but instead, he used stones which were hit together to make fire. The author was uncertain of referring to making fire, potentially encouraging young readers to imitate. Additionally, the author also thought that it did not make sense for the boy to save people from Kishikishi's stomach while there was fire, because there was no fire in this version.

Another change was the boy in the original story did not have a name. The author gave the boy the name Penda, an Oshiwambo name, which means "the person who is brave or simply the brave warrior." It was important to give the boy not only a name but also an important name, because he was the hero of the story. In addition to this, children always wanted to know the name of the boy in the story. The word Kishikishi means monster in Oshiwambo and it also means Albino in Oshiwambo. The author wanted an illustration of Kishikishi which is not too scary to children, and which does not have any color similar to an Albino person, thereby avoiding stigmatization. The green color was selected because the Kishikishi lives in the forest, and it fits perfectly with the forest.

A major change was to publish the story in English rather than in its original language Oshiwambo. Even though the Kishikishi story is originated from the Oshiwambo-speaking people found in the Northern part of Namibia, it was important to write the first version of the Kishikishi book in English so that all the Namibian children regardless of their mother tongue could learn and enjoy the story.

4.1.2 Feedback Collection

Feedback on the book was collected using semi-structured interviewing with a convenience-based sampling. Interviews were conducted face to face or telephonically. In 2016, we donated books to the grade 2 and 3 classes at People's Primary School (PPS) with one of these books being Kishikishi. A month later, we visited the same school and interviewed the teachers to obtain their feedback. Opinions from parents of young children were collected at different events such as the Namibia Book Fair, and personal conversations. Some parents would casually call author 1 to show their gratitude for documenting the stories they grew up listening to.

4.1.3 Impressions Expressed

During the Namibia Book Fair, one parent expressed that her 4-year-old son was scared of the Kishikishi monster when she first took the book home. Minutes later, the boy asked for the book pointing and giggling, "Kishikishi", "Kishikishi". Later, it became his favorite bedtime story. Another parent who expressed that she grew up listening to the story of Kishikishi whose son is also named Penda contacted the

Fig. 4 Storytelling session in school, Windhoek

author through the telephone and mentioned how excited her son was to see his own name in a book for the first time. The researchers also asked children during the PPS workshops why they like the Kishikishi story, some children answered that they like it because its scary. When something is scary its not boring. One child said, "I like to be scared, it's fun to be scared." They also said they like the song and the repeating rhythm. In summary, the book format maintained the evocation of being scary and attractive at the same time for the reader. Additionally, it created hero identification for namesakes, as the name Penda is very common in Namibia.

In 2016, author 1 visited three primary schools in Windhoek and delivered a live ly Kishikishi-storytelling performance (Fig. 4). Observations of the audience were noted. After the storytelling, many children usually try to mimic the narrator's singing. This has been confirmed by a number of teachers who stated that the children enjoyed the singing part with the repeating rhymes, "I'm the only one in this land." "I'm the only one in this land." "It's me and you in this land." "It's me and you in this land". Thus, the listener's experience is enhanced through participation (singing) and rhythm besides the entertainment of the narrator's performance.

4.2 Kishikishi on the Digital Community Notice Board

A digital community notice board is a technology tool intended for creating and sharing of public information. Having successfully engaged in authoring workshops with children, yet not developing innovative and alternative forms of "innovative digital books", we introduced a digital community notice board in a school where children had no prior experience with technology.

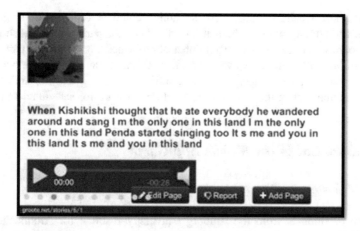

When Kishikishi thought that he ate everybody he wandered around and sang I m the only one in this land I m the only one in this land Penda started singing too It s me and you in this land It s me and you in this land

Fig. 5 The story of Kishikishi as it appears on the notice board

As a platform, we adopted an open-source digital community notice board originally developed with an Australian indigenous community. This notice board was designed with particular consideration of the communities' inclination for orality and storytelling [21], which made it a perfect candidate for hosting the story of Kishikishi and presenting it in Namibian schools.

We uploaded Kishikishi onto the notice board (Fig. 5).

The story was composed of photos, text, and audio. A special feature of the notice board is that if the audio correspondence with the text it will highlight the words as it plays in a karaoke style.

4.2.1 Notice Board in Use

In 2016, a 2 h workshop with 23 children from a local school in Windhoek was held. The children were all part of the dancing afternoon activity program, aged between 9 and 14, grade 4–6. The students were grouped in 4 with one facilitator per group. They were first asked to think of their favorite book and what makes reading enjoyable. Then they were asked to make up their own story and be creative in the "form" they shape the content in, to make it more fun to read. One group of learners was introduced to the community notice board. The children enjoyed looking through the content, in particular, they liked hearing the audio with the text highlighting. The children showed interest in the story, and they were encouraged to create their own stories. A number of features of the notice board used as storytelling tool promise to be useful in the Namibian setting, such as the karaoke feature, and the fact that it is uploaded to be shared on a bigger screen thereby upholding a community activity. Also, the easiness for children to create their own story is convincing.

Since then, we have introduced the notice board at further workshops with children and another with teachers at a local school. As part of the workshops, the notice board was introduced with a number of preloaded stories and the participants were requested to write their own story. In both the instances, the workshop participants were eagerly creating their own stories suggesting that the notice board should become part of the school infrastructure allowing for scheduled activities.

4.3 Kishikishi in the Mobile App Game

4.3.1 The App

A group of students from the Aalborg University Institute for Architecture and Media Technology in Denmark developed a running prototype of a Kishikishi App game. It was based directly on the book version maintaining its graphics and text. It was subdivided in scenes to read followed by an interactive challenge. For example, in scene 1, the player is provided with a paragraph taken from the Kishikishi storybook to read (Fig. 6). Above the paragraph, there is an option to play the animation. The animation contains Kishikishi running chasing and eating the people. The monster also sings in a male voice, "I'm the only one in this land."

The app game design used different features to involve the player in the story. First, the player enters their name which then becomes the name of the hero in the story. Second, as the player reads through the story, at the end of each scene the player can acquire reward arrows which when accumulated can defeat the monster (Fig. 7).

However, if not enough arrows are gained the monster will eat up all the children at the end. Thus, the player determines the outcome of the story.

Fig. 6 Scene 1 with text

Fig. 7 Image illustrating the challenge

4.3.2 App Evaluation by Namibian Children

Four girls aged between 10 and 12 from a school with which we have a collaboration agreement and ethical clearance to work with attended the evaluation session at the university premises. The children were briefed and completed an informed consent specifically designed for children. Then, one by one, they were seated at the tablet with the game on and recorded with a 360 camera to record their facial expression and their interactions with the tablet. The children were left to explore and navigate by themselves (Fig. 8).

Fig. 8 The children playing the app game and filling the evaluation forms

4.3.3 Results

Three girls focused on the animation above the text and kept on attempting to interact with it by randomly pressing on the images and buttons. They only scanned over the text and could not solve the challenge and did not gain the needed arrows. One of the four girls, however, took all her time to read through the text yet could also not solve the challenge. We observed that the animation distracted the children from reading rather than encouraging them. Moreover, all the children indicated that they loved the feature that their name was given to the hero, making them feel part of the story. Equally, they did not like the fact that they were all swallowed by the monster after having failed to solve the challenges. They requested for the app to be loaded on their parents' mobile phone. Once the app was taken to their school for further free time to spend with, the four girls made sure that this time they read, solved the challenge, and successfully defeated the monster. Thus, given enough time, the children did eventually read the story. Even though this app has a voice singing, the children did not mention if they liked it or not.

4.4 Kishikishi Augmented Out of the Book

4.4.1 The Augmented Reality App

The Kishikishi Augmented Reality App was designed and developed by a group of students from the Faculty of Computing and Informatics at the Namibia University of Science and Technology (NUST). In this implementation, the reader holds the cell phone over the different pages of the real book which serves as markers in the app. For each page, the corresponding part is read out by a small girl's voice while animated 2D images of the specific scene are displayed with the monster jumping up and down, shaking trees, etc. (Fig. 9).

4.4.2 Augmented Reality Testing

Six girls aged 10–12 came to the university to evaluate the app. Four of the six girls have also tested the Kishikishi in the mobile app game. One by one, they were seated at a table holding the cell phone while a student was holding the book and turning pages. It was recorded with a 360 camera for later analysis.

The children were fascinated by the augmented reality animations as they had never seen such in their life. They really enjoyed the app but were also complaining about having to hold the cell phone in a certain position. They gladly listened to the story rather than having to read it for themselves and liked the voice. Some children were mimicking the reader's voice. They liked the animations with the monster

Fig. 9 Augmented reality book

moving around. Though did not appreciate the monster eating children. All in all, the children thought it was "cool and fun". While this app was testing for the application of augmented reality, it did not encourage reading per se.

5 Discussion

The audience's experiences are an important element as we explore the five different interpretations and media of a traditional tale. We examined the listener and reader's preferences and identified themes to be considered in further designs of technologies.

5.1 Performative Aspects

In the story told or read to the children, the audience captivation was created through performative actions, such as narrative styles, voices and singing, and varying content. The voices and singing were incorporated in all three technologies with different emphasis. In all three instances, the children showed much appreciation to be able to "listen" rather than having to read. Also, the singing along and mimicking was a significant factor showing engagement with the story. The children expressed that the girl's smooth voice helped them follow the story.

5.2   *Illustrations and Animations*

While imagination is deemed to be an important factor in story reading, smaller children do need illustrations in order to connect to the story in their own time and terms. Thus as much as the children liked the illustrations in the book, they also appreciated the moving and augmented illustrations in the two apps. The children were also amused by the animations of Kishikishi chasing the people and shaking the tree, thus played it over and over again. While it is supported that animation can enhance children's memory and comprehension of stories [16], we also observed that it distracted the children from reading and focusing on the story.

5.3   *Stimulation and Engagement*

Some of the adults who participated in the storytelling study expressed that the storytelling with their parents helped them enjoy the tension, fuel curiosity, and stir imagination. The digital notice board used in the participatory workshop inspired children to create their own stories and thus promoted creativity. The children also felt a sense of accomplishment and proud to see their own work on the notice board. The game app stimulated children to carefully read in order to solve the quiz to gain enough arrows to defeat the monster. In the app game, personal participation was further induced through the reader's name becoming the hero's name, which allowed the children to identify themselves within the story. The children expressed that they felt as they were part of the story because the children's name appears in the book replacing the hero in the story.

   None of the children liked the idea of Kishikishi swallowing them up at the end of the story. Because the children who first interacted with the app, did not pay much attention to the text when they played the app the first time, at the end of the game they were all swallowed by the monster. All the kids were disappointed about the idea of being swallowed by the Kishikishi. Thus when they played the app the second time, they concentrated and made sure that they read and understood the story and instructions. They felt victorious once they defeated the monster, and they were ready to play again. This confirms [15], statement, that multimedia enhancement and interactivity may add great value to the children's e-reading experiences.

5.4   *Bonding*

As expressed by one of the adults, the closeness with the mother created a memorable experience which is equally provided by bedtime story reading. Doubtful is whether the technologies making human interaction redundant can recreate those feelings. Different designs would need to be explored equally engaging adults and children into stories simultaneously. First developments have been showcased by Samsung with their VR Bedtime Stories app, which is targeted at bridging the physical distance between parents and children Ref. [22].

6 Conclusion

This paper presented a study exploring audience experiences of the same story expressed through different media. We acknowledge that indigenous storytelling maintained a long history of oral traditions in Namibia. With only recent introduction of writing and technologies mainly supporting the written words, no reading culture could have been established by now. We postulate that by learning from listener experiences we can design more appropriate technologies promoting a reading culture in Namibia. We realized the significance of performative aspects as well as illustration and animation design and features allowing for stimulation and engagement. The latter vary between offering interactive elements to simple identification mechanisms.

We suggest that, if appropriate technologies are developed they can improve reading experiences of indigenous stories in the long-run overcoming novelty effects. We are equally conscious of constraints of current designs not focusing on important aspects such as bonding and inter-human relationships, which have been the basis of storytelling and story reading to children. We consider technologies such as the presented notice board, supporting collaboration, by its design, to be promising tools to reinstate bonding experiences across generations. Thus, we will be evaluating techniques and features focusing on the four identified themes to inform future designs of technologies aiming at enhancing reading experiences.

Acknowledgements We particularly thank the student developers of the reading game and the augmented reality app. We further thank the children who participated in the app evaluation sessions.

References

1. Tuwe, K.: The African oral tradition paradigm of storytelling as a methodological framework: employment experiences for African communities in New Zealand. In: African Studies Association of Australasia and the Pacific (AFSAAP) Proceedings of the 38th AFSAAP Conference: 21st Century Tensions and Transformation in Africa (2016)
2. Itenge-Wheeler, H., Kuure, E., Brereton, M., Winschiers-Theophilus, H.: Co-creating an enabling reading environment for and with Namibian children. In: Proceedings of the 14th Participatory Design Conference: Full papers, vol. 1, pp. 131–140. ACM (2016)
3. Clark, C., Rumbold, K.: Reading for Pleasure: A Research Overview. National Literacy Trust (2006)

4. Colombo, L., Landoni, M.A.: Diary study of children's user experience with EBooks using flow theory as framework. In: Proceedings of the 2014 Conference on Interaction Design and Children, pp. 135–144. ACM (2014)
5. Tashaya, C.: Teenagers only read textbooks retrieved. From: https://www.newera.com.na/2014/02/05/teenagers-read-textbooks/ (2014)
6. Picton, I.: The impact of eBooks on the Reading Motivation and Reading Skills of Children and Young People: A Rapid Literature Review. National Literacy Trust (2014)
7. Schilit, B.N., Price, M.N., Golovchinsky, G., Tanaka, K., Marshall, C.C.: The reading appliance revolution. Computer **32**(1), 65–73 (1999)
8. Zhao, Y., Qin, Y., Liu, Y., Liu, S., Shi, Y.: QOOK: a new physical-virtual coupling experience for active reading. In: Proceedings of the Adjunct Publication of the 26th Annual ACM Symposium on User Interface Software and Technology, pp. 5–6. ACM (2013)
9. Rubegni, E., Landoni, M.: Supporting creativity in designing story authoring tools. In: Proceedings of the 14th International Conference on Interaction Design and Children, pp. 287–290. ACM. (2015)
10. Grasset, R., Duenser, A., Seichter, H., Billinghurst, M.: The mixed reality book: a new multimedia reading experience. In: CHI'07 Extended Abstracts on Human Factors in Computing Systems, pp. 1953–1958. ACM (2007)
11. Sieck, J.: Information and communication technology in culture and creative industries. In: EVA 2015, pp. 31–33, Saint Petersburg (2015)
12. Sanchez, S., Dingler, T., Gu, H., Kunze, K.: Embodied reading: a multisensory experience. In: Proceedings of the 2016 CHI Conference Extended Abstracts on Human Factors in Computing Systems, pp. 1459–1466. ACM (2016)
13. Colombo, L., Landoni, M., Rubegni, E.: Design guidelines for more engaging electronic books: insights from a cooperative inquiry study. In: Proceedings of the 2014 Conference on Interaction Design and Children, pp. 281–284. ACM (2014)
14. Schafer, G.J., Green, K.E., Walker, I.D., Lewis, E., Fullerton, S.K., Soleimani, A., Zheng, X., et al.: Designing the LIT KIT, an interactive, environmental, cyber-physical artifact enhancing children's picture-book reading. In: Proceedings of the 12th International Conference on Interaction Design and Children, pp. 281–284. ACM (2013)
15. Cingel, D., Blackwell, C., Connell, S., Piper, A.M.: Augmenting children's tablet-based reading experiences with variable friction haptic feedback. In: Proceedings of the 14th International Conference on Interaction Design and Children, pp. 295–298. ACM (2015)
16. Zhao, S.: Feeling Stories: Enriching Story Listening Experience for Children with Haptic Feedback (2014)
17. Elago, S.: Namibian children poorly read? https://www.newera.com.na/2014/07/09/namibian-children-poorly-read/ (2014)
18. Murray, C.: A study of language related factors impeding the English reading comprehension of Namibian first year University students (Doctoral dissertation) (2013)
19. Wikan, G., Mostert, M.L., Danbolt, A.M.V., Nes, K., Nyathi, F., Hengari, J.: Reading among grade six learners in Namibia and Norway: an investigation of reading habits and attitudes of learners in the Khomas and Oshana regions of Namibia and the Hedmark region in Norway (2008)
20. Itenge-Wheeler, H.: Kishikishi the Bad Monster. Yambeka Children Media, Windhoek (2012)
21. Soro, A., Brereton, M., Taylor, J.L., Hong, A.L., Roe, P.: Cross-cultural dialogical probes. In: Proceedings of the First African Conference on Human Computer Interaction, Nairobi, Kenya, pp. 114–125 (2016)
22. Nudd, T.: Samsung made VR bedtime stories for kids and parents who can't be together in person. Live storytelling app places them in the same fantasy. http://www.adweek.com/creativity/samsung-made-vrbedtime-stories-kids-and-parents-who-cant-be-together-person-171166/ (2016)

A Contemporary Expression of the Namibian San Communities' Past and Present Sufferings Staged as an Interactive Digital Life Performance

Kileni Fernando, Tertu Fernandu, Simpson Kapembe, Kamati Isay and Japeni Hoffeni

1 Introduction

Marginalization affects many tribes and subgroups of populations across the globe. Marginalization diminishes self-esteem and hampers self-actualization, which could be strengths that enable those ostracized to thrive. Namibian San groups currently still suffer from marginalization, despite numerous efforts by the Namibian government, non-governmental organizations (NGO's), and individual advocates. Factual and personal accounts are plentiful in the form of books, other written materials, documentaries, videos and radio broadcasts, all reminding the Namibian society of the past and current injustices. In a further attempt to reach out to the national and international public in fighting against marginalization, we (a group of San youth) have co-produced a digital live performance entitled: 'Follow my Shadow, See me to Suffer; Track my Spirit, Empathise with Me: Uncovering Marginalization via a Live Healing Performance'. This was done in form of a live choreography, which merges a projected prerecorded film of the ostracized grieving shadow together with a live enactment of the empathizing spirit [1]. The performance was staged at the International Conference on Culture and Computer Science in October 2016, Windhoek, Namibia (Fig. 1). Conceptualizing, choreographing, rehearsing and eventually performing this piece in

K. Fernando (✉) · T. Fernandu · S. Kapembe · K. Isay · J. Hoffeni
//Ana-Djeh San Trust, Windhoek, Namibia
e-mail: kileni.fernando@gmail.com

T. Fernandu
e-mail: ftertu6@gmail.com

S. Kapembe
e-mail: skapembe@gmail.com

K. Isay
e-mail: kamatiisay@gmail.com

© Springer Nature Singapore Pte Ltd. 2018
D. S. Jat et al. (eds.), *Digitisation of Culture: Namibian and International Perspectives*, https://doi.org/10.1007/978-981-10-7697-8_13

Fig. 1 Authors of this chapter during the ICCCS 2016 performance

front of an audience allowed for a new mean of reaching out; it allowed us to convey a strong message of what desirable actions should be undertaken to undo past discriminations and to move forward together as equal partners.

This article is an extension of the transformative performance now presented as a written piece airing different voices. We first elucidate elements of the Namibian San's history and point out perceived injustices from our own perspective as members of the San tribe in present-day Namibia. The associated collective memories and individual experiences have shaped the narrative in content and expression of the interactive digital performance. We share the original proposal, written by Daniel Cabrero and Tertu Fernandu [1], then describe in detail the production process, as well as the performance itself. Having received positive feedback from the audience, we intend to continue the fight against marginalization by digital and performative means. A short commentary by our collaborating editor, Heike Winschiers-Theophilus, helps position our performance in the sphere of digital artistic expressions that aim to change societal ills. Lastly, we reflect on our performance and propose a way forward.

2 The San in Namibia

Namibia is estimated to be home to about 30,000 San, which is less than 2% of the country's population. The San have mostly settled in the eastern parts of the country; individuals and families live on commercial farms and in different towns. They are well known for having been nomadic hunter-gatherers and to be among the oldest tribe on the continent; San are seen as technically gifted, artistic, clever, skilled hunters and powerful healers [2]. Yet in contemporary Namibia, the San face many forms of discrimination, including prejudices such as being drunkards, childish, incapable of sustaining themselves and primitive. Even the term 'San', which has negative connotations, was designated for a set of various tribes with dissimilar languages [2]. We prefer to be distinguished and identified by our language affiliations, such as Ju/'hoansi, !Xung, Naro, Hai//om, Khwe, N/oha, and ! Xoo. However, the term 'San' has been agreed upon as a unifying name of the above-mentioned tribes and has been established nationally and internationally.

2.1 Marginalization Issues

According to Suzman [2], the San 'are regarded as one of the most disadvantaged ethnic group compared to other groups in Namibia on almost every socio-economic indicator'. With a strong drive to reposition the San in mainstream society, we are focusing our efforts on four areas, namely the current lack of agency, land, and education, as well as the ongoing stigmatization.

2.1.1 Lack of Agency

We have very few San leaders who can represent the San communities at a national or global level. Considering that our educational attainment is below the nation's average, very few San have the opportunity to complete their studies let alone become leaders. Consequently, their representations at national or international decision bodies, addressing concerns directly affecting the communities, is mostly absent. Their voices are rarely heard directly, and mainly others speak on their behalf; thus, continuously suppressing the Sans agency. With an accumulated loss of self-confidence and a lack of understanding of human rights, the San do not speak out and lay claim their rights. To make matters worse, the San people are not given the freedom to choose their chiefs and leaders, but the government appoints chiefs for the San people.

Under the umbrella of 'empowering the San', numerous NGOs and initiatives have attempted to 'do good' without consulting the San themselves and understanding what 'good' would mean to the communities. For example, a number of agricultural projects supported by the government and organizations such as the GIZ (German development agency) have been established were San communities were relocated to a farm and engaged into farming activities such as planting, harvesting, etc. However, these projects which are by nature top-down and often donor driven, do not take into consideration the cultural pre-dispositions, skills and likings of the San. As such attempts to convert hunter-gatherers into farmers without adequate training have received much resistance. Projects are recorded as failures, often leaving the impression that the San are not reliable, accountable and teachable, adding to the already existing stereotypes.

On the other side, the value of the San's indigenous knowledge, skills, and practices have been well recognized worldwide. Yet without an appropriate regulatory system in place; intellectual property rights have been violated many at times. One of the most famous incidences has been the patenting of the active ingredient of the Hoodia plant. This plant has been used by San communities for centuries as an appetite and thirst oppressing substance on hunting journeys. However, it was patented in the US and commercialized as an appetite suppressant for the obese, without acknowledging the San or having benefit sharing mechanisms in place. While a policy on traditional and indigenous knowledge has been drafted, many practical questions remain unanswered, such as what regulations on communal benefit sharing will be in place and in which way might they be counterproductive to grass root innovations. Thus, concern has been expressed by the San communities, regarding recordings, research activities and results, ethical principles, as well as models of benefit sharing.

2.1.2 Lack of Land

The land has been a contentious issue in Namibia for long. As such the San Development Website states that:

Due to the encroachment of the European settlers with their farming economies, the san people were dispossessed of their land and their traditional way of life has been severely destabilized. Consequently, they have been marginalized and started living in some of the most inhospitable terrains in the country, mainly surviving by hunting wild game and gathering roots and wild berries [3].

In contemporary Namibia, the land issue has not been resolved as yet to the satisfaction of many. Illegal grazing and fencing are the main challenges in communal lands were San people are living and most of the San people do not own land.

2.1.3 Low Level of Education

Current statistics reveal that San learners in Namibia have the lowest education outcomes, with less than 1% finishing their secondary education. Many explanations and reasons are given to explain this phenomenon. The most common reason given by San parents and learners for not attending school relates to poverty; an inability to pay expenses associated with school, including school and hostel fees (despite the exemption of school fees), books and other school-related items, clothes and toiletries, and bedding. In addition to poverty, San students often face severe discrimination and stigmatization from other students, teachers, school officials and hostel staff. Most San children live in villages or settlements that are remote from the schools, thus they stay far away from their families. Furthermore, there is a remarkable cultural mismatch between school and home, including both language differences and important cultural and social differences. Other explanations for the lack of San participation in schools include inappropriate curricula for indigenous learners, a lack of San teachers and role models, and teenage pregnancies.

While there are many reasons for the low educational success rate of San learners, the situation has severe impacts on the San communities' development. For one, they cannot compete in the formal job market and are thus highly vulnerable to exploitation. They experience difficulties accessing information, dealing with official paperwork, and developing general skills, capacities and confidence, thus being trapped in a vicious circle.

2.1.4   Stigmatization

Surrounded by stigmas and stereotypical characteristics, such as laziness, stupidity, childishness, the San often grow up assuming the position of the marginalized victim or the fighter continuously leading a counter-narrative. With clearly distinct physical features and often being petit in nature, San children are bullied at school more than others. Accounts of San children being discriminated at school and university by teachers and other learners, at workplaces and also at other public services are many. Even when San make it through the formal education system, they still face enormous difficulties in obtaining formal employment because of the stigma attached to them and their communities. We often do not know and understand our basic human rights, which allow other people to discriminate against us. San people are called names such as 'Vaduni, kwankaras (people who consume everything in one go leaving nothing for tomorrow), Mkuruha (people who have lived for long in the bush)' by other majority ethnic groups in Namibia.

2.2   Support Initiatives

As a minority and marginalized ethnic group in Namibia, the San currently receive much international attention, with a focus on establishing their rightful position within mainstream society as well as preserving their rich cultural heritage. Meanwhile, a number of local initiatives have joint forces in the fight against marginalization in an attempt to undo previous injustices. However, most San organizations in Namibia are donor bound, which creates further dependencies and challenges of sustainability. Below, we describe a few of the Namibian initiatives that exist for the purpose of fighting marginalization of the San.

2.2.1 Namibian San Council

The Namibian San Council is an association which was established in 2006 and comprises of different San communities in Namibia. The San Council is running a project with the Museum Association of Namibia, in collaboration with the Museum Africa where San artifacts are displayed. The artifacts displayed in the Museum are from the San who live in Namibia. This is a way of reviewing the history of the San culture, to preserve our history, and to empower our youth.

2.2.2 //Ana-Djeh San Trust

In 2014, San youth in Windhoek have formed a non-profit non-governmental organization called //Ana-Djeh San Trust. The name //Ana-Djeh is a word derived from !Xung, one of the San dialects, which means 'new light'. The main aim is to promote the San's right to education and to preserve the cultural heritage of the San communities. The organization is engaged in numerous outreach activities, including rural school visits, empowerment workshops with rural and urban San youth, and the production of information material in form of booklets. //Ana-Djeh San Trust recently launched an inspirational role model pamphlet by the San for the San.

Concerned with the well-being of the individuals within the communities, // Ana-Djeh San Trust leads a counter-narrative to overwrite a widespread negative and discriminatory image of the San. At the same time, the trust actively addresses current issues of dispute, such as the lack of agency, right to land and education in the light of latent discrimination.

2.2.3 Nanofasa Conservation Trust

This organization was established in Norway by Aleksandra Orbeck-Nilssen and was joined by the co-founder of //Ana-Djeh San Trust this year. It has the aim of decreasing dependencies and preserving tradition and culture. The #TakeItOFF Campaign is a global awareness movement encouraging people to take off labels that have been put on us and return to what is honest, true and sacred in our lives. The backbone of the Campaign is a 1200 km long expedition #Sanwalk, where Aleksandra Nilssen, the activist and founder of Nanofasa, walked from the east to west of Namibia with San huntsmen, !ui and Kamache. The trek took place in the traditional way of the San people, with Aleks expected to survive by living largely of the land by going back to nature and its rich deep roots.

3 The Interactive Digital Performance

As each organization is following different means of creating awareness and initiating change, //Ana-Djeh San Trust youth have engaged in a digital journey of expression.

3.1 Original Inspiration and Plan

The following section is an edited excerpt from the original proposal submitted to the ICCCS 2016 by Daniel Cabrero and Tertu Fernandu [1], who got inspired by the 'Theatre of the Oppressed' [4] and shadow dances [5] as a means to express the San's ongoing marginalization. The Theatre of the Oppressed [4] examines the way in which poetry, drama, protagonists, antagonists, empathy and other elements and devices are utilized in theatre since its inception. This publication ultimately offers an approach to artistically address issues of subjugation via political means of expression. Ultimately, The Theatre of the Oppressed provides a potential space to the subjugated because theatre is determined by society much more stringently than the other Arts. This is due to its instant contact with public and its great power to convince [4].

Emulating the above premises the artwork proposed in this paper aims to find how theatre can be situated at the service of the oppressed; how they can express themselves and that by using the theatrical and technological language San groups can discover new, restorative concepts against marginalization.

The combination of screen projection and live performance is an emergent theatrical technique. An example of this comes from [5], where projected shadows and live entertainers are choreographed via an interactive performative representation. The artistic combination of screen projections and live routines can provide ostracized societies with tools to perform interplays that combine dualities like issues with marginalization versus capabilities and strengths as antagonized by the San groups above [1]. Hence, this mixture of screen projection and live performance is proposed to enable the San group to (1) mirror themselves as they see their marginalization before others via a projection; (2) then counteract such feelings by casting their abilities, dreams and drives live, and (3) to later heal their feelings of ostracism. 'Follow my Shadow, See me to Suffer; Track my Spirit, Empathise with Me' is an artistic attempt to make a group of San aware of the potential and prospects their customs, skills and dreams hold, while also making audiences aware of and empathising with the current feelings of the San groups.

To realize this objective a series of prerecorded imagery first conveys shadows (i.e. marginalization issues) faced by the San. A set of silhouettes and other elements projected onto a screen portray how the San are perceived as being incapable, unreliable, drunken, primitive, childlike, etc. These were formed in response to the following questions: Why are you uneducated? Why are you discriminated and bullied? Why are you uncivilized? Why not open to technology and modern life-style? Why are you afraid to try and explore new things? Why are you exploited? Why are you the weak tribe in the world? [1].

Subsequently tracking the spirit (i.e. strengths) leads the San to respond to the above via a live performance inspired by a task in which the group of San wore masks of anonymity and conveyed the following messages: I am proud of being a San; I feel lucky for being a San; I love to defend rights of people, especially San; I want to change discrimination against San.

Combining screen projections and live routines, the San can face their feelings of stagnation and challenge themselves via positive self-representations. This ulti-mately intends to heal the San from such ostracizing bearings.

3.2 The Production Process

Tertu Fernandu and Daniel Cabrero discussed the idea of the interactive perfor-mance and called fellow San youth to participate in the performance production. At the first meeting, five San performers (including Tertu) attended. Daniel Cabrero showed one of his earlier movie productions comprising of flamenco dances, fol-lowed by a shadow dance movie on YouTube [5] to provide us with inspiration and to show us what is possible. Daniel shared his research on the creation of Personas in different ethnicities, including the San community [6]. To push the agenda Daniel Cabrero pointed out what he had read about the San, namely that they are humble and live in peace and harmony, but also that they are ignorant, drunkards, and childish. He asked us about our opinions and feelings regarding these representa-tions. We let him know that we were very upset and felt provoked. However, this also gave us the energy to correct this representation and to create a counter-narrative. We took a paper where we wrote and/or drew about how we were living in the past, and how we want to live in the future. Then, we shared these amongst each other and had a lively discussion about all kinds of issues, such as the Botswana border and other contentious matters. During the discussion one of us took notes and another was drawing. Looking at the notes and drawings we selected a set of specific topics and ordered them in a timeline. We wrote up a rough storyline of approximately 20 pages. Later it was rewritten and organized into parallel scenes, which would either be voiced, displayed on the video, or performed (see script below).

Considering that none of us had traditional attire here in town, we rented the clothes from the National Theatre of Namibia. Unfortunately, the clothes were made out of linen and not leather as the original traditional attires. Other utensils were collected from the bush, such as sticks and reed.

The video was produced through shooting, cutting and editing a series of short clips, combined with clips and pictures taken from the public domain on the World Wide Web. A full session was dedicated to the scripting, rehearsing and shooting of the video clips. As agreed upon, these depicted different scenes, such as ladies collecting veld food, hunting scene, domestic working, as well as a drunken San lady throwing bottles away. All scenes were performed in front of a white banner. The original idea was to transform the clips into shadow scenes, yet it was decided to leave them in their original lighting. Daniel then cut and edited the video and read the voice over script. The video was shown to us for feedback and change requests. Considering the short time frame we were happy with the product. We then launched into multiple sessions of performance rehearsals were we refined stage actions, such as the trick of the bottle thrown in the video and caught on stage by a real actor at the moment.

In summary, the interactive performance comprised of elements of the San history, present-day issues and future plans. It was personalized through individual points of interest, messages to be conveyed, as well as artistic and cultural elements, as an expression to share our joy and struggles with the public.

3.3 The Performance

The performance was staged as part of the opening programme of the ICCCS 2016 conference at the Safari Hotel in Windhoek, Namibia. The prerecorded video was displayed on a large screen mounted behind the stage, where the actors performed in front of the conference participants and invited guests. Most notable was the presence of the Minister of Information, Communication and Technology. The following table shows the scenes, with the corresponding voice-over, video images, and performance (Table 1).

The performance received a great round of applause and positive feedback from the audience. The minister reminded the audience of the marginalization of the San, as well as the value of our knowledge. He further praised our skills and performance in his opening speech. He promised to ensure connectivity for all remote indigenous villages throughout Namibia, allowing for a fruitful information and knowledge exchange. We felt very proud of our achievement of producing this digital interactive performance, of performing it, and getting our message to an international audience.

On a critical note, we admit that the performance has much space for improvements. For example, the current voice-over is read by Daniel Cabrero, a non-San, and thus it produces a kind of contradictory message in terms of wanting to hear the 'San voices'. The editing of the video was extremely rudimentary with the clips still showing the edges of the background banner. Though some of the audience thought it was done in purpose as a specific artistic form of expression. Thus more work will need to be put in the video editing. However, at this point the video is not in the possession of any of the authors, thus we need to learn to take greater ownership of our materials.

Fig. 2 Scene 1.1 of performance (authors of the chapter)

Table 1 Scenes of the performance

Scenes	Voice over	Video images	Performance
1.1	Once upon a time in Southern Africa, there was a group of people called San We all spoke different dialects	Three photos of San depicted on a map of southern Africa	Two women sitting with crops, three men hunting over the stage (Fig. 2)
1.2	These groups were living in peace and harmony, and were known as skilled hunters and gatherers	Moving images over southern African map depicting san in action	Same as above
1.3	We were living in an egalitarian society where decisions were made collectively	Image of San around the fire and hut in the background	Performers leaving the stage
1.4	Education was practical and children disciplined without violence This was a very happy community	Self-recorded clips of san hunting, picking crops, etc.	Empty

(continued)

Table 1 (continued)

Scenes	Voice over	Video images	Performance
1.5		Self-recorded clips of san hunting, picking crops, etc.	San man talking to the audience: 'But one day all of this happiness began to vanish And these peaceful San communities were relegated as the marginalized communities in Southern Africa'
1.6	'Where are you going?' 'no you cannot this is the Botswana border'	Self-recorded clips of san woman walking In front of Namibia map towards the border where a person on the other side asks:	San woman talking to the audience: 'We decided to keep living our lives a hunters and gatherers However, when we tried to move to other places, we were told that we cannot' A san man comes on stage and moves San man points to the east
1.7	Then other tribes came with domesticated animals and farming and cropping; and they blame us because, as hunters and gatherers that we are, we hunted their animals and collected their crops; so they regarded us as thieves, and they beat and enslaved us	A map filled with cattle and other domesticated animals in between self-recorded clips of San	San scratching their heads and leaving the stage (Fig. 3)
	'Do this, and that, and this...'	White man filling half the screen with a pointing finger saying	San woman fulfilling different household jobs as a maid
1.8	Working under pressure is negatively affecting us. And when we are told to do many things at once, it becomes far too many, for what we are insulted and discriminated		Woman walking to the middle of the stage... Screaming out: 'enough, enough'

(continued)

Table 1 (continued)

Scenes	Voice over	Video images	Performance
1.9		Self-recorded clip of the same woman drinking in a bar She throws a bottle	Woman says: 'Now I feel lonely and sad because I am feeling less human. So when I come home, instead of letting it all out, I turn to alcohol —then I become violent'
1.9		Self-recorded clip with community members coming to comfort the drunk woman, they stand all together in a half circle	Man jumps on stage having caught the bottle and says: '…which is neither good for me, nor for my family. For this, community policies can help and support me in living a life together as we San used to live; and share all wisdom with the Nation and the world' Man leaves the stage
1.10	This is a different kind of leadership that we are used to We used to NOT have chiefs and bosses but a respectful house of the household	White man on left side of screen, San sitting in a circle in front of a tree, and San elder on the right side	Man walks on stage saying: 'This allowed us to be democratic, for what we felt very lucky' and hands over San constitution to the VIPs in the audience
1.11	Today we feel equally lucky that sustainable development projects come to us However, we need to be consulted and involved from the very beginning of the project We also need continuity in the projects	Three men standing and observing, White man with suitcase negotiating with San woman, shaking hands, point all directions, leaving… San woman wondering…	
		San discussing in a circle matters	San woman walking up and down on stage saying: 'we also believe that having our own community policies developed will help us to share our traditional knowledge, and to sustain community development projects in today's world…'

(continued)

Table 1 (continued)

Scenes	Voice over	Video images	Performance
		Book	'...Now you have seen how we lived, how we were transformed, and how we want things to be done' All five performers on stage each saying one part of the following: 'Are you willing to listen to us', 'to understand us', 'and to work together with us', 'to improve the livelihood of the San', 'and to learn and live together?' (Fig. 4)
			San walking on stage in line singing a traditional song

Fig. 3 Ownership discussion of authors of this chapter

Fig. 4 Final scene of the performance depicting authors of the chapter

4   Digital Artistic Expressions of Sufferings

The following section is an insert by Heike Winschiers-Theophilus, as an editor and interaction designer currently working with us on cultural technology developments.

The purpose of this short insert is to place the current digital performance in context with other similar projects. We distinguish two aspects, namely the narrative itself as well as the means of digital expression. The San have a long history of narratives being told by 'the others' without their voices being heard directly. Truna [7] assumes a critical stance on the story told of Cwi Nqane, a San from Tsumkwe, who won a Samsung sponsored trip to Korea upon having won a video game at the Windhoek showgrounds. Two storylines go through the media, one presenting technology as a savior to the indigenous communities and one as destructive, while none allows for Cwi to appropriate technology in his own terms and tell his own story [7]. However, been given a digital platform to express themselves, Sabiescu [8] reports on one Romani group she has been co-designing self-portraying websites with, that chose to describe themselves entirely in form of a counter-narrative. Thus the emphasis of the self-portray was to discard mainstream stereotypical accounts, such as the Roma are thieves, dirty, and irresponsible. Similarly, the performance presented in this article contains elements of narratives in response to mainstream allegations, while striving for a multicultural perspective.

The quest for effective means of transforming society, by changing the attitudes and behaviors of mainstream society, to cease marginalization, abuse and discrimination is ongoing. For example, based on a similar means of expression as the performance presented here, Stroh and Mbonambi [9] performed a theatrical piece in front of an endless looping slide show depicting single suffering woman faces at a time with dramatic musical effects. The act aimed at reminding the audience of the atrocities committed in ongoing gender-based violence through a shocking and memorable audience experience. Ndjibu et al. [10] constructed a cultured interactive technology hut (see chapter in this book), which takes the participants through an equally distressful experience in which they are confronted with the reality of gender-based violence. In both the cases, the audience is left troubled, as the interactive installations do not allow for closure nor suggest actions. The San performance takes advantage of the multidimensionality afforded by technology, in terms of expressing simultaneously the suffering and suggesting a solution. Thereby they leave the audience with worded behavioral instructions regarding future actions. In an attempt to reach a wider audience, to instil self-confidence, and initiate an ongoing dialogue within the society they are currently exploring emerging technologies, such as augmented and virtual reality. First conceptualizations of cultured technologies are being co-designed with the authors, cherishing traditional and indigenous elements while living a modern and urban lifestyle [11]. In order to support a wider societal transformation, more complex and refined digital expressions need to be developed, allowing for deeper user experiences. Thus, building on the current production of the San performance, technologies should be harnessed to initiate an ongoing dialogue resulting in long-term effects.

5 Reflections and Way Forward

Firstly, we would like to comment on the original intent of the endeavour as expressed by Cabrereo and Fernandu [1] to leverage the San's 'skills to make the youth aware of their strengths and possibilities by holding on to their history, tradition, skills and drives as active contextual imperatives, and as organic components in the equation of community self-engagement and societal self-development'. This is very much in line with our initiated actions at the // Ana-Djeh San Trust, which aims to promote cultural pride, restore self-esteem and provide opportunities to succeed in mainstream and modern life. As the San continue to be marginalized, it has been very difficult for us to be recognized in the world. We have been ignored but we are not giving up and will keep on fighting for our rights.

One of the initiatives has been this very specific performance, which was educational, entertaining and at the same time brought out the talents and the creativity of the performers and the producer. San audience could relate to the story having experienced the very same. While the other audience could now understand what the San went through and what their aspirations are, giving clear guidelines for future collaborations. The technology infusion brought new light to a story told so many times. It demonstrated the San's ability to make use of modern technologies thus was unique and novel to the audience. It indeed built up the performers' confidence and solidarity. It was visual and interactive and amplified the voice of the San, serving as an example to fellow San yet equally educational to the rest of the nation, highlighting the importance of the San culture and history. We believe that through the use of technology the audience was more captivated and listened more carefully to the San. Thus the San need to understand the power of technology, which we can use to amplify our voices, educate the nation including our own communities and reach out to international audiences to tell our own story and future aspirations. Thereby, the history can be rectified and the truth is known.

However, technology is new to the San in Namibia. Although a few of us use basic technology such as phones, radios, TV, cameras, computers, etc. We still need more exposure to different technologies to empower ourselves, to preserve and promote the San culture and to use technology as a platform to amplify our voices. The urban San youth is using social media platforms to share information and to debate San community issues. However, most of the San communities in rural areas do not have access to or knowledge of technologies such as smartphones. Often chances are only given through donor agencies or government initiatives with limited access due to high prices of connectivity and devices. We suggest to initiate a technology empowerment programme which will train rural san in the use and development of technologies, which will improve their well-being.

We, the authors, are grateful to have been exposed to new digital forms of expressions, such as this digital interactive performance and other technologies such as augmented and virtual realities, internet of things, gesture-based inputs and many more. We still feel overwhelmed by the new technologies we have seen such as the augmented and virtual reality, games, sound and music applications and even wearable organs. At this point, we cannot quite grasp the endless opportunities given and the possibilities of merging technology with our rich cultural heritage as everything is still novel, unfamiliar and amazing to us. We are currently in the process of designing new digital cultural expressions and San value-based technologies in collaboration with students from the Namibia University of Science and Technology. This will hopefully allow us to position ourselves in the digital and real world, as well as reach out to our fellow San youth by setting examples and opening up new opportunities.

Acknowledgements First of all, we would like to acknowledge our co-performers and producers, Appolia Dabe, Esau Kamati, Japeni Hofeni, Simson Kapembe, and Daniel Cabrero without who this production would not have been possible. Further, we would like to thank Prof Heike Winschiers-Theophilus for the editorial assistance in putting this chapter together. We further recognize the financial support of the NCRST for the digital production as well as NUST, Faculty of Computing and Informatics as the organizer of the ICCCS 2016 conference. Special thanks to Namibian government for establishing San division in the government and recognized San people as an indigenous community in Namibia. To our donors, Open Society Initiative of Southern African (OSISA), Finish embassy Namibia, our partners Party Project, Ubuntu Foundation, and Namibian University of Science and Technology (NUST). We would also like to express our gratitude to //Ana-Djeh San Trust, and Women Leadership Center, in particular, Ms Liz Frank, as well as everyone who contributed for the establishment of //Ana-Djeh San Trust.

References

1. Cabrero, D., Fernandu, T.: Follow my shadow, see me to suffer; track my spirit, empathise with me: uncovering Khoisan Marginalisation via a Live Healing Performance. In: Proceedings of the International Conference on Culture and Computer Science 2016, Windhoek, Namibia, Oct 2016
2. San development. http://www.sandevelopment.gov.na/
3. Suzman, J.: Regional assessment of the status of the San in Southern Africa. Report Series in Suzman, J., Legal Assistance Centre (LAC), Windhoek (2001)
4. Boal, A.: The Theatre of the Oppressed, 3rd edn. Pluto Press, London (2008)
5. Thaitd85.: Gruppe Pilobolus Amazing Shadow Dance (2011). https://www.youtube.com/watch?v=FYftvseVzuI
6. Cabrero, D., Winschiers-Theophilus, H., Abdelnour-Nocera, J., Kapuire, K.G.: A Hermeneutic inquiry into user-created personas in different Namibian locales. In: Proceedings of the 14th International Participatory Design Conference (PDC'16), Aarhus, Denmark, pp. 101–110 (2016). https://doi.org/10.1145/2940299.2940310
7. Turner, J.: African Gamer: Whose story is it anyway? In: Bidwell, N.J., Winschiers-Theophilus, H. (eds.) At the Intersection of Indigenous and Traditional Knowledge and Technology Design, pp. 35–66. Informing Science Press, Santa Rosa, California (2015)
8. Sabiescu, A.: Mainstream narratives and counter-narratives in the representation of the other: the case of the Romani ethnic minority. In: Bidwell, N.J., Winschiers-Theophilus, H. (eds.) At the Intersection of Indigenous and Traditional Knowledge and Technology Design, pp. 67–88. Informing Science Press, Santa Rosa, California (2015)
9. Stroh, J., Mbonambi, B.: I rock woman/woman beats drum installation. In: Proceedings of the 13th Participatory Design Conference (PDC): Short Papers, Industry Cases, Workshop Descriptions, Doctoral Consortium papers, and Keynote abstracts, vol. 2, pp. 151–152. ACM Press, New York (2014)
10. Ndjibu, R., Peters, A., Winschiers-Theophilus, H., Namhunya, F.: Gender-based violence campaign in Namibia: traditional meets technology for societal change. In: Proceedings of the 2017 CHI Conference Extended Abstracts on Human Factors in Computing Systems, pp. 1024–1029 (2017)
11. Kauhondamwa, M., Winschiers-Theophilus, H., Fernando, K.: Towards design inspirations for cultural technologies from explorative workshops with San Youth, HCIXB 2017 workshop at CHI 2017. Denver, Colorado (2017)

Technological Aspects of Presenting the Cultural and Historical Content in Multimedia Information Systems

Nikolay Borisov, Artem Smolin and Valentina Zakharkina

1 Introduction

Ongoing upgrading of information and multimedia technologies offers more advanced solutions for representing cultural and historical content in multimedia information systems. The systems can thus become more interactive and informative, as well as include new types of multimedia content (such as video 360°, interactive applications, etc.).

In the narrow sense of the word, a multimedia information system is a specifically structured web portal with the following components:

- Multimedia content (images, videos, video 360°, animation, etc.);
- Database with the options of editing and updating;
- Administration system.

The online resources that represent the objects of cultural heritage are always addressing a very wide range of audience. Apart from the experts in the particular field (historians, archeologists, linguists, architects, experts in cultural studies, etc.), they also target the so-called 'unsophisticated' users (students and other people searching for certain information). We believe that the cultural missionary mission of a resource is highly important, and that makes it imperative to design the interfaces that stimulate effective work with the content and encourage participation and learning [1].

N. Borisov (✉) · A. Smolin · V. Zakharkina
ITMO University, Saint Petersburg, Russia
e-mail: nikborisov@gmail.com

N. Borisov · A. Smolin · V. Zakharkina
Saint Petersburg State University, Saint Petersburg, Russia

© Springer Nature Singapore Pte Ltd. 2018
D. S. Jat et al. (eds.), *Digitisation of Culture: Namibian and International Perspectives*, https://doi.org/10.1007/978-981-10-7697-8_14

Introduction of interactive interfaces into a project that includes substantial multimedia content calls for the adequate server and client solutions. Server solutions provide for software generation of the pages after the database query, functioning of the content manager, division of access rights, etc. Client solutions are end user oriented, and have to represent the content in the most visually attractive way. Thus, the presentation of data as either interactive map or a timeline helps not just to visually accentuate the entities and the links, but encourages the user to look further in order to obtain more detailed information.

The basic server options are provided by most of the modern Content Management System (CMS); however, the more sophisticated situations might call for the design of a customized server software module. The choice of a CMS is, for sure, determined by the structural complexity of the resource and the range of the end user interface solutions that have to be implemented.

Client software solutions imply a fluid mergence of three formal descriptions: page structure (HTML), visual representation of structural entities (CSS), and functionality of individual elements (JavaScript). Incidentally, a number of functional solutions for modern browsers can be implemented without the JavaScript program scenarios. For instance, such common elements as drop-down menus or pop-up notes can be described at the CSS level. Still, even in those cases, JavaScript should preferably be used to facilitate cross-browsing.

Today, most of the software JavaScript solutions are based on the JQuery library that supports cross-browsing and offers an impressive choice of selectors, events, and methods (JQuery API), as well as JQuery UI plug-ins that provide individual functional elements of the interface. To address specific issues of display on mobile devices, JQuery designers offer yet another program library, JQuery Mobile.

Some issues of client functionality can be resolved at the level of JQuery solutions, while certain interface solutions require either time-consuming programming or usage of additional predesigned software modules.

The strategy of using external libraries and modules is determined both by the functional concept of the resource and the designer's preferences. Most of them opt for comprehensive solutions, and the highly popular Bootstrap framework that offers a great software implementation of dozens of standard functional and decorative options is worth mentioning here. Still, certain designers tend to look for alternative solutions, rather than limit themselves to the typified ones, however spectacular they might be.

The process of selecting software modules for a specific task often leads to finding (and sometimes even designing) customized interface solutions. We believe that the balance between using successful typified solutions and the search for the new, even though untested ones, gives impetus to the emergence of new interface ideas and respective software solutions.

2 Multimedia Information Systems for the Conservation of Cultural Heritage

A good case study of a multimedia information system for the conservation of cultural heritage is "Multimedia Information System Architecture and Murals of the Novgorod Church of Transfiguration of Our Savior on Nereditsa" (http://www.nereditsa.ru). The project of the multimedia system, supported by the Russian Humanitarian Research Foundation, was designed in 2007–2009, by a team from St. Petersburg State University, in cooperation with the State Russian Museum and the State Novgorod Integrated Museum and Reservation [2].

The Church of Our Savior on Nereditsa Hill near the city of Novgorod is one of the most renowned monuments of ancient Russian culture. The church, commissioned by Prince Yaroslav Vladimirovich, was built in 1198, and a year later, in 1199, its interior was decorated with frescos. The frescos' exceptional cultural value, excellent preservation and unusual, almost unique iconography brought international acclaim to this monument [3]. In 1992, UNESCO put the Church of Our Savior on Nereditsa on its World Heritage List, together with a number of other monuments from Novgorod and its area

Unfortunately, the Church and the frescoes suffered greatly during the Second World War. More than 80% of the frescoes were irretrievably lost, so the question arose about the virtual restoration of the frescoes of the Church of Our Savior on Nereditsa Hill based on the picturesque copies of frescoes of the beginning of the twentieth century. The project was devoted to solving this problem and presenting results in the Internet.

The multimedia portal offers structured and diverse information on the unique monument: a historical survey of its creation, a description of the specific architectural properties of Ancient Novgorod and the Church of Transfiguration of Our Savior on Nereditsa, the description of the frescos, an electronic library of research data on the history of fresco paintings, bibliographical data. Because of the abundance of diverse data, this resource can be categorized as an academia-and-research type. However, the resource is also accessible to the "unsophisticated" users who take interest in Russian history and culture.

One of the portal's multimedia components is an interactive FlashMap with hyperlinks to the descriptions and images of the key sites of the area, that are located close to the Church of Transfiguration of Our Savior on Nereditsa.

The key component of the multimedia information system is the 3D historic reconstruction of the architectural ensemble and the frescos of the Church of Transfiguration of Our Savior on Nereditsa Hill. At the primary stage of the reconstruction, an authentic historic recreation of the object (both its exterior and interior) was made. After that, the 3D model was used for superimposing unique digitized images of the frescos (images are kept at the State Russian Museum) on the respective sections of the model of the Church, using 3D graphics. One of the major challenges was to align the digital copies of the flat images of the frescos with

Fig. 1 Frescoes of the Church of Transfiguration of Our Savior on Nereditsa Hill (fragment)

the curved surfaces of the Church's interior. The results of the virtual restoration of the Church of Our Savior on Nereditsa are presented in the "3D Reconstructions" section of the portal (Fig. 1).

Apart from the results of the 3D modeling, the designers share their customized method of 3D reconstruction—their work on the project is described in detail and illustrated by a video.

Any digital humanities multimedia information system commonly features two components: structured informational content and the results of virtual reconstruction (2D, 3D or 4D), both available online.

A relevant case study, where, as we believe, the results of the virtual 3D reconstruction play a very prominent part, is the website of the project "Virtual Reconstruction of the Moscow Nunnery of Our Lady of Passion (Mid. seventeenth– early twentieth century): Analysis of the Spatial Infrastructure Evolution Through 3D Modeling" (http://www.hist.msu.ru/Strastnoy/). The website was designed at the Department of Historic Informatics, Historical Faculty, Moscow M. V. Lomonosov State University [4].

The main goal of the project was to provide a virtual reconstruction of a unique historical and cultural site in Moscow, the Nunnery of Our Lady of Passion. The Nunnery was built in 1649, in compliance with the Royal Decree on the foundation of the "maiden" Nunnery of Our Lady of Passion. Later the name of the Nunnery was also given to the adjacent square (Square of Our Lady of Passion), one of the most significant sites in the city. In the eighteenth and nineteenth centuries, the Nunnery went through several major reconstructions and several devastating fires. After the fire of 1812, the Nunnery was completely rebuilt, the new bell tower was constructed over the gate, with the hipped roof and the clock, of a unique architectural design. The Nunnery had evolved into one of the city's major ecclesiastic centers. It incorporated a school for the girls, a library and a hospitium.

In 1931, Square of Our Lady of Passion was renamed Pushkin Square. Hardly anything has been preserved there to remind us of the historic look of Square of Our Lady of Passion back in the seventeenth or early twentieth centuries.

The principal outcome of the project is the historic virtual reconstruction of the Nunnery of Our Lady of Passion with the adjacent architectural ensemble of Square of Our Lady of Passions, featuring three temporal strata: turn of the sixteenth–seventeenth centuries, the 1830s and early twentieth centuries.

The main informative component of the website is the section "History of the Nunnery of Our Lady of Passion" that features a survey of its history, based on several published sources. There are also general data on the project: an annotation, the project's structure and information about the project team. The bibliographic component is to be found in the section "Publications and Presentations by the Team Members".

Otherwise, the structure of the website has a direct connection to the virtual 3D reconstruction of the Nunnery. The section "Virtual Reconstruction: Sources" is the archive of the records used for designing the virtual reconstruction (topographic plans, blueprints, inventories, etc.); they highlight the historical accuracy and authenticity of the recreated structures of the Nunnery of Our Lady of Passion.

The section "Technologies of Virtual Historic Reconstruction" details the process of reconstructing the architectural monuments, and offers general operational guidelines for such projects.

Apart from 3D modeling, other technologies, such as photogrammetry, laser scanning, and aerial footage were used for making the virtual 3D reconstruction of the site.

Finally, the section "Results of the Virtual Reconstruction" is a compendium of the resulting multimedia and interactive matter, used for the visualization of the Nunnery and adjacent historic and architectural ensemble of Square of Our Lady of Passion at several time samples. In this section, the user can view, in interactive online mode, both the virtual reconstruction of the Nunnery and the Square as a whole, and the 3D models of individual buildings and structures.

Addressing several interactive maps (for various time samples), designed with flash technology, the user can view the complex as a whole and obtain a historical reference for each of the buildings.

Besides, the use of Sketchfab technology adds the option of interactive (in 3D) examination of individual buildings (Fig. 2), accessing information on them through the use of special markers, and downloading the images of certain structures in *.pdf format. In this format, sectional view of the objects is available; besides, dimensions of the architectural monuments can be projected on the 3D model.

Fig. 2 Sobor of Passion Virgin (1910 year)—3D virtual reconstruction

The virtual tour of the complex is available in two formats:

- Video format—viewing the virtual tour of the reconstructed monument in the movie format;
- Location, designed with the use of Unity 3D graphic engine, offering an interactive walk through the site.

Another key component of the project is the augmented reality mode [5]. The main idea of designing the application was to project the virtual historic reconstruction and the available source-study data on the modern urban environment. In order to create the software shell with the elements of augmented reality, panoramic shots were filmed (and stitched together in PtGui); they offer an all-round view of the sites of today's Pushkin Square from 15 base points at different locations. After that, the final version of the application was assembled in Kolor Phototour Pro 2. The final version of the application takes the user on a virtual tour of the modern Square of Our Lady of Passion, and thus introduces him to its present-day look; he can also utilize the option of projecting historic layers of the urban environment from a certain time period on today's landscape.

3 Multimedia Information System for Museum Communities

As we discuss various multimedia information systems, we should always keep in mind the mobile platforms, for they offer an excellent opportunity to represent various information resources in the format that can be used, for instance, in tourism (eTourism). Location-based service that uses various technologies for defining the specific location (GPS, satellite systems, WiFi, etc.) can provide interactive navigation through a cultural heritage site.

One of the relevant case studies is the resource "Open Karelia Network" (Fig. 3), a system that provides information on museums (http://openkarelia.org/); it is designed within the framework of the project "Euregio Karelia—Museum Hypertext" [6]. The system is an open one, which means that various museums of Russia and Europe can join it. The museums that have joined the Open Karelia museum network have their own web portal that is optimized for viewing from various devices. Currently, 12 entities, 8 of them museums, are involved in this project.

Content can be fed into the system in two ways: manually and through automatic import from various open reliable sources that offer updated and verified information.

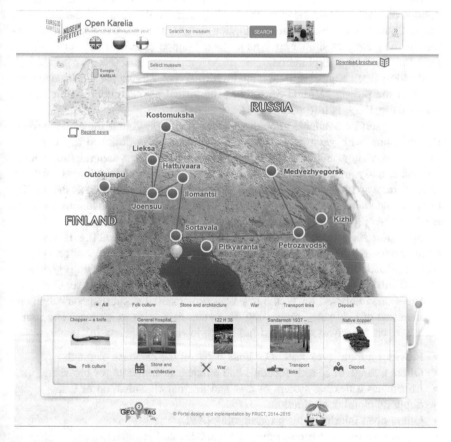

Fig. 3 Open Karelia network (homepage)

The main purposes of the system are [6] the following:

- To improve visitor attraction of the venues through mutual advertising of the museum collections and new approaches to electronic representation, all the above build up the visitor interest;
- To create a virtual interactive extension of the galleries space, by reconstructing the lost or temporarily inaccessible artifacts and objects of cultural heritage;
- To facilitate and optimize the process of information tracking and managing the exhibitions.

The main information component on the homepage of the web interface for Open Karelia system is the map of Euroregion Karelia, with the icons that show the location of the museums—members of the Open Karelia network. The map highlights logical links between different collections. The links unite the exhibitions and collections into various theme categories.

The collections are united through the description of their exhibits, with the options of viewing their location and binding them to the map and the time axis. Each artifact has a card with its description, image, and the list of related tags, as well as the gallery of similar artifacts in the exhibition of the current museum, as a guideline for further exploration.

Besides, Open Karelia system includes virtual reconstructions. For instance, the result of the project "Virtual Sortavala", the virtual reconstruction of the city of Sortavala in 1939, is also featured [7].

Another service available through the Open Karelia system is the audio guide to the museums, with geographic references. The service is designed to inform the prospective visitors about interesting cultural heritage sites, natural monuments, museums, and various infrastructure objects located at a certain limited distance from them. Any objects from the Open Karelia database can be used as the binding ones. As the visitor moves along the route, he receives audio notifications about the nearby objects [6].

Open Karelia system is based on Geo2Tag platform. Geo2Tag is the most popular open-source LBS platform in the world [8]. The platform can be used for building desktop and mobile applications for processing (or just using) geographical and map data and integration with popular social networks and services [9].

The system is based on Web 3.0 + LBS principles, it supports geolocation and mechanisms of automated processing of content from various sources. The source code is open for downloading and has the following parameters [6]:

- Provides a multilevel system of links between the database elements;
- Offers a range of hi-tech methods and efficient instruments for browsing;
- Effectuates a flexible system of tags and internal classification of data;
- Supports cloud configuration;
- Offers open interfaces for programming (API);
- Offers instruments for designing new modules and extensions.

4 Multimedia Information Systems with Virtual Reality Technologies

Another instrument for the improvement of the interactivity of multimedia information systems, are hardware–software complexes based on the systems of interactive immersion into virtual environments. This implies the use of various virtual reality headsets that offer the high level of user immersion into the multimedia and information environment.

Using a desktop hardware–software complex, of the "computer + virtual headset (e.g., HTC Vive)" type, the user can take a tour of a virtually reconstructed cultural heritage site, visit a virtual museum, with the option of tactile virtual contact with the exhibits, try out the simulator of a reconstructed historical mechanism, etc.

A good case study that showcases the use of virtual environments to augment a multimedia information system is the web portal that has been designed as a part of the project "Ancient Fortresses of the Northwest of Russia Multimedia Information System" (http://nwfortress.ifmo.ru) [10].

The system of ancient fortresses in the Russian Northwest, was built between the thirteenth and fifteenth centuries and formed a robust defense shield. It protected Old Russia's borders from foreign invaders (belligerent Swedish feudal lords and knights of the Livonian Order), provided access to the Baltic Sea, and ensured Russian sovereignty over the country's remote Finnish-speaking parts [11]. Some of the fortresses have been preserved, they are fortification monuments and popular tourist centers of Leningrad region (Koporye, Korela, Ivangorod); others still exist, but in ruins (Tiversky Town, Yam).

The team of this project consisted of the experts from ITMO University (Design and Multimedia Center, Department of Graphic Technologies), as well as the history researches from St. Petersburg State University and the curators of the museums that now function in the former fortresses.

The multimedia information system «Ancient Fortresses of the Northwest of Russia» is a website which consists of historical, archeological, and other materials regarding the five fortresses in Northwest of Russia: Koporye, Yam, Korela, Ivangorod, Tiversky town. In addition to relevant text materials, the website also contains various other forms of multimedia, including photo galleries, videos and virtual three-dimensional reconstructions, virtual tours, and social graph.

A social graph is a graph where the nodes represent social objects, and the ribs represent social ties between them. The interactive graph of the "fortress-researcher" relationship was designed on the basis of the data pool collected as a part of the project. The user can access additional information on the objects from the social graph, and then get redirected to the relevant pages of the site. For modern browsers, the rendering of the ribs of the graph is done by special software, in SVG vector format. A special information structure was designed to create the graph, it represents the social ties between the "Fortress" objects and "Research Staff" objects.

The project involved designing virtual 3D reconstructions of five fortresses of the Northwest, and subsequently, the respective locations were posted on the web portal. The fortresses were modeled in Autodesk 3D Studio Max, with subsequent export into Unity 3D graphic environment.

The fortress of Korela was selected as the venue for the virtual interactive tour in 4D format, because the virtual historic reconstruction of the fortress (late seventeenth–early eighteenth centuries.) and its current exterior could easily be aligned (Fig. 4).

The resulting product is the virtual interactive tour of the present-day Korela fortress with a private guide, in video 360° format, with the option of interactive choice of the direction of further exploration from the key points of the tour. We have also designed a "leap in time" from the video 360° format, featuring the present-day view of the fortress, into the 3D format of the historical reconstruction, with the option of interactive visit to the reconstructed objects of the fortress and subsequent return to the respective key points of the tour in video 360° format. This interactive virtual 4D tour was designed for the Oculus Rift DK2 virtual reality headset.

While planning the filming of the tour in video 360° format, we have superimposed the exterior of the present-day fortress on its reconstructed exterior of the late seventeenth–early eighteenth centuries. We have selected the key points that do not coincide with the unpreserved reconstructed virtual objects, and chartered the routes between them. The walks along these routes were filmed on the site in video 360° format, in back-and-forth mode, to provide the user with the option of backtracking to the initial point of his virtual walk.

Fig. 4 3D virtual reconstruction of Korela fortress

We have recorded, in video 360° format, video files of two types, "stationary" and "motion" ones:

- "Stationary" formats are static videos, loop rolls (running for 30 s) that keep playing until the user selects the direction to his next destination;
- "Motion" format is the video recorded while walking along the route.

The route can be selected by aiming a semi-transparent "aiming sight", aligned with the user's gaze, at a special marker, who activates an animation that shows the time that will elapse before the respective action takes place. If the gaze is "averted" before the end of the animation, the marker glides to the initial position.

The video in the "motion" format, featuring the walk along the route, is activated once the route is selected; as soon as the destination is reached, another stationary video, filmed at the end of the route, is activated.

One of the challenges we had to face while designing the 4D virtual tour was to integrate a large number of fairly high-resolution video files into the Unity3d system, as well as to ensure the playback and switching between them. To implement these options, we used RenderHeads AV Pro Windows Media plug-in. This plug-in allows to seamlessly playback of the video with the required resolution, as well as to superimpose the video onto any surface. Since the footage filmed in video 360° format has equidistant scanning, a sphere with the inwardly inverted normals was used as the projection surface [12].

We also used the sprite animation technology. The video file was broken into frames and converted into a table, which was interpreted by the Unity3d graphic environment as a sequence of images that were subsequently animated using the in-built animation instrument from Unity3d.

To facilitate the interactive control of the virtual tour, the following hotkeys were provided:

- Rewind the current video file of the tour, to jump to the next control point;
- Return to the beginning of the virtual tour in 360° video format from any control point.

To switch from the virtual 3D tour in 360° video format to the virtual 3D reconstruction, a "hotkey" was programmed, that offers the option of moving from any control point of the video tour in video 360° format to the same point of the virtual 3D reconstruction.

In the virtual 3D reconstruction, control keys that are typical for the majority of the 3D computer games are used for the interactive navigation of the fortress.

To return to the present-day video tour in 360° video format, a special portal has been designed for each control point.

The tour begins with an introductory video with the credits, then the guide greets the user and welcomes him or her to the unique historical site that has been preserved until nowadays. This experience adds to the in-depth emergence into the virtual space.

5 Multimedia Information System "Architectural Ensemble of Solovetsky Monastery in the Period of Its Highest Prosperity (XVI–XVII Centuries)"

One of the key aspects of the modern multimedia information systems is the combination of interactivity with various related technologies. The experts from ITMO University, together with the research staff of the Solovetsky National Historic and Architectural Museum and Natural Reserve, supported by a grant from the Russian Humanitarian Research Foundation, have designed the information multimedia system featuring the ensemble of the Solovetsky Monastery: http://solovky.ifmo.ru [13].

There is a large number of unique historic religious sacred sites within the Russian Federation, that is still being used for the initial purpose and attract special attention of pilgrims, tourists, researchers, etc. One of such sacred sites is definitely the Solovetsky Monastery, listed as a Highly Valuable Object of Cultural Heritage of the Peoples of the Russian Federation [14].

The Solovetsky Monastery holds an exceptional place of honor in the Russian history and culture. It was founded in the fifteenth century, as the residence of the spiritual followers of the "father of the Russian monasticism", Holy Sergey of Radonezh, and soon evolved into the ecclesiastic, cultural, political, and economic capital of the Russian North. The missionary efforts of the Solovetsky clergy led to the proliferation of Christian faith along the endless vastness of the Russian Arctic Circle area. The Solovetsky Monastery played the key role in stimulating the migration of the Russian population to the White Sea area. The Monastery was instrumental in repelling the foreign invasion of Pomorye in the late sixteenth century.

The seaside monastery made a major impact on the emergence of the economy and marine practices of Pomorye. It thus gave impetus to the exploration of the Arctic Ocean by the Russian seafarers and to turning Russia into a great Arctic power.

In the Middle Ages, the Russian government delegated important foreign and military policies to the Solovetsky Monastery, and the monastic community left a substantial legacy in the history of Russia. The Solovetsky Monastery was the place where the paths of many major historical figures of Russia had crossed—spiritual leaders, ecclesiastic and political activists, writers. For centuries, the Solovetsky Monastery was a major pilgrimage destination. A powerful image of the monastic archipelago can be traced in the prerevolutionary literature and visual arts.

The Monastery that was founded on the uninhabited islands and evolved into a major power center, still stands as an inspiring national symbol of creativity and overcoming historic challenges; it is one of the country's major sanctuaries.

The Solovetsky Monastery is a major part of the Russian cultural legacy, primarily because of its outstanding architectural monuments and extensive collection of icons, votive objects, pieces of applied art, manuscripts, blackletter books, and other documents.

The monks of Solovki were particularly proud of their Treasury that ranked amid the most outstanding collections of ancient Russian art. Only the libraries of some major monasteries could compete with the Solovetsky Library in the importance and number of manuscripts and old-printed and handwritten books.

The special importance of the historic, cultural and natural legacy of Solovetsky Archipelago led to the foundation of the Solovetsky Museum and Natural Reserve (1974), as well as to its inclusion into the list of the Highly Valuable Objects of Cultural Heritage of the Peoples of the Russian Federation. Session sixteen of the UNESCO Committee for the Protection of Cultural and Natural Heritage added the architectural ensemble of the Solovetsky Monastery to its World Heritage list.

Historic, cultural, and natural complex of Solovetsky Islands is a unique entity, with the extremely well-preserved ecclesiastic and residential buildings, fortifications, auxiliary and hydraulic structures, roads, etc. The complex evolved between the sixteenth and early twentieth centuries. The main component of the historical and cultural complex of the Solovetsky Monastery is the central ensemble that includes the fort, the churches, residential buildings, auxiliary and hydraulic structures, workshops, and production units.

Virtualization of the cultural heritage objects pursues the following goals:

- Virtual reconstruction of the object, in order to demonstrate what it looked like in the past epochs. For this purpose, it is necessary to have the adequate amount of content, such as blueprints, archival images, engravings, etc.
- Virtual conservation of the object in its current state, to preserve it in the virtual format for posterity. In this particular case, the main technologies used for the purpose are 3D scanning and photogrammetry.
- Design of interactive products with the use of virtual and augmented reality technologies.

The above mentioned tasks can be combined in various modifications, for the purpose of representing a certain cultural heritage site in the most comprehensive way. The results obtained are used to meet a specific goal, to design an information resource with the specific structuring of the historic and research data. Using the technologies of augmented reality, information support for the virtual tours of the cultural heritage sites can be designed for smartphones.

The main components of the Multimedia Information System "Architectural Ensemble of the Solovetsky Monastery in the Period of Its Highest Prosperity (sixteenth–seventeenth centuries)" are [13] the following:

- Unique historic data, represented thematically in the respective section "History";
- The archives of the historical sources used in the working process, to emphasize the scholarly component of the project;
- The 3D virtual reconstruction of the architectural ensemble of the Solovetsky Monastery in sixteenth–seventeenth centuries;
- The virtual spherical panoramic tour of the architectural complex;

- A multimedia library of relevant video and photo data on the history and current state of the Solovetsky Monastery;
- An interactive 4D tour of the Solovetsky Monastery ensemble.

At the initial stage of the project, the curators of the Solovetsky Museum and Reserve compiled a bibliography of required sources (ca. 220) on the history and architectural complex of the Solovetsky Monastery. They were consolidated into an archive. The virtual reconstruction of the Solovetsky Monastery in sixteenth–seventeenth centuries was made with high historic precision because of the abundance and diversity of available academic and historic sources: the Monastery's inventories beginning with 1514 and up to the early twentieth century, a huge bulk of other historical sources available at the main archives of the Russian Federation, a vast number of visual records (icons, engravings, lithographs, photographs, including the color ones) dating back to the period from mid-sixteenth to early twentieth centuries, records of the archeological excavations of the Monastery site from mid-1960s till nowadays. Besides the project of the restoration of the architectural ensemble of the Solovetsky Monastery, that includes its axonometric models in sixteenth–nineteenth centuries, as well as architectural measurements, graphs, sections, projects of the restoration of all the major monuments of the Monastery's ensemble.

The architectural complex of the Solovetsky Monastery includes: the church complex (Transfiguration Cathedral, Church of St. Nicholas, Church of Assumption with the refectory and treasury, the gatehouse Annunciation Church, Church of St. Philip that has been fully rebuilt at a different location); the complex of auxiliary structures (the Mill, the Drying Chamber, Kitchens, Fur Chamber, Icon-Painting Chamber, Tailors' Chamber), as well as two residential buildings for the monks, the Cloisters of the Annunciation and the Sanctifier. The complex is surrounded by a unique fortification wall, made of boulders, with eight towers (White, Archangelskaya, Povarennaja, Kvasovarennaya, Nikolskaya, Korojnaya, Uspenskaya, Pradilnaya) and eight strips of fortification walls.

The virtual reconstruction of the architectural ensemble of the Solovetsky Monastery in sixteenth–seventeenth centuries became necessary because the initial architectural view of the monastery was much distorted by the reconstructions of the eighteenth–nineteenth centuries, as well as by the irreparable damage inflicted in the period when the Solovetsky Special Prison Camp was located on the site. The current restoration strategy implies that the late-period reconstructions of most of the monuments will be preserved, that is why the virtual reconstruction is the only way to show the ancient ecclesiastic ensemble in its entity and integrity to the community of the researchers of the Russian culture and the public at large.

The virtual reconstruction was based on the archival data and carried out in close cooperation with the research staff of the archive of Solovetsky State Museum and Reserve. Besides, the photo and video footage of the Monastery in its current condition was used as the auxiliary data.

One of the challenging issues was a vast number of discrepancies between the drafts made by various groups of researchers at various times. Whenever the problem arose, the most reliable drafts were selected by the researches from the Solovetsky Archive. This was the case with the roof of the Cathedral of Transfiguration of Our Savior. Three options were outlined, including the modern view, and the most credible one was selected. The data on the changes that were not documented in the drafts was also provided by the Archive.

3D Studio Max software package was used for the modeling. The main peculiarity and challenge in the reconstruction of the walls and the towers of the Solovetsky Monastery fort was the unique structure and texture of the materials these objects are made of. The challenge was to render the masonry (boulders) with utmost precision. Every wall has its own type of masonry, with boulders of different sizes—this is determined by the special historic features of each structure and the technologies of the time, these special features had to be taken into account [15] (Fig. 5).

Photogrammetry methods and the method of generating of extrusion maps and normal maps based on photographs were chosen as the most appropriate for the reconstruction of such textures.

At the first stage, three-dimensional support models of fortress towers and walls between them were created according to the drawings. In a number of cases, there were discrepancies between the data in the drawings made at different times by different restoration groups.

These problems were analyzed together with a team of professional architects and employees of the Solovetsky Museum and optimal solutions were worked out.

Part of the objects [Korozhnaya tower, Spinning tower, some walls (spindles)] has been restored from photographs using photogrammetry technology. As a result, high-polygonal models of areas of objects were obtained, with the shape reproducing the forms of real objects with a high degree of accuracy.

From the modeled towers and wall elements, heightmap and normalmap maps were produced and applied to previously created low polygonal copies of the models of these objects. Also, texture maps were done.

Fig. 5 Virtual 3D reconstruction of Solovetsky Monastery

Special "patches" based on existing textures were created in the graphics editor for parts of objects that were not included in the photo because of the impossibility or difficulty of access.

Thus, thanks to the photogrammetry technologies, it was possible to obtain three-dimensional models of a high degree of reliability, both in terms of geometry and texture maps, in order to obtain information on the shape of real objects and transfer it to reference models.

For a number of objects, high-resolution texture maps (about 35,000 pixels on the long side for the spindles) were manually combined from the available photographs for use as textures on models.

In order to optimize performance, reduced copies of textures (16K, 8K, 4K) were created to use them at distances that do not require high resolution. In order for the objects that were bouldered to not look flat, on the basis of the received images, height maps and normal maps were generated using special software to be applied to reference models modeled on drawings.

Another difficulty was the use of height maps to "extrude" parts using the Displacement algorithm. Since the obtained maps did not cover 100% of the whole object, in the places of sharp transition of the form (loopholes, joints of objects), the algorithm gave an unacceptable result, "tearing" the model.

To solve the problem, additional masks were created for all objects based on the texture scan, which, when mixed with the previously obtained height maps, eliminated the emerging unwanted artifacts. The texture of the brick was also generated using photographs.

The structures were positioned on the landscape modeled from the topological plan and existing section plans of the Monastery's territory. All the possible changes in the relief have been taken into account.

The main interactive element of this multimedia information system is an interactive map located at the homepage of solovky.ifmo.ru. The map is the chart of the Solovetsky Monastery in sixteenth–seventeenth centuries, and currently, it features 15 hotspots, the so-called "presence spots" (Fig. 6).

To design the interactive map, we have created a software module that enables the site editor to add new presence spots and edit the relevant data. Both a block of information and media elements in various formats can be attached to each spot. In the current version of the site, the options of 360° Video representation and 3D scenes visualization are available.

The interactive map is a virtual interactive 4D tour of the Solovetsky Monastery; it mainly concentrates on the architectural highlights of the Monastery's ensemble.

The virtual interactive 4D tour is structured as a map of the Solovetsky Monastery that is divided into sectors. In each sector the user can select one of the following viewing formats:

- Virtual tour in video 360° format—present times;
- Virtual tour in 3D reconstruction in video 360° format—sixteenth–seventeenth centuries;
- Textual illustrated information about each sector.

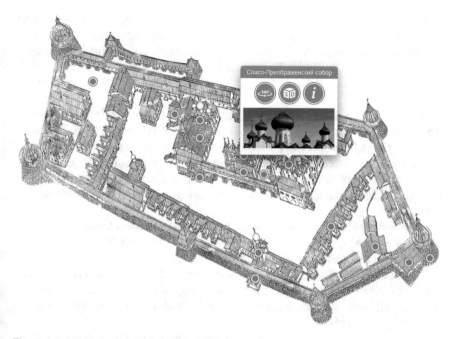

Fig. 6 Interactive map of the Solovetsky church complex

This virtual interactive tour gives the user a chance to experience an in-depth personified immersion into the Solovetsky Monastery.

The first component is a short tours in video 360° format: a professional guide speaks about the architectural significance of the site of the Monastery located at the respective presence spot. To create this virtual interactive tour of the architectural ensemble of the Solovetsky Monastery, we filmed local tours of fifteen sites within the Monastery grounds, using the video 360° technology.

Video tours in 360 video format were filmed in cooperation with the Video360Production Project, using a custom-developed two-camera system with Entanya Fisheye Lenses.

All the artistic and technological challenges of filming the video tour in video 360° format arise from the special features of the technology. Watching this video, the viewer allegedly stands on the same spot as the camera or the cameraman, he is able to take in all the space covered by the camera, as well as to interactively control the direction of his gaze. When the video is viewed on the computer, the mouse is used for controlling, while when it is viewed through various virtual reality headsets (Oculus Rift, Samsung Gear VR, etc.), the viewer just turns his head.

In planning the filming of each of the episodes of the tour in video 360° format, the timing of the viewer's ability to comfortably process the interactive virtual reality of video 360° has to be taken into account. According to the current standards, the duration of 2–15 min is recognized as the reasonable comfortable length.

One of the typical faults of video 360° is the distortion of the image at the upper and lower end of the frame. To counter that, the height and the location of the camera have to be calculated with utmost precision, especially if there are people in the frame.

The second element of virtual interactive tour of the architectural ensemble of the Solovetsky Monastery is the 3D visualization of the view of the Solovetsky Monastery from the respective presence point, based on the digital reconstruction of the monastery of sixteenth–seventeenth centuries, with the option of a 360° survey. Thus the concept of a 4D tour is implemented: from one and the same location the user can "visit" two different time strata, our days and sixteenth–seventeenth centuries.

The third element offers the historical background, in textual format, with photos highlighting the special architectural features of the sites of the Solovetsky Monastery at this particular presence spot.

The resulting product is the information multimedia portal that features a wide range of multimedia elements (3D reconstructions, video 360°, an interactive map, etc.), as well as the informative and educational content on the history of Solovetsky Archipelago.

To design the web portal that would allow to store and efficiently access all the data of the multimedia information system that features the architectural and historic monuments of the Solovetsky Monastery, one of the most popular noncommercial platforms, CMS Drupal, was used.

The software solutions for the interactive elements of the resultant Web resource can be provisionally divided into three categories:

- The elements that are typical for a number of resources, with the typical client solutions (menu, tooltip, drag and drop manipulations, scrolling position processing, etc.). The programming of the interactivity of these elements can easily be done on the level of JQuery, with the additional options provided by frameworks, e.g., Bootstrap. Customized software modules also emerge. In this project, Superfish Menu module was used, as well as the small and elegant Tipso module that offers tooltips for interactive maps.
- The elements that are equally typical for representing certain data formats, yet offer a wider range of interface solutions. The natural sample is an image gallery. Even though an image is the most common element of the modern Web resources, the options of image display are very diverse and, as a rule, necessitate the selection of specific software modules.
- Fairly complex interface elements that necessitate special settings and server support for the organization of the data by content manager. Thus, many successful JavaScript solutions for interactive graphs, maps, charts, and diagrams can be further improved through integration with the respective server modules for popular CMSs. In this project, such module was designed for the interactive map. The content manager determines the coordinates of the objects, inputs the

informative illustrated text, anchors the video fragments and 3D scenes. Using the available data, the server scenario forms the visible and initially hidden elements of the map. The functionality is ensured by the client software scenario that uses the software modules Tipso (tooltips) and FancyBox (output of data blocks in overlay).

Software solutions used for the presentation of artwork deserve special analysis. Scanned archival data and photographs of the current state of the sites are crucial for the cultural heritage resources, and they have to be structured for comfortable viewing. One trivial option should not be neglected: the insertion of the image "as it is", in its original size, into a block of text; however, it is worthwhile to mention the options that require certain software support at the server level, as well as the software client solution. The main options are as follows:

- Displaying a set of miniatures, with the option of activating each of them for viewing the full-size image. The full-size image is displayed in an overlay. It is a very practical solution, for it gives the user a chance to get the initial summary of the visual data. The software solution can be based on the numerous clones of the once-revolutionary Lightbox. In this project, FancyBox software module was used, that allows to display in overlay not only just the images, but also the data structured in HTML.
- A compact solution that allows to simultaneously display both the set of miniatures and the full-size image. The main image and the miniatures are displayed in size-limited blocks, in certain versions, scaling and detail enlargement are available. A positive sample is JGallery that offers the options of numerous settings and viewing modes.
- Instantaneous display of one image from the set. Typical solutions are offered by numerous modules with the slider option. This option is very widely used, for it looks very attractively on the small screens of the mobile devices. The designers often choose it for decorative purposes. However, there is no option of viewing the whole set of images, at least on the miniature level, which drastically reduces the informational value of this solution.

In designing the web portal for the architectural complex of the Solovetsky Monastery, we tried to meet the following requirements:

- Storage of the website's main content and administration parameters in the database;
- Representation of media elements from a wide range of formats;
- Divided rights of access to the content and the website parameters; specified roles with respective privileges;
- Updating and editing of the site via web interfaces accessible to respective roles;
- The option of follow-up by the content editors without special education or special skills of working in the global network;
- The option of generating the database structure on the level of creating new entities with their own sets of fields;

- Software generation of a display of information blocks, as the result of addressing the database entities by field filtration;
- Realization of the designer idea in the display of pages of different types, with the option of subsequent correction.
- Realization of the adaptive versions of displaying the site on a wide range of gadgets, including mobile devices.

The final version of the project's web portal meets all those requirements. Multimedia information system "Architectural Ensemble of Solovetsky Monastery in the Period of its Highest Prosperity (sixteenth–seventeenth centuries)" is available online at http://solovky.ifmo.ru.

6 Conclusion

Modern information and multimedia technologies offer unlimited options for full-scale visual representation of cultural and historical data. The efforts of the research teams working in technologies, humanities, and other fields, to create multimedia information systems based on the historically credible content and supported by hi-tech digital solutions will definitely lead to the ongoing improvement of the educational, academic, and research of online resources.

This work was supported by the project Multimedia information system "Architectural ensemble of the Solovetsky monastery in the period of its highest prosperity (XVI–XVII centuries)" (Grant 16-01-12022, Russian Foundation for Humanities).

References

1. Borisov, N., Smolin, A., Zakharkina, V.: Interactivity in multimedia information systems for cultural heritage. In: Proceedings of the FRUCT'20, pp. 562–568. FRUCT Oy, Finland (2017)
2. Borisov, N., Shvemberger, S., Shcherbakov, P.: 3D modeling as a tool for creating information systems related to historical and archaeological monuments. In: X All-Russian Joint Conference "Internet and Modern Socity", 23th–25th Oct pp. 68–71. Saint Petersburg, Russia (2007) (in Russian)
3. Bulkin, V.: The transfiguration church on Nereditsa and the Novgorod Architectural School of the XII century. In: Church of the Savior on Nereditsa: from Byzantium to Russia, pp. 33–50. Moscow, Russia (2005) (in Russian)
4. Borodkin, L., Zherebyatiev, D., Mishina, E., Ostapenko, M., Moor, V., Kim, O.: Methodology and sources of virtual reconstruction of Moscow historical centre: Strastnaya square, 1830s. In: EVA 2015 Saint Petersburg: Electronic Imaging and the Visual Arts. International Conference, pp. 95–102, June 24–25, St. Petersburg, Russia (2015)
5. Mironenko, M., Moor, V.: Geoinformation systems and 3D-reconstructions. In: Historical Informatics, pp. 4–18 (2015)

6. Museum Network "Open Karelia". http://fruct.org/sites/default/files/files/Brochure_Open Karelia.pdf
7. The Virtual Sortavala. Web: http://virtualsortavala.jns.fi/
8. Balandina, E., Balandin, S., Koucheryavy, Y., Zaslavskiy, M.: Role of mobile OS and LBS platform in design of e-tourism smart services. In: Proceedings of the UBICOMM 2016, The Tenth International Conference on Mobile Ubiquitous Computing, Systems, Services and Technologies, pp. 172–177. IARIA (2016)
9. Geo2Tag. Web: http://www.geo2tag.com/
10. Borisov, N., Smolin, A.: Virtual reconstruction of the ancient Russian fortress koporye. In: Proceedings of the Third International Conference "Digital Presentation and Preservation of Cultural and Scientific Heritage" DIPP2013, pp. 147–152. Veliko Tarnovo, Bulgaria, 18–21 Sept 2013
11. Kirpichnikov, A.: Stone fortress of Novgorod. Publishing House "Science", pp. 4–5. Leningrad (1984) (in Russian)
12. Borisov, N., Smolin, A., Shcherbakov, P., Trushin, V.: Design of interactive virtual environments. Interactive virtual 4D tour of korela fortress. In: EVA 2016 Saint Petersburg: Electronic Imaging and the Visual Arts. International Conference, pp. 84–89. St. Petersburg, Saint Petersburg, Russia, 23–24 June 2016
13. Multimedia Information System "Architectural ensemble of Solovetsky Monastery in the period of its highest prosperity (XVI–XVII Centuries)" http://solovky.ifmo.ru/
14. Osipenko, M.: Solovetsky Monastery: history and shrines, p. 676. Solovky (2014) (in Russian)
15. Borisov, N., Smolin, A., Volkov, O., Trushin, V., Shvemberger, S., Logdacheva, E., Zakharkina, V., Tserbakov, P.: Specificity of 3D Modelling in the projects for preservation of cultural heritage. In: EVA 2017 Saint Petersburg: Electronic Imaging and the Visual Arts. International Conference, pp. 75–81. Saint Petersburg, Russia, 22–23 June 2017

Part IV
Interactivity in Culture Experiences

A Cultured Interactive Installation to Probe Gender-Based Violence in Namibia: The Tales of Nali Technology Hut

Ruben Ndjibu, Naska Goagoses, Heike Winschiers-Theophilus, Anicia Peters and Fannes Namhunya

1 Introduction

Gender -based violence (GBV) is a global societal ill, occurring across cultures and countries around the world [1]. Horrifically, one in three women experience some form of GBV in their lifetime [2]. GBV is defined as a harmful act, perpetrated against a person based on their socially ascribed gender; most often GBV is committed by men against women and children, who are ascribed to a subordinate societal status and increased vulnerability [3]. GBV and violence against women are often used interchangeably, because most violence is perpetrated by men against women [4]. Violence against women continues to be a pressing problem across the world, undermining women's fundamental rights, such as dignity, access to justice and gender equality. The impact of violence against women reaches far beyond the individuals immediately involved, i.e. the victims and perpetrators. It affects

R. Ndjibu (✉) · H. Winschiers-Theophilus · A. Peters
Namibia University of Science and Technology, 13 Storch Street,
Windhoek, Namibia
e-mail: rubendjibu@yahoo.com

H. Winschiers-Theophilus
e-mail: heikewinschiers@gmail.com

A. Peters
e-mail: anicia.peters@gmail.com

N. Goagoses
Carl von Ossietzky University of Oldenburg, Ammerländer Heerstraße 114,
26129 Oldenburg, Germany
e-mail: naskagoagoses@gmail.com

F. Namhunya
University of Namibia, 340 Mandume Ndemufayo Avenue, Pioneerspark,
Windhoek, Namibia
e-mail: ftnamhunya@gmail.com

© Springer Nature Singapore Pte Ltd. 2018
D. S. Jat et al. (eds.), *Digitisation of Culture: Namibian and International Perspectives*, https://doi.org/10.1007/978-981-10-7697-8_15

families, communities and society at large. Even in the present, most countries are unable to deal with the phenomenon effectively [1]. Although many actions have been taken to reduce GBV such as dissemination of information, legal and civil actions and promotion of preventive measures [5], there is still a lot to be done. According to Doris Bartel, a Senior Director of Gender and Empowerment at CARE USA [6], GBV is such a complex issue; it requires numerous services and difficult coordination among services; furthermore, numerous resources need to be combined to form multifaceted solutions.

Though being a global ill, there are local differences in the act, spread and causes of GBV. 'There is no archetypal attacker—but there are cultural patterns of movement and behaviour in each community, as well as regional and local discourses of sexuality and violence' [7]. Social and cultural factors translate into attitudes towards violence against women [8]. Namibia has a great diversity of cultures, which are mainly dominated by a patriarchal system. Many rural communities in Namibia do not have much experience with women who take on professional roles, remain unmarried and live away from their families [8]. In many court cases of GBV in Namibia, men still defended the maiming or killing of female partners as their perceived right to chastise a woman, which is allegedly part of their distinct culture [9]. Although correlations between GBV and social–cultural values have been recognized, this has not yet led to possible measures to combat the overwhelming trend of violence, nor to deconstruct conflicting value systems in Namibia [10]. Though the Namibian Government has made great strides in gender equity in the government and private sector [8], gender inequalities are still believed to be the root of violence against women in Namibia.

In an effort to reach out, present-day advocacies on public education, cultural learning and campaigns on social issues in Namibia have sought to harness passive communication channels, including newspapers, television, radio, advertising, public service announcements, direct emails and the Internet [10]. Recently, there has been a proliferation of websites designed specifically to persuade or motivate people to change their attitudes and behaviours towards a certain topic [11]. Social media can also be a powerful tool to change norms and attitudes that endorse sexual violence. With this in mind, two of the authors (Namibian men), launched an online social media campaign titled 'The Tales of Nali', which advocates cultural learning and raises awareness on pressing social issues in Namibia. The campaign included a series of self-produced video clips, which highlighted societal ills such as GBV (in different forms). These went viral with more than 500,000 views and triggered numerous online debates. However, the social media campaign has not sufficiently leveraged technology to move beyond creating awareness to achieve a long-term cultural change. We postulate that based on a vast wealth of cultural practices in Namibia and technology as a change agent, that we can deploy public art in form of a cultured interactive technology installation to address GBV. Thus, we designed and built a traditional technology hut, which transformed 'The Tales of Nali' into a public interactive technology installation. The aim of the installation was to probe GBV in Namibia, to establish values and attitudes associated with GBV. Specifically, we achieved this through a role simulation technique within a traditional setting.

2 Related Work

2.1 Technology to Combat GBV

The spread of mobile technology and the Internet has great potential to combat GBV at a scale never seen before [6]. As more women find themselves with increasing access to mobile technology and the Internet, the technology world attempts to provide women with more and better tools to help them stay safe [12]. Technologies like SMS networks, GPS monitoring systems, radio and television programs, have been appropriated in order to give women information, support, and surveillance, to increase their security [5]. Furthermore, mobile phones and the Internet give women freedom—to speak to whomever they want, whenever they want. It also increases their mobility, for example through crowdsourced tools like maps of assaults, and tools which improve the reporting of crimes [6]. Multiple projects have engaged in reporting and mapping experiences with sexism and crime, through user participation and awareness campaigns. Personal safety applications such as Circle of 6, Everyday Sexism, HarassMap and Hollaback, are being disseminated in multiple markets to help women send an SOS signal to friends, family and emergency services. Technologies help bring everyday experiences of sexism and assault to light through real-time reporting and counter-mapping. In many instances, data reported via these technologies has resulted in local law enforcement changing their routines and resource to create a safer environment for women [12].

Yet [7], warns from an overly optimistic thinking in which ICT is seen as a saviour in reducing GBV. She problematizes the dilemma of designing technologies to prevent, protect and support post-trauma experiences of GBV. 'We are designing for criminal events that should not happen to anyone, but do—in a wide variety of socioeconomic, political and cultural contexts. There is no "standard" or "normal" rape, which calls into question the efficacy of a uniform design in response to sexual assault' [7]. Besides a fictive feeling of momentous safety, a technological standardization of such acts risks the fostering of societal acceptance of crime and women lacking agency. Buskens [13], reminds us of the power of a transformative approach over a conformist or reformist design. 'In assisting women to conform to existing gender relations and society as it is, designers will inevitably contribute to maintaining and strengthening the status quo' [13]. The author exemplifies this with technologies such as the SHE wear, an electric anti-rape underwear introduced by engineers, built as a direct reaction to the December 2012 gang rape and murder of Jyoti Singh in India [14]. Reformers, as [13], describes, do not directly challenge established socio-economic contexts yet 'reform existing gender relations in the hope that this will influence the male-female gender relations so that rape will not occur anymore'. On the other hand, designers following a transformative approach recognize 'systemic gender biases not only as a problem in itself, but also a symptom of a deeper problem plaguing human societies' [13]. Thus, the author suggests the design and use of technologies that allow for a re-conceptualization of the self, as proposed by Light [9]. In line with a transformative approach, we are exploring designs with the intent to trigger a wider societal evolution with a definite attitude and behaviour change in regard to GBV.

2.2   The Potential of Public Art and Interactive Technologies

The making of public art has occupied a special position amongst human activities in many cultures globally [15]. The role of public art installations has become an essential tool to enliven, inspire and intrigue, motivate and provoke people in the public space. Public art can be interpreted as artworks situated in public spaces with free access to an audience of public users and communities of interest [16].

Public art installations can exist in urban centres, suburbia, rural regions, cyberspace, contexts of augmented realities and economic spaces of international flows [17]. Public art has expanded towards forms of socially engaged public art practices in many disciplines, such as computer science and multimedia design. According to Benford et al. [18], public art installations can also be used as a medium to create spaces that are discomforting to the audience. This, in turn, creates a frame for engagement with challenging themes, provoking audiences to reflect on their responses and feelings. Artistic works that employ discomfort to confront challenging themes may set an appropriate tone, demand personal commitment, avoid trivialization and promote empathy and respect. With increased possibilities of digital means of expression and technologies providing targeted user experiences, interaction designers can purposefully create discomfort. This can help produce a more entertaining, enlightening, socially bonding cultural experience and technology designers can employ combinations of visceral and cultural discomfort by distorting control and social relationship [18]. For example, an interactive theatre installation entitled 'I Rock Woman/Woman Beats Drum', created a feeling of distress among the audience to highlight the ever-growing social ill of GBV in Namibia [19]. The installation was designed to take the audience through a new and awkward experience of performance art; through a singular space, the installation was used to explore the journey of abused Namibian women through art, song, film, poetry, and visual landscapes. These types of tools, combining art and technology, will give us the greatest ability to change the social scenery and the asymmetries that are embedded in these. Public art and technologies have the unprecedented potential to reach all of its intended audiences.

3   Namibian Context

In the recent years, GBV has taken on endemic proportions in Namibia [20]. A multi-country study revealed that in Namibia more than one-third of ever-partnered women reported having experienced physical or sexual violence at

the hands of an intimate partner at some point; with 31% reporting physical violence and 17% sexual violence [21]. Over the past years, violence escalated to
numerous 'passion killings' among partners and exes, with as many as 36 reported
in 2014 and 48 in 2015 [22].

3.1 Causes of GBV

Several research studies attempted to investigate root causes for GBV, but the
problem is multifaceted. Studies have had contradictory results regarding attitudes
and beliefs towards GBV; this may be due to the large variances in demographics,
including age, ethnicity and socio-economic status. For example, studies have
shown that women with no education experienced far more violence (47%) than
educated women (26%) [23]. High correlations have been found between alcohol
and GBV, with 71% of violence perpetrated against women included alcohol abuse
was recorded [23]. However, alcohol cannot be attributed as a cause of GBV, as
there are underlying characteristics, such as jealousy, self-esteem, possessiveness,
power and control which have been found to drive GBV [23, 24].

Culture, on the other hand, seems to be a strong contender as one of the causes of
GBV. Although some studies found disparities for the cultural acceptance of GBV
in Namibia [24, 25], there are numerous occurrences and studies which support the
role of culture. Interviews with perpetrators of domestic violence revealed that older
men did not view their actions as abuse but as culturally acceptable behaviours [26].
All of the perpetrators had witnessed violence amongst their parents when growing
up, and a substantial amount was subjected to violence themselves [26]. In some
instances, men have defended the assaulting and murdering of their female partners
as their perceived right to punish a woman, which allegedly is part of their culture
[3]. The payment of lobola (a bride price), which is still done in several communities, is often perceived as the man having ownership of his wife, thus giving him
the rights of control. A survey of university students found that 82% think the belief
that women are owned by a partner or husband is still prevalent in Namibia [25].
Furthermore, in some Namibian cultures, being beaten was traditionally viewed as a
sign of love [26].

One suspected cause for the high pervasiveness of GBV in Namibia is the
prevalence of traditional attitudes. UNFPA [2], found that in Namibia around 28%
of men and 21% of women considered beating to be acceptable in their culture. This
view was also shared by university students, were 50% of men and 30% of women
respondents said that traditional customs and laws customs justify violence against
women [25]. However, in an earlier study, only 15% of university students agreed
that beating women is part of African culture and heritage [26]. This is also
reflected in the attitudes held towards domestic violence, with both women (26%)
and men (22%) agreeing that there are occasions in which wife-beating is justified
[23]. Numerous other studies have reported similar trends and statistics, concerning
the appropriateness of domestic violence [26].

Furthermore, the changing dynamics within the society has been deemed a likely cause for the increase in GBV. It is believed that violence against women has intensified due to the changing status of Namibian women, with equal rights for both men and women. This equality threatens the men's desire to keep up the tradition of being the head of the household, just as their fathers were. Coupled with insecurities, due to poverty and unemployment, men are more likely to reassert their dominance and status by using violence. However, as alluded to elsewhere, Ministry of Health and Social Services [23] revealed that educated women (26%) experience far less violence than uneducated women (47%). Culturally accepted concepts of masculinity and femininity, which have been subject to change, are also believed to be a causing factor in GBV [26].

3.2 GBV Legislative Framework

The country has an extensive national legislative framework that is designed to deal with GBV. Despite such a comprehensive regulatory system GBV records have increased over the years. Legislative instruments addressing GBV include among others the Namibian Constitution, the Labour Act of 2007 (sexual harassment), the National Gender Policy (2010–2020), the Married Persons Equality Act of 1996, Combating of Domestic Violence Act of 2003 and the Combating of Rape Act of 2000. Even within these legislative frameworks, cultural aspects are seen. The National Gender Policy of 2010 states that the adopted legal reforms address issues of economic and social injustices that result from former discriminatory cultural practices, historical imbalances and patriarchal ideologies. The introduction of the Combating of Domestic Violence Act resulted in many debates within the Parliament, with culture being raised several times [26]. While the Deputy Minister stated that the Bill is an indication of the failure of the Namibian cultural, religious and family values, some colleagues argued that the Bill was instead a sign that Africans were gradually losing track of their traditional values. They maintained that such laws will divide families, and should not be implemented to solve 'petty things' that occur in the home. However, other members of Parliament asserted that the Namibian culture does not condemn violence and should stop being used as an excuse for inequality. The Deputy Minister of Justice firmly asserted that in cases where Namibian traditions and culture conflict with the Namibian Constitution and statutory laws, they are deemed invalid. Hon. Gurirab stated that 'we must not see culture and tradition as static and must be prepared to discard those practices in our cultures which serve no purpose in the day and age we live' [26].

3.3 GBV Interventions

Although Namibia has a comprehensive legislative framework to handle GBV, there is an obvious gap between its enforcement and social transformation. In

March 2014, after a series of so-called passion killings, the Namibian Head of State declared a National Day of prayer against violence. The initiative was received with mixed feelings and opinions by the nation. While some applauded the spiritual turning, others criticized the lack of worldly actions. It brought forward numerous debates, highlighting contradictory speculations, myths, believes, values and attitudes around the topic. Moreover, it also displayed helplessness and the lack of appropriate solutions. Under the mounting public pressure and a call for action, a number of initiatives emerged. The First Lady of Namibia launched the Zero Tolerance Media Campaign against GBV in July 2015, as well as a national #BeFree campaign. Furthermore, the country also participates in the annual '16 Days of Activism against GBV' campaign which is part of an international campaign started in 1991 [1].

In 2015, an online interactive campaign titled 'The Tales of Nali' was launched by two of the authors. The campaign advocated cultural learning and raised awareness on pressing social issues in Namibia, using social media and Internet platforms [27]. Through its promotional initiatives, the campaign has reached out to more than 500,000 online audiences (mostly Namibians) on platforms such as Facebook, YouTube, Twitter, Google+ and WhatsApp. Although having succeeded in reaching a large audience, the campaign has not sufficiently leveraged technology to move beyond creating awareness to achieving long-term cultural change. The Tales of Nali technology hut was conceptualized as part of a wider research initiative to investigate the values and attitudes of the Namibian population, in order to design an informed technology campaign with the intent of breaking the cycle of violence.

4   The Tales of Nali Technology Hut

4.1   Physical Description

The Tales of Nali technology hut is an interactive installation that combines cultural probes and technology to engage the public in the topic of GBV. The hut is modelled to look like an Oshiwambo/Rukavango cultural homestead, and includes some of the items traditionally found there (e.g. baskets, wooden stools). Similar looking huts and items are also used by other tribes in Namibia and on the African continent. Through an artistic flair, it was made to look like a circular brick hut with a straw roof, although it is mainly built out of Styrofoam and cloth. The hut measures two metres in height and covers an area of 6.3 m squared (Fig. 1).

The inside walls of the hut contain collages with paintings outlining the Namibian indigenous cultures, landscapes and articles extracted from the local newspaper about GBV issues in the country. The following paintings are found on the walls of the hut (Fig. 2).

Fig. 1 The exterior view of The Tales of Nali installation

Fig. 2 The interior wall of the hut painted with scenes relating to Namibian cultures, landscapes and GBV messages

Image 1—portrait of a Rukavango man in his traditional attire close to his livestock and homestead. In the portrait, the man is seen striking at the outcry hand of GBV in Namibia with a spear.

Image 2—portraits of a compilation of GBV messages extracted from the local newspapers about GBV issues in Namibia. The image is designed to look like a

Namibian map with a hand of GBV articles from the newspapers. This image is referred to as the outcry hand of GBV in Namibia.

Image 3—portraits of a San/Khoisan ethnic man, with a bow and arrow walking in the Namib deert. In the portrait, the San/Khoisan is also striking at the outcry hand of GBV in Namibia with a bow and arrow.

Image 4—the portrait shows a traditional homestead, ant hill and palm trees, which is a common landscape from the northern parts of Namibia mainly in the Oshiwambo, Herero, Rukavango, Zambezi and Kunene ethnic regions.

Image 5—portrait image of an Oshiwambo woman in her cultural attire, harvesting mahangu (pearl millet) in the field.

Image 6—portrait of a landscape with a river flow, which is popular to the ethnic groups from the northern part of Namibia within the Kunene, Kavango and Zambezi regions.

A traditional local ambience was created by appealing to different senses such as smell and auditory. A unique scent of Omumbiri, the powder traditionally associated with OvaHimba people was used. As well as recordings of Ovambo music, playing men and women clapping hands and singing are moderately played inside the hut but heard outside. The items used to decorate the surroundings of the hut installation are as illustrated in Fig. 3.

Fig. 3 Items used to decorate the hut

Item 1—Calabash, is a vine-grown fruit, which can either be harvested young and used as a vegetable, or harvested mature, dried and used as a bottle, utensil or pipe. When dried, calabashes are often used in the homesteads of many Namibian ethnic cultures to store beverages, water, milk, seed, food, etc.

Item 2—Palm tree fruits, are fruits that are harvested from the palm trees and are popular to many ethnic groups from the northern part of Namibia within the Oshiwambo, Kunene, Kavango and Zambezi regions.

Item 3—Kalimba instrument, a musical instrument that is popular amongst many ethnic groups in Namibia, especially by the San/Khoisan ethnic group.

Item 4—Woven basket, is a popular tool used by many ethnics in Namibia, especially by the Oshiwambo ethnic group. The tool is used to carry and store food.

Item 5—The tales of Nali album cover artwork. The album cover is used inside the hut to promote the 'Tales of Nali' online campaign. The audio content from the album is also used to play the traditional ambient sound in the hut.

Item 6—The Omumbiri powder, traditionally associated with OvaHimba people. The powder is used to create a unique scent inside the hut and surroundings.

Item 7—Face masks designed in a shape of a cheetah, a wild animal that is found in many parts of Southern Africa, and Namibia holds the largest population of Cheetah in the world. The masks were often used to decorate the participants during photo shoot session at the installation site.

The interior layout of the hut is as illustrated in Fig. 4. The technology setup consists of a client–server architecture. The server is positioned in proximity to the hut but not obviously visible to the participants. The server machine comprises of a database (MySQL) to store the data from the interactive application, web-server

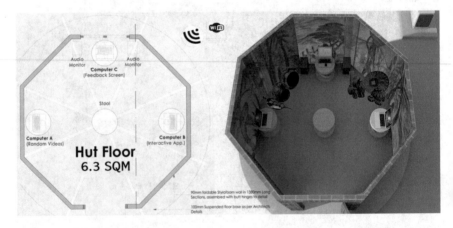

Fig. 4 Interior layout of the technology hut

software (glassfish server) to host the interactive application (Java web application) and multimedia (images, videos and audio) used inside the installation. A local network using a wireless router connects the server to the three laptops (A, B and C) positioned inside the hut.

4.2 User Experience Inside the Hut

Computer A plays a loop of three video films portraying a rape, a passion killing and GBV at home. The videos were scripted and recorded by two of the authors. They were specifically produced for a social media campaign. Computer B presents an interactive computer application simulating the rape and capturing the users' answers while taking them through the different screens (see Fig. 5a–e).

Computer C displays in a random sequencing text answers provided by previous participants (see Fig. 6).

5 The Hut in Action

5.1 Event Descriptions

The hut installation was set up at four different places, at which we recorded data and made small adjustments to reach the final application described above. The hut was first displayed in October 2016 at the International Conference on Culture and Computer Science (ICCCS) in Windhoek, Namibia [27]. The attendees of the conference were mainly national and international academics, however a few politicians and cultural heritage officers were also present. Approximately 15 participants interacted with the role simulation inside the hut. In November 2016, the hut installation was set up again, this time for the #BeFree Activation Conference in Windhoek, Namibia. The conference focused on youth-related topics and was attended by youth (i.e. mostly teenagers), parents and stakeholders. At this conference, approximately 30 participants interacted with the installation. The third exhibition, held in March 2017, was during two workshops with marginalized and unemployed youth in Havana, an informal settlement in Windhoek. At the workshop, 36 participants interacted with the installation. Lastly, we set up the hut in the library foyer of the Namibia University of Science and Technology in Windhoek. In April 2017, approximately 77 students interacted with the hut installation; their ages ranged between 17 and 39, and 47% were male. In all cases, at least one researcher was standing next to the hut.

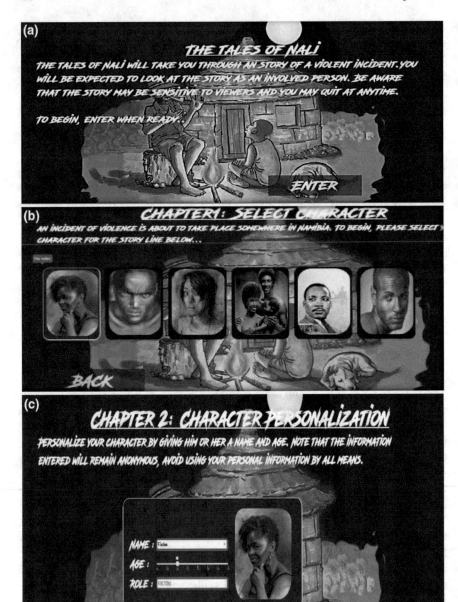

◄**Fig. 5 a** The first screen contained an introductory text, which informed participants that they would be viewing a sensitive film about a violent incident. Furthermore, they are told that the application requires them to view the film as an involved character. **b** Upon clicking the enter button, they were asked to select a pictorial character from whose perspective they wished to see the film; namely the victim, the perpetrator, an eyewitness, a family member of the victim, as an institution or a friend of the perpetrator. **c** Before watching the film, the participants had the option of either viewing the entire event or only segments thereof (i.e. before, during or after the event). **d** Participants then watched the short film. The film is about a perpetrator who stalks a young woman in a shop. He follows her as she takes a shortcut through the riverbed and sexually assaults her. The perpetrator is seen running away and the victim sits crying on the ground. At the end of the film, the victim is seen standing on a bridge and reminiscing about the terrible event. **e** After watching the film, the participants were asked a set of open-ended questions pertaining to the event; for each, they could write a response in a provided text field. Participants were asked what they would do, how they feel, what tool or item they would want, how they could avoid the crime being in the position of the chosen character and why they selected the character they did

Fig. 5 (continued)

Fig. 6 Computer showing randomly sequenced text answers provided by previous participants

5.2 The Hut in Context

The interactive technology hut installation drew a lot of attention at the conferences, workshops and the library. Below we examine and discuss some of the experiences of the participants and common feedback we received.

5.2.1 Outside the Hut

At the conferences and workshops, although the hut was among many exhibits, it still fascinated passers-by and provoked interaction. Participants were asked what had attracted them to the hut and made them interact with the installation. The following features were named:

- The arts and crafts aspect, with all the materials and tools used to construct the installation.
- The artistic appeal that created the hut's physicality.
- The unique scent of the powder traditionally associated with OvaHimba people.
- The objects displayed around the hut, such as the masks and the calabash.
- The sound of men and women clapping, singing and dancing to a traditional song.

The researchers who were coordinating the presentation of the installation onsite were tasked to ensure maximum participation and engagement with the public. Thus, they often invited any curious participants who were caught gazing at the installation to participate in the entire experience. Some participants approached the researcher by the hut and inquired what the hut was all about. There were a few participants who were very interested in finding out about the materials used to construct the hut, especially the brick-looking wall structure. Researchers and participants engaged in discussions about GBV in Namibia and the scope of the study and installation, as they queued outside the hut waiting for their opportunity to interact with the installation. Due to the limited number of participants allowed inside the hut at a time, many waiting participants found other forms of interacting with the installation such as taking photos, selfies and videos next to the installation. However, some participants left due to the long time taken by individuals within the hut.

5.2.2 Inside the Hut

Before entering the hut, a researcher guided the participant through the upcoming experience. The researcher informed the participant about the purpose of the installation and the research, explained the design, assured that there would be anonymity of the provided answers, and gave information about the upcoming interaction. The researcher followed the participant inside the hut to explain the detailed layout and start the technology application. An average session took about 5 min; however, some participants took up to 10 min. The most common character choice was the victim and the witness, and more than 50% of the participants opted to watch the entire film. An analysis of the answers provided by the participants to the five questions is beyond the scope of the current chapter.

6 Reflections

Many participants were provoked by the visuals and storyline of the rape film, which resulted in various reactions and emotions. Upon exiting the hut, most participants engaged in discussions with the researchers, reflecting on their experiences. A large number of participants showed interest, wanting to know more about the installation and the study. To encourage discussion, the researcher asked participants how their experience was, what they found interesting during their interaction, how easy or difficult their experience was, what could be improved about the installation, and how often they discussed GBV with other people. After the conversation, the answers were noted down and at times audio recorded. Below we describe some identified themes, which commonly reoccurred in the discussion held with participants after their experience.

6.1   Relatedness/Realism

'The experience was beyond what I expected; I was personally involved in the GBV incident'. This quote from a participant at the university library shows how open some of the participants were to discuss and reveal their involvement. One of the aims of the installation was the creation of an understanding of the act of violence and provide an insightful experience; in the discussions, participants confirmed that this was indeed successful. Another participant at the university library stated, 'Impressive, I was able to internalize GBV through the interactive environment inside the hut'. Participants at the university and conference affirmed that prior seemingly distant news now felt more real, 'The experiment was very insightful and shocking. The video was almost real and reflected on what we read about in newspaper every day'. and 'The video was very relatable (rape)'. Considering the rising number of shocking atrocities of GBV reported in the news across the country, many people are aware of the situation and could relate it to the current campaign. Participants of the #BeFree Activation Conference reported that 'at school there is a program dedicated to teaching learners about gender-values and moral' and that 'as part of the debate team, GBV is a big topic of discussion during the debate session'.

There were also some individuals who stated that they would invite people or close relations, who were previously victims or were affected by GBV, to participate and interact with the installation. A small number of participants, specifically females, exited the hut and refused to discuss their interactive experience. In the data recorded in the hut, we found that approximately 22% of the participants have been personally involved (directly or indirectly) with cases of GBV. Thus, it could be that for some of the participants the visuals might have triggered some memories of personal traumatic experiences that they did not wish to discuss. Another explanation could also be due to the shame of GBV and specifically of rape [25]. If the participants associated so much with the victim they might either be too ashamed or too angry to talk about it, especially given that the researchers at the hut were mostly male.

6.2   Discomfort

While on the one side the enclosure of the hut ensured privacy, some participants felt frightened of both the space and the topic of the experiment. One university participant described that she felt 'A bit frightening to sit inside the hut alone because it's a bit dark inside'. Emotional discomfort was also observed with most participants showing signs of anger, sadness and/or disappointment; this was evident in their tone of voice and body language. Although the technology hut installation was designed to accommodate only one participant at a time, often participants wanted to go in together or as a small group. Occasionally the researchers allowed pairs or smaller groups of three participants at the same time; these were mainly female participants. Thus it was suggested to 'increase size of the hut so that more than one person can conduct session at the same time'. Participants also felt physical discomfort, especially elderly and bigger people complained about the small entrance and that they needed to bend in order to enter the hut. The volume of the sound was not controlled by the participant, which was also discomforting to some.

6.3 Role-Taking

After selecting a character, participants were asked to answer all further questions in the hut installation as if they were this character. The data revealed that participants were indeed able to do this, as they gave answers that closely corresponded with their choice of character. For example, one participant who chose to be a perpetrator answered, 'Try to silence my victim by grabbing her and covering her mouth so she cannot cry for help', while another wished he had a pillow to smother her screams in response to the question what she/he as the perpetrator would do. A participant, who had chosen to be the institution, stated that they could avoid the crime 'by implementing stricter laws to those who commit these crimes, to set an example for others to fear committing such crimes'.

Occasionally participants described 'difficulty in identifying the best character choice to put you through the interactive session, I wish I could try other characters'. This curiosity in interacting with the installation from the perspective of another character was quite common. A number of participants asked to enter the hut multiple times, to 'try out' the interaction with another character. We allowed this, considering that the intention was for participants to experience the act from different perspectives and express their thoughts and feelings from the point of view of that character.

The current video depicting a rape only shows the perpetrator and the victim, and none of the other characters make an appearance. A participant stated, 'Interesting, however I was expecting to see the character that I have chosen in the video'. Thus, the video would need to include at least the felt presence of the other characters to increase role identification and in-action experience. Alternatively, different videos containing corresponding characters could be made available.

6.4 Technical Judgments

Generally, participants did not have any difficulties operating the interactive installations. Participants expressed that 'the application is user friendly and does not require a lot of computer knowledge to interact' and 'I liked the design of the application. It was easy; it is like playing a normal computer game'. Whenever a participant took longer than expected, the researcher went inside the hut to inquire if there were any difficulties with the application. The majority of participants completed their interactive sessions without external assistance and longer interaction times were ascribed to a high commitment on the side of the participant. They took time internalizing the topic and contents of the application, and answering open-ended questions is always associated with longer time periods.

Some participants were disappointed in the use of older computer equipment, such as laptops: 'I was expecting to see cool interactive technologies inside, perhaps you can use interaction technologies such as touch screens or pads'. With a more permanent structure, touch devices should be integrated within the probes of the installations to make the technology disappear within the design [28]. Other participants complained about the font and readability, which should be re-assessed. One participant more critical to details remarked that 'the questions are not relating to the characters, e.g. an institution asked to answer "how do you feel?" during an event. This question is more suitable to an eye witness character'.

Participants from the ICCCS Conference, who were mainly researchers, were intrigued by the possibility of collecting viable information by recording participants inside the hut, they suggested installing 'video cameras inside the hut to record body language and reactions of participants during the interactive session'. Indeed, at some point the authors did intensely discuss having cameras present [27]; however, even if consent was to be given by the participants beforehand, the installation would lose its sense of privacy and anonymity, which was deemed more important.

The younger participants at the #BeFree Activation Conference were more fascinated and interested in the technology, and were less engaged in the topic of GBV; in comparison to adult participants who showed interest in mitigating GBV and embracing the technological intervention. Youth who had computer studies as a school subject, experienced the hut installation as an eye-opener, seeing how technology can help tackle important problems and transform societies. Some expressed pursuing Computer Science at university in their future.

6.5 Transferability

Many of the discussions revolved around how the artistic design and technology can be used to address other social problems in Namibia, apart from GBV. For example, a participant suggested to 'include different provoking videos with different themes or topics to expand awareness'. Participants, who were social workers, admired how the subject of GBV was embedded in the installation and recommended that the installation could be used in other fields of the social sciences, especially in outreach programs and behavioural research. They suggested replicating the technology hut and installing it at public places, like shopping malls or social gatherings. They maintained that this could result in obtaining valuable data for national policy planning and informing the law reform on issues like GBV or corruption.

6.6 Ethical Concerns

Considering the sensitivity of the matter we assured ethical compliance with the institutional regulations. Each participant entering the hut was warned about the violence depicted in the videos and the possible distress it could create. They were further informed about privacy and the option to leave at any moment. To ensure a full immersion in the experience, the participants were not explicitly informed about the logging of their answers. However, they were cautioned not to enter data leading to personal identification. The participants could maintain their privacy being alone in the hut, unless they explicitly requested another person to join them. In most cases, a social worker or institutional councillor was on the premises to which participants could be referred to in case of distress. Upon exit of the hut, participants were asked whether they would like a picture of themselves with the installation, whether it should be uploaded on social media and whether they would like to be tagged. Most participants were eager to be pictured on social media.

7 Conclusion

Overall, we consider the public interactive installation to have been successful in terms of probing gender-based violence at the exhibitions. Despite a number of technical and logistical challenges experienced we received much positive feedback for the initiative as such. From a research perspective, we consider the data collection method to be worthwhile pursuing allowing for a deeper engagement with societal cultural values and transformation.

7.1 Methodological Advantages

The hut installation presented a methodological advantage in collecting valuable data about GBV in Namibia. The hut installation provided participants with the feeling of anonymity and privacy, which we believe, influenced the detailed diversity and openness of the given answers. Furthermore, the installation showed GBV in a very familiar surrounding but discomforting light which reflects its true nature, but is often not captured in research probing for values and attitudes. The design enabled participants to easily embody the concept and take on the role of a chosen character. Instead of simply asking participants what they think about GBV or what they think an involved character would think, we provided them with an insightful opportunity to take the perspective of a character through role-playing. In this way, we obtained valuable data regarding their behaviours, feelings, need for possessions, and strategies on how such crimes could be avoided. Last but not least, participants showed a tremendous amount of engagement and commitment to the hut installation.

7.2 Traditional and Cultural Aspects

Having the topic of GBV embedded in a traditional setting, we created an opportunity for participants to experience the interaction in a setting that they are familiar with. Usually, such a setting should create feelings of safety and comfort, but can also create feelings deeper emotional feelings like hurt, joy and sadness. Having these traditional surroundings and allowing participants to interact individually and privately with such an intense topic definitely influenced the answers provided by participants, which is exactly what we wished for. The traditional setting and simulated interaction further lent realism to the experience. Furthermore, displaying GBV in the shell of a cultural context should promote in participants the idea that change within themselves or the society can only happen if tackled at the roots. Culture provides societies with their core values and attitudes, and thus this needs to be taken into consideration when evaluating and combating a societal problem.

The emotional impact of the experience inside the installation needs to be moderated as often the experience felt was so real that participants, especially women, came out crying. The installation will in future incorporate appropriate actions to mitigate the traumatic impact of the interaction.

7.3 Societal Transformation

The hut installation can be seen as a stepping stone for future campaigns on GBV. The interactive nature allows participants to not only be perceived as passive vessels which get pumped with the message that GBV is bad, but also allows them to voice their opinions and contribute to a societal turning. It provides a new perspective on the monotonous and psychologically distant topic of GBV, which is provided to the nation through news broadcasts.

The hut installation demonstrated the overwhelming desire of participants to help reduce GBV, in whichever way they feel possible; thus it is important to harness this collective energy and provide future opportunities to change the culture of violence currently devastating the country. The installation reflected a unique scenery and environment, attracting many participants. Instead of hosting single events to inform and combat GBV, future campaigns can set up similar installations in public spaces. A larger and more diverse audience would be reached and given a voice.

7.4 Future Work

The discussions with participants during the exhibition of the technology hut were very insightful regarding future research, improving the design and expanding the campaign against GBV. Participants praised the installation as an ideal technology to uncover values of GBV, and experts reckoned that the installation has the potential to inform policy and law reform in mitigating GBV. Other societal ailments, which may also be coupled with cultural aspects, could be investigated and combated with similar technologically infused cultural installations.

Although the hut installation initially served only as a platform to probe GBV, we found that participants experienced the event as insightful not just informative. The data and interpretations provide us with a deeper understanding of the values and attitudes towards GBV which can also be used to design transformative and persuasive technologies.

References

1. UN Women 1a.: 16 Days of Activism (2016). http://www.unwomen.org/en/what-we-do/ending-violence-against-women/take-action/16-days-of-activism
2. UNFPA: http://www.unfpa.org/gender-based-violence
3. IASC: https://interagencystandingcommittee.org/gender-and-humanitarian-action-0/documents-public/guidelines-gender-based-violence-interventions-7
4. Ali, T., Charles, R., Middernacht, Z., Rahimdil, W., Townsend, J.: Tackling gender-based violence with technology. Case study of mobile and internet intervention in developing contexts. http://hirondelleusa.org/wp-content/uploads/2014/09/STATT-Tackling-GBV-with-Technology.pdf
5. López, J.R., Hayna, S.L., Marvelia, G.J.G.: AME-C raising awareness for a life free of gender violence. In: Proceedings of the 2013 CHI Conference Extended Abstracts on Human Factors in Computing Systems, pp. 2579—2584. AMC Press, New York (2013)
6. Wilson Center: Gender-based violence and innovative technologies: opportunities, challenges, and ethical considerations (2013). https://www.wilsoncenter.org/event/gender-based-violence-and-innovative-technologies-opportunities-challenges-and-ethical
7. Sterling, S.R.: Designing for trauma: the roles of ICTD in combating violence against women (VAW). In: Proceedings of the Sixth International Conference on Information and Communications Technologies and Development: Notes, vol. 2, pp. 159–162. ACM Press, New York (2013)
8. Peace Corps Namibia: Diversity and cross-cultural issues (2014). https://namibiapc.wordpress.com/diversity-and-cross-cultural-issues/
9. Light, A.: HCI as heterodoxy: technologies of identity and the queering of interaction with computers. Interact. Comput. 23(5), 430–438 (2011)
10. Ndjibu, R., Peters, A., Winschiers-Theophilus, H., Namhunya, F.: Gender based violence in Namibia. Traditional meets technology for societal change. In: Proceedings of the 2016 CHI Conference Extended Abstracts on Human Factors in Computing Systems, pp. 1024–1029. ACM Press, New York (2017)
11. Chatterjee, S., Price, A.: Healthy living with persuasive technologies: framework, issues, and challenges. J. Am. Med. Inf. Assoc. 16(2), 171–178 (2009)

12. Borgstedt, Y.: 4 Ways technology is boosting the fight against gender-based violence. http://www.huffingtonpost.com/yann-borgstedt/four-ways-technology-is-b_b_7756240.html
13. Buskens, I.: Infusing a gender perspective in indigenous knowledge technology design: some reflections and suggestions. In: Bidwell, N., Winschiers-Theophilus, H. (eds.) At the Intersection of Indigenous and Traditional Knowledge and Technology Design, pp. 297–315. Informing Science Press, USA (2015)
14. Wilkinson, I.: Shocking! Indian engineers introduce electric 'anti-rape' underwear (2013). http://www.thedailybeast.com/this-is-not-hazing-this-is-rape-a-texas-towns-football-nightmare
15. Heilbrun, J., Gray, C.: Economics of Art and Culture. Cambridge Press (2001)
16. Zebracki, M., Summer, A., Speight, E.: Publics and the city. Public Art dialogue. Making public campus art: connecting the university. J. Publ. Art Dial. **7**, 6–43 (2017)
17. Cartiere, C., Zebracki, M.: The Everyday Practice of Public Art: Art. Space and Social Inclusion. Routledge, London (2016)
18. Benford, S., Greenhalgh, C., Giannachi, G., Walker, B., Marshall, J., Rodden, T.: Uncomfortable user experience. How to create and resolve discomfort for a thrilling and memorable experience. Commun. ACM **56**(9), 66–73 (2013)
19. Stroh, J., Mbonambi, B.: I rock woman/woman beats drum installation. In: Proceedings of the 13th Participatory Design Conference (PDC): Short Papers, Industry Cases, Workshop Descriptions, Doctoral Consortium papers, and Keynote abstracts, vol. 2, pp. 151–152. ACM Press, New York (2014)
20. Britton, H., Shook, L.: I need to hurt you more: Namibia's fight to end gender based violence. Signs J. Women Cult. Soc. **40**(1):154–175 (2014)
21. World Health Organization: Understanding and addressing violence against women: intimate partner violence (2012). http://apps.who.int/iris/bitstream/10665/77432/1/WHO_RHR_12.36_eng.pdf
22. Sevenco, F.: Letter from Africa: Namibia's battle with passion killings (2016). http://www.bbc.com/news/world-africa-35705739
23. Ministry of Health and Social Services: Namibia Demographic and Health Survey 2013. http://www.mhss.gov.na/files/downloads/891_DHS.pdf
24. Badcock, J.: Gender and violence in Namibia. Namibia Human Development Report 2000. http://wwwisis.unam.na/hivdocs/unicef/Socio-economic/Namibia%20HDR%202000%20PDF/Namibia%20HDR%202000_06_violence&gender%20factors.pdf
25. Ruppel, O.C., Mchombu, K., Kandjii-Murangi, I.: Surveying the implications of violence against women: a perspective from academia. In: Ruppel, O.C. (ed.) Women and Custom in Namibia: Cultural Practice Versus Gender Equality? pp. 119–129. Konrad Adenauer Stiftung, Windhoek (2008)
26. Legal Assistance Centre: Seeking safety: domestic violence in Namibia and the combating of domestic violence act 4 of 2003. Windhoek (2012)
27. Ndjibu, R.: Beyond awareness of gender-based violence in Namibia. A culture change through mediated technology intervention. In: International Conference on Culture & Computer Science (ICCCS). Windhoek, Namibia (2016)
28. Reitsma, L.: Enabling design to disappear: the design process of StoryBeads. In: Bidwell, N., Winschiers-Theophilus, H. (eds.) At the intersection of indigenous and traditional knowledge and technology design, pp. 205–217. Informing Science Press, USA (2015)

Gesture Recognition-Based Human–Computer Interaction Interface for Multimedia Applications

Svitlana Antoshchuk, Mykyta Kovalenko and Jürgen Sieck

1 Introduction

The concept of Virtual Reality, in one form or the other, has existed for more than a century, starting from the introduction of Wheatstone Stereoscope back in 1838. With the launch of the Oculus Rift Development Kit Virtual Reality entered the marketplace for consumers. Now with the recent rapid growth and development of the wearable computing devices, the appearance of affordable virtual reality devices, as well as the recent innovation in the information technology have renewed the interest towards virtual reality and augmented reality applications.

The emergence of virtual environments brings in a whole new set of problems for user interfaces. The unveiling of 3D objects and worlds in which the user is engrossed allows people as scientists, engineers, medical doctors and architects to envision composite structures and systems with eminent degrees of quality and naturalism. Shutter glasses furnish a stereo or 3D view of the scene, which is no longer limited to a cave or desktop monitor. It is also possible to use a large table, projection screen or room.

One of the most important tasks of a virtual reality system is to provide a user with an ability to control their environment and interact with the virtual objects that

S. Antoshchuk · M. Kovalenko (✉)
Odessa National Polytechnic University, Ave. Shevtchenko 1F, Odessa 65044, Ukraine
e-mail: kovalenkonv@opu.ua

S. Antoshchuk
e-mail: asg@opu.ua

J. Sieck
University of Applied Science Berlin, Wilhelminenhofstr. 75A, 12459 Berlin, Germany
e-mail: juergensieck@acm.org

J. Sieck
Namibia University of Science and Technology (NUST), 13 Storch Street, Windhoek, Namibia

© Springer Nature Singapore Pte Ltd. 2018
D. S. Jat et al. (eds.), *Digitisation of Culture: Namibian and International Perspectives*, https://doi.org/10.1007/978-981-10-7697-8_16

are used to augment the real or virtual scene. Two approaches are commonly used to identify the hand gestures: device based and vision based [1]. The device-based method makes use of wearable devices, sensors for hand orientation and finger motion, as well as controllers to interact with the virtual environment including game controllers, virtual reality headsets and electronic gloves [2], as well as other kinds of devices. The common feature of these kinds of approaches lies in their use of additional hardware and expensive devices, which might not always be available or affordable.

Though the vision-based method requires only a camera, making the interaction between the human and machines adaptable without any use of the extra device. The problem faced by the recognition system is the background needs to be invariant, light problems, the distance of the users from the camera and the orientation of the camera. In this paper, we focus on the visual-based approaches that use a variety of visual sensors as well as specialised image processing algorithms to locate and track human limbs and then use the extracted visual and motion features to provide interactivity.

Vision-based hand gesture interface has been attracting more attention due to no extra hardware requirement except the camera, which is very suitable for ubiquitous computing and emerging applications. The main advantage of using hand gestures is to interact with computer as a non-contact human–computer input modality. Vision has the potential of carrying a wealth of information in a non-intrusive manner and at a low cost, therefore it constitutes a very attractive sensing modality for developing perceptive user interfaces. Research that uses the Kinect sensor [3] and another one that employs the Leap Motion system [4] are examples of the aforementioned category. Proposed approaches for vision-driven interactive user interfaces are used for problems like head tracking, face and facial expression recognition, eye tracking and gesture recognition.

In this paper, we propose an approach based on hand detection and tracking, as well as gesture recognition, to interact with a virtual environment and augmented reality objects, that uses a simple colour camera as an input device.

2 Related Work

A large amount of research can be found dealing with the problem of hand gesture recognition. One of such research papers [5] details a robust scale, translation and rotation-invariant approach that uses a curvature space method to find the boundary contours of the hand. Its downside is high computational demand. Another research describes a hand-pose estimation technique that uses skeleton images acquired by calculating the hand's centre of gravity and finding the fingertips, which are located by finding points that are furthest from the centre [6]. This information is used to build a skeleton image and recognise simple hand gestures. One more research [7] attempts to apply a hand gesture recognition approach to interpret sign language.

Other research uses a Kinect device for real-time gesture recognition. In this research, a finger emphasised multi-scale descriptor is proposed to represent the noisy and articulated hand shape segmented from the Kinect image. To fully utilise hand shape features, this descriptor incorporates three types of parameters of multiple scales, which emphasise the finger features. Hand gesture recognition is then achieved with both dynamic time warping algorithm and backpropagation neural network [8].

Gesture recognition finds application in the virtual reality (VR) systems to provide the user with a way to interact with the virtual environment. For instance, a virtual reality system that uses gesture recognition is presented by Zhao et al. [9] where they build a feature vector using Fourier descriptors and perform hand segmentation by employing Gaussian distribution to build a complexion model in the YCbCr colour space. The feature vector is fed into a backpropagation neural network for the actual gesture recognition and the approach, in general, boasts an improved successful recognition rate. The weakness of the approach was a high sensitivity to shadows and highlights. A similar idea was presented in a paper by Sepehri et al. that used hand as an interface to interact with the virtual and physical space [10].

Another paper described an approach to recognise a pointing gesture [11]. It required the user to wear special clothes with markings and was based on the binocular stereo vision principle.

In a paper by Freeman and Weissman, an interesting approach was presented. They use hand gesture recognition for a remote control of a television [12]. Unfortunately, the paper only describes recognition of one simple gesture, which is an open palm facing in the direction of the camera. A novel sign language and air-writing real-time recognition method was proposed that uses the leap motion sensor [13]. In the approach, a support vector machine (SVM) classifier has been used to differentiate between manual and finger-spelling gestures. Next, two BLSTM-NN classifiers are used for the recognition of manual signs and finger-spelling gestures using sequence-classification and sequence-transcription-based approaches, respectively.

Analysing the existing systems and approaches we can summarise that hand segmentation and tracking are the most important and challenging steps of any vision-based real-time gesture recognition. We need to consider many factors such as environmental noise, light conditions, different skin-tones, speed of hand motions and occlusions [14]. This still remains a challenging task and the demand for a lot of research activities. For instance, an approach to hand tracking was recently introduced that uses a novel algorithm called the tower method where skin colour is used in conjunction with the hidden Markov model for robust hand segmentation [15].

3 Hand Detection and Tracking

3.1 Hand Detection

The first stage of hand detection is finding and locating the hand candidates, i.e. the regions on the image that have a high probability of containing the user's hands. Just as in our past paper [16] we used the Viola–Jones cascade detector for the hand detection. The reason for choosing that particular algorithm is its high speed and robustness, as well as a high detection accuracy [17]. After we have located the hand candidates on the image, the candidates are then verified using the colour histogram approach.

The main requirement for the process of detecting the small areas on the image where hand candidates are located is that it has to work in real time. This means that ideally, it should not take more than 40 ms. The other requirement is, of course, the high detection rate of the candidate detection process. The Viola–Jones approach that we selected for this task meets both our requirements.

The Viola–Jones cascade detector is widely used in many object-detection applications, with face detection being its chief application. Depending on how the approach is trained, it can also be used for the detection of other objects like road signs, human silhouettes or hands.

As explained in the original research [17], the detector uses grayscale images as input. The sliding-window approach is utilised to process the entire image while searching for the hand candidates. The detection process itself is built as a cascade of weak classifiers, constructed with AdaBoost using a large set of two-dimensional features that feed into the main classifier. The weak AdaBoost classifiers can be computed quickly thanks to using integral images, where every image element contains the sum of all the pixels from the current location to the upper left corner of the image.

The training process for these weak classifiers in the Viola–Jones detector is performed to ensure a very high rate of successful detection as well as a low rate of false positives. Unlike in our previous research [16], in this application, we demand a higher accuracy of our hand detector, so in this case is the successful detection rate and false positives rate for the training are set to 99.9 and 1.0% respectively.

As stated in the original research paper [17], organising the classifiers into a cascade allows the most likely hand candidates to be passed along the stronger classifiers on the next level where they are further considered, while the least likely regions that do not contain hands will immediately be rejected. This means that most regions of the image that definitely do not contain hands will be rejected at the beginning of the detection process, thus, along with the high speed of the feature computation, allowing real-time hand detection with a high accuracy.

To increase the efficiency and accuracy of our cascade detector compared to our previous implementation [16], we have trained our cascade detector using a set of 5000 positive samples of hands taken from pictures of 30 different people and a set of 9000 negative samples not containing visible hands. We have also switched from using the Haar features to using more computationally expensive yet more efficient histogram of oriented gradients (HOG) features. The software used for the training was MATLAB due to its convenience and relatively fast training process.

After the training, we have obtained a cascade detector with four levels of classifiers and a 0.01 false alarm rate. Additional cascade level provides a more accurate hand detection and ensures fewer false positives.

For our applications that use our hand gesture recognition approach, we used the OpenCV [18] implementation of the Viola–Jones cascade classifier. An example of real-time hand detection on a video stream from a camera is shown on Fig. 1.

Once the positions of the hand candidates have been located in the image, each of the candidates is verified by using skin-colour histograms [16]. The aim of this is to determine whether a colour pixel has the colour of human skin or not. Using this approach allows us to make our hand detection process stable against the cases where hands in the image might have different skin tones (white, pink, yellow, brown and black), where the lighting might change rapidly in the scene, as well difficult cases where the background might have a tone similar to the colour of the skin [19].

As part of our skin-histogram approach we use, convert the hand candidate region of the image into the HSV colour space, because, unlike RGB, it does not have the problem of not providing valid information about the skin colour due to the luminance effects. In the HSV colour space, the colour information is represented as hue (colour depth), saturation (colour purity) and value (intensity or brightness of the colour). The hue and saturation or even just the hue values provide the necessary information about the colour of the skin, sufficient for building a colour histogram and segmenting the correct region in the image that should ideally coincide with the detected hand candidate.

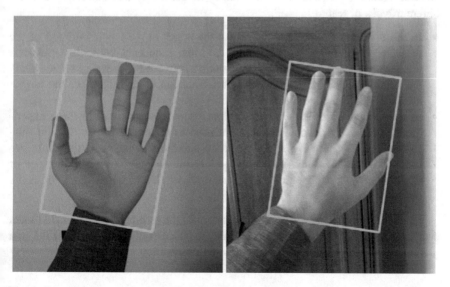

Fig. 1 Example of hand detection from both sides

3.2 Hand Tracking

Having detected the hand position, the model-based tracking of the hand position is performed in the consecutive frames using the unscented Kalman filter (UKF) [20].

First, a hierarchical hand model approximately representing the anatomy of a real human hand is constructed that has 27° of freedom (DOF) corresponding to the degrees of freedom of a real human hand. The DOFs included in the hand model are the following: six for the overall posture of the hand, four for the positions of each finger and five for the thumb positions. Beginning at the bottom end of the palm and ending at the fingertips, we define the coordinate system for each quadric surface relative to the previous coordinate system in the hierarchy.

We use basic shapes to model the hand: a truncated cylinder closed by half-ellipsoids at its ends for the palm, and cone segments for each phalanx of the fingers. The joints are represented by truncated spheres. The joints connect the phalanxes, while fingertips are represented by hemispheres. Each shape has its parameters to set up proportionally to a real hand.

Our approach adjusts the parameters of the hand model automatically in order to match the posture of the hand that we derive by our detection algorithm described in the previous chapter. After that, the constructed model and the unscented Kalman filter algorithm are used for the tracking of a hand in the video.

In the experiments, we use two dynamic models, one with a constant velocity, and the other with a constant acceleration. Linear transformations are used to describe the dynamic models. The observation function introduces nonlinearity into the model. We obtain the observation vector Z by projecting the model into the view of the camera and finding local features along the vectors normal to the contour. Additive Gaussian noise is used to model the system noise. We use two different types of features:

- In the first set of experiments, we use the edges in the neighbourhood of the projected contour as features, while the input sequences consisting greyscale images are used. We perform a convolution between the intensity values along the normal vector are convolved and a Gaussian kernel and label the largest absolute value as edge location.
- In the second set of experiments, colour sequences are used. In these experiments, the local skin colour edges are used as features. We use a colour histogram in HSV space to classify the pixels into the skin and non-skin pixels. We only take the measurements from points on the silhouette for this set of experiments and use the point of transition from skin to non-skin colour as the observation.

This information is used to continuously adjust the parameters of the hand model such as position, scale and rotation in order to successfully project the model in a particular pose in order to obtain a predicted observation vector.

We then construct the observation vector using the extracted features of intensity edges and skin-colour edges. We obtain the predicted observation vector in the UKF algorithm by projecting the hand model corresponding to the state into each image and averaging these observation vectors. Our approach provides four degrees of freedom for the tracked hand motion: translation in the axes and rotation about the z-axis. We use the first order process to model the dynamics of the hand, which means we use position and velocity. An example of this is shown in Fig. 2.

Using the UKF algorithm with a hand model, as opposed to other pixel-based tracking algorithm such as Camshift, provides us with a more precise hand position and rotation, as well as more detailed information on the position of each finger. Moreover, using the model allows us to better track each finger individually and tell different fingers apart, i.e. determine if it is the index finger that is outstretched or the ring finger. Information like this makes a larger range of options possible for our human–computer interaction interface.

The information about the hand position, as well as the model parameters corresponding to the fingers can be extracted and used for gesture recognition. In particular, we extract the hand movement speed and direction, the number of outstretched fingers and the angles between fingers to construct a feature vector used in the gesture recognition algorithm.

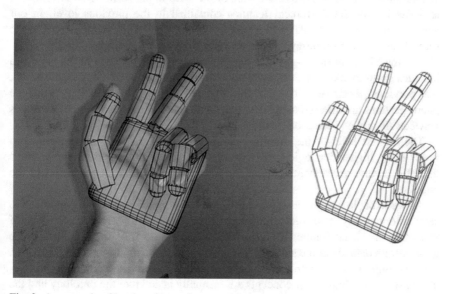

Fig. 2 An example of hand tracking using a model

3.3   Gesture Recognition

The allowed gestures can be divided into two groups: movement gestures and posture gestures. The posture gestures use the information about the hand posture, i.e. the spatial orientation of the hand and the fingers, to recognise gestures.

For the hand gesture recognition, we have to introduce a novel approach [16], based on a modified Bayesian network that we semi-automatically construct with the help of a domain ontology. The aforementioned ontology is built as a hierarchical decomposition of a domain or a field or application represented as a set of concepts and the relations between them. The ontology also contains a set of logical expressions used for inferring new knowledge, assumptions and decisions. Thus in our application, the concept of a hand gesture is represented as an ontology of four abstract levels describing components of a gesture.

On the first level of the ontological hierarchy, we have the visual descriptors and features of the hands, derived from the video processing stage. These include the direction, angle and movement speed of the hand, the orientation of the hand in space, the number of outstretched fingers (number of fingertips) and the relative angles between fingers relative to the hand's centre of mass.

On the second level of the ontology, we have the concepts that describe the general nature of the gesture or the state of the hand in the scene. This information is derived from the movement features contained in the previous level. In our applications, we include states like 'static', 'swipe right' and 'swipe down' in the second level of the ontology, which we refer to as macro-gestures.

The third level of micro-gestures describes the specific postures of the hand and includes gestures like 'fist', 'thumbs up', 'devil horns', etc. The information from the previous levels is fed onto the logical rules in the ontology and the micro-gestures are inferred using data like the number of detected fingertips, angles between fingers and hand orientations.

The highest level of the ontology combines the concepts in the previous two levels using higher tier logical rules to infer the complex gestures. Some gestures that also involve movement also use the information from the lowest level of the ontology.

As we wrote in our previous paper [16], we use a supervised training approach to semi-automatically construct the gesture ontology. This process consists of extracting the visual features from the training video data and matching them to the ground-truth data about the gestures, also contained in the training set. In this paper, we have improved the approach by implementing an automated ontology refitting, during which the higher tier concepts are manually added into the ontology and the entire hierarchy is checked for consistency.

Our semantic-probabilistic approach uses a Bayesian network to perform gesture classification, which is constructed and trained automatically using our ontology and its hierarchy as a basis. A Bayesian network can normally be described as a directed acyclic graph (DAG), where the arcs represent the conditional dependence and independence between the nodes of the network, or, in our case, the concepts of the gesture ontology. The weights on the arcs are the conditional probabilities of the dependence between the network's nodes [21].

Typically for a neural network, the Bayesian network also has input nodes and output nodes. In our application, the low-level concepts of the ontology, i.e. the visual descriptors, are fed into the input nodes of the network. Because the Bayesian network's input nodes should normally be represented as discrete states, we have quantised the possible range of values for each value of the visual descriptors into four intervals. To build the Bayesian network from the ontology and train its structure we use the K2 algorithm [21] which belongs to a class of greedy search algorithms. This means that it must search the entire space of all possible network structures and find an optimal one by minimizing a scoring function.

The K2 algorithm starts with a network that has an initial random ordering of the nodes. To compute the score of the network structure candidate and avoid over-fitting the Bayesian Information Criterion (BIC) [22] was used. The BIC criterion uses the Minimum Description Length (MDL) approach to approximate the marginal likelihood. An example of a trained Bayesian network structure is shown in Fig. 3.

After the Bayesian network's optimal structure has been found, we need to train the network's parameters, i.e. the graph's weights. We used the maximum likelihood estimation approach utilising the log-likelihood on the training data [22].

The Bayesian network with the trained structure and parameter can finally be used to recognise hand gestures in the video stream [16]. The classification results are presented in the form of a list of gestures sorted in the descending order of the gesture probability. The gesture at the top of the list has the highest likelihood of being the correctly classified hand gesture. Figure 4 shows several examples of hand gesture recognition.

The movement-based gestures are detected when the hand is moving with a significant speed, at which point the hand posture is ignored. We are able to

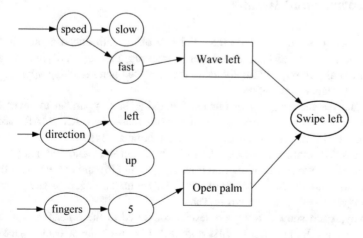

Fig. 3 A fragment of network structure to recognise a gesture 'swipe left'

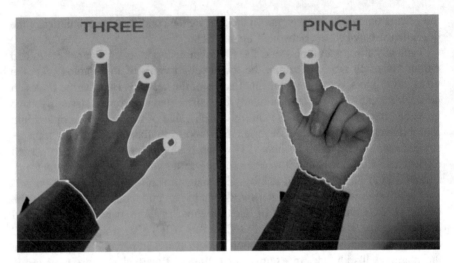

Fig. 4 An example of posture-based gesture recognition

recognise simple movement-based gestures as swiping in eight cardinal directions, as well as more complex gestures where the hand movement trajectory describes a predefined shape. We use the '1$ Recogniser' algorithm for the latter [23].

The $1 Recogniser is a two-dimensional single-stroke recognition algorithm designed for rapid prototyping of gesture-based user interfaces. In machine learning terms, it is an instance-based nearest-neighbour classifier with a Euclidean scoring function, i.e., a geometric template matcher. Despite its simplicity, the 1$ Recogniser requires very few templates to perform well and is very easy to deploy.

4 Experimental Results

In this chapter, we demonstrate the efficiency of the introduced approach first by testing the accuracy of hand and fingertip tracking, then by verifying the gesture recognition algorithm, and finally using the proposed hand tracking approach in an augmented reality application.

We analyse the accuracy of our hand tracking in comparison to several other existing approaches. The first one is a general markerless AR (MAR) approach based on real-time 3D reconstruction using Kinect [24]. The second one is a markerless AR approach that uses GrabCut to detect trackable features [25].

We use the Dexter-1 hand motion tracking dataset [26] and the reprojection error measure to estimate the accuracy of our AR system. The average and variance of the reprojection error are shown in Table 1.

Our approach shows very good results compared to the other two approaches, especially considering that the first approach [24] uses the Kinect device which

Table 1 Average and variance of reprojection errors	Method	Average RMS error (pixel)	Variance
	Our approach	4.19	4.10
	[24]	3.95	4.23
	[25]	5.86	14.77

Fig. 5 Example of fingertip position tracking. Every finger is tracked separately

greatly increases the accuracy of hand tracking. An example of fingertip tracking is shown in Fig. 5 where we visualise a track-line for the previous fingertip positions. Here we are using an additional Kalman filter to smooth the fingertip track lines by eliminating the 'noise' in the fingertip positions between frames. This also allows us to stabilise the position of the virtual objects later in the AR application.

Mapping the fingertip movement to the input control of an application, including a virtual reality environment, provides the user with an ability to interact with the computer system via hand movements, using a simple colour camera and no additional hardware.

In the next step, we analyse the validity of our gesture recognition approach. Our approach allows to differentiate between eight swipe gestures, nine posture based gestures (numbers from 1 to 5, 'pinch' gesture, 'thumbs up' and a fist) and eight shape based gestures (rectangle, star, circle, etc.).

The sensitivity/precision metric [27] was used to estimate the efficiency of our hand detection process. This metric allows us to determine how accurately our approach locates the hands on the image by considering the regions of false and true negatives, as well as true and false positives. Figure 6 describes the basic principle of the metric.

In this particular example, the A-region is the ground-truth data representing the ideal hand detection. The B-region is an example of the actual hand detection/

Fig. 6 The principle idea of the metric. The intersection regions are used for the calculations

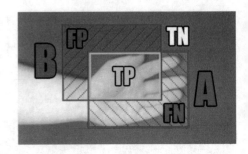

tracking by the implemented system. The intersection of these regions is the true positive (TP), i.e. the only pixels of the image that were correctly detected by the system.

The following equation is used to calculate the sensitivity metric that shows the proportion of positives that are correctly identified as follows:

$$\text{Sens} = \frac{|\text{TP}|}{|\text{TP}| + |\text{FN}|}, \tag{1}$$

where TP is the amount of true positives—pixels that were correctly classified as belonging to the region, containing the hand; and FN is the amount of false negatives—pixels that do belong to the hand region, but were not detected.

The next equation calculates the precision metric that measures the proportion of negatives that are correctly identified as follows:

$$\text{Prec} = \frac{|\text{TP}|}{|\text{TP}| + |\text{FP}|}, \tag{2}$$

where FP is the amount of false positives—pixels, that were incorrectly classified as belonging to the hand area.

Thus, to measure the detection accuracy of our approach we need to perform test-runs of our system, processing every frame of the video, detecting and tracking all hands, comparing the results to the ground-truth data and then calculating the sensitivity and precision metrics.

The results of the experimental testing against a dataset of prerecorded and annotated videos [16] are summarised in Table 2.

Finally, we tested our approach in an augmented reality application. Here the information about hand position, orientation and scale are used as a 'marker' for the

Table 2 Quality of the gesture recognition

Gesture type	Precision (%)	Recall (%)
Swipe gestures	96.2	97.3
Posture gestures	93.7	94.1
Shape gestures	98.6	95.4

(a) (b)

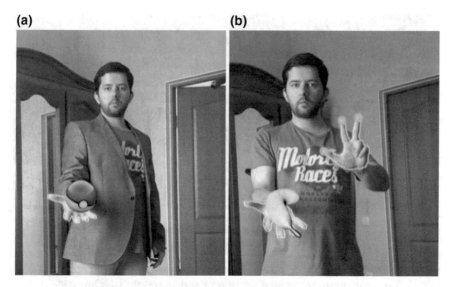

Fig. 7 Visualizing a virtual object upon the user's hand

placement of a virtual object (Fig. 7). In this example we also use the gesture recognition as a method of interaction with AR systems, allowing the user to swap between different objects using hand gestures (Fig. 7b).

The approach was tested on the high-resolution video stream (1280 × 720) and runs in real time, showing the performance of 22.3 frames per second on average, and provides stable positioning of the virtual objects on the user's hand, with this exception of the cases when the hand is occluded. The approach works well when the plane of the user's hand lies parallel to the camera's field of vision, however in the cases when the hand is parallel to the ground a small degree of error can be observed.

5 Proof of Concept and Applications

The gesture recognition approach presented in this paper provides a reliable and easy to use human–computer interaction interface and can have various applications.

Virtual Reality Interface. With the appearance of new virtual reality headsets such as Oculus Rift, HTC Vive and Samsung VR, a problem of providing a way for the user to interact with the virtual environment efficiently. Using handheld wireless controllers is currently the most widespread solution, although it has its shortcomings. Gesture recognition, using Leap Motion is a newer trend and it has many advantages, but the main problem is a very limited field of view and the limited distance. Using cameras for visual hand tracking and gesture recognition as a way of interacting with

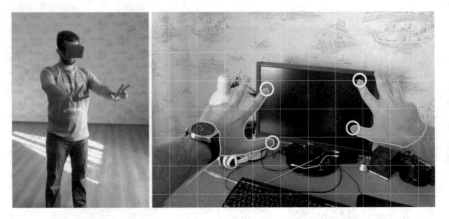

Fig. 8 Using the head-mounted smartphone camera to control the virtual environment

the virtual environment could be an alternative solution, with several cameras positioned at strategic locations around the user or perhaps on the user himself.

Using a camera, mounted on the virtual reality headset, or a camera directed at the user wearing a virtual reality headset can provide such a way of interaction between the user and the virtual environment. An example of such application is shown in Fig. 8.

In this example, we are using the Google Cardboard with a smartphone that has a simple VR application installed. The smartphone camera is facing forward so that the user's hands are in its field of view. The application performs the hand detection and gesture recognition as well as the translations into control instructions for the Virtual Reality environment.

Multimedia Application. Another possible application for our approach is the information systems for cultural institutions. Information technologies and augmented reality has been used to enrich the experience from visiting an art gallery or a museum for several years. Providing a user with a way to interact with the media content available at the location through an embedded screen with a camera, is a possibility of integrating the hand tracking and gesture recognition technology.

Gesture interaction has made its way into interactive digital exhibits in museums and other cultural institutions for example for information, education and entertainment. Using gesture recognition for gaming applications is another way of attracting the interest of young visitors, as it allows them to virtually interact with the exhibits, without actually disturbing them and at the same time providing a learning experience.

6 Conclusion

In this paper, we have presented a fast, robust and efficient approach for hand detection, tracking and gesture recognition. The hand detection involved hand candidate detection using the Viola–Jones cascade detector. Then we performed hand tracking using the unscented Kalman filter algorithm and a hand model that we constructed using simple geometrical shapes that have several degrees of freedom to simulate movement.

We then used the information about the hand movements to recognise hand gestures using a semantic-probabilistic approach. As part of this approach's pipeline, we use a semi-automatically constructed ontology that describes the domain of gesture recognition in terms of concepts and relations between them. The concepts in the ontology are hierarchically divided into several levels of abstraction. The approach then uses this ontology to automatically generate a Bayesian network and train its structure and parameters. The network then can be utilised to classify the hand gestures and even more complex situations in the video. The semantic-probabilistic approach allows reliable recognition of short time micro-gestures as well as more complex gestures and gesture-sequences.

To provide our gesture recognition approach with a wider array of features, we have also implemented the recognition of shape based gestures, or 'air-drawings', using the 1$ Recogniser algorithm. This is a geometric matching algorithm that uses a Euclidian scoring function to compare the user-provided air-drawings with a set of predefined templates. The algorithm shows good results in experimental and synthetic tests and works well with our gesture-based human–computer interaction approach.

We performed the experimental testing of the developed approaches, namely we have tested the accuracy of hand and fingertip tracking and validated the gesture recognition approach using the precision-sensitivity metric and then tested the efficiency of our hand tracking and gesture recognition approach in an augmented reality application by first comparing it with two state-of-the-art solutions using the reprojection error measure. We then performed some experimental tests of the Augmented Reality approach by placing the 3D objects on the user's hand. The location, orientation and scale of the hand is used as a marker for the placement of virtual objects, and hand gestures are used to provide interaction between the user and the virtual environment. Our application presents a more effective and user-friendly methods of human–computer interaction intelligently with the usage of hand gestures. Functions of mouse-like controlling of movement of the virtual object have been replaced by hand gestures.

Lastly, we have provided a list of possible scenarios and use cases that can potentially benefit from the integration of our hand tracking and gesture recognition approaches. The first application is using the developed gesture recognition approach to provide a way for the user to interact with the virtual environment when experiencing virtual reality using a headset like Oculus Rift. The camera is either mounted on the headset itself or watches the user from the side, allowing the recognition of gestures and using them as controls for the virtual reality application.

The second application is the use of hand tracking based Augmented Reality technology in museums and exhibitions. The visitor can get a better look at the exhibits or art-pieces through a large wall-mounted screen and interact with the object using gestures in the cases when direct contact with the object is impossible or prohibited.

7 Future Work

The presented approach provides an efficient and user-friendly way of human–computer interaction and has many possible application outlines in the previous section. However, the accuracy and robustness of the hand tracking and gesture recognition could be further improved by adding another dimension to the input video. This means either adding a second calibrated camera, giving us the stereo-view of the user's hands, or using a depth-sensor so we can work with a more accurate and indicative 3D representation of the user's hands.

Using a multi-camera approach with different points of view can potentially solve the problem of the limited field of view, where the user is forced to keep always his arms to a position where the camera can see them. This, of course, presents a challenge of combining the data from different cameras and finding correspondence between different views.

Finally, the accuracy and stability of the Augmented Reality approach can also be improved, which would require upgrading the hand tracking algorithm and improving the object-to-hand mapping approach.

References

1. Itkarkar, R.R., Nandi, A.V.: A survey of 2D and 3D imaging used in hand gesture recognition for human-computer interaction (HCI). In: 2016 IEEE International WIE Conference on Electrical and Computer Engineering (WIECON-ECE), Pune, pp. 188–193 (2016)
2. De Jesus Oliveira, V.A., Nedel, L., Maciel, A.: Proactive haptic articulation for intercommunication in collaborative virtual environments. In: 2016 IEEE Symposium on 3D User Interfaces (3DUI), Greenville, SC, pp. 91–94 (2016)
3. Sreejith, M., Rakesh, S., Gupta, S., Biswas, S., Das, P.P.: Real-time hands-free immersive image navigation system using Microsoft Kinect 2.0 and Leap Motion Controller. In: 2015 Fifth National Conference on Computer Vision, Pattern Recognition, Image Processing and Graphics (NCVPRIPG), Patna, pp. 1–4 (2015)
4. Invitto, S., Faggiano, C., Sammarco, S., De Luca, V., De Paolis, L.T.: Interactive entertainment, virtual motion training and brain ergonomy. In: 7th International Conference on Intelligent Technologies for Interactive Entertainment (INTETAIN), 2015, Turin, pp. 88–94 (2015)

5. Chang, C.-C., Chen, I.-Y., Huang, Y.-S.: Hand pose recognition using curvature scale space. In: IEEE International Conference on Pattern Recognition (2002)
6. Utsumi, A., Miyasato, T., Kishino, F.: Multi-camera hand pose recognition system using skeleton image. In: IEEE International Workshop on Robot and Human Communication, pp. 219–224 (1995)
7. Aoki, Y., Tanahashi, S., Xu, J.: Sign language image processing for intelligent communication by communication satellite. In: IEEE International Conference on Acoustics, Speech, and Signal Processing (1994)
8. Yang, J., Zhu, C., Yuan, J.: Real time hand gesture recognition via finger-emphasized multi-scale description. In: 2017 IEEE International Conference on Multimedia and Expo (ICME), Hong Kong, Hong Kong, pp. 631–636 (2017)
9. Zhao, S., Tan, W., Wu, C., Wen, L.: A Novel Interactive Method of Virtual Reality System Based on Hand Gesture Recognition, pp. 5879–5882. IEEE (2009). ISBN: 978-1-4244-2723-9/09
10. Sepehri, A., Yacoob, Y., Davis, L.: Employing the hand as an interface device. J. Multimed. 1 (7), 18–29 (2006)
11. Guan, Y., Zheng, M.: Real-time 3D pointing gesture recognition for natural HCI. In: Proceedings of the World Congress on Intelligent Control and Automation, China, pp. 2433–2436 (2008)
12. Freeman, W., Weissman, C.: Television control by hand gesture. In: IEEE International Workshop on Automatic Face and Gesture Recognition, Zurich (1995)
13. Kumar, P., Saini, R., Behera, S.K., Dogra, D.P., Roy, P.P.: Real-time recognition of sign language gestures and air-writing using leap motion. In: 2017 Fifteenth IAPR International Conference on Machine Vision Applications (MVA), Nagoya, pp. 157–160 (2017)
14. Erol, A., Bebis, G., Nicolescu, M., Boyle, R., Twombly, X.: Vision-based hand pose estimation: a review. Comput. Vis. Image Underst. 108, 52–73 (2007)
15. Bao, P., Binh, N., Khoa, T.: A new approach to hand tracking and gesture recognition by a new feature type and HMM. In: International Conference on Fuzzy Systems and Knowledge Discovery. IEEE Computer Society (2009)
16. Kovalenko, M., Antoshchuk, S., Sieck, J.: Real-time hand tracking and gesture recognition using a semantic-probabilistic network. In: Proceedings of 16th International Conference on Computer Modelling and Simulation, Cambridge, pp. 269–274 (2014)
17. Viola, P., Jones, M.: Robust real-time object detection. Int. J. Comput. Vis. 57(2), 137–154 (2004)
18. Open Computer Vision Library. Retrieved from 26 June 2016. http://sourceforge.net/projects/opencvlibrary/
19. Tayal, Y., Lamba, R., Padhee, S.: Automatic face detection using colour based segmentation. Int. J. Sci. Res. Publ. 2(6), 1–7 (2012)
20. Wang, X., Wang, J.: Simulation analysis of EKF and UKF implementations in PHD filter. In: 2016 IEEE 13th International Conference on Networking, Sensing, and Control (ICNSC), Mexico City, pp. 1–6 (2016)
21. Cooper, G., Herskovits, E.: A Bayesian method for the induction of probabilistic networks from data. Mach. Learn. 9(4), 309–347 (1992)
22. Murphy, K.: Dynamic bayesian networks: representation, inference and learning. Ph.D. thesis, University of California at Berkley (2002)
23. Wobbrock, J.O., Wilson, A.D., Li, Y.: Gestures without libraries, toolkits or training: a $1 recognizer for user interface prototypes. In: Proceedings of the ACM Symposium on User Interface Software and Technology, Newport, Rhode Island, pp. 159–168, 7–10 Oct 2007
24. Apolinário, A.L., Giraldi, G.A., Macedo, M.C., Souza, A.C.: A markerless augmented reality approach based on real-time 3D reconstruction using Kinect. In: Workshop of Works in Progress (WIP) in SIBGRAPI 2013, XXVI Conference on Graphics, Patterns and Images, Salvador, Brazil (2014)

25. Khandelwal, P., Swarnalatha, P., Bisht, N., Prabu, S.: Detection of features to track objects and segmentation using GrabCut for application in marker-less augmented reality. Procedia Comput. Sci. **58**, 698–705 (2015)
26. Sridhar, S., Oulasvirta, A., Theobalt, C.: Interactive markerless articulated hand motion tracking using RGB and depth data. In: Proceedings of the IEEE International Conference on Computer Vision (2013)
27. Baumann, A., Boltz, M., Ebling, J.: A review and comparison of measures for automatic video surveillance systems. EURASIP J. Image Video Process. **3**, 280–312 (2008)

Diagnostic and Interactive e-Learning Application for Children with Reading Weakness Based on Eye Tracking

Oliver Weede and Robin Heisterkamp

1 Introduction

We present a diagnostic and interactive eye tracking application for transfer of cultural knowledge, that is analysing the reading task, user's attention, relaxation and potential mind wandering. The application is designed for children with the aim of helping them to acquire reading skills. According to the analysis of their eye movements, the system adapts the displayed content. We designed the application for the use in museums, schools, education centres and (ADHD) learning institutes. The analysis is based on measurements of an affordable consumer eye tracking device which makes it possible to apply the system in many different contexts. Especially schools in rural areas of countries that are in transition from traditional lifestyles toward the modern lifestyle can benefit greatly from an automated system that children enjoy. While designing the system we kept this user experience goal in mind. However, in the first instance, we designed the system as an exhibit for Namibian museums, like the Owela Display Centre of the National Museum of Namibia. It is a museum of ethnography and natural history. The diagnostic and interactive eye tracking application is telling a story about indigenous hunter-gatherer people representing the first nation of Southern Africa. It tells a story about their life by presenting text and images. After short phases of reading, the system offers interactive sections that involve the learner. It asks questions about the text and includes game-like training phases for relaxation and mental focus. To our best knowledge, there is no adaptive training system, which measures mental focus and

O. Weede (✉) · R. Heisterkamp
Hochschule für Kunst, Design und Populäre Musik Freiburg (HKDM),
Haslacher Str. 15, 79115 Freiburg, Germany
e-mail: Oliver.Weede@HKDM.de

R. Heisterkamp
e-mail: Robin.Heisterkamp@Student.HKDM.de

© Springer Nature Singapore Pte Ltd. 2018
D. S. Jat et al. (eds.), *Digitisation of Culture: Namibian and International Perspectives*, https://doi.org/10.1007/978-981-10-7697-8_17

reading skills to provide an individual training. Besides improving reading skills, the system aims to transfer knowledge about Namibian cultural heritage.

Worldwide, the number of children with reading difficulties increases. There are several reasons which lead to reading and writing difficulties. While developmental dyslexia is regarded as hereditary [1] and training can just mitigate the synthons, other forms of reading and writing difficulties are temporary and treatable. The causes are psychological, physiological and sociocultural. One of the sociocultural causes is an overstimulation by extensive media consumption or use of instant messaging systems [2]. Media consumption of children is rapidly increasing in a critical age where they learn to read and write. The fast sequence of visual and auditory stimuli in computer games and television and the parallel use of electronic media lead to an increasing number of children with attention deficit hyperactivity disorders (ADHD), which is strongly related to reading and writing disorders [3, 4]. Radach et al. [4] state that ADHD affects the viso-motoric skills. While looking on small and flat screens, the eye muscles hold the eyes in a fixed position. The eye muscles that are responsible for moving their eyes, side to side, forward and backwards and up or down are rarely used. These factors cause weakness in eye movements and affect the ability to read. Of course, another critical factor is the motivation of young persons to read. Depending on the causes of reading disorders individual specific therapeutic programmes are needed to empower the reading and writing skills.

According to the analysis of the eye movements, the presented system includes individual training sessions for improving the reading skills. The interactive character of the application surely motivates young learners to read.

1.1 Interactive Museum for Namibia

Several approaches were presented for preserving and transferring indigenous knowledge (e.g. [5] or [6]) and integrating interactive applications into museums with the aim of attracting young people for visiting cultural institutions in Namibia.

Motion tracking via a Kinect sensor is used to create a "Virtual Welcome Guide" that interacts with the visitors of an exhibition. If the visitor enters a room the media actor, shown on a screen, welcomes the guest. Its eyes follow him/her. If the visitor leaves too fast, the guide tells the guest to come back. If the visitor is interested in the artefacts shown in the museum, the media actor indicates a gesture of approval. Figure 1 shows the Virtual Welcome Guide in action [7].

RFID technology can be used to locate visitors in a museum to identify the artefacts that interested them the most by monitoring the duration of their stay in front of the displayed artefacts. As a "Persuasive Souvenir", a photo of the visitor taken at the entry point will then be displayed on a screen with the artefact s/he was interested in. The visitor can share the photo on social platforms [8].

Fig. 1 Virtual welcome guide for an interactive museum. States: left, middle, right, approval gesture, welcome gesture, come back gesture

To display additional information on smartphones, a wireless system for indoors localisation was presented which uses iBeacons attached to artefacts for locating visitors' smartphones. The approach was evaluated in the Independence Museum of Namibia [9].

To provide information about rock art in outdoor museums like in the Twyfelfontein area in Namibia a crowdsourcing platform was created, where visitors can access and provide information about the images engraved on the rock surfaces via a smartphone [10]. Images of rock art with the geolocation and a description of the painting are stored in a database. A picture taken on a smartphone is compared with the images of the database of the same location to find a best fitting result. We suggest a combination of the AKAZE and the ORB algorithm and a 2-Next Neighbour Classifier for a simple image classification running on a smartphone. Figure 2 shows complementary key points of AKAZE and ORB. We also suggest using colour descriptors of the HSV and the CIELAB colour space as features for the classifier.

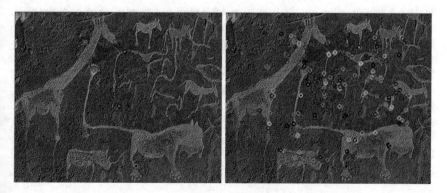

Fig. 2 Image classification of rock art. Left: Key points of AKAZE. Right: Key points of ORB

The purpose of the mentioned installations and applications is to enhance the interest of visitors by feeling connected through an interactive design. The same holds for the diagnostic and interactive eye tracking application for improving reading skills presented here.

1.2   Eye Tracking Applications

Applications that use eye tracking can be categorised as either diagnostic, interactive or a combination of both.

In the *diagnostic type*, eye tracking is used for collecting data for conducting empirical studies of human perception, cognition, information processing or behaviour. Especially the reading task has been analysed for many decades now. An overview of reading in relation to eye movements can be found in Rayner et al. [11, 12]. The authors also presented an influential review of eye movements and attention in scene perception and visual search [12]. Walker et al. [13] presented a diagnostic system that analyses eye movements of children and adults as they view paintings at the Van Gogh Museum, Amsterdam to find out whether eye movements are driven mainly by the intrinsic characteristics of a painting, or by the knowledge, expectations and intentions of the viewer. In the field of human–computer interaction, diagnostic applications are used for evaluating usability and user experience. Poole and Ball [14] present an overview of derived eye movement metrics. These indicators mostly include fixation-, saccade- or scan path-derived features. For example, more fixations on a particular area indicate that it is more noticeable, or more important, to the viewer than other regions. Other fields of application include market research, analyses for advertisements and product design and web analyses. Examples of diagnostic applications with broader interpretations include human activity recognition (e.g. [15]) and emotion recognition. For example, the system presented by Raudonis et al. [16] can distinguish four emotional states based on the eye movement.

In the *interactive type*, eye movements are used as input device, mostly to replace a mouse, allowing the user to interact with a computer using only the eyes. Applications for environmental control and communications in the field of assistive technology were created. For example, gaze-controlled communication and interaction for disabled persons.

In the *hybrid type*, both the approaches are combined resulting in an adaptive or perceptual user interface. A diagnosis is used to adapt the systems' behaviour, instead of an offline analysis of eye gaze to study attentional processes or a system that uses eye movements as input devices for direct manipulation. Furthermore, hybrid applications are closed-loop systems that respond to attention, workload, behaviour, emotional or cognitive states in real time. Examples are e-Learning and tutoring systems. For instance, Hutt et al. [17] were able to detect mind wandering, a ubiquitous phenomenon characterised by an unintentional shift in attention from task-related to task-unrelated thoughts. The diagnosis is used to adapt the behaviour of an intelligent tutoring system, e.g. pausing an educational video and asking a content-specific question.

1.3 Saccades, Fixations and Blinks

While reading a text (or viewing a scene), eyes do not move continuously (along a line of text) but make short, rapid movements of both eyes, intermingled with short moments where the eyes are relatively stationary, the eye *fixations*. Rapid movements backwards in the linear text order are called *regressions*, whereas the forward movements are called *forward saccades*. Rayner et al. [11, 12] reported mean fixation durations of 225–250 ms for (silent) reading, 180–275 ms for visual search and 260–330 ms for scene viewing.

During a fixation, new information is encoded by the cognitive processing system, during rapid movements no encoding takes place. Because of a saccadic suppression, some milliseconds before and after a saccade no information is processed. Due to this reason, the minimum fixation duration is about 80 ms. While reading, the distance the eye moves in each saccade of about 20–40 ms is in average 7–9 characters. During the saccade, no new information is acquired. The purpose of most saccades is to move the eyes to the next viewing position. The cognitive system is searching for the next items to process [11].

According to Rayner et al. [11], there is considerable variability in fixation points and saccades between readers and even for the same person reading a single passage of text. For example, slow readers show longer average fixation durations, shorter saccades and more regressions. Around the fixation point, we can only see a few letters with full acuity. The letters between two successive fixations are determined by our ability for pattern recognition, strongly based on our reading experience. Fixation durations are increasing while reading complex texts with a high degree of difficulty. Although most regressions are very small, only skipping back two or three letters, much larger regressions can represent confusion in the higher level processing of the text. Readers often make such regressions in response to comprehension difficulty, but small regressive eye movements (respectively small forward saccades) also frequently occur when the eyes moved a little too far forward (respectively not far enough) in the text and a small correction is needed. When an item has to be processed again, a so-called *post-target fixation* is needed [11].

The duration of a blink is on average 100–150 ms. Actual blink rates are individually very different and depend on a variety of various factors. Many people blink around 10–15 times a minute, some have a higher frequency, but blinking can also decrease to 3 or even fewer blinks per minute.

2 Description of the Eye Tracking Application

As exemplary content, our application presents a story about the life of the Gwi, one of the individual nations of the indigenous hunter-gatherer people of southern Africa. Various terms, including San and Bushmen, have been used to refer to them collectively. The presented story is inspired by a novel of the Namibian author Giselher Hoffmann [18].

The system presents reading tasks and interactive sections that involve the learner. It asks questions about the text and includes game-like training phases for relaxation and mental focus, since children with reading difficulties are often not able to fixate on one point accurately, and kids with ADHD have, due to unintentional shifts in attention, challenges in focussing on one task. While reading skills are measured during the system displays text on the screen, mental states like attention, relaxation and mind wandering are measured in relaxation and point fixation tasks. Questions are included to capture reading comprehension automatically. The learner should answer the questions by looking at a particular area of an image or animation (multiple choice menu). When he/she looks at the specific area for more than 3 s with at least one fixation with a duration of over 300 ms, he/she chooses the specific answer. If the learner cannot respond to the question correctly, the system gives feedback and presents the current text section again. When reading problems are measured, the system displays the text differently.

As exemplary content the application displays the following text:

The Gwi live in the vast expanse of the Kalahari Desert. They have learned to survive in the wilderness. Have a look at the Kalahari Desert and the Gwi family.

(*Relaxation task* starts: The system presents photos of the Kalahari. Some images contain members of the Gwi. Each picture is presented for 15 s. At the end of the task, the system provides feedback about the relaxation.)

The Gwi live by hunting and gathering. In the great drought, it is hard to find water holes. To get water, they dig up specific roots and wring the water from it. In the morning, they collect water from the grass when it is wet with dew. Often an empty ostrich egg is used to collect the water. In their millenary tradition, they have learned to preserve the environment. They always leave some roots over, even when they are still a little bit thirsty. At night, a watchman stays awake to guard the family group. Imagine, you are this watchman. Be present! Keep calm and look into the moon until the dawn begins.

(*Point fixation task* starts: A small moon in a nightly sky is shown. Parameters for the point fixation task are computed (c.f. Sects. 4 and 5). When the learner succeeds in fixing his/her gaze at the moon, it slowly sets, and dawn begins. The scene is getting lighter. Figure 3 shows the starting scene of the point fixation task on the left side and an intermediate state on the right side where the moon is nearly set. The OpenGL animation contains four layers. The foreground landscape on a day, the sky as the background scene, the moon as a moving object in between both layers and a fourth layer used for a crossfade: An image of a nightly sky containing stars that is slowly faded out via the alpha-channel until it is fully transparent.)

Fig. 3 Point fixation task. Moon observation activity. Successful point fixation of the moon drives the animation. Slowly the moon sets and dawn begins. In the end, it is a new day

The Gwi are great hunters who have learned to read animal tracks very well. With bow and arrows, they are hunting antelopes and share everything with their family groups. In the evening, they sit around the fire and tell each other exciting stories of the day, stories about their forefathers, about animals or hunting experiences. Look into the fire, can you see what the Gwi are telling each other? (Comprehension question: When a learner looks into the fire for more than 3 s a herd of elephants occur. When it takes too long until the learner looks into the fire, comprehension problems are assumed.) While hunting it is important to be attentive and to discover whether there is a lion around who is also interested in the prey. When the Gwi discover a herd of elephants, they hurry up to disappear because they fear these big and mighty animals. The Gwi are experts in reading animal tracks. They know precisely which track belongs to which animal. They can also find out how old the tracks are. Look at these animal tracks and remember them. This is the track of a lion. (A lion's track is shown.) An elephant's track looks like this. (An elephant's track is shown.) This is the track of a springbok. (A track of a springbok antelope is shown. The system proceeds in showing randomly chosen tracks of its database.) Imagine you are a Gwi hunter. Find the track of the springbok. (Comprehension question. Several tracks are displayed. The learner should select the right track by looking at it for more than 3 s. Figure 4 shows an example of animal tracks for the visual search task. The animal tracks are drawn according to the illustrations of Liebenberg [19].)

Fig. 4 Comprehension
question. Identifying animal
tracks. The learner should
choose the springbok track by
looking at it for more than
three seconds. Top row from
left to right: elephant, giraffe,
lion; middle row: cheetah,
kudu, baboon; bottom row:
springbok

3 Empirical Study for Skill Evaluation

We derived the metrics for skill evaluation used in the described application from a
series of experiments. First, we define potential features for measuring reading
skills and second, features for measuring the quality of the performed interactive
activities in the application: the relaxation task and the point fixation task
(c.f. Fig. 3).

3.1 *Empirical Study to Measure Reading Skills*

In the first experiment, we analysed eye movements of persons with and without
reading weakness to derive criteria for reading skills and to discover individual
difficulties of weak readers. We conducted a study with 12 test persons: two skilled
readers at the age of 8–12 without reading difficulties, five children at the age of 8–12
that consulted a therapist due to reading problems and ADHD, one reader at the age
of 30 with reading disorder and four skilled readers at the age of 20–45 years. All
test persons had to read the same text consisting of 7 lines and 47 words. We
displayed the text with double line spacing (2.66 cm), Courier New font with a letter
width ("letter-space") of 0.95 cm on a 15″ display with 1920 × 1080 pixel.

3.2 *Empirical Study to Measure Different Activities*

In the second series of experiments, 11 test persons—adults at the age of 21–60 years —were asked to perform four different tasks. Each of the tasks induces various states of mind. Activity, relaxation, stress and focused attention. We measured eye movements during the test persons performed the tasks to identify potential features that distinguish the different activities respectively the various states of mind. The four activities are:

(T1) *Reading task*: Persons are advised to read a text of 430 words,

(T2) *Relaxation task*: Persons are advised to view images of landscapes shown for 30 s while performing a Jacobson relaxation task for 6 min

(T3) *Stress task*: Persons are instructed to see a slideshow of 20 sweeping Futurism paintings while listing to a piece of stirring, churning and dramatic contemporary music: Wolfgang Rihm's "Hamletmaschine". The pictures, randomly switched in a period of 3 s, emphasise speed, technology and violence. The duration of the task is 2 min.

(T4) *Point fixation task*: Persons are asked to fix their gaze at a particular point on the screen for a duration of 90 s.

The parameters derived from the point fixation task (T4) are used directly in the application to measure the quality of the learner while performing the point fixation task of the application (Moon observation activity, c.f. Fig. 3). The nearest mean classifier is used to compute the score. The relaxation task (T2) and the stress task (T3) are used to measure the level of relaxation in the scene viewing tasks of the application.

For both the studies, we computed the mean and the quantiles of all features. If the confidence intervals of both groups are non-overlapping, we conclude that the parameter can significantly distinguish the categories. All parameters presented in the results section can separate the classes.

4   Features for Skill Evaluation

First, we segment saccades, fixations and blinks out of the gaze points obtained from the tracking device. Then we compute potential features.

4.1 *Preprocessing for Feature Extraction*

A consumer tracking device (Tobii EyeX Sensor) captures the eye movements. It uses near-infrared light to track the eye movements. The points on the screen where the reader's eyes are looking at (gaze point) are measured and transformed into pixel coordinates on the screen (resolution 1920 × 1080). After calibrating the eye tracker, sub-centimetre precision is achieved. The average sample rate of the system is about 60 Hz.

The mean gaze locations of both eyes are computed. We obtain a sequence of gaze locations, the scan path, $(\mathbf{g})_i = (x, y, t)_i$, $i = 1, 2, 3, \ldots$ with x and y coordinates and time stamps t.

We segment blinks, saccades and fixation from the raw data stream. Eye blinks are extracted by regarding the time difference between valid gaze locations. During an eye blink, we do not obtain any data from the eye tracking device. If the gap is larger than 50 ms, we assume an eye blink. After we get the next valid gaze location, we estimate the duration of the blink. We included a retrigger threshold of 80 ms for blinks.

For determining the fixations, we iterate through the gaze locations $(\mathbf{g})_i$. When the movement is stable (positions in a circle with a radius of 0.6 times a letters space and a velocity below one letter space per 20 ms) for a minimum of 80 ms and a maximum of 2 s, we assume a fixation. If the gaze location is stable less than 80 ms or the velocity is above the velocity threshold, we assume a saccade. The data structure for fixations consists of a starting point t, a duration d and an average position, computed as the mean of the gaze locations belonging to the fixation. By performing this clustering, we obtain a sequence of fixations $(\mathbf{f})_j = (x, y, t, d)_j$, $j = 1, 2, 3, \ldots$ The data structures for saccades and blinks just contain a timestamp and a duration.

We need to take the layout and the reading direction into account to analyse regressions and forward saccades during a reading task. We assume a linear script, horizontally written in a left-to-right and bottom-to-top order. The reader starts with the first word written on the top-left, reads the first row horizontally, from left to right with successive rows going from top to bottom. With slight adaptation, it is possible to apply the presented criteria for reading skills for other writing directions. We also assume a layout with full justification (left and right aligned) and a specified line spacing. For measuring the forward and backward movements while reading, we regard the text as a linear sequence, starting with the first letter in the first row from left to right, followed by the second row from left to right, etc. Blue

Fig. 5 Justified text with fixations (dashed blue circles), forward saccades in a linear order (thick blue arrows), page break saccades (red dashed arrows), one regression (black thin arrow in the row zero)

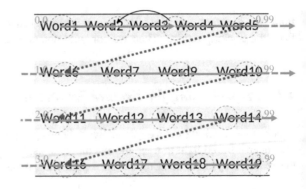

arrows in Fig. 5 illustrate the forward movements in a linear order. Following the line break is a forward saccade regarding the linear text order. Figure 5 shows one larger backward movement (regression) from word 3 back to word 2.

We define a one-dimensional real-valued function $l(i)$ that represents a text position at time t of sample i. The integer value of $l(i)$ represents the vertical position in the text. The digits after the decimal point represent the horizontal position. The function is defined in a way that a letter in row i has an integer value of $i - 1$: For example, the value 0.0 represents the left side of row zero and 0.99 the right side of the top row. The green numbers in Fig. 5 show example values of $l(i)$.

To obtain the rows of the gaze locations $(\mathbf{g})_i$, we iterate through the samples $i = 1, 2, 3, \ldots$ and choose the row with the minimum distance to a horizontal line through the letters of a row. For each sample i, we remember the row of the last sample $i - 1$. We just accept changes in a row, if a threshold of 0.5 letter spaces is exceeded, because readers can see a region with few letter spaces around the fixation points with full acuity.

The digits after the decimal point are computed as x-value of the gaze location i divided by the line width. For this computation, the coordinates are transferred into a relative coordinate frame with its origin in the top-left of the first letter.

After this preprocessing stage, we can compute the parameters for skill evaluation and task characterisation.

4.2 Criteria for Reading Skills

All in all, we examined 30 features. By comparing the median and confidence intervals, we decide whether the features are significant and can be used as metrics for skill evaluation. Here, we just present the significant features and group them into four criteria.

Criterion 1: Duration and Path length: The duration of the reading task is computed by subtracting the timestamp of the first fixation of the first word from the timestamp of the last fixation of the last word. The duration is measured in seconds.

The scan path is computed by iterating through the gaze locations $(\mathbf{g})_i$ and summing up the Euclidean distance of the gaze location of sample i and sample $i + 1$. This distance in pixels is divided by an idealised scan path, just containing a horizontal line for each line of text and a diagonal from the end of a line to the beginning of the next line. Hence, we express the scan path as a ratio of the measured path to a shortest or idealised path. It is assumed that skilled readers do not perform unnecessary eye movements and should have a shorter path length.

Criterion 2: Number of Saccades, Regressions and Post-Target Fixations: We assume that groups of skilled and weak readers can be distinguished by their number of saccades, regressions and post-target fixations.

The number of computed fixations and saccades is counted. The number of forward saccades is computed by iterating through the function $l(i)$ for all samples i. The value $l(i)$ is compared with $l(i + 1)$ to determine whether the movement is a forward saccade or regression. If the distance is below 1.5 letter spaces, the movement is counted as a small saccade (respectively small regression). Otherwise, we regard it as a large saccade (respectively large regression).

For each movement, we also store whether it occurs at the beginning of a line (first 20% of a line width), at the ending of a line (last 20%) or in the middle.

The number of post-target fixations is computed by summing up the number of small forward saccades, small regressions and large regressions.

Criterion 3: Line following: We assume that weak readers have problems following a line of text and that it is hard for them to follow a line break efficiently. In contrast, skilled readers should only show vertical movements at line breaks, while their fixations follow the lines of text horizontal. Experienced readers should be able to move accurately to the next line after reaching the end of a text line.

To measure the capability of following a line of text, first, the sum of vertical differences between all succeeding samples i and $i + 1$ is computed. It is the "y-scan path" of the reading task. Then, the number of vertical line switches is counted. Again, we distinguish between line switches at the beginning, the middle and the end of a line. The number of vertical switches is computed by comparing the integer value of $l(i)$ and $l(i + 1)$ during the reading task including a threshold for acceptance.

If a reader is not able to estimate the right horizontal position of the beginning of the next line, he/she most likely performs small forward or backward saccades to process the letters of the first word in the new line. To measure this amendment, we compute the number of post-target-fixations at the beginning of a line.

Criterion 4: Text covering: It is important to analyse, which parts of the text are not regarded and which parts are seen longer than necessary. To measure the text covering, we consider all text positions **p** starting from the first letter in the first row to the last letter in the last row. For each text position **p,** we iterate through the sequence of computed fixations. If the distance of a fixation location to the point **p** is below a threshold of four letter spaces, then point **p** is seen with full acuity. We sum up the duration of these fixations for each text position **p** to estimate the overall time spent in gazing at the particular text position. We obtain a function that captures the time allocated for each text position l. To measure text positions that are observed more than necessary, we compute the area of the function above a horizontal line of 250 ms (roughly an average fixation duration). If the curve is below the horizontal line, the associated text positions are not observed enough. If the curve is above the line, the corresponding text is observed too long.

4.3   Criteria for Activity Recognition

As potential criteria for activity recognition, we analysed the mean fixation duration, the skewness of the fixation durations, the mean saccade duration, the mean duration of blinks, the standard deviation of blink durations, the skewness of blink durations, the mean times between to succeeding blinks and its standard deviation.

Due to the fact, that blink durations vary strongly from person to person and depend on physical factors like wet or dry eyes. We also compared the relative change of the same person regarding different tasks.

5 Results

5.1 Reading Skill Criterion 1: Duration and Path Length

Skilled readers usually read faster. The average duration ratio is 16.1:33.8 s. The variance in the group of the weak readers is large. The scan path of the skilled readers is shorter (ratio 2.2:3.2). Thus, experienced readers perform less unnecessary eye movements. The findings indicate an efficient search. Table 1 shows the 25% quantile, the median and the 75% quantile for the parameters of Criterion 1.

5.2 Reading Skill Criterion 2: Number of Saccades, Regressions, and Post-target Fixations

Experienced readers perform fewer saccades (72.0:108.5). We observed both, fewer forward saccades (60:70.5) and fewer regressions (10:22.5). When we just take regressions in the middle or the end of a line into account, the result is remarkable: Skilled readers perform in average eight times fewer regressions than weak readers. The eyes of poor readers often move too far, and they need backward corrections. Accordingly, skilled readers also need fewer post-target fixations (24.0:41.5). Test persons with reading weakness perform more larger forward saccades at line beginnings (10:7 letter spaces). Table 2 shows the medians and the range of values.

Table 1 Duration and path length. Median and quantiles

	Weak readers	Skilled readers
Duration	33.8 (22.8–54.1)	16.1 (16.1–16.3)
Scan path	3.2 (2.8–4.1)	2.2 (2.2–2.3)

Table 2 Saccades, regressions and post-target fixations

	Weak readers	Skilled readers
Saccades (total)	108.5 (93.5–147.4)	72.0 (66.9–72.0)
Forward saccades	70.5 (64.2–102.9)	54.1, 60.0, 60.0
Regressions	15.0 (22.5–38.1)	10.0 (9.2–15.1)
Larger regressions in middle or end of a line	8.0 (4.1–12.6)	1.0 (1.0–1.9)
Post-target fixations	41.5 (33.1–84.8)	24.0 (20.6–29.1)
Larger forward saccades at line beginning	10.0 (9.3–10.7)	7.0 (6.2–7.0)

Table 3 Line following

	Weak readers	Skilled readers
Horizontal movements	16.6 (8.6–26.0)	7.0 (6.7–10.3)
False line after line break	5.0 (4.5–5.5)	0.0 (0.0–1.7)
Wrong first word in new line	16.2 (13.2–21.5)	8.0 (6.3–8.9)

5.3 Reading Skill Criterion 3: Line Following

Experienced readers show less horizontal movements (7.0:16.6) and no line switches at the beginning of a text line (0.0:5.0). They can follow the lines much better than weak readers. After a line break, skilled readers move to the appropriate position in the new line, resulting in fewer post-target fixations at the beginning of a line (8.0:16.0). Table 3 shows the medians and the 25% and the 75% quantiles of the parameters of Criterion 3.

5.4 Reading Skill Criterion 4: Text Covering

There is no significant difference in skipping words. In contrast, there is a substantial difference regarding text positions which are observed more than necessary. Skilled readers seldom spent more than 250 ms for reading a word (30.7:76.5).

In contrast to the parameters shown in Tables 1, 2, 3 and 4 which distinguish both the groups of readers, we could not find a significant difference in other regarded parameters, like the average distance between two fixations.

A comparison of the 15 and 85% quantiles of the groups of weak and the skilled readers shows that the most robust parameters are reading duration, number of saccades, especially forward saccades in the line beginning, false x-positions after a line break and text passages with too much fixation duration. Since the parameters presented in this section depend on the length of a text, the values should be divided by the number of words (in our case 47) to obtain generic values.

Table 4 Text covering

	Weak readers	Skilled readers
Letters regarded too much	76.5 (63.5–116.7)	30.7 (27.0–34.0)

5.5 Criteria for Relaxation, Point Fixation and Mental Focus

The results of the reading task especially show that it is essential for weak, young readers to learn to fix their gaze at a certain point and to decrease the overall movement of their eyes. Due to an analysis of potential features computed during the four experimental tasks—reading, relaxation, stress, and point fixation (T1–T4) —we could obtain a set of features that characterise a successfully performed point fixation task, and we acquired features that can identify a relaxed state of mind during scene viewing.

Fixation duration is significantly different *for all* four tasks: the reading task, the relaxation task, the stress task and the point fixation task. Figure 6 shows the probability distribution of fixation durations for the four tasks.

In addition to the fixation duration, of course, we could observe the shortest scan path in a time window of 10 s for the *point fixation task*. So, the eyes are moving slower compared to the other tasks. It can also be distinguished from the other tasks by the skewness of the fixation durations (compare Fig. 6) and the skewness of blink durations, significantly fewer blinks per minute and shorter saccade durations.

The *stress task* can be distinguished from the *relaxation task* by the following three absolute parameters. As mentioned the fixation duration is different: With a median of 306 ms, the fixation durations of the stress task are lower than 575 ms fixation duration of the relaxation task. Also, the duration of the saccades is significantly shorter for the relaxation task. Last, the scan path per time window (velocity of eye movements) is shorter for the relaxation task.

In addition to the absolute criteria, we measured more blinks per minute during the stress task compared to the relaxation task (median ratio 1.3:1 with 0.14 quantile of 1.1:1 and 0.86 quantile of 1.6:1) while comparing the results of the same person in different tasks.

Fig. 6 Probability distribution of fixation duration in four different tasks: (T1) reading task, (T2) relaxation task, (T3) stress task and (T4) point fixation task

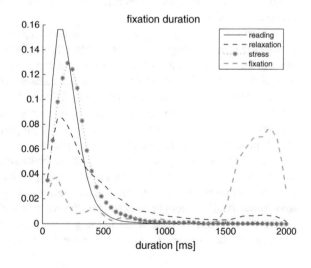

Table 5 Most important features for detecting the four tasks. Median and (0.16, 0.84)-quantiles

	Reading task	Stress task	Relaxation	Point fixation
Fixation duration (ms)	225 (196–248)	306 (258–326)	575 (462–775)	1511 (1176–1720)
Fixation duration skew	1.8 (1.6–2.4)	2.2 (1.5–2.8)	1.5 (0.8–2.1)	−1.0 (−1.8 to −0.3)
Velocity (pixel/s)	1252 (1160–1567)	1085 (970–1319)	551 (469–769)	282 (198–358)

The mentioned parameters are the most important significant features. Other features like the duration of blinks or the standard deviation of times between blinks are not significantly different. Our tracking device with 60 Hz sampling frequency can not measure short saccade durations of about 30 ms accurately enough to answer the question whether saccade durations may discriminate all four tasks.

Table 5 summarises the most important features for distinguishing the four tasks.

6 Discussion and Conclusion

It is possible to distinguish skilled readers from persons with reading weakness according to the four presented criteria for reading skills. We have also shown that the four activities—reading, scene viewing under stress condition, relaxation and point fixation—can be distinguished by features derived from eye movements.

The results of the reading task especially demonstrate that it is crucial for the young learners to learn how to fix their gaze at a certain point and to decrease the overall movement of their eyes. The designed point fixation task embedded in the presented story (Moon observation activity, c.f. Fig. 3), where learners obtain rewards for slow eye movements can help them to acquire valuable skills, not only needed for reading.

In summary, weak young readers move their eyes to fast. They have problems finding the right line beginnings. Often they start reading a line too fast. Maybe they want to be finished soon. Forward saccades at the start of a line are usually longer than eight letters. So not all letters have been observed. Regressions are needed. Sometimes poor readers are also not able to follow a line of text. After a line break, weak readers tend to change to a wrong line or a false first word. They need post-target fixations for correction. In a plotted scan path, it is easy to observe the search process for finding the right line beginning.

In the next line, the process starts again: at the beginning, the readers hurry up, do not get all aspects right, they slow down, have problems following the line break and need many corrections for finding the right starting point for reading the next line. Weak readers strongly tend to read the same letters again and again.

We assume that an individual training programme designed according to the analysis of the presented interactive e-Learning application can contribute to enhancing reading skills. Because there is a tendency to be overwhelmed by a page of text, we reduce the number of words per page when we measure reading difficulties. If large vertical movements are observed, we present the text with a larger line spacing and choose alternating text colours for each line to help the learners while following a line. When the system observes many long forward saccades, it automatically selects a smaller text width. If the scan path is too long, the learner might benefit from more fixation tasks similar to the Moon observation activity to obtain a direct feedback.

We plan to extend the content presented by the system to provide a continual pleasureful user experience. For example, other aspects of the cultural heritage of Namibia could be included. A long time study with learners should be performed to provide evidence that the system can help students improving their reading skills sustainable.

References

1. Grigorenko, E.L., Wood, F.B., Meyer, M.S., Hart, L.A., Speed, W.C., Shuster, A., Pauls, D. L.: Susceptibility loci for distinct components of developmental dyslexia on chromosomes 6 and 15. Am. J. Hum. Genet. **60**(1), 27–39 (1997)
2. Levine, L.E., Waite, B.M., Bowman, L.L.: Electronic media use, reading, and academic distractibility in college youth. CyberPsychol. Behav. **10**(4), 560–566 (2007). https://doi.org/10.1089/cpb.2007.9990
3. Willcutt, E.G., Pennington, B.F., Boada, R., Ogline, J.S., Tunick, R.A., Chhabildas, N.A., Olson, R.K.: A comparison of the cognitive deficits in reading disability and attention-deficit/ hyperactivity disorder. J. Abnorm. Psychol. **110**(1), 157–172 (2001)
4. Radach, R., Günther, T., Huestegge, L.: Blickbewegung beim Lesen, Leseentwicklung und Legasthenie (2012) http://www.allgemeinepsychologie.uni-wuppertal.de/
5. Winschiers-Theophilus, H., Jensen, K.L., Rodil, K.: Locally situated digital representation of indigenous knowledge: co-constructing a new digital reality in rural Africa. In: Strano, M., Hrachovec, H., Sudweeks, F., Ess, C. (eds.) Eighth International Conference on Cultural Attitudes Towards Technology and Communication 2012, pp. 454–469 (2012)
6. Gallert, P., Winschiers-Theophilus, H., Kapuire, G.K., Stanley, C., Cabrero, D.G., Shabangu, B.: Indigenous knowledge for Wikipedia: a case study with an OvaHerero community in Eastern Namibia. In: Awori, K., Bidwell, N.J. (eds.) Proceedings of the First African Conference on Human Computer Interaction (AfriCHI'16), pp. 155–159. ACM, New York (2016)
7. Weede, O., Muchinenyika, S.H., Muyingi, H.N.: Virtual welcome guide for interactive museums. In: Proceedings of the 13th Participatory Design Conference (PDC'14), vol. 2, pp. 167–169. ACM, New York (2014)
8. Muchinenyika, S.H., Weede, O., Muyingi, H.N.: Persuasive souvenir. In: Proceedings of the 13th Participatory Design Conference (PDC'14), vol. 2, pp. 175–176. ACM, New York (2014)
9. Kandjimi, H., Muyingi, H.N., Sieck, J.: A usability study of indoor micro location-aware interactive guide application in a museum: the Namibian independence museum. In: Franken-Wendelstorf, Lindinger, Sieck (eds.) Kultur und Informatik: Reality and Virtuality. vwh Verlag Werner Hülsbusch (2016)

10. Amugongo, L.M., Muyingi, H.N., Sieck, J.: Designing a crowdsourcing platform for Rock-art and graffiti images. In: Franken-Wendelstorf, Lindinger, Sieck (eds.) Kultur und Informatik: Reality and Virtuality. vwh Verlag Werner Hülsbusch (2016)
11. Rayner, K.: Eye movements in reading and information processing: 20 years of research. Psychol. Bull. **124**(3), 372–422 (1998)
12. Rayner, K.: Eye movements and attention in reading, scene perception, and visual search. Q. J. Exp. Psychol. (Hove) **62**(8), 1457–1506 (2009)
13. Walker, F., Bucker, B., Anderson, N.C., Schreij, D., Theeuwes, J.: Looking at paintings in the vincent van gogh museum: eye movement patterns of children and adults. PLoSONE **12**(6), e0178912 (2017)
14. Poole, A., Ball, J.B.: Eye Tracking in Human-Computer Interaction and Usability Research: Current Status and Future Prospects. Encyclopedia of Human-Computer Interaction. Idea Group Inc., Pennsylvania (2005)
15. Bulling, A., Ward, J.A., Gellersen, H., Troster, G.: Eye movement analysis for activity recognition using electrooculography. IEEE Trans. Pattern Anal. Mach. Intell. **33**(4), 741–753 (2011)
16. Raudonis, V., Dervinis, G., Vilkauskas, A., Kersulyte, G.: Evaluation of human emotion from eye motions. J. Adv. Comput. Sci. Appl. **4**(8) (2013)
17. Hutt, S., Mills, C., White, S., Donnelly, P.J., D'Mello, S.K.: The eyes have it: gaze-based detection of mind wandering during learning with an intelligent tutoring system. In: 9th International Conference on Educational Data Mining, Raleigh, NC, USA, pp. 86–93 (2016)
18. Hoffmann, G.W.: Die Erstgeborenen. Hammer Verlag (1991). ISBN-13: 978-3872944504
19. Liebenberg, L.: A Field Guide to the Animal Tracks of Southern Africa. David Philip Publishers (Pty) Ltd. (1990). ISBN: 978-0-86486-132-0

ColourMirror—Connecting Visitors with Exhibits by an Interactive Installation

Zsófia Ruttkay

1 Introduction

In the age of the Information Technology revolution, we witness not only the proliferation of digital assets and online services in daily life, but also profound challenges to the traditional forms of cultural heritage preservation and the institutions dedicated to it [1]. In particular, museums are in transition, from being the 'temple' of knowledge and cultural assets to a forum where the tangible and intangible heritage triggers conversations between the past and present, between the museum and its visitors, and also among the individual visitors [2–4]. The visitor is no longer considered a consumer, but a participant, on a number of different levels [5–7].

Digital technologies offer an arsenal of possibilities to liven up exhibitions, to trigger visitors' curiosity and get them involved, and to reach out beyond the walls to increase impact and to attract new audiences. Museums are starting to harvest the opportunities. For earliest examples, see [8, 9], for recent developments, check out the annual conferences.[1] Still do not exist enough studies of the benefits of digital installations, apart from their entertainment value for (young) visitors. Do they also learn, do they become more interested in cultural heritage, do they come to value museums more? We firmly believe that well-designed digital installations can serve

---

[1]Museum and the Web: https://www.museumsandtheweb.com/ Museum Next international conferences: https://www.museumnext.com/

Z. Ruttkay (✉)
Tech Lab, Moholy-Nagy University of Art and Design Budapest, Bertalan Lajos utca 2, Budapest 1111, Hungary
e-mail: ruttkay@mome.hu

© Springer Nature Singapore Pte Ltd. 2018
D. S. Jat et al. (eds.), *Digitisation of Culture: Namibian and International Perspectives*, https://doi.org/10.1007/978-981-10-7697-8_18

all these purposes. One must be aware that the introduction of technology merely for its own sake may even work against the basic objectives of museums, e.g. if people come to play with new technologies, without focusing on the exhibits and confronting their key messages, or if an installation appears too 'childish' to certain types of visitors who, thus, feel excluded. However, the essence of good design is hard to figure out and formulate because of the diversity of content and messages in different museums, the lack of settled methodology of measuring success in the aforementioned dimensions, and because several factors play a role in the evaluation of an installation, such as the design of the UI and UX, the quality and quantity of the content, and the spatial and logical integration of the installation into the structures of the exhibition. Thus, a detailed account of the design and usage of an installation helps to establish a new, interdisciplinary field, and nuance the picture about the potentials of digital technologies in museums. The lessons are relevant for all major players: the creative and the computer scientists involved, and the staff of the museum. The Cleveland Museum of Art's detailed follow-up report and conscious strategy for re-design is an example in this respect [10].

In our TechLab, we have been designing, implementing and—occasionally— evaluating installations for leading museums in Hungary.[2] We have been working with a dozen of partner museums both in the framework of our interdisciplinary *Digital Museum* courses[3] and through commissioned works prepared for exhibitions. In both the settings, we are motivated to support the message of an exhibition, the—explicit or implicit—needs of the visitors of all kinds, and last but not least, to comply with the aesthetics of the physical space and the topic of the exhibition, by hiding, as much as possible, the electronic components.

In this paper, after exploring the above-mentioned challenges in more detail, we discuss one of our most recent and most complex museum installations as a case study. The ColourMirror is a multifunctional digital installation with three components, accompanying an exhibition where objects are arranged by their dominant colour. We discuss the experience and the working of the 'magical' mirror, where visitors get to see an exhibit next to their own image. They may send and distribute this special 'selfie'. The collected data is visualized in several ways, giving insight into the objects and colours recalled by prior visitors.

We report on an exploratory empirical study of usage and visitor experience and discuss its results. We also reflect on the museum staff's reaction to this unusual item. We finish the article by outlining further work and application potentials that have a broader relevance.

---

[2]For information and videos on a list of our museum projects, see http://techlab.mome.hu.
[3]See http://techlab.mome.hu/dimu.

1.1 Museums and Their New Audiences

The communication, learning and leisure habits of the generations growing up with the Internet and mobile devices have changed drastically [11, 12]. These potential future visitors to museums may be characterized by the following features:

- a preference for (audio) visual materials over text,
- fast and parallel processing of (small) chunks of information,
- a need for activity,
- a preference for discussion and self-expression instead of authoritative (academic) statements,
- living online, connected, all the time,
- a masterly handling of digital devices and services.

For these generations, the traditional nineteenth-century setting and protocols of museums are not appealing. This is strikingly visible from the result of an inquiry in which university students in art and design were asked to write down the first three words that came to their mind about a museum (see Fig. 1).

But behind many of the issues raised here there are—and in fact, there have been for quite some time—inherent problems that may become more articulated with the increase in visitor numbers and diversity. The following phenomena will be familiar both to visitors and to museum staff:

- The so-called 'museum fatigue', caused not only by the difficulty of *orienting oneself* and by the distances and stairs to be walked (typical in traditional museums), but by the overwhelming *amount of exhibits*.
- People spend little time *examining individual exhibits*: they take a quick photo, a selfie (if allowed), they are in a hurry 'to see everything', or wander around as

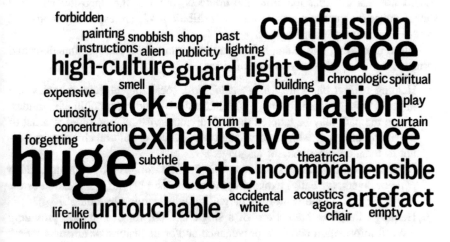

Fig. 1 Words associated with the museum by university students

they do not receive enough clues to explore the exhibition and make sense of it for themselves [13].

- Visitors are reluctant *to read the textual information* offered, both the 'object descriptions' which are professional and of identical nature for each object, and the lengthier introduction at the beginning.
- There is a limited availability of affordable *souvenirs to take home and give away*, to recall the visit, typically constituting magnets, notebooks and small office utensils.
- Once visitors have seen an exhibition, they receive no means of remaining in touch, they are not motivated to do so, nor to return and to consider the (future of) the museum as a matter of personal concern.

1.2   Potential Uses of Digital Technologies in Museums

Digital technologies can be exploited both to serve the needs of the new generation of visitors and to remedy—one or more—anomalies of the museum visit. We emphasize that even without any digital device it is possible to reach several goals. For instance, an experienced museum guide can orient, inform, keep interest alive, adjust the depth, length and wording of his/her explanation to suit individual visitors, and challenge them to give their own opinion. But there are far more visitors than guides, so digital devices and solutions can take over several of these functions. Different types of applications such as multimedia guides, quizzes and touchscreen-based explanations are finding a place in museums.

It is more exciting to invent entirely new, poetic or 'magical' experiences that would not be possible without a digital arsenal. These novel experiences—often involving emotions, the joy of bodily movement or cooperation between visitors—should not distract attention from the artefacts, but just the opposite; and they should underline the main message of the exhibition. We are especially motivated to invent such unique applications.

Before discussing one example in detail, we sum up the possible functions and forms of digital applications in an exhibition:

1. Helping to *find one's way in an exhibition*, localizing objects or topics and offering paths tailored for individual interest—by audio or multimedia guides, where the path may be tailored to the individual visitors (e.g. offering a list of top attractions, suggesting topics to suit age, gender or cultural characteristics—not to mention the choice of languages).
2. Helping to *investigate and understand individual exhibits*—by showing hidden parts or layers, (visually) explaining the mechanism behind, the creation or the usage, by putting the visitor in charge through 'learning by doing'.
3. Helping to *explore the context* of a single exhibit, for example by providing layered information about its provenance and/or its historic or artistic context,

or by presenting a (virtual) collection of similar artefacts, even from other collections and countries.

4. Facilitating *active learning*—by quizzes or single- or multi-player games.
5. Enabling a *playful physical activity*, also in order to break the monotony of the visit.
6. Facilitating *remembering and creative re-use*—by enabling visitors to take (special) photos and share them instantly, by offering access to high-resolution photos of the exhibits online, possibly accompanied by further background information.
7. Making the visitor *identify emotionally* with the topic, protagonists and stories in an exhibition—the means for which may vary from controlling motion, bringing to life the 'heroes' of an exhibition or taking decisions on their behalf, or following a story from the point of view of any particular character. The general atmosphere, realistic or abstract sound and light installations may also induce emotions.
8. Urging the visitors to *form and voice their own opinion*—by taking decisions and voting as part of the exhibition visit, with witty physical or virtual instruments fulfilling the role of a query or a guest book.
9. Inducing *discussion between visitors*—multi-user and spacious installations with a role for onlookers can also fulfil this function.
10. *Reaching out* to potential visitors—by placing a catchy installation at the entrance of the exhibition, or outside of the museum building.
11. *Getting visitors involved*—by asking them for contribution to an exhibition or a collection of own objects, stories, creative ideas or pieces.

Space does not allow for a detailed discussion of the above functionalities (nor some others); but see further [14]. We will reflect on these functions in connection with our application in the final discussion.

2 The ColourMirror

The ColourMirror is an interactive digital installation that was created for the exhibition 'In the Mood for Colours' at the Museum of Applied Arts in Budapest.[4] This exhibition, which was the last one before the museum closed for several years of renovations in Fall 2017, was based on an unusual curatorial concept, presenting almost 400 artefacts (glass, ceramics, textiles, furniture) arranged according to their most dominant colour, in three rooms—red, green and blue.

The museum asked the interdisciplinary team of MOME TechLab to create an engaging and playful installation which would prepare visitors for the colour-centred exhibition, before they entered the exhibition rooms. They gave complete freedom to the design team; the only constraining factor was the physical

---

[4]http://szintukor.imm.hu/en/.

space available. After exploring different ideas that would allow visitors to experiment with RGB colours or to explore the linguistic expression and the emotional and symbolic connotations of colours, the museum staff chose for a transmedial interactive application to bring the exhibits into focus in a playful way.

The very basic idea of our installation is similar to the one of the Make a Face! application, where the visitors recalls a portrait from the collection which is similar to his/her facial expression [15]. In [16], the authors present a 'digital souvenir', a photo compiled of the image of the visitor and the exhibit he/she spent the most time with. We also exploited a similar idea of a digital souvenir.

2.1 The Three Functions

The ColourMirror is placed in a separate room with two doors opening to a corridor, which visitors pass through before they enter the exhibition. In the corridor, a short text in Hungarian and in English explains the installation and invites visitors to give it a try. (Initially, we provided no other written instructions in the room, neither printed nor displayed.)

Besides creating an engaging interactive installation, we also wanted to reflect on the visitor's data and to offer them a digital souvenir as a reminder of their experience, and of the exhibition. We created an installation consisting of three units, on three sides of the room, serving the following functions:

1. When entering the room, the visitor is faced with a *mirror-like interactive installation* that responds to the visitor by displaying one of the exhibits.
2. On the side wall, as visitors move forward in the room, *animated data visualizations* may be observed on large displays.
3. Next to the exit, there is a touchscreen from which visitors can *send off an email with their own 'mirror image'* that also shows the object that was assigned to them.

2.2 Mirroring the Visitor with the Object that Matches Him/Her the Best

In the darkened room, there is an installation resembling a full-length dress mirror. Behind this semi-transparent mirror there stands a display of the same size, and at the bottom of the mirror, there is a hidden Kinect camera. At first, the mirror shows a dazzling mixture of moving colours in order to catch the eye of the visitor. When the visitor stands still in front of the mirror, (s)he is scanned by the camera. The few seconds of this scanning process are indicated visually in the mirror, after which there appears an exhibit in the upper right-hand corner of the mirror next to the

Fig. 2 A visitor in front of
the ColourMirror

silhouette of the visitor, which is filled with stripes representing proportionally the
six dominant colours that result from an analysis of his/her captured silhouette
image. A one-sentence explanation (also in two languages) states that the object is
the exhibit that is the most similar in colour to those of the visitors (see Fig. 2).

When a visitor enters, stands still or leaves, this is perceived by processing the
amount of movement (the number of changing pixels) in a dedicated capture area in
front of the mirror. The silhouette of the person is extracted through depth analysis
of the 3D image taken by the Kinect camera. The colour photo of the visitor is
processed in a similar way as the object photos (see Fig. 2).

The visitor is offered the artefact from the collection of exhibits that matches his/
her colours the best. The implicit DB query of the artefacts is based on preprocessed
information about the colours of each artefact in the DB. For each object, there is
also a good-quality photo available, in 3 × 8 bit colour representation and with the
background removed. In order to reduce the number of colours for fast query
purposes, we reduced the number of colours for each object to six by standard
colour quantization [17]. In all computations, we used CIELab representation,
which is more suited to model the human perception of colour similarity. For
computing the similarity of individual colours, we used the CIE94 measure [18].

For each object, next to the full-colour photo, we also stored the six reduced colours and the percentage of the presence of each of these in the entire image. Hence a *colour palette*, consisting of six colours and six percentages, was obtained for each artefact and stored in the DB. From the scanned image of the visitor, a colour palette was obtained each time in a similar way.

The best match for the visitor's palette was obtained by the following steps:

1. The correspondence of the colour palette of the visitor with that of the kth object was characterized by a number h_k for each of the objects in the database:

   (a) Using the CIE94 measure, the colour distance c_{ij} of each of the 36 pairs (6 in the colour palette of the visitor paired with 6 in that of the object) was quantified.

   (b) Indicating by p_i and p_j the percentages in the colour palette of the visitor and in that of the object, respectively, a representative distance r_{ij} of the colour pairs was computed by taking into account the occurrence of the two colours:

   $$r_{ij} = c_{ij} * \min\left(p_i/p_j, p_j/p_i\right).$$

   (c) Then, by taking into account the r_{ij} numbers for the 36 pairs of colours between the two palettes, we picked the 'best match'—that is, the best pairing of the 6 colours in the object and the visitor—using the Hungarian method algorithm [19], which provided the number h_k.

2. From all the objects, the one with the lowest h_k value was selected as the best match and shown in full colour on the display of the mirror.

2.3 Sharing the Mirror Image

Before leaving the room, visitors passed by an interactive display showing the images that had been taken most recently by the mirror. Here, they could select their own mirror image and send it to themselves by email. (For this purpose, we installed WiFi in the room.) We wanted to offer a simple and fast means to 'take home' the mirror image, also as an alternative to the fashionable selfies that are often shot in museums. Moreover, the email contained more information than had been shown in the mirror, including a more detailed description of the selected object and the codes of the six colours in the visitor's palette.

The visitor obtained the content of the email by activating a URL and could also share the content with others via Facebook, Twitter or email by clicking on a button. About half of the visitors used this option. We found, however, that many of the images were spread further on Facebook.

2.4 Data Visualizations

On a large display, slightly animated data visualizations were shown in a loop, allowing visitors to reflect on past scans in four different views, one after the other:

1. In the *Catwalk*, the past ten scan results were shown, appearing in a 2.5D catwalk presentation, where the visitors' colour palette silhouettes walk alongside their corresponding object (see Fig. 3).
2. In the *Calendar*, the palettes of all visitors of the past 30 days could be seen in a matrix-like arrangement. This view gave an impression of the dominant colours of the clothes of visitors (see Fig. 4).
3. In the *Statistics*, a visual impression of the statistics of different colours in past periods was given.
4. In the *Extremes* view, the 'most colourful' and the 'most red/green/blue' visitor's colour palette was shown in their silhouette, differentiating between adults and children by a guess based on the height of the scanned person (see Fig. 5).

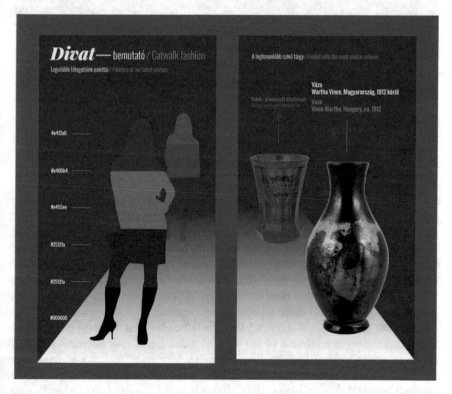

Fig. 3 The result of past scans in the Catwalk view

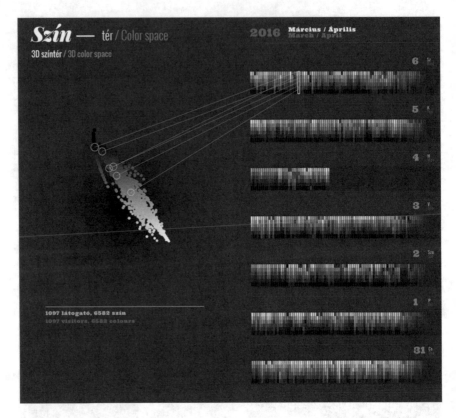

Fig. 4 The calendar view

3 Visitors' Emotions, Behaviour and Opinion

In the case of novel—and usually rather expensive—digital installations, it is very justified to ask whether the investment was worth the trouble. Usually, a digital installation is regarded as modern, and it is praised by the media for this reason. But how to grasp the real benefits for the museum: based on feedback in the visitors' book (which is still in use)? In terms of the number of visitors? Or of the time spent with the installation? Or how they behave, what emotions they reveal? Or what they think of it? Through some measure of what visitors really learnt, thanks to the installation? How should these aspects be aggregated?

From the perspective of the designers, the efficiency and the ease of the interaction and the appropriateness of the user interface are of also interest—and they may turn out to work differently than expected. Moreover, one should remember that feedback from different people may differ based on static as well as time-based dynamic personal characteristics. With all this in mind, we conducted a small-scale study, trying to explore several of the above aspects.

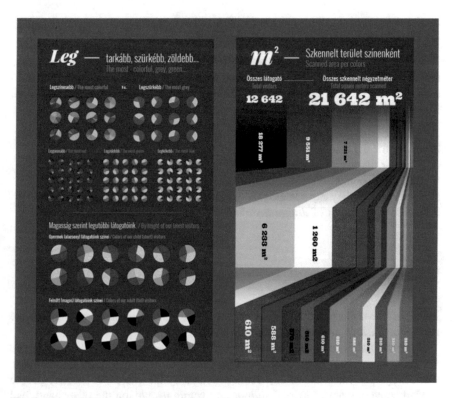

Fig. 5 The statistics and the extremes views

3.1 The Empirical Study

We collected data from 135 visitors. Their age group, nationality, gender and type of visit (individual or in a couple, family or group) was also recorded. We also interviewed six museum guards who had been observing and helping visitors for months and four guides offering special activities for young visitors, by asking open-ended self-completed questions.

The major body of the research was carried out by means of recording observed behaviour in the room of the ColourMirror, and by a short interview just after visitors had left the room. The data was collected during the winter months, in 2-h recording sessions both during the week and on weekends, by four coders who had received some initial training. The observer, sitting in a corner inconspicuous as a museum guard, registered data on a tablet in a Google form, considering:

1. *the type and number of scans* (some people modified their dress, pose, formed groups);
2. *the emotions observed* (expressed by the face of the visitors, sometimes by their body language, and very often also verbally);

3. the amount of attention paid to the *data visualizations*;
4. whether the visitors *emailed their mirror image*.

In the interview, the visitor was asked a few questions. The answers were registered by the interviewer in the same online form, ticking on choices characteristic of the answers. Spontaneous additional remarks from visitors were typed in. The interview addressed, among others:

1. *recall* of the (first) received object;
2. *liking* for the received object;
3. whether the visitor would *track down* the object in the exhibition;
4. how they thought the ColourMirror *worked*;
5. in what way they *experienced* the ColourMirror installation;
6. what they thought of *digital installations in museums* in general.

3.2 Major Findings

Based on the collected empirical data (shown in Tables 1 and 2), we sum up the major conclusions around four general questions.

How did people use the ColourMirror? About half of the visitors observed *did not know what to do* in the room, so they asked for assistance from a guard (one was always present in the room). From accounts by the guards, even more people needed some amount of help. *Children and young people*, on the other hand, had hardly any difficulty and they were the ones to invent ways to receive different objects (e.g. by changing their dress or forming groups). Also foreign tourists, who were less hurried and had usually read the description outside, were more at ease in general, than Hungarian visitors. As we discovered, it was here that many of the subjects met an interactive museum installation for the first time in their life, and some regarded the Mirror as an exhibit to be watched but not to be used. People over 60 complained several times about the lack of detailed written instructions on what to do, and about a fear of becoming awkward in public with such an

Table 1 Summary of visitors' data concerning the ColourMirror and the object shown

Aspect	Distinct categories with occurrences (%)		
Emotion displayed	Happy	Neutral	Other
	72.6	17	10.4
Recall of the received object	Very good	Satisfactory	False or none
	71.5	24.4	4.1
Satisfaction with the object	Pleased	Neutral	Unsatisfied
	72.6	20.2	7.2
Would track down the object	For sure	Perhaps	Not
	81	10.7	8.3

Table 2 Summary of visitors' opinion about the ColourMirror and digital installations in museums

Question	Answers with occurrences (%)		
How does the ColourMirror work, in principle?	Correct answer	Approximate	Incorrect/no idea
	33.3	36.7	30
How do you characterise the ColourMirror?	Great, funny	Modern	For youngsters
	80.6	27.3	6.5
What do you think of digital installations in museums?	Motivates to visit	Do not care	Dislike the idea
	77.6	18.4	4

installation. They asked for assistance from the guard. As a reaction to this somewhat unexpected outcome, we added more instructions to the display, telling visitors what to do.

As for the engagement with the installation, *children and teenagers* spent more time in the room, were at ease and kept experimenting (e.g. by changing their dress or forming groups), while people above 60 often needed assistance to get started, and hardly went for more than a single scan.

The *data visualization could not compete for attention* with the mirror itself: people, in general, did not look at all the four visualizations and found some of them (Extremes, Statistics) difficult to interpret. However, foreigners (e.g. tourists) spent a larger amount of time observing and discussing the visualizations.

From the point of view of the *design and the technical solutions*, we (the designers and programmers) spotted some anomalies that visitors usually did not notice. It turned out that certain types of textiles (corduroy, shiny leather) fooled the detection of a motionless visitor, as their reflection was constantly changing. Due to the lack of light in the windowless room and the low quality of the built-in camera of the Kinect, the scanned colours were not always true to life. The complex selection criteria made sure that the many visitors who wore dark colours also received an object. On the other hand, the colour of the skin was always taken into account, which made it difficult at times to interpret the match even if somebody was wearing at least some bright colours.

How did people experience the ColourMirror? Visitors enjoyed the experience: they were smiling or laughing (72.6%) or pleasantly surprised (7.4%) when their object showed up. If they were with someone else, they also made emotionally charged comments about the objects.

Children and young adults became especially engaged, made further scans, and experimented with changing their dress or altering their pose. Some children spent more than 10 min in the room, and several visitors returned later for a second try.

We also expected that the ColourMirror would confront visitors with their clothing habits, and with the tendency of Hungarians to wear dark colours. We have some clear but anecdotal evidence for this: some people did return in different outfits and commented on the dominance of grey and dark colours of the visitors shown in the data visualizations.

How did people perceive the object they were assigned? More than 95% of the visitors *could recall the object*, over 71% of them very well (describing its details, quoting its textual description).

A majority of the people (72%) *were happy* with the object they received. When they were not, the negative linguistic connotations of certain objects as well as gender mismatches (a man receiving a woman's dress) were mentioned as reasons for disliking it. In the case of indifference, aesthetic aspects were sometimes mentioned.

81% of the people *planned to track down 'their' object*—even in cases when they did not like it. Hence the 'mirrored object' served as an entry anchor to the nearly 400 exhibits.

People *identified with the object*—they mostly used terms such as 'I am a jar' in spontaneous outbreaks, and in the feedback in the visitors' book. This identification was beyond expectations: people were eager to seek (and find) psychological and life-style references in the object they received. People talked spontaneously and passionately about their feelings and assumptions, even to strangers.

What did people think of the ColourMirror, and of digital installations in museums? Only about one-third of the subjects had the right idea about the working of the mirror, one-third had no idea or gave very strange answers (assuming for example that it was based on an X-ray scan, or an analysis of their shape). This result really surprised us, as it was explained in a text outside the entrance of the room how the installation functioned, and also on the mirror whenever an object got displayed. It seems that many of the people did not read these texts at all (though we did not explicitly check this).

A vast majority (above 80%) of the subjects did like the ColourMirror and found it a joyful, funny, enjoyable experience. They liked to find such a cheerful installation in a place as 'serious' as a museum. More than a quarter (also) described it as 'modern'.

For a vast majority of the subjects (more than 77%), digital installations offer an additional motivation to visit a museum.

Did people share digitally the object they received? Only about half of the visitors sent their mirror image to themselves. Those who did not were mostly above 50, and they explained that they do not use social media. On the other hand, we traced the sent images and found that they spread quickly over Facebook. Thus, the visitors themselves spread the news about the exhibition.

Some visitors wanted to know more about the object they received. For this purpose, after the study, we expanded the email in which the mirror image was forwarded with a textual description of the object.

3.3   Feedback from the Museum Staff

During the 16 months of the exhibition, we received much positive feedback in the media (even in television), and also from museum professionals. We conducted a small survey with the six guards who were on duty in the room, and four people who were organizing activities for children in the museum. The qualitative answers from the guards were in line with the major findings suggested by the empirical data. They all liked the installation very much, and enjoyed that—finally—it put them in a more interesting role than just disciplining visitors: their help was needed and appreciated, and they strayed into conversation with visitors. They were also pleased that—in the huge staff of the museum—they were addressed as competent people in the research.

The animators reinforced the impression that children loved the installation. The only problem they had was the inevitable queuing effect, when complete classes visited the exhibition. They found that similar digital installations should become a regular item with all exhibitions. The management and direction of the museum were very pleased by the free PR due to the mirror images of artefacts that were shared by visitors on Facebook. They were planning to use the ColourMirror in dedicated campaigns and to provide more publicity, for e.g. data visualizations on the website of the museum, but after all this has not happened so far.

4   Discussion

The ColourMirror is a novel and unique installation. However, several of the lessons learnt are of a general scope.

1. People can engage and even identify with objects if they encounter them in a playful context. Besides 'having fun', we managed to focus their attention on a singular exhibit, and by this, get them interested in the exhibition.
2. The installation turned visitors (and guards) into participants. It evoked discussion even among visitors who did not know each other. It helped to increase the impact of the exhibition.
3. It connected artefacts with an everyday aspect of the life of the visitors (that is, how colourfully they dress). In this way, it also underlined the major message of the exhibition—the rich use of colours in past centuries.
4. The ongoing development of the enabling technologies (e.g. small and cheap sensors, powerful processors in mobile devices, the scaling of image processing, Internet and wireless communication) open up entirely new domains of applications. A novel, surprising and engaging installation can serve several of the objectives listed in the introduction, and possibly even better than more direct types of application that have already been in use in museums.

The empirical study revealed that with a single installation, we could accomplish 5 of the 11 potential functions listed in Sect. 1.2, namely:

- facilitating *active learning*,
- enabling a *playful physical activity*,
- making visitors *emotionally involved*,
- inducing *discussion between visitors*,
- *reaching out* to potential visitors.

The ColourMirror itself can be used in other public spaces than the museum—this would also provide a way to 'keep in touch' with the collection of the museum, which will be closed to the public for several years. On the other hand, the same idea could be adopted for other collections, especially for paintings. Also, the colour-based query could serve the basis for different campaigns and competitions, e.g. who is able to receive from the mirror objects that rarely appear as a query result, or appointing the most colourful visitor of a certain period.

In such a new field of application, the possible genres, the criteria of good design and success and the methods of evaluation all have to be established. This is especially difficult compared to the traditional fields of application of computer science (such as banking or manufacturing) for the following reasons:

1. The collection, the mission and the audience of museums are significantly different.
2. In the process of creating applications, there has to be a close collaboration and a mutual understanding of each other's disciplines, working methods and values between museologists/curators and computer scientists/programmers, and this must be extended to other players (visual designers, museum educators, marketing experts), each of whom have their own objectives.
3. Data collection and evaluation of digital installations is (still) rarely done, connected to a lack of resources and the short time-span of temporary exhibitions.

Acknowledgements The ColourMirror was designed and implemented by an interdisciplinary team: Zoltán Csík-Kovács, Ágoston Nagy, Gáspár Hajdu, Gábor Papp, Bence Samu and Zsófia Ruttkay. We are thankful for Szilvia Silye for her contribution to the design and execution of the empirical study. We are also grateful to the staff of the Museum of Applied Arts in Budapest, and to Dániel Kiss for his help with preparing this article.

References

1. Crowley, D., Heyer, P.: Communication in History: Technology, Culture, Society. Routledge, London (2016)
2. Anderson, G. (ed.): Reinventing the Museum: The Evolving Conversation on the Paradigm Shift, 2nd edn. AltaMiraPress, Plymouth (2012)

3. Drotner, K., Schrøder, K.: Museum Communication and Social Media. Routledge, London (2013)
4. Gombrich, E.H.: The museum: past, present and future. Crit. Inq. **3**, 449–470 (1977)
5. Kidd, J.: Museums in the New Mediascape: Transmedia, Participation, Ethics. Ashgate, Surrey (2014)
6. Parry, R.: Museums in a Digital Age. Routledge, London (2010)
7. Simon, N.: The Participatory Museum. Museum 2.0, Santa Cruz (2010)
8. Grinter, R.E., Aoki, P.M., Hurst, A., Szymanski, M.H., Thornton, J.D., Woodruff, A.: Revisiting the visit: understanding how technology can shape the museum visit. In: Proceedings of the 2002 ACM Conference on Computer Supported Cooperative Work, pp. 146–155. ACM (2002)
9. Ferris, K., Bannon, L., Ciolfi, L., Gallagher, P., Hall, T., Lennon, M.: Shaping experiences in the hunt museum: a design case study. In: Proceedings of the 5th Conference on Designing Interactive Systems: Processes, Practices, Methods, and Techniques (DIS'04), pp. 205–214. ACM, New York (2004)
10. Alexander, J., Wienke, L., Tiongson, P.: Removing the barriers of gallery one: a new approach to integrating art, interpretation, and technology. In: Museum and the Web 2017 (2017). https://mw17.mwconf.org/paper/removing-the-barriers-of-gallery-one-a-new-approach-to-integrating-art-interpretation-and-technology/
11. Jenkins, H. (ed.): Confronting the Challenges of Participatory Culture: Media Education for the 21st Century. The MIT Press, Cambridge (2006)
12. Palfrey, J., Gasser, U.: Born Digital. Basic Books, New York (2008)
13. Serrell, B.: Paying attention: the duration and allocation of visitors' time in museum exhibitions. Curator: Mus. J. **40**(2), 108–125 (1997)
14. Bényei, J., Ruttkay, Zs.: Renewal of the museums in the age of digital technologies (In Hungarian). In: Tímea, A., Pörczi, Zs. (eds.) Mediaculture Without Borders (In Hungarian), pp. 51–80. Wolters Kluwer Complex, Budapest (2015)
15. Alexander, J., Barton J., Goeser, C.: Transforming the art museum experience: gallery one. In: Proctor, N., Cherry, R. (eds.) Museums and the Web 2013. Museums and the Web, Silver Spring (2013). http://mw2013.museumsandtheweb.com/paper/transforming-the-art-museum-experience-gallery-one-2/
16. Muchinenyika, S.H., Weede, O., Muyingi, H.N.: Persuasive souvenir. In: Proceedings of the 13th Participatory Design Conference, vol. 2, pp. 175–176. ACM, New York (2014)
17. Heckbert, P.S.: Color image quantization for frame buffer display. Comput. Graph. **16**(3), 297–307 (1982)
18. Mokrzycki, W., Tatol, M.: Color difference Delta E—a survey. Mach. Graph. Vis. **20**, 383–411 (2011)
19. Kuhn, H.W.: The Hungarian method for the assignment problem. Nav. Res. Logist. Q. **2**, 83–97 (1955)

Printed in the United States
By Bookmasters